The KING'S *favour*

For
A.C. Whitehead
who made it possible.

The
KING'S
favour

Three eighteenth-century monarchs and the favourites who ruled them

J.J. MANGAN

ALAN SUTTON

First published in 1991

First published in this edition in the United Kingdom in 1993 by
Alan Sutton Publishing Ltd · Phoenix Mill · Far Thrupp · Stroud
Gloucestershire

British Library Cataloguing in Publication Data

Mangan, J.J. *1928–*
The king's favour: three eighteenth-century monarchs and
the favourites who ruled them.
1. Monarchs, history – Biographies – Collections
I. Title
929.7

ISBN 0–7509–0456–9

Typeset in Bembo 11/13pt.
Typesetting and origination by
Alan Sutton Publishing Limited.
Printed in Great Britain.

Contents

Part III – The Cyclops

Acknowledgements

A biographical study such as this, which primarily concerns itself with the intimate lives of famous people, must by its nature owe an immense debt to scholarship in the general field. I regret that I have been able to acknowledge only constantly consulted, major sources in the bibliography. Nor have I given adequate credit to the eighteenth-century letter-writers, diarists and antiquarians, whose vivid, graceful chronicles have been my unfailing inspiration.

I have received aid and comfort from a circle of friends and collegues whose kindness and patience, in the face of my monomania, is beyond reward. Among the many, I must thank Jody Randall and Carl Griffasi. My gratitude to Terry Moore, a gentleman of rare gallantry, for perspective when I needed it; to my agent, Anita Diamant, for expert guidance, graciously given; and to Paris and Marcia Flammonde for their unflagging generosity and love.

J.J. Mangan
Brooklyn 1991

A Word About Money

Because money is among the most troublesome of human inventions, translating prices of a particular time into present-day prices is a risky business. No handy booklet exists. Nor do monetary experts, when closely examined, agree on much.

Such lack of clarity is particularly vexing when writing about the ladies and gentlemen found in this book. They were among the great spendthrifts of all time and to tell their stories without details of their extravagance translated into modern-day terms would be pointless.

Writers have used the price of a loaf of bread, or a workman's daily wages to convey 'money's worth'. However, most aristocrats of the eighteenth century never purchased a loaf of bread, nor did they have any idea what a workman might earn.

Courtiers and the propertied classes of most periods understood, however, the price of gold as do investors today.

Even the 'golden constant', as it has been called, is only really useful for rough translations of value from century to century. Gold has withstood wars, revolutions, devaluations and revaluations, with greater integrity than most standards, but not perfectly. The author hastens to disavow any claim to precision, therefore, in comparisons of antique and present-day money in this book. They were arrived at with reference to the price of gold, using the following simple formulas:

Prices in English pounds of the early 1700s were multiplied by fifty to arrive at prices in pounds sterling and by a hundred for US dollar prices of the late 1900s.

Prices in French *livres* of the early 1700s were multiplied by 2.175 to arrive at prices in pounds sterling and by 4.35 for US dollar prices of the late 1900s.

Prices in imperial gold rubles of the mid-to-late 1700s were multiplied by 12.92 to arrive at prices in pounds sterling and by 25.65 for US dollar prices of the late 1900s.

The reader's indulgence is appreciated.

Introduction

In 1794, George IV, then the Prince of Wales, granted a sixteen-year-old acquaintance, George Bryan Brummel, a cornet's commission in the prince's own regiment, the 10th Hussars. Brummel, from a stuffy, middle-class background, had little to recommend him to fashionable London but his new friendship with the prince, his insolent wit, and impeccable taste in clothes.

Brummel quickly dominated the London scene. As Beau Brummel, he popularized dark, tight-fitting suits, corsets for men, long trousers instead of knee breeches, and, in a giant step forward, the frequent use of soap and water.

The Beau gave the prince, who was paunchy and hopelessly *démodé*, a few pointers. It was enough to gain the royal favour. They saw each other daily. George watched in awe as Brummel arranged and rearranged his elaborate, starched cravat, insisting on a perfect fold, if it took all morning to achieve. The prince worshipped his friend, and made no sartorial decisions without consulting him. In fact, he made few moves of any nature without the Beau's advice. The favourite dined, wined and weekended with the cream of the English aristocracy. His bills were paid, his credit with his butcher, his baker, and especially his tailor, was unlimited. His landlord bowed him out, the porters at the gambling clubs like White's and Brooks's bowed him in.

Finally, Beau Brummel and Prince George quarrelled. Their spatting reached a climax when they attended, separately, the same ball. They met, face to face. George, by now the Prince Regent, pointedly ignored his friend and spoke to Lord Alvanley, who was standing beside Brummel. Brummel, in a moment of historic fury, lost his head. His voice carried through the room as he asked his companion, 'Alvanley, who is your fat friend?'

It was the end of Beau Brummel's career. Frozen out of society, he was driven into a debtor's exile in Caen, where he ended his days in abject poverty. Sadly, he became a little unhinged and very shabby.

Pity the poor Beau. Had he lived in the reign of James I, he might not have been ruined. In 1615, James's favourite, Robert Carr, the Earl of Somerset, quarrelled with his royal patron, privately and publicly. Somerset, who was gorgeous, scorned James's physical condition, which was repulsive. The king's tongue, too big for his mouth, lolled when he talked; his crippled legs were too weak to support his weight.

Somerset attempted to blackmail James, actually, when he and his wife were brought before the Star Chamber for the murder of a rival courtier, Sir Thomas Overbury. The favourite had Overbury sentenced to the Tower of London. His lethal wife, Lady Frances, arranged Overbury's assassination with a poisoned enema. Public shock forced James to put them on trial, but he could not bring himself to see his favourite hang. He pardoned them both.

The difference between Brummel's position and Somerset's was clearcut. George IV, who kept a mistress, favoured Brummel solely because he admired the Beau's brilliant taste. He would not or could not forgive Brummel's public insult. James I, a homosexual, was helpless to resist his yearning for Somerset's strapping Scots body. In the end, he was willing to wink at murder.

No tie binds like lust.

This book is about sexual favourites. Of the non-sexual kind, it is enough to note that taste in royal companions has been as diverse as the temperaments of kings and queens themselves. Over the centuries, lonely monarchs have sought special friendships with dandies, bishops, generals, philosophers, rakes, dwarfs, gossips, ghillies, and a vast swarm of political connivers.

The Majesties chose their *amours* from an equally mixed bag: sexual favourites have been variously passionate, cold-blooded, brave, gifted, glamorous, pious, profligate, handsome, beautiful and – with surprising frequency – stupid, quarrelsome, and homely.

All reached the peak of their careers at the throne. The perks of a royal love affair were lavish: servants, jewels, carriages, titles, estates and so on. Proximity to the crown conferred social status, at least with the broad-minded circles at court. There were drawbacks, to be sure. Tenure was uncertain, royalty being as likely to stray as anyone else. Retirement, too, was chancy, since it usually entailed the death of a patron and the accession of an unfriendly heir.

The worm in the apple was frustrated ambition. To be so near to sovereign power, yet to be denied its uses, would have tried the patience of a saint. Few favourites were patient, and none at all were saints.

In seventeenth-century England, the beautiful playmates of Charles II, Barbara, Countess Castlemaine, and Nell Gwynn, were ferociously ambitious but remained concubines and nothing more. In France, the *maîtresses* of Louis XIV, de la Vallière and de Montespan, even his morganatic wife, Madame de Maintenon, might yearn for power but they achieved little more than control of the occasional church appointment. No one ruled Louis's France but Louis. In faraway, frozen Russia a camp-follower named Martha Skovronsky Glück Johan serviced the lieutenants of Peter the Great and the czar himself, but she achieved power only when she became Peter's legal wife, widow, and the Czarina Catherine I.

Then, between the Glorious Revolution of 1688 and the French Revolution of 1789, the eighteenth century ushered in a series of royal favourites who ruled as if to the purple born. In the historical era which historians like to call the Twilight of Princes, the same three monarchies, England, France, and Russia, accepted the governance of whores and minions. Monarchs were lax, for one reason or another, and ministers not yet fully empowered. It was an invitation to opportunism, and government fell into the hands of impudent nobodies whose principal qualification was their performance in the monarch's bed. The favourites usurped supreme authority – even the power to wage war. Thomas Carlyle, in the nineteenth century, called the phenomenon 'harlotocracy'.

In 1714, the English, having decided to import a king from the German electorate of Hanover, were startled to discover that their new monarch allowed his elderly, ugly mistresses to run the country.

'German George' was the great-great-grandfather of the Prince of Wales who favoured Beau Brummel. When he became George I, founder of the English House of Hanover, George was best known to Englishmen as a ducal mercenary who fought against Louis XIV. Worldly Londoners had also heard about Hanover as the 'Venice of Germany'. George's father, who liked his vice, had copied the Italian Sodom. The Hanover carnival became an annual Bacchanal which drew hell-raisers from every corner of Europe.

George I stepped ashore at Greenwich accompanied by his two dragon mistresses. They were the rotund Baroness Sophia Charlotte von Kielmannsegge, who became the English Countess of Darlington, and skinny Ehrengard Melusina von der Schulenberg, who was ennobled as the Duchess of Kendal. The dreadful pair guarded their lover against Englishwomen, complained loudly about the barbaric customs of the English – and stole. Immune to reprimand because of their royal connection, they looted Queen Anne's jewellery, requisitioned gargantuan quantities of furniture, food, and wine from the royal commissaries, and grabbed anything and everything valuable that was not nailed down.

The mistresses' greed aggravated an awkward period of royal

adjustment. The king spoke no English. His English ministers spoke no German or French. For a time, the Prince of Wales acted as translator, but even that trickle of communication dried up, when father and son squared away for an historic feud. The king actually plotted to have the prince deported or killed. The squabble became so embarrassing that the Duchess of Kendal and the Princess of Wales patched it up, at least for public consumption. (The two men continued to snarl at each other in private.)

From George I's standpoint, his residence in St James's was more a bivouac in enemy territory than a reign. He never really trusted his new subjects. (They had, after all, cut off Charles I's head.) He was homesick for Germany, went abroad often, stayed away as long as he dared, and returned only when he ran short of funds.

Into the vacuum created by his neglect marched the Countess of Darlington and the Duchess of Kendal. The duchess was especially bossy, ordering the ministers about, meddling in Parliamentary affairs, speculating in the City, and growing enormously rich.

The audacious old woman bought and sold the highest offices in the kingdom. Sir Robert Walpole, who liked her, called her 'as much a Queen of England as ever any was, though she would sell the king's honour for a shilling to the highest bidder'.

She helped defraud the nation at large, in the financial swindle of 1720 known as the South Sea Bubble. The country was swept up in an eight-month frenzy of speculation, during which promoters of the South Sea Company and hundreds of smaller 'Bubbles' made fortunes for themselves and their friends, and nearly destroyed the English economy. The duchess, who was on the payroll of the South Sea Company, pulled the king himself into the scandal.

George I died in 1727 on a junket to Hanover, struck down by a supper of water-melons. The fat Countess of Darlington predeceased him; the rich, thin Duchess of Kendal survived him until 1743. She kept a pet raven, the story goes, which she believed was the reincarnation of her royal lover.

This odd reign had one golden result. Sir Robert Walpole, who became the first English 'prime' minister under George I, managed to keep the peace and continue it into the reign of George II. For two untroubled decades, England and her ancient enemy, France, lived in shared prosperity.

Walpole's truce encompassed the minority of Louis XV, beginning with the regency of the boy's uncle, Philippe, Duc d'Orléans. The regency French, exhausted by half a century of bloodshed under Louis

XIV, threw themselves with abandon into the enjoyments of peace. Paris became the scene of an eight-year-long public orgy, with the regent himself as master of the revels. Orléans was a brilliant politician by day, who drank himself senseless night after night; an atheist who dabbled in satanism; a fond father who had an incestuous love affair with one, or possibly two, of his daughters.

He gave his blessing to a totally dissolute society until 1722, when he was forced to re-open the château of Versailles, in preparation for Louis XV's thirteenth birthday, his coronation, and the inevitable royal wedding to follow. It was, however, Orléans's successor, the Prince de Condé, who found the boy-king a bride.

She was Marie Leczinska, the daughter of the ex-king of Poland, a princess so poor that Condé's mistress had to lend her chemises for her wedding progress. Marie did the job queens are supposed to do, bearing ten children, six of whom survived infancy. Her husband remained a permanent adolescent, handsome, athletic, without any purpose in life more serious than the pursuit of game.

Serious business for more than an hour or two bored him. When he was bored, he grew morbid. Corpses, graves and disease preyed on his mind. His elderly tutor, Cardinal Fleury, obligingly made the king's light schedule lighter still, and governed France.

In 1732, Louis went hunting for a mistress. Like George I in England, he was strangely selective, seducing the ugliest women in France, the three Nesle sisters, Mesdames de Mailly, de Vintimille, and de Lauraguais.

A fourth Nesle sister, the beautiful Duchesse de Châteauroux, was a 'kingmaker'. When the War of the Austrian Succession broke out in 1740, Châteauroux pushed and prodded her lover to the battlefront. Louis found war almost as exciting as the hunt, but his interest did not long survive the death of the duchess in 1744.

That winter, he was hunting near Versailles, when the royal chase was disrupted one day in the forest of Sénart, by a pretty woman driving a phaeton. She appeared again, as the goddess Diana, at the royal ball celebrating the dauphin's marriage. Louis's heart was lost, to the twenty-four-year-old wife of a minor *bourgeois* official, le Normant d'Étoiles. Born Jeanne Antoinette Poisson, she would rule France for twenty years as the Marquise de Pompadour.

Pompadour was a poor *maîtresse*, physically, dosing herself with aphrodisiacs for the half-dozen years they were lovers. She could, however, lift the paralyzing ennui that haunted the king, in the time he spent away from the chase, the gaming table, and sex.

She stage-managed every day, every hour of his life, like scenes in a never-ending *divertissement*. Pompadour acted, sang and danced for Louis. She acquired a succession of châteaux and rustic hermitages, where she kept him busy with plans, designers, workmen, inspection tours. Eventually, Louis set up, in a cluster of houses near Versailles, the *Parc aux Cerfs*, a brothel reserved for his exclusive use. Pompadour left the pimping to others, but she stepped in when needed, to retire girls who had outlived their usefulness, and dispose of their bastards.

While Louis fornicated his way into the annals of lechery, Madame de Pompadour ruled France. She presided at a daily meeting of the ministers, sitting in the single chair she allowed in the room. Louis's lieutenants, many of them of ducal and princely rank, stood.

Her enemies fought back with twenty years of slander, paying the street *chansonniers* of Paris to scribble an endless stream of filthy verses and pamphlets. The campaign spattered the king with the mud aimed at his *maîtresse*, but failed to dislodge her.

Austria's pious empress, Maria Theresa, paid court to Pompadour. Frederick II of Prussia detested her. When their mutual hatred ignited the Seven Years War, Pompadour took control of the French high command. She actually supervised the armies from Versailles, handing out the plummy commands to her friends.

France lost. Pompadour's bitter legacy was the Treaty of Paris in 1763, which stripped the nation of her American and Indian colonies. The marquise spent her last days heart-broken to see France militarily insignificant, insolvent, a second-rate power. Even her personal holdings, which had drained the French treasury of thirty-six million livres, were ready for the auction block. There were only thirty-seven *louis d'or* in her desk on the day of her death.

Pompadour was France's last political mistress, and certainly the most powerful. Louis's last *maîtresse*, the lovely, expensive Madame du Barry, took no interest in affairs of state. A *fille publique* who barely missed being labelled a prostitute in the police records, she was exuberantly sexy, mad for diamonds, and amused at the scandal her reception caused among the prudes at court. The ramshackle reign was left in the hands of a caretaker ministry as Louis and his magnificent blonde enjoyed the years of his decline to the fullest. She and his daughters, Mesdames, were at his bedside when he died quite horribly, in 1774, of smallpox.

Du Barry, a few years later, found herself in the Place de la Révolution, screaming in uncomprehending terror as she was carried to the guillotine. In death, she left little more than a memory, of beauty and outlandish extravagance.

Madame de Pompadour, ironically, was memorialized by her enemy, Frederick the Great. She was one of the three women Frederick mocked by erecting their statues to hold up the dome of his palace at Potsdam. The others were the empress Maria Theresa of Austria, and a minor German princess, Sophie of Anhalt-Zerbst, whom Frederick had helped to become the Czarina Catherine II of Russia.

It was Frederick who brought Sophie to the attention of the Czarina Elizabeth, Peter the Great's daughter. At fourteen, the princess was shipped to St Petersburg and a dreadful marriage to the Russian grand duke Peter. He came to power as Peter III, infuriated the nobles with his pro-Prussian policies, and in 1762 was deposed and killed.

Catherine II assumed the throne. Highly sexed, she took lovers along the way. Her second lover, Stanislas Poniatowski, she later created king of Poland. Her third, Gregory Orlov, helped engineer the *coup d'état* which made her czarina, but could not endure life as Catherine's minion. Fearing he could ruin her, she began the practice of placating her lovers with enormous parting gifts. Orlov and his successors were bribed into retirement with palaces, country estates, thousands of serfs, diamonds by the fistful, art treasures, enormous pensions.

Her fears were not entirely unfounded, for in the eyes of many conservative Russian boyars, Catherine was a usurper. She ruled by her wits, embarking on a strategy of conquest to expand Russia to the ancient borders of Byzantium. Catherine annexed the Ukraine first. Then, acting with the King of Prussia and the Empress of Austria, she partitioned Poland. Her generals fought the Turks to a standstill. In 1773, she crushed the Pugachevschina, the great rebellion led by the cossack Emelyan Pugachev. Rebels were crucified in wholesale lots. Pugachev himself was drawn and quartered.

On the heels of Pugachev came Gregory Potemkin, the outrageous, one-eyed 'Cyclops', would-be monk, warrior, Catherine's favourite of favourites. Now the usurper, Catherine, was, lovingly, usurped. She could deny Potemkin nothing, allowing him to rule her southern empire as czar in all but name.

Their sexual affair was fiery, immensely satisfying to the czarina, but ended after only two years. Potemkin was too often absent, conquering the new territorial prize of the Crimea, while his mistress fidgeted in St Petersburg.

A series of handsome, muscular young officers filled Catherine's arms in his absence. They were true minions, in no way supplanting

Potemkin except in the physical satisfaction of the czarina. She promoted each in turn to the position of aide-de-camp and pretended she was improving their minds. One or two tried to topple Potemkin. Only the last succeeded.

In 1787, with her latest aide-de-camp at her side, trailing a circus troupe of officials and diplomats, Catherine left St Petersburg on an unforgettable tour of her empire. The trip, part vacation, part imperial progress, was a stupendous show-and-tell by Potemkin of his accomplishments in 'New Russia'. The journey lasted six months and nearly emptied the Russian treasury. Potemkin paraded happy peasants, freshly built Crimean cities, and a new Black Sea fleet. He succeeded in entering the language with the phrase *Potemkinsche Dorfer* ('Potemkin villages'), a synonym for gigantic fraud.

The selection of a power-hungry new favourite, Plato Zubov, in 1791, brought Potemkin racing back to St Petersburg from a resumption of the Turkish war. He made his last bid for Catherine's favour, only to be refused. Potemkin died on the road to a peace conference with the Turks.

Zubov, twenty-two, sold his virility to Catherine, sixty, for unquestioned control of the empire. He demanded Potemkin's ministries, his diplomatic portfolios and army commands, the viceroyship of his southern provinces, even his medals.

Catherine died in 1796, after a reign of thirty-four years, unable to prevent her son, Paul I, from ascending the throne. (To the last minute, she hoped to displace him with her grandson, Alexander.) Plato Zubov was 'allowed to travel'. Paul, who worshipped his dead father, installed a Prussian-style military state. He attempted to rewrite history, publicly ignoring Peter III's deposition and the reign of Catherine II. Zubov returned in 1801, to join in the murder of the czar, in the Michael Fortress.

With Zubov passed the age of the great political favourites. It was a gaudy accident of history, which made heroes and heroines of the men and women who enjoyed, often degraded, and sometimes glorified the king's favour. There would be beauties in later centuries, and gallants, who became the darlings of the throne, but the time of the sexual usurper was at an end.

Part I

THE ELEPHANT
AND
THE MAYPOLE

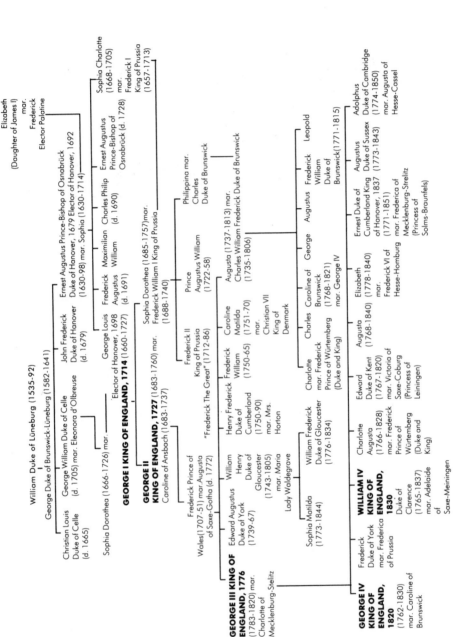

The House of Hanover (From 1535 to 1850)

Chapter One

The Venice of Germany

O ffered a bouquet of roses, England's 'four Georges' grasped the thorns. This quartet of kings, who reigned between Queen Anne and King William IV, shared an incomprehensible passion for homely women. Not that the Georges themselves were particularly god-like – they tended to be red-faced and corpulent – but with the throne of England as part of the package, one assumes the goddesses of the day made themselves available. The Georges ignored such distractions again and again as they paid court to trolls.

George I, whose life and reign is the primary concern here, was the unrivalled champion in their quest for awfulness. When the London mob first laid eyes on the elderly mistresses he brought with him from Germany in 1714, they howled in derision. The wits instantly nicknamed fat Baroness Kielmannsegge 'The Elephant' and skinny Fraulein von der Schulenburg 'The Maypole'. The two old hags were never equalled for ugliness or greed.

George II's grand passion was Henrietta Howard, Lady Suffolk, who was as plain as a post and nearly as deaf as one. Happily, their affair had no adverse effects on his marriage to Caroline of Ansbach. Clever, attractive Caroline did the thinking for George, almost from the moment they met in 1705.

George III, in 1761, actually winced at his first sight of Charlotte of Mecklenburg-Strelitz. He married her, got used to her resemblance to a monkey and fathered fifteen children by her. Their marriage had nothing to do with King George's loss of his American colonies, or his tendency, later in life, to hold conversations with trees. His insanity was caused by a genetic disease called hepatic porphyria.

George IV, in 1795, nearly fainted from the stench when the

slatternly Caroline of Brunswick was presented to him. George was Prince of Wales at the time and avid for a bigger allowance from Parliament. He ignored half a dozen delightful princesses on the European marriage market and, smelly or not, Caroline became the Princess of Wales. They treated Europe to a lurid divorce trial.

The Georges tended to be evil-tempered (the exception was George IV, who was a charmer) and shared a pop-eyed, double-chinned profile. Their sameness of name, of course, gives us the familiar term for the elegant architecture of eighteenth-century England. It is called 'Georgian' because, until 1830, it was axiomatic that the king was George and a George was king.

Georges II, III and IV are, unfortunately, outside our purview. There are tales worth telling of their years on the throne, but none can match, for cheerful sin, the exploits of the early generations. The family history, a preposterous tangle of poison plots, infidelities, incest, murders, mistresses (including the astonishing old concubines of George I) seems deliberately contrived for comic effect.

As a guide for the uninitiated, the figures in the German parade which led to the succession of George I in England are:

Great-grandfather William (1535–1592),
the pious Duke of Lüneburg;
Grandfather George (1582–1641),
the warrior Duke of Brunswick-Lüneburg;
Uncle George William (? –1705),
duke of Celle and George I's father-in-law;
Father Ernest Augustus (1630–1698),
the reprobate Duke and first Elector of Hanover;
Mother Sophia (1630–1714),
Electress of Hanover and granddaughter of James I;
George I (1660–1727),
King of England and founder of the English House of Hanover.

Their family name was Guelph. They ruled a cluster of postage-stamp-sized duchies in Germany as the House of Brunswick-Lüneburg until late in the seventeenth century. Then, from Vienna, the Holy Roman Emperor Leopold I elevated George I's father, Duke Ernest Augustus, to the rank of imperial elector.

The electorate of Brunswick-Lüneburg, or Hanover as it came to be known for its capital city, included about eight thousand square miles stretching from the North Sea to the Harz Mountains. It was a tidy, prosperous realm. Three quarters of a million hard-working Hanoverians mined silver and copper in the mountains and tended herds of fat cattle and sheep on the plains below.

When the elector George Louis became King George I, he thought to impress his new English subjects with his German inheritance so he established his dynasty in England as the House of Hanover. (He also sensibly dropped the 'Louis'. Louis XIV of France, his namesake, was universally loathed across the North Sea.)

The dukes had always been sharply divided on the question of style. Great-grandfather William, Duke of Lüneburg, whose father once studied with Martin Luther, ran his little duchy like a monastery. Duke William decreed prayers and hymns at all hours of the day, sermons during meals and harsh penalties for bad language, horseplay and drunkenness.

George I's grandfather George, duke of Brunswick-Lüneburg, couldn't abide German provincialism in general or great-grandfather William's churchiness in particular. He escaped on a Grand Tour, visiting England and the court of Elizabeth I. His talent was soldiering, which he proved with distinction under Christian IV of Denmark, the Emperor Ferdinand II and the Swedish King Gustavus Adolphus. Grandfather George's prowess at arms in the Thirty Years War put Hanover on the European map. He was allowed to add the famous Abbey of Hildesheim to the duchy as his portion of the spoils. When his turn came to be duke, the old warhorse settled down to a court as prim and prayerful as his father's before him.

His sons displayed a taste for the high life. Some favoured the beery *gemütlichkeit* that passed for riotous living in German courts of the time, some hankered after foreign pleasures.

George I's father, Duke Ernest Augustus, was spellbound by Venice, which was, in its heyday, a glittering blend of Monte Carlo, the Parisian Left Bank and Sodom. When he inherited the Hanoverian title and treasury, the duke did his best to transform his backwater capital into the Venice of Germany. Hanover achieved considerable notoriety as the wickedest city of the north. Its libertine duke was the first to adopt the most exotic new luxury or the most infamous new vice. Tourists flocked in. They gawked at relics of the Crusades in the refurbished *schloss* on the Leine River; drove out to the summer palace of Herrenhausen for the magnificent gardens; floated on the canal in imported Venetian gondolas; attended the new opera house; and lost their inhibitions in a gaudy annual carnival.

Carnival swept all before it during the winter months from Advent until Lent. The humblest dwellings were gaily decorated. Even servants and tradespeople affected wigs and fancy dress. For arriving guests of noble enough lineage, the duke turned out his personal carriages. The holiday-makers were borne to the Leine Palace in great, lurching, gilded coaches drawn by six or eight geldings in velvet harness. A guard of honour of jack-booted troopers in scarlet, silver and gold trotted alongside.

The entertainments which awaited the duke's visitors were spectacular, sometimes outlandish. Torch dances, particularly, astonished first-time revellers. Couples paced off the intricate steps as they balanced flambeaux six feet high, paused to eat, drink, make love and danced on. At daybreak, they snatched a few hours' sleep, only to begin again the following night. A single dance might last a week.

In the court theatre at Herrenhausen the classical allegories so dear to seventeenth-century audiences were performed, if not for their absurd plots and windbag sentiments, certainly for their spectacle and costuming. Italian musicians piped in garlanded shepherdesses. Chirping songs, the maidens gave a tantalizing show of bare arms and legs as they danced. Handsome, muscular heroes of antiquity joined in their pastoral fun. At the climax of the performance, a fantastically painted *deus ex machina* clanked down from the flies bearing Duke Ernest Augustus's current lady love disguised as a goddess. Her creamy breasts and buttocks all a-jiggle behind a yard or two of transparent lawn, she struck a pose and delivered a high-falutin address. The audience applauded wildly, and the duke suffered an attack of itchy fingers.

Of all the carnival pleasures by far the most popular was the masquerade, which imitated the elaborate masked routs of Venice. A barely-controlled madness took hold in which every impudent social breach was permitted, every lustful fantasy was fulfilled. The domino was democratic. Masked, all men were equal and equally debauched.

The upright Lutheran burghers of Hanover were ravenous for sex, of course, and the boldest masqueraders prowled like animals in rut. Among the gorgeously costumed carnival kings and queens, birds and beasts, Italian Punchinellos and Spanish infantas, sexual invitations were open, urgent and rarely rejected. For a night, women especially could throw off all restraints and emulate the goatish eroticism of their menfolk. Class barriers came tumbling down. In this cushioned alcove, a tavern girl could be found panting beneath a prince; in the next, a well-endowed footman performed astride his noble mistress. Entertainments were lewd, often nothing more than sexual tableaux and contests.

Masquerade had its sinister side. There were unexplained pregnancies and embarrassing diseases, which destroyed love affairs and marriages. The masked assassin seized the opportunity to stalk his victim among the merry-makers. Unknown duellists settled their scores in blood.

If the duke's court prided itself on Italian vice, its dress, its manners and its speech were French. At the time, this held true for the entire civilized world, which was enthralled by the magnificence of the French king, Louis XIV.

Louis XIV was the bully of Europe. Almost from the moment he took personal control of France on the death of Cardinal Mazarin, the *Grand Monarque* grabbed territory from his smaller neighbours. In 1667, he tested his strength against the decaying kingdom of Spain and took over a huge chunk of the Spanish Netherlands. His *mousquetaires* swarmed down on Holland in 1672, but the tough Dutch prince, William of Orange, fought them and won. Two years later, Louis gobbled up Franche-Comté. In 1681, it was the turn of Alsace.

An assault on Germany was inevitable. In 1688, the French king promised the imperial crown, then in the possession of Habsburg Austria, to the elector of Bavaria. His help was requested in conquering the small German states in the Austrian orbit. Among these client states was Hanover, the source of troops that had frustrated French ambitions in the past. With his property squarely in the path of the French armies, Duke Ernest Augustus of Brunswick-Lüneburg was a marked man.

Like the rest of Europe, George I's father hated the great Bourbon, fought him and slavishly copied him. French displaced Latin as the language of his court. The only food fit to eat was French. So also were the wines, dishes and crystal of his table.

People were especially avid for French dress. The seventeenth century degenerated into a sartorial silly season as otherwise sober, reasonable men pranced about in satin breeches, high heels, lace cuffs, cocked hats and powdered perukes. Ladies risked pneumonia in ever-deeper *décolletage* and corseted themselves to the point of suffocation. Fashionable husbands risked bankruptcy to adorn their wives in the brocades and *bijoux* favoured by King Louis's mistress of the moment.

William Makepeace Thackeray, whose rollicking essay, 'The Four Georges', is the model of all succeeding Hanoverian chronicles, described Louis's imitators with the greatest zest:

Every prince . . . had his Versailles, his Wilhelmshöhe or Ludwigslust; his court and its splendours; his gardens laid out with statues; his fountains and waterworks and Tritons; his actors and dancers and singers and fiddlers; his harem, with its inhabitants; his diamonds and duchies for these latter; his enormous festivities, his gaming tables, tournaments, masquerades and banquets lasting a week long, for which the people paid with their money, when the poor wretches had it; with their bodies and very blood when they had none; being sold in the thousands by their lords and masters, who gayly dealt in soldiers, staked a regiment upon the red at the gambling table; swapped a battalion against a dancing girl's diamond necklace; and, as it were, pocketed their people.

War was the family trade. George I, when he was Prince George Louis, took it up enthusiastically, captaining the foot soldiers his father trained and sold to the highest bidder. Like many of the Baltic principalities, Hanover functioned as a sort of rustic weapons factory which cranked out regiments of soldiers from a seemingly endless supply of big, robust farm boys. Disciplined manpower was the weapon of choice of the day.

Mostly they died fighting the French, but they were available for slaughter against any foe at all. When his latest extravagance threatened to empty the ducal pockets, Duke Ernest Augustus would fill an order for soldiers. The purchaser might be the Austrian emperor, the elector of Saxony or whoever was feeling bellicose. George Louis or one of his four brothers would officer such campaigns, princely mercenaries for hire to any royal house willing to pay their salaries. In one typical transaction, the duke sold off seven thousand troops under his son, Prince Max, to the seigniory of Venice for action in Greece. Fewer than fifteen hundred marched home again.

Faced with such blood-curdling careers, it is a wonder that any of the Guelphs survived to sit on the ducal throne. As it happened, three sons were killed in combat and one wound up in Italian exile. Prince George Louis alone seemed to prosper as a warrior. From his very first campaign at the age of fifteen, he preferred the boisterous life of the bivouac, the battles – and the whores – to the more discreet, if equally earthy, pleasures of the court.

He was quite good at his craft. In action against the Turks on the Danube, he commanded forces of ten thousand men and more. (A pair of black body servants, Mustapha and Mahomet, were part of the booty from that campaign. They saved his life during the siege of Vienna in 1685. In gratitude, he took them into his service.) The hot-tempered little prince with the bulging blue eyes distinguished himself in Italy and on the Rhine. Veteran campaigners compared him favourably with old grandfather George in the Thirty Years War.

Returning from these expeditions, George Louis's domestic felicity was arranged by a woman with ample credentials for the task. She was Clara Elizabeth, Countess Platen, his father's mistress. The daughter of an importunate Hessian nobleman, Count Carl Philip von Meissenbach, Clara was a baggage of the lowest sort. She racketed around the European capitals for years, seeking position, horizontal or otherwise, in any royal establishment that would have her. In Paris, as Mademoiselle von Meissenbach, she hoisted her skirts in the direction of Louis XIV. She was run out of France for her pains, on orders from Louis's favourite. Clara eventually drifted north to Hanover, drawn by tales of the jolly court the duke kept. When she arrived with her younger sister, Catherine Marie, they possessed little more than a trumped-up introduction or two, and the clothes on their backs.

The sisters instantly bedded and wedded a pair of promising courtiers. Clara snared Frank Ernest Platen, who was George Louis's governor; her sister landed John Busche, governor of one of the younger sons. Soon, Platen graduated from shepherding the son to advising the father, and the new Countess Platen paraded her soiled charms before Duke Ernest Augustus in one of the endless court fêtes. She was an entertainer of few gifts but she performed brilliantly by the duke's standards when she took her curtain call in his bedroom. Count Platen was obliging. His wife became the duke's *maîtresse en titre*, over perfunctory objections from his duchess, Sophia. Clara clung to that position until the old duke died, survived him and watched her daughter set sail for London with his son.

By the time Prince George Louis came into the market for flesh, Clara was showing signs of wear. The army that had marched through her bed had left its boot-marks on her heavily painted face. There were horrified whispers of a dreadful disease that made her garish make-up necessary; it is likely she shared syphilis with Duke Ernest Augustus. Although she used her harlot's skills to hang on to the duke, there was no hope of personally seducing his son, much as she might have liked it.

Without hesitation, the old doxie turned procuress. George Louis's taste in tarts was not exotic, nor was there a lack of likely ladies at Court. They enraptured Lady Mary Wortley Montagu, a visiting English diarist who observed the delights that stirred men's loins in Hanover:

I am now in the region of beauty. All the women have literally rosy cheeks, snowy foreheads and necks, jet eyebrows, to which may generally be added coal black hair. These perfections never leave them to the day of their death, and have a very fine effect by candlelight; but I could wish they were handsome with a little variety. They resemble one another as Mrs Salmon's Court of Great Britain [a wax museum] and are in as much danger of melting away by too nearly approaching the fire.

At first, Countess Platen tried to interest George Louis in her sister Catherine, now Frau Busche. Catherine was quickly discarded. Whatever bloom had once been on that rose had long since fled. Other candidates for George Louis's favour proved equally unsuitable, not due to fussiness on the prince's part, but because 'La Platen' insisted on a high degree of craftiness to carry out her schemes.

Determined to ensnare George Louis with a mistress of her choosing, the countess succeeded in planting a perfect deputy in the younger Guelph's bed. She paired him off with Baroness Sophia Charlotte von Kielmannsegge, wife of the master of the horse in the Hanover court, a lady of truly monumental attractions. George Louis, who fancied fat, was instantly and permanently smitten.

Horace Walpole, the diarist and son of the great Whig minister must be thanked, for an inimitable characterization of Kielmannsegge when she called on Walpole's mother in London:

Lady Darlington, whom I saw at my mother's in my infancy, and whom I remember by being terrified at her enormous figure, was as corpulent and ample as the duchess [the Duchess of Kendal, the king's other mistress] was long and emaciated. Two fierce black eyes, large and rolling beneath two lofty arched eyebrows, two acres of cheeks spread with crimson, an ocean of neck that overflowed and was not distinguished from the lower parts of her body, and no part restrained by stays – no wonder that a child dreaded such an ogress, and that the mob of London were highly diverted at the importation of such a seraglio . . . food for all the venom of the Jacobites; and indeed nothing could be grosser than the ribaldry that was vomited out in lampoons, libels, and every channel of abuse, against the sovereign and the new court and chanted even in their hearing about the public streets.

Kielmannsegge was commonly known to be Clara's daughter by Duke Ernest Augustus. (With sly humour, the duke permitted Kielmannsegge, who was almost certainly his bastard, to bear the same name as his legitimate daughter, Princess Sophia Charlotte.) When her status as George Louis's mistress became common knowledge, the possibility that she was his half-sister added a special *frisson* to the affair. Fortunately for George Louis's reputation, Countess Platen's promiscuity blurred his new mistress's parentage just enough to give the lie to charges of incest. The prince, who cared little for such niceties anyway, found Kielmannsegge exactly the type dearest to his heart: friendly, complaisant and *zaftig*.

She was also a dedicated spendthrift. From her plump hands, her husband's modest income went scattering to the winds, followed by a substantial fortune she acquired from her mother, Countess Platen. When her paramour George Louis succeeded to the electorate, the baroness waited with bated breath for his weekly handouts. According to the historian Tolland, George 'was wont to keep strict account of the Electoral expenses, which he defrayed in person on Saturday nights'.

Roly-poly Kielmannsegge was Prince George Louis's consolation when he took to wife his first cousin, Princess Sophia Dorothea. The princess was the daughter of his uncle, Duke George William of Celle, and his gorgeous French Huguenot wife, Eleanora d'Olbreuse. An only child, Sophia Dorothea had been raised to adore all things French and despise her German relations. She was even more beautiful than her mother, and spoiled rotten.

Ostensibly, the marriage had been negotiated by the brother dukes. Subtler minds than theirs had concocted it – Countess Platen at Osnabrück and George William's first minister, Baron Andreas Gottlieb von Bernstorff, at Celle. For once, Duchess Sophia allowed anger to overrule good business sense. She considered a connection with her hated sister-in-law Duchess Eleanora so detestable, she was willing to permit her niece's fortune to slip away from the family, in a marriage to the prince of nearby Wolfenbüttel. Not so Clara Platen. The duke's mistress was loath to see millions of thalers lost forever to the Hanover treasury (and her own pockets). For months, she planted hints in Duke Ernest Augustus's ear. Bribes, including a famous jewelled gold snuff box, won over Baron Bernstorff. Bernstorff, in turn, undertook to persuade his master, Duke George William, of the desirability of Sophia Dorothea's marriage to her cousin.

Suitably prompted, George William unveiled his master plan to his already half-persuaded brother. Let us make the family estates whole again, he cried, through the union of our children! Ernest Augustus agreed. To no one's surprise, he immediately bewailed the empty state of his treasury. Insolvency was his second nature.

George William's proposal was greeted with disgust by everyone but his brother. The prospective bride was anguished. Both mothers-in-law were outraged. The groom came out roaring,

'No Frenchwoman!'

No Frenchwoman, indeed, if his mother had anything to do with it. George Louis's bride-to-be was, for want of a less pejorative term, an ex-bastard. Her parents' left-hand marriage was not formalized until April 1676, when Sophia Dorothea, aged nine, was declared legitimate by proclamation of the Emperor Leopold. The emperor paid his war debt to her father with a dowry of fifteen thousand imperial crowns. In 1680, the imperial dowry failed to impress Duchess Sophia. She insisted her son, as the heir to an up-and-coming German duchy like Hanover, deserved a bride of better quality.

The duchess herself was from threadbare but impeccable lineage, a daughter of the beautiful, luckless Queen Elizabeth of Bohemia and a granddaughter of James I of England. Hoping to stake a claim to what she regarded as his rightful English inheritance, she hustled her son off to London to woo Princess Anne of York.

Prince George Louis was a disastrous suitor. He refused to learn even a few polite grunts in English and mortally offended his Stuart cousins. Anne of York received him only after exhausting every possible delay. Once they met face to face, she found excuses to be elsewhere. Her fat, silent little German suitor was a beau only a mother could love. Duchess Sophia described her eldest son with pathetic regret, 'The Brunswicker who is *fort doux* and makes [me] love him because he is so ugly.' Princess Anne eventually married George of Denmark.

Some years later, Sir Geoffrey Kneller did the best he could with the new English monarch in an official picture. The great portraitist painted George I fair-skinned. (One assumes nothing disturbed the sitting to provoke the famous beet-red face of the Guelphs.) Kneller thinned his royal subject's pudgy cheeks and made his blue eyes look a fraction less like a bullfrog's. No artist could do much, unfortunately, with the tiny, tightly pursed Guelph mouth. In the portrait, it is clamped shut in exasperation, ready to bellow over infractions by troopers, courtiers, mistresses or wives.

George Louis returned to Hanover in 1682 still balking at 'the Frenchwoman', but his uncle had been persuasive in his absence, setting forth the girl's merits in the only language clearly understood by the Guelphs. Nearly half a million thalers in various payments and promises made the princess of Celle an ideal daughter-in-law, in the eyes of Duke Ernest Augustus. Duchess Sophia did her arithmetic, forgot St James's for the moment, and added her blessing. George Louis had to succumb. According to the duchess,

'He did not like it, but the money tempted him as it would anybody else.'

It was most emphatically not a love-match.

Chapter Two

The Frenchwoman

P rince George Louis of Hanover, twenty-one, and Princess Sophia Dorothea of Celle, sixteen, were wed in the bride's apartments on 21 November 1682. They departed for the groom's ancestral home ten days later in a spectacular procession of one hundred coaches-and-eight, escorted by both ducal families, the brilliantly costumed wedding guests, a regiment of cavalry, trumpeters, outriders, pages and footmen, these last all dressed in red and blue with silver buttons. Citizens of the two duchies lined the thirty-mile route to cheer the party to its destination.

As several generations of romantic novelists have pointed out, a loveless marriage had been consecrated and a gothic tragedy was about to unfold. It need never have happened if Sophia Dorothea had only known how to make friends. Or keep her mouth shut.

The new Princess of Hanover displayed a nitwit genius for self-destruction. If she had deliberately set out to goad her husband into a permanent fury and set most of the court, including her mother-in-law, against herself, Sophia Dorothea could not have succeeded better. Her prince was plainly unhappy with his 'Frenchwoman' but he knew his dynastic duties; he was willing to give the marriage bed a try as long as it didn't interfere with his enjoyment of Baroness Kielmannsegge. He reckoned without his wife's tongue. The quick wit in which her parents delighted, he felt as a lash.

Sophia Dorothea had heard about his dalliance with Frau Busche but mistakenly assumed that his premarital high jinks were at an end. When she discovered he kept a current mistress whose sheer size made her impossible to ignore, the princess turned shrew, dragging the whole sordid mess into public. She staged a scene in which witnesses described her as a 'wildcat' who shrieked her loathing of her husband, his fat whore, his parents and all things Hanoverian.

Raging, demanding that she be returned forthwith to Celle, tearing at her husband with astonishing strength, the beautiful bride from Celle swore she would not bow to what the court saw as her husband's sexual prerogatives.

After that, her husband paid his conjugal visits warily. The couple's quarrelling was constant and vicious. It is a tribute to George Louis's persistence that he somehow managed to impregnate his wife. In between her hysterical outbursts and her husband's military expeditions, she gave birth to a son, George Augustus, in October 1683.

The heir was greeted publicly with cannonades and tumultuous cheering. In private, with the exception of the two enormously pleased grandfathers, the family's reaction to the blessed event was decidedly sour. A shaky reconciliation – or more accurately, an armed truce – was arranged between the princess and her young husband, who returned as quickly as possible to the less hazardous business of slicing up Frenchmen and Turks. Duchess Eleanora, the baby's maternal grandmother, wept. The birth destroyed the last hope of bringing her daughter back from hated Hanover. Duchess Sophia was also rankled by her grandson's birth. She saw the babe as a source of power over her husband, Duke Ernest Augustus, held by her aggravating daughter-in-law. An heir was an heir, however. Sophia was correct in her dealings with Sophia Dorothea, albeit cool.

The duchess's coolness turned to ice when the princess managed to embroil herself with her husband's treacherous younger brothers, Frederick Augustus, Maximilian William, and Charles Philip. In the 1680s and 1690s the young princes bitterly contested their father's new policy of primogeniture. Eldest-take-all was one of the rules of the game if Ernest Augustus, who had succeeded as Duke of Hanover in 1679, wished to achieve his ambition to be an elector of the empire. German custom parcelled out bits and pieces of an inheritance to each surviving son. Under the new rule, the duchy was handed intact to a single heir, George Louis. As they saw their prospects fade, his brothers turned to conspiracy.

Sophia Dorothea's infant son benefited enormously from the change, but she defied common sense by welcoming the young rebels to her apartments and her sympathies. Gus was tossed out in 1685. Max played a deadlier game and tried to assassinate his father with poisoned snuff. He escaped the headsman's axe by a whisker and fled.

When Gus was disinherited, only luck and her father-in-law's prurience saved the young princess. The old lecher, barely able to keep his hands off his tempting niece, pooh-poohed the evidence against her. He actually invited Sophia Dorothea to join him and Countess Platen on an Italian holiday.

Duchess Sophia was forced to watch her penniless son ride off to certain death as a common mercenary, while her husband and daughter-in-law kicked their heels in Venice and Rome. She could not help but be grimly pleased when Sophia Dorothea returned from her travels in the south to find George Louis infatuated with another mistress.

The prince's new love was Ehrengard Melusina von der Schulenberg, an extraordinarily tall, aggressively vulgar noblewoman who was one of his mother's maids of honour. Schulenberg was sallow, emaciated and so ill-favoured, even the duchess was at a loss to understand her attraction for her son. According to Horace Walpole,

> The duchess of Kendal . . . when mademoiselle Schulenberg, was maid of honour to the electress Sophia . . . though by no means an inviting object – so little, that on an evening when she was waiting behind the electress's chair at a ball, the princess Sophia said in English to Mrs Howard (later countess of Suffolk), then at her court: 'Look at that mawkin, and think of her being my son's passion!'

A numerous, war-like clan, the Schulenbergs were known for their claim to have given the Holy Roman Empire 'four marshals, twenty-five generals, six ministers, and four bishops'. Fraulein Schulenberg's brother, Count Johan Mathias, had fought his way in and out of the armies of the emperor, the Duke of Savoy and the King of Poland. At the end of his career, he defended the flag of the Republic of Venice, where he died in 1747.

The gawky giantess's relatives, including Count Johan, possessed distinguished reputations, chests full of medals, and little else. They were poor as military mice. When she was invited to be the duchess Sophia's maid of honour, Ehrengard Melusina set out from her family's dilapidated castle in Saxony without a backward glance.

In Hanover, she expected creature comforts and three meals a day; she was overwhelmed by her good fortune when George Louis seduced her. Amazingly, the liaison lasted, producing a pair of 'nieces' along the way.

George Louis's new conquest sent his wife into paroxysms of rage. One suspects her protests would not have been so shrill if her husband's choices had not been so grotesque; he seemed deliberately to taunt her with the repulsiveness of his two strumpets. Bony Schulenberg and mountainous Kielmannsegge, seen together, were the ugly sisters in 'Cinderella' come to life.

In the end, Sophia Dorothea was forced to accept her husband's freakish harem. There must have been a patch-up for at least a night or two because a daughter, also named Sophia Dorothea, was born to the couple in 1687. At that point their marriage disintegrated completely. During the parties celebrating the baby's birth, one of their routine spats escalated into open warfare. Bystanders had to pry George Louis's fingers from his wife's beautiful neck.

Countess Platen could barely conceal her pleasure as she watched from the sidelines. She had suffered a season of the princess's tongue in Italy, where the battle lines were drawn between them from the moment Sophia Dorothea identified the countess as the match-maker who had arranged her woeful marriage. The fading wanton was the target of the young beauty's cruellest remarks. Clara Platen gave as good as she got, defending her position with the duke. In her opinion, he spent entirely too much time admiring his daughter-in-law's cleavage.

Within her little clique, the princess mixed gossip about 'La Platen' with the renewed palace conspiracy. The plotting princes, whispering once again in her boudoir, were a ready audience.

Spies behind every tapestry and under every bed in the Leine Palace kept the countess fully informed. Her fury mounted day by day when she heard herself described as an elderly, vice-ridden hag whose day was done, a disgusting *cocotte* beneath the attention of the aristocratic young princess from Celle. Sophia Dorothea's perverse talent for inspiring hatred at last turned lethal. Clara Platen was her adversary in a classic female struggle for power – and for the same lover.

He was Count Philip Christopher von Königsmarck.

Philip was an aristocratic cutthroat from Sweden, a member of the same set of international freebooters that had spawned Clara Platen. His connections in Hanover were excellent. A brother-in-law, Count Carl Gustaf Lowenhaupt, was a general under the Duke of Celle. Philip himself was no stranger, having served, many years before, as a page in the court of Celle. To the shy lad's embarrassment, the tiny Princess Sophia Dorothea had developed a crush on him.

Philip was taller, handsomer, and not at all shy when he returned from a career as a free-lance soldier of fortune. He trailed a lurid reputation, acquired in the armies and bedrooms of Europe. The Swedish *condottiere* and his older brother Charles John were brushed with suspicion in a notorious English murder case. Philip's brother escaped the noose only by grace of his foreign citizenship. They were both urgently requested to quit the country.

Philip returned to Hanover a practised seducer, debauchee and duellist. Thanks to his brother's timely death fighting the Turks, he was also rich. All these qualifications sweetened his introduction to the court in the summer of 1688 by his comrade-in-arms, Prince Charles. With the prince's friendship came the duke's patronage, and the rank of colonel in the army. Philip quickly became Prince George Louis's boon companion. The glamorous Swede was the older son's kind of man, a battle-hardened officer and eager whoremonger. He acquired an imposing mansion not far from the Leine Palace, where he set up housekeeping with his sisters Aurora and Amelia Wilhelmina, who was Count Lowenhaupt's wife.

As indiscriminate as he was immoral, Philip had barely set foot in Hanover before he was entangled in Countess Platen's bedclothes. She was weatherbeaten, true, but he understood her value in dealing with the duke. She was also disposable, in his eyes, marked for the scrap-heap the moment he lined up his sights on Prince George Louis's beautiful young wife.

Contemporary paintings of Sophia Dorothea were destroyed after her disgrace, but one or two survived, hidden and secretly cherished by her children. There is one, very *décolletée*, that pictures her in her teens, charmingly dressed for a costume ball as a wood nymph with a wreath in her hand and flowers twined in her abundant dark hair. In another, more formal, portrait with her little dog, she is modestly decked out in an ermine trimmed gown and pearls. Her curls fall around a flirtatious, somewhat thin young face with an adorable dimpled chin. The eyes dominate both portraits, big, thickly lashed and deep as the sea. Her colouring is delicious, creamy and apple-cheeked. She was a pippin, as ripe for plucking as one of the sweet, tempting fruits that grew in the duke's orchards.

Philip and Sophia Dorothea flirted. He pleaded. She sighed. They pledged. He wrote love letters. She wrote love letters. (All used as evidence later, by the bushel-basketful, despite the amateurish codes they used.) Their romance was semi-public, for the silly things were incapable of keeping a secret. They paraded their infatuation under George Louis's very nose, although the princess probably remained physically chaste until 1690 or 1691. Philip, meanwhile, peddled his talents in the bedroom to the Platen woman and went tomcatting abroad, when warfare convulsed the Continent in 1688 and 1689.

Louis XIV's aggressions generally were good business for the mercenaries of Hanover. They now joined battle against him on the side of the newly-powerful alliance of Emperor Leopold and William of

Orange. King William had just chased James II from the throne of England. King Louis, who nursed an old grudge against the Dutchman from his defeats in 1672, sheltered the Stuart refugees in Paris and took up James's cause.

The war suddenly turned into a personal agony for Duchess Sophia when the French armies hacked their way through the Rhine Palatinate. They displayed a ferocity seventeenth-century Europe had never seen before, devastating the countryside, looting cities, butchering civilians. When French troops sacked Heidelberg, Sophia lived through days of terror for her brother, the Elector Palatine Charles Louis. In 1689, the enemy burned Heidelberg Castle to the ground. Then Louis invaded Holland and Germany. Sophia feared as much for her girlhood friends in the Hague, where her mother Queen Elizabeth had held her tattered court, as for her family in Hanover.

To complicate matters, the Turks went on a rampage at the emperor's back door. Troops were needed everywhere at once. Dukes George William and Ernest Augustus, with most of Ernest Augustus's sons, departed for the fighting in the Netherlands. Count von Königsmarck rode off on an expedition to Constantinople, at the side of Prince Charles.

Out of all this death and carnage, a dainty bonus dropped into Philip's lap – he added the lovely Sophia Dorothea to his sexual conquests. As the Hanover regiments fought, the princess waited in a fever of apprehension with the rest of the court. There were days of agonizing silence. Then a trickle of confused, frightening rumours. Then a messenger arrived carrying the news of a Turkish victory in the Morea, in which young Prince Charles had died but handsome Philip, dear Philip, had escaped with his life. She was uninterested in the fate of Charles, or her husband, or her father and father-in-law. Philip von Königsmarck was alive and galloping home to crush her in his arms!

He barely unbuckled his sword in Hanover before he took her. Their flirtation became a torrid physical affair; it was as if all the hot blood shed in battle served only as a loving cup for the scoundrel and his royal mistress.

The domestic triangle originally cornered by George Louis, Sophia Dorothea and fat Kielmannsegge now resembled a crowd scene. Thackeray did wry justice to the *dramatis personae*:

The characters in the tragedy, of which the curtain was now about to fall, are about as dark a set as eye ever rested on. There is the jolly prince, shrewd, selfish, scheming, loving his cups and his ease (I think his good humour makes the tragedy but darker); his princess, who speaks little but observes all; his old painted Jezebel of a mistress; his son, the electoral prince, shrewd, too, quiet, selfish, not ill-humoured, and generally silent, except when goaded into fury by the intolerable tongue of his lovely wife; there is poor Sophia Dorothea, with her coquetry and her wrongs, and her passionate attachment to her scamp of a lover, and her wild imprudences, and her mad artifices, and her insane fidelity, and her furious jealousy regarding her husband (though she loathed and cheated him), and her prodigious falsehoods; and the confidante, of course [Sophia Dorothea's lady-in-waiting, Eleanora von Knesbeck] into whose hands the letters were slipped; and there is Lothario, finally, than whom . . . one can't imagine a more handsome, wicked, worthless reprobate.

The lovers' passion blazed all the hotter for smouldering unfulfilled for so long. Philip was given command of the palace guard, which provided him with an open door to Sophia Dorothea's bedroom. They clung together in breathless, snatched moments when her husband was in residence; when the prince lingered with Kielmannsegge or Schulenberg or went campaigning in the field, they made love the night long.

When the couple was separated for a day, an hour, a minute, the love letters fluttered between them. Frau Knesbeck played postman, rushing the day's guilty scribblings back and forth with less and less concern for her mistress's safety as the months stretched into years.

There were lovers' quarrels, of course. The Swede was beside himself with jealousy when the princess appeared at her husband's side in the electoral celebrations of 1692. As the young couple was elevated to the rank of Electoral Prince and Princess, the thought that his mistress might share her bed with her legal husband tortured her seducer. He wrote:

Electoral Princess, . . . apparently the Electoral Prince invested you last night with this honourable title. Has his love-making more charm now that he has achieved higher rank? I cannot sleep for rage when I think that an Electoral Prince has robbed me of my charming mistress. This morning I would have offered congratulations on your newfound dignity, but I doubt whether your husband had done his duty; judging by his eagerness to see you again, the 'investiture' would have to have been at six in the morning. I hope that this letter will bring fresh memories, immediately after your electoral pleasures . . . Alas! I do not dare leave you with a souvenir of what we have had together; it would seem so meagre (I use the word *meagre* because a song says: 'Alas, my prince, how meagre is your love-making') – that you no longer can remember it.

Jealousy flared up again when Philip strayed briefly with the Duchess of Saxe-Eisenach. Sophia Dorothea lashed out in a bitter frenzy, as only she could. Miserably contrite, he pleaded for her forgiveness in an appropriately desperate letter:

I do not deserve your haughty airs; the sacrifice I have made for you of the Duchess of Saxe-Eisenach at least deserved a glance. You can see for yourself that I hardly look at her . . . I can only throw myself on your mercy. . . . What torment for me to miss the society of my adored one! What a night I shall spend! *Grand Dieu!* what was I thinking about? What demon possessed me? . . . When will you send me an answer? For the love of Heaven, let me have one soon.

There was no mistaking the answer she gave him, which prompted Philip to send this giddy note the morning after:

I slept like a king, and I hope you did the same. What joy! what rapture! what enchantment have I not tasted in your sweet arms! Ye gods! what a night I spent! The memory of it blots out all my troubles, and for the moment I count myself the happiest man on earth.

A single daily scribble was not enough. That same afternoon Frau Knesbeck went scurrying to her mistress with the following:

. . . I have never loved you so much before. You have never appeared to me so altogether lovely. With crossed hands and bended knees I thank you for all you have vouchsafed unto me. Suffer me therefore to see you again today, and do not put me off. I should die.

Knees appear with curious frequency in their correspondence. Philip's favourite farewell to the chestnut-haired princess was, '*Adieux, émable Brune. Je vous embrasse les jenous.*' '*Les jenous*' popped up again, in another letter of reconciliation:

. . . if you will allow me to come to you and kiss your knees and ask your pardon for all my suspicions, I shall be overjoyed. I am punished enough for them, God knows; for I have been sick unto death with grief and rage, and I had no news of you.

The apologists who later tried to defend the princess's innocence ignored sheaves of her love-letters, which ranged from the impetuous to the embarrassingly explicit:

Yesterday I received two of your letters, one very different from the other. One filled me with ecstasy. If I had held you in my arms I could have devoured you with kisses then and there. I will begin by answering all the nice and charming things you say. . . . There is madness indeed in the passion I have for you. I cannot understand how any one can love as I love. . . .

Another favourite theme was romantic death. Sophia Dorothea was certain she would not outlast her lover, should he be killed. When a mutual friend passed away, she wrote,

I heard yesterday of the death of La Court's brother. It was a shock, for I thought of you. Like you, he was young, he was well, yet now he is dead. You cannot imagine my sad reflections: I fear for you more than ever. If you truly love me, be careful of yourself for my sake; for if anything happened to you, what would become of me? I would not stay a moment in this world, life would be impossible.

Philip, not to be outdone, boasted of the flamboyant death he planned for himself. He went into grisly detail in a letter from his regiment:

I hope after all these assurances you will not ask me again whether I love you. If you still doubt it will kill me. But I must tell you I have a consolation here, close to me, not a pretty girl but a bear, which I feed. If you should fail me I will bare my chest and let him tear my heart out. I am teaching him that trick with sheep and calves, and he doesn't manage it badly. If ever I have need of him – God help me! I shall not suffer long.

Their letters recorded stormy departures, tearful reunions – all the usual trappings of such liaisons. The love affair of the Frenchwoman and her Swedish scallawag went its foolhardy way through 1692 and 1693.

The point is, nobody much cared.

In a court as amoral as Hanover, the private lusts of public persons provided their enemies with diverting gossip and little more. The elector licked his lips over the latest reports of Countess Platen's spies and chuckled as she rushed to him with intercepted billets-doux, but he did nothing. Shrewd little George Louis knew perfectly well that his wife was sleeping with his friend. He diddled his trollops, bided his time and did nothing. Word of the princess's misconduct quickly travelled the thirty miles to her parents in Celle. Her mother wrote warning Sophia Dorothea to be more discreet, but she did nothing.

Both lovers were shielded from the inevitable reckoning, she by the elector's amused indulgence, he by the reluctance of both the elector and Prince George Louis to lose a first-rate officer. Even when the pair became a public embarrassment, the family looked the other way. Sophia Dorothea wept openly for her beloved when he was away soldiering. Philip repaid her in cheap coin by dragging her name – and Clara Platen's – into drunken tales of his sexual exploits, bawled out to his drinking companions during a visit to Dresden in 1694.

Wearing such public horns stretched the prince's patience to the limit.

Philip returned from his Dresden trip with a secret commission as a general in the army of Saxony. His sister Aurora, who had become the mistress of the Saxon elector Augustus the Strong, secured the post for him. Philip bemoaned his inability to support his princess. Aurora pleaded his case to her royal paramour. Augustus, eager to secure the services of a fine officer, promised sanctuary, a handsome income, and a splendid new military career.

The affair underwent an abrupt change. In the eyes of Hanover, the Saxon army commission was an act of high treason by a trusted colonel. Philip's treachery was more than matched by Sophia Dorothea's political indiscretions. Flaunting her French sympathies, she declared that she would rather be a marquise in France than a princess in Germany. The 'Frenchwoman' actually proposed to her lover that they seek protection from Louis XIV. Casting about for a refuge closer to home, she suggested that they flee to Wolfenbuttel, where the duke was Prince Max's erstwhile ally in the poisoned snuff conspiracy. The question became less and less what grounds the prince would use to cashier his friend and divorce his wife, than when he would get around to doing it.

Retribution began to stir when Philip publicly blamed Clara Platen for his financial troubles. Even Sophia Dorothea had enough wit to insist that he stay on cordial, if not intimate, terms with the countess. Königsmarck would have none of it. He spilled out his hatred of Clara in a scalding letter to his mistress:

My greatest grudge is against Countess Platen, and on her I will avenge myself for she is the source of all my misfortunes. I will seek out her son, pick a quarrel with him and despatch him to the next world. After that I will tell everybody how she persecuted me, tell them also all the foolish things I once did with her, and then, if the Duke still shuts his eyes, the first time I meet her off her dung-hill I will insult her publicly, so that as long as she lives she will never dare show her face in public again. But how small such a revenge is in comparison with the harm she has done me! For she robs me of the only joy I have in the world. I lived only for you, I wore your chains with joy; you were my joy, my divine beloved, my all. Imagine what misery this jade of a woman brings upon me. If I were the Lord of Creation I would sacrifice her, fling her to the bears, let the lions suck her devil's blood, let the tigers tear out her cowardly heart. I would spend day and night seeking new torments to punish her for her black infamy in separating a man who loves to distraction, from the object of his love . . .

The countess got her hands on the letter almost as quickly as the princess. She dismissed the vituperation but the threat to her son goaded her into action; Königsmarck, one of Europe's finest swordsmen, would surely have killed young Platen. Sophia Dorothea, with inspired ineptitude, added heat to the feud with a new round of name-calling. The two star-crossed twits ignored their precarious position – and Countess Platen's very real power with the elector.

Chapter Three

A Most Wonderful Wickedness

The original scheme to entrap Philip and Sophia Dorothea was not terribly menacing, as worked out by the elector and his son. Once Countess Platen took a hand, their plan turned vengeful and bloody.

Prince George Louis was to absent himself on a mission to Berlin. He was fairly certain that his wife and her paramour would seize the opportunity to elope. In his son's absence, the old elector expected to catch the lovers in the act, charge and cashier his treacherous colonel and bring divorce proceedings against his daughter-in-law.

At the start, everything went according to plan. Great public fanfare accompanied the prince's departure for Berlin. By 1 July, the entire court of Hanover was in residence for the summer at Herrenhausen. Lingering in the nearly-empty Leine Palace, Sophia Dorothea acted out her role as if rehearsed. She crammed her jewels and personal possessions into a carriage and waited nervously for Philip. Sometime before midnight, he hurried from his home to the palace for their last rendezvous.

The elector, alerted by Countess Platen, sent armed men to take Count von Königsmarck into custody. It was hoped that the arresting party would apprehend him *in flagrante delicto* with the electoral princess.

From this point on, the descriptions of the night's events are as various as they are sensational. There is no doubt Philip was ambushed, but by whom he was attacked and where it happened is anybody's guess.

In one story he was set upon by a party of four armed bravos led by the estate manager of Osnabrück, a man named Montalban. A second tale involves three attackers, two Germans and an Italian. Depending on which account you read, he faced his assailants on the lonely road to the Leine Palace, in the Hall of Knights of the palace, or in the princess's bedroom itself. A sensational *roman à clef* written by Duke Antony Ulric of Wolfenbüttel, an amateur novelist, pictured Philip surprised in the princess's bed, springing into action in his nightshirt. A minority report from the memoirist Horace Walpole dismissed swordplay entirely and described him being strangled. Most stories are in agreement that the assassins had their hands full. Philip defended himself fiercely, wounding one or more of the men before he was finally vanquished.

In one highly coloured version of his death, Countess Platen stepped out of the shadows to sneer at her betrayer as he lay mortally wounded. The handsome, dying cavalier cursed her. She ground her heel into his mouth.

What happened to Königsmarck's corpse was as conjectural as how he came to be one. Some writers believed the dead man was cast into the swift, black waters of the Leine river. Others envisioned a gruesome end in the palace latrines, with a dusting of quicklime. Duke Antony's *Roman Octavia* described the body being walled up. In Thackeray's version, his carcass was burned the next day. A macabre account that went the rounds of the French court told how the murderers dragged their victim from the roadside and thrust him, wounded but still breathing, into a red-hot furnace. (A puzzling touch, since it was midsummer.) Walpole reported the discovery of Philip's skeleton under the floor of Sophia Dorothea's dressing room by an alterations crew refurbishing the Leine Palace for George II.

On one point only, the stories are unanimous. After his steward saw him leave his residence Sunday night, 1 July, the dashing Swede was never seen again.

When he did not put in an appearance by Tuesday, his secretary, George Conrad Hildebrandt, became alarmed. He wrote to the count's new employer and protector, the Saxon elector. A tremendous howl was heard from the elector's mistress, Aurora von Königsmarck, and her sister, Countess von Lowenhaupt. (The Electress Sophia called them 'the witches from Dresden'.) Through the Elector of Saxony, they demanded that the officials in Hanover produce their brother at once. The Elector of Hanover answered truthfully that he had no idea of the count's whereabouts.

Meanwhile, Princess Sophia Dorothea was an unwilling guest in the castle of Ahlden near Celle. Her lady-in-waiting Eleanora von Knesbeck had been clapped into a fortress in the Harz Mountains. The elector ordered a systematic search for the Philip–Sophia Dorothea letters, wherever they could be found.

An official version of the count's disappearance was issued by the Electress Sophia, who set a greater store by public opinion than most of the family:

> The Königsmarck affair was like this: he was gloomy in the evening and pretended he was going to bed, but his secretary saw that he went out alone, and when he did not return for four days they went to Marshal Podewils and told him their master was lost. They hunted for him everywhere but could not find him. The Duke had his things sealed up, but they took his correspondence. . . . We must take comfort in thinking that God does all for the best. If the wife cannot endure her husband she is better from him than with him.

Her announcement stirred up more whispers than it stilled. Gossip flew from court to court across Europe. Königsmarck's disappearance was a most wonderful wickedness, the latest in a long string of outrages committed by the upstart Guelphs. Calls for an investigation from Saxony, Denmark and Wolfenbüttel sent the elector of Hanover scrambling before Emperor Leopold in an attempt to quiet the outcry. The family fretted lest the scandal wreck their hopes of an English succession.

Prince George Louis accomplished what he started out to do. He divorced his wife. Advised by Count Platen and Baron Bernstorff, the same bureaucrats who originally promoted the marriage, he used a simple and effective stratagem to end it. He wrote to Sophia Dorothea, inviting her to take her place at his side once again, with special mention of her duties in the marriage bed. His letter ignored Königsmarck, adultery and pro-French sympathies.

The princess refused. She foolishly asked to return to her parents at Celle, whereupon her father was shown a selection of her steamiest love letters. He declined to receive his daughter. A rump tribunal presided over by Platen and Bernstorff pronounced her guilty of 'malicious desertion'.

On 28 December 1694, the marriage was officially dissolved. Sophia Dorothea, who took up enforced residence in Ahlden Castle, was to be known henceforth as the duchess of Ahlden. She remained in the castle, except for a few months spent at Celle when French armies seriously menaced Ahlden, for the rest of her life. Twenty-eight when she arrived, the duchess died at the age of sixty, on 13 November 1726.

Sentimental apologists have made a heart-rending case for Sophia Dorothea, picturing her as a blameless, melancholy wife from whom fortune and children were torn by a scheming husband who threw her into durance vile. The actual facts are less gothic.

A moat circled her castle, it is true, but the big, comfortable sixteenth-century country house on the banks of the Aller was far from being a fortress. Nor were the duchess's circumstances cruel in the slightest. Cavalry troopers accompanied her carriage on short fair-weather outings to the tiny village, but any lady of her rank went abroad with a military escort. A courtesy call was paid twice a day by the superintendant of the castle, who became, in time, an old friend. Her court was small but not inconsequential; more than thirty persons kept the duchess amused. There seems to have been a fussy anxiety about her health, with physicians at the ready to treat the slightest sniffle.

The prisoner, if such she was, was maintained in luxury. No expense was spared for her table or the comforts of the household. Her allowance (which her partisans fail to mention) was generous. Devoted to French fashion, the duchess purchased new gowns frequently and made fairly lavish acquisitions of jewels. Captivated by her brilliant costumes and melted by her smiles as the lady of Ahlden swept past in her coach and six, the villagers became quite partisan about 'their princess'.

In her long incarceration, Sophia Dorothea was refused only three things: permission to speak to whomever she pleased, freedom to travel and the right to raise her children.

The first taboo was intended to prevent her from drumming up political support. Considering the troubles her chatter had brought down on her head, the ban on conversation may have been a kindness to the talkative duchess. Small talk with the village rustics was included in the prohibition – no great loss. In fact, it added a charming touch of mystery to the lady of the castle. Year after year, she rode out among the locals, cheerful, beautiful and silent. In her last decade at Ahlden, even this rule was relaxed. She was allowed to hold monthly receptions for her neighbours and welcomed visits from her mother, Duchess Eleanora of Celle.

Forbidding Sophia Dorothea to travel seemed punitive since her parents' home was only twenty miles away, but the possibility that the former electoral princess might impulsively decamp to Versailles, say, to spread her own version of the Königsmarck scandal was a prospect too embarrassing to contemplate, even for a family inured to disgrace.

The loss of her children was a tragic necessity. If her disregard of their welfare as she romped with Philip von Königsmarck did not dictate her separation from them, the family's effort to save the reputation of her young son and salvage the English succession did. Even before his adulterous mother entered Ahlden castle, the smart talk in London dubbed Prince George Louis's son 'Young Königsmarck'.

Little George Augustus so resembled his mother in boyhood that his father could not bear the sight of him. The young prince, aged eleven, and his sister, aged seven, were given into the care of their paternal grandmother, the Electress Sophia. After her husband died in 1698, the electress took particular comfort in her grandchildren and retired to the summer palace at Herrenhausen to devote her time to their rearing.

His unwanted children securely tucked away with his mother, George Louis began his electorate. A certain amount of carping could be heard that his court was a drab affair compared to that of his extravagant father. His cousin, the razor-tongued Duchesse d'Orléans, wrote:

> . . . pleasure is no longer to be seen in Hanover, for this Elector is so cold he turns everything to ice . . . he knows nothing of what is princely as I have seen in all his doings.

But Carnival was kept, and except for the intrusion of a certain soldierly coarseness, the electoral court had no difficulty warming to its new prince and his ways. Acceptance among his fellow sovereigns came as the ghost of Königsmarck was laid. The electors seated the new ruler in the Imperial College, where his father had never gained admission.

George Louis made his amends and settled his scores. The Platens went. However useful Platen had been in the divorce from Sophia Dorothea, there was no forgetting or forgiving the fact that the count and his scheming wife had promoted George Louis's ghastly marriage in the first place.

Condolences on his father's death from the Duchess of Ahlden were ignored, as were all her attempts to communicate. Her tear-stained pleas for reunion with her children received no answer. Divorce, to the new elector, was divorce. Mention of his ex-wife was prohibited in his presence, nor were his son and daughter permitted mementos of their mother. To all intents and purposes she did not exist.

He was brutal with his mother-in-law. When he inherited the Duchy of Celle on his uncle's death in 1705, George Louis entered the city in triumph. The widow, the other hated 'Frenchwoman' in his life, was unceremoniously driven from her castle to live out her days in a tiny residence at Lüneburg with a handful of attendants.

The new elector was even-handed, even magnanimous toward his remaining brothers. He ignored the years of intrigue, even the poisoned snuff incident, brought Max home from Rome and restored both him and his brother Christian to army commands. His youngest brother, Ernest Augustus, became his constant companion, basking in the affection the elector could not bring himself to bestow on his son. When the elector became King George I and head of the Church of England, Ernest Augustus succeeded him as Lutheran Prince-Bishop of Osnabrück.

The Guelphs presented a united front, or what was left of one, as they rode off to fight Louis XIV in the War of the Spanish Succession.

It has been remarked that George Louis was loyal. Under his rule, Hanover never wavered, as the new conflict between the Austrians, their English and German allies, and the hated Bourbon monarchy see-sawed across Europe. Hanoverian regiments gave a splendid account of themselves under the command of the elector and his brothers. They defended the Low Countries and fought as far afield as the Danube. (Prince Christian was drowned in it during a retreat.) Precious reinforcements dispatched by George Louis gave the Duke of Marlborough the edge he needed in 1704 to achieve his immortal victory at Blenheim. Small wonder that the elector was in high favour with the English in general and Marlborough in particular.

After the victory, Duke John came calling with his duchess Sarah to thank his feisty little German ally – and sniff out preferment, should the English succession come to the House of Hanover. The Churchills, a supremely supple pair of courtiers, fawned on his mother as they flattered the elector. For the moment at least, it was Sophia, not George Louis, who would take up the English orb and sceptre when Queen Anne died. (Meningitis had carried off the little duke of Gloucester in 1700. In 1702 William III's horse stumbled in a mole hole, threw him and killed him.) The dowager electress was as coy as Marlborough was unctuous, feigning disinterest in her own prospects and doing her son's cause no good at all.

Sophia's Jacobite sympathies had been public knowledge for decades. By her own admission, she maintained a correspondence with James II in Paris during the years her husband and sons were fighting off his protector, Louis XIV. She was full of sympathy for James's exiled son, 'the poor Prince of Wales', actually urging his claim to the English crown at the expense of her own son. In a letter to one English diplomat, she dismissed George Louis as too unpopular to govern the English and heaped praise on the Old Pretender. 'The Prince of Wales is not a bastard . . . he has learned and suffered so much for his father's errors that he may make a good King of England.' When William III, whose life had been devoted to keeping male Catholic Stuarts off the throne, met Sophia at Loo in 1700, the Act which would eventually make kings of her heirs was already being debated in Parliament. She was maddening in her modesty, sighing that if she hoped for a crown, 'it must be a heavenly one'.

If all this was not exactly treasonous, it was disloyal to a ridiculous degree, ample cause for the elector to hate his mother. He snubbed her and banished her to Herrenhausen. She was too popular to abuse publicly, so he was forced to treat her with respect on the state occasions that marked the march of the Guelphs towards their English destiny.

One such occasion was the wedding of the heir, George Augustus, in 1705. It was a match arranged by the dowager electress, who displayed perceptible malice in her selection of a bride. Princess Caroline of Ansbach delighted the prince and infuriated the elector. Too coarse-featured to be called a beauty, Caroline nevertheless had the attractions needed to please her earthy twenty-two-year-old husband: she was blonde and blue-eyed with a radiant pink complexion and superb breasts. She was also tartly intelligent. The elector found to his dismay that his witty new daughter-in-law was a painful echo of his shrewish ex-wife. After one or two encounters, he referred to her as '*cette diablesse Madame la Princesse*'.

Just to be irritating, the dowager electress drummed up foreign honours for her newlywed grandson. Prince George Augustus was voted English citizenship by Act of Parliament and, in 1706, was invested with the Garter by Queen Anne. The queen went further, creating him Baron Tewkesbury, Viscount Northallerton, Earl of Milfordhaven and Duke of Cambridge. The elector choked with jealousy to see such honors showered on his son, but he could do nothing for fear of offending the English court.

Whom the elector disdained, of course, his mother adored. She kept the young couple at her side in Herrenhausen for the birth of her great-grandson, Frederick Louis, and for the succession of little princesses who followed, Anne, Emily and Caroline. To brighten prospects for her grandson and his wife, if not for her son, she stopped protesting her lack of royal ambitions long enough to receive Lord

Halifax in 1707. The English envoy came to share with Queen Anne's 'first subject and heiress' the queen's joy at the union of Scotland and England. The dowager electress Sophia, now in her mid-seventies, was a dutifully joyful heiress. Her own heir, the elector, was grumpy, but accepted the Garter from Halifax.

A few months later, he was reduced to impotent rage when his detested son became an authentic hero in the Battle of Oudenarde. As an officer under the Duke of Marlborough in the great Allied victory of 1708, George Augustus was as fierce as any Guelph in history. He fought on foot when his mount was shot out from under him, slashing his way into the French with no thought but for glory. A new royal legend started when the poet Congreve celebrated the 'young Hanover brave' in verse:

> In this bloody field, I assure you,
> When his warhorse was shot
> He valued it not,
> But fought still on foot like a fury.

The elector put an instant stop to the heroics, yanked the prince from military service and refused his repeated requests to be returned to action. (It was thirty-five long years on the sidelines before the prince, as George II, rode into battle once again at Dettingen.)

George Augustus was brave but not bright. It quickly became apparent that his wife Caroline would be the guiding genius behind the couple's future career. She soothed his tantrums (he was given to kicking his wig and hat around the room) and persuaded him, as his grandmother could not, to learn English. Although heavily accented, his modest command of the language would serve him splendidly in later years as Prince of Wales.

For the moment, the family manoeuvred gingerly between wooing the Whig politicians in London and angering Queen Anne. The queen was dying, but hated being reminded of it; she was slowly drowning in laudanum, to which she was addicted, and fat. Guelph hopes faded when Sarah Churchill overreached herself in her domineering management of the befuddled queen in 1711. Her husband, the Duke of Marlborough, grandest of the Whig grandees, was dismissed as commander-in-chief. The queen expressed her dislike of the Whig-sponsored Guelphs, but did not change the Act of Succession. A muted sigh of relief could be heard in Hanover.

In 1714, the dowager electress Sophia died unexpectedly, just seven weeks before Queen Anne. She was laid to rest in the chapel of the Leine Palace without ever setting foot on the English earth she regarded as her native soil.

Across the Channel, the queen realized that Sophia's death meant that the boorish little German prince who had once made a botch of wooing her was about to inherit her throne. From her deathbed, she angrily forbade any member of the House of Hanover to visit London – and almost immediately died. At the last, the pitiful queen's bulk was so colossal she had to be hoisted about with a chair-and-pulley. Anne was buried in Westminster Abbey, some said, in a square coffin.

In due course, messengers arrived in Hanover to announce, '*Die Königin Anne ist tot!*' The little continental electorate and the great island kingdom now shared a single ruler.

When the Act was passed thirteen years before, the officials who scouted Europe for royal talent knew exactly whom they wished to see on the English throne. It was the electress Sophia. She was an attractive princess whose aristocratic profile would look well on the coinage; a well-travelled sophisticate who could contend with diplomats in four modern languages and classical Latin; a lively woman of many enjoyments who even in old age was as eager for a dance as a dispute with a philosopher. The cheap press in London might refer to her as 'the German' and 'Old Sophy' but those who knew better looked beyond the pinched and pious court of Queen Anne to a brilliant new era under 'the merry *débonnaire* princess of Germany'. With English expectations screwed up to such a pitch, the Elector George Louis came as a shock.

Chapter Four

His Hideous Mistresses

W hen Londoners realized their new king was an utterly graceless little Teuton who spoke not a word of English, they mocked him unmercifully. Coffee-house wits made up howlers in German dialect; Grubb Street scribblers vied with each other concocting slanders for the *Daily Courant* and the *Evening Post*; urchins ran after the royal carriages everywhere, shrieking taunts at 'German George' and his retinue.

The butt of their jokes came to town in September, 1714. George I landed at Greenwich from the royal barge sent out to pick him up, when fog prevented the yacht *Peregrine* from navigating the Thames.

George I squinted through the mists at a new London populated by new Londoners. He was now fifty-four years old. When he was five, the Great Plague of 1665 killed more than one hundred thousand, or one in every three, Londoners. Mass graves engulfed whole neighbourhoods, put the citizens to flight and gave the city an all but unrecognizable new face. Less than six months later, the Great Fire of 1666 completed the transformation. Charles II fought the blaze personally, galloping through the inferno scattering guineas by the fistful to his bucket brigades. He was powerless to save London. More than thirteen thousand houses went up in smoke, together with nearly every landmark of the medieval city.

During George's only previous visit in 1680, the new St Paul's had consisted of a few rough courses of stone, roofless and domeless. All around there was a hubbub of construction as the metropolis raised itself out of the ashes. Now Londoners worshipped in Sir Christopher Wren's magnificent cathedral. The city, much of it, was rebuilt in a graceful style of architecture named for Queen Anne but introduced by William of Orange. Recent houses were actually built with brown brick imported from Holland, their front doors canopied in the Dutch manner. They lined spacious new squares and straight new streets alongside new royal parks laid out in imitation of the formal gardens of Versailles.

The mansions of the rich clustered along the banks of the Thames. River frontage, with private landings and watergates, was much sought after, for city people looked upon the river as their central boulevard. The eighteen-oar royal barge was only the most elaborate of the luxurious private craft that skimmed back and forth. Watermen in hundreds of little wherries supplied public transport. London Bridge provided the only foot crossing, an ancient span groaning under a superstructure of shops and houses which threatened to topple into the water – and sometimes did. Westminster Bridge would not be built until the reign of George II.

London's population was lustier than ever. Satin-clad, bejewelled aristocrats lurched through the mob in sedan chairs on their way to a hundred destinations of the flesh: to the uproarious Southwark Fair in September; to the streets around Shepherd Market for the May Fair ('the chiefest nursery of evil'); to Covent Garden with its phalanx of bawdy houses. Drinking, gaming and sex (with child prostitutes, as often as not) were the principal entertainments, along with public hangings and bare-knuckle boxing, bull-baiting and cock-fighting. In the country the hunt, in hot pursuit of anything that moved, reigned supreme. In town dining or, more accurately, gorging on mountainous evening meals, was the preferred diversion of the day. To keep abreast of affairs, everyone congregated in the city's coffee- and chocolate-houses. A Swiss visitor, Misson de Valberg, wrote:

> These houses are extremely convenient. You have all Manner of News there: You have a good Fire which you may sit by as long as you please; you have a Dish of Coffee, you meet your friends for the Transaction of Business, and all for a Penny, if you don't care to spend more.

Etiquette had improved not a whit. Rich or poor, educated or ignorant, gentleman of quality or street-corner tough, the typical Londoner cursed constantly and with relish.

The snobs in Parliament and court dismissed George as a bumpkin. They tittered behind their lace cuffs at his awkwardness and his army manners, raised eyebrows at his locked-up wife and thought his mistresses were absolutely priceless.

His ministers, or the Lords of the Cabinet Council, as they were called, complained bitterly about their master's ignorance of English. They sputtered that it gave the Germans who surrounded him a monopoly of his time. George I had no English and wanted none. His French was fluent, as befitted a Continental monarch; he regarded English as the backwater tongue of an untutored nation of sailors. The fault lay with the stupid Englishmen who refused to learn the lingua franca of the time. For thirteen years, the king of England and most of his ministers addressed the nation's business by means of hand signals and fragments of schoolboy Latin.

If the English were vexed with their strange new king, George I was openly suspicious of his new subjects, both before and after his coronation. His uneasiness was shared by gaunt old Fräulein Schulenberg – she was forty-eight now, or fifty-six, or sixty, if you counted unkindly – who balked at leaving Hanover and voiced the most violent objections to George risking his electoral neck among savages, even for a kingdom.

Along with their other faults the English had been known to kick out their kings, even kill them. A shudder of horror still reverberated through Europe over the beheading of Charles I in 1649. George owed his own succession to the betrayal and ejection of James II in 1688.

Ehrengard Melusina blubbered her fears to her lover. When she actually stood in the dust watching George's carriage drive off, the poor thing went a little daft. She staggered about the gardens at Herrenhausen, weeping buckets of desperate tears as she embraced the linden trees and the statues, swearing that she, for one, would never leave them.

Baroness Kielmannsegge was driven to desperation by much more practical matters. When her creditors heard of George's departure, they instantly camped on her doorstep, refusing to vacate until their bills were paid in full. There was no other way out for the baroness, except to follow her master. Somehow, she disguised herself (a major undertaking, considering her dimensions) and hot-footed it in pursuit of George. Schulenberg heard of her rival's departure, wiped away her tears and hurried off in Kielmannsegge's wake, gathering up her 'nieces' along the way.

The hysterical creatures caught up with their protector before he reached the Channel. He greeted them warmly and soothed their fears of regicide.

'Oh,' he told them, 'I have nothing to fear, for the king-killers are all my friends.'

His barge slid into Greenwich on 29 September 1714 and the court trooped down to greet him. The assembly did not inspire confidence. Many of the noblemen who knelt to their new sovereign, including the nimble-witted Duke of Marlborough, had undergone a lightning switch of loyalties from Catholic King James to Protestant King William. They could switch again. Mercifully, the ceremonies were in English, so, to George I, their oaths of loyalty were incomprehensible and easier to swallow.

William Thackeray painted a picture of the welcoming pageantry impossible to surpass:

He brought with him a compact body of Germans, whose society he loved, and whom he kept round the royal person. He had his faithful German chamberlains; his German secretaries; his negroes, captives of his bow and spear in Turkish wars; his two ugly, elderly German favourites, Mmes. of Kielmannsegge and Schulenberg, whom he created respectively Countess of Darlington and Duchess of Kendal. The duchess was tall and lean of stature, and hence was irreverently nicknamed the Maypole. The countess was a large-sized noblewoman, and this elevated personage was denominated the Elephant. . . . One seems to be speaking of Captain Macheath, and Polly, and Lucy. The king we had selected; the courtiers who came in his train; the English nobles who came to welcome him, and on many of whom the shrewd old cynic turned his back – I protest it is a wonderful satirical picture. I am a citizen waiting at Greenwich pier, say, and crying hurrah for King George; and yet I can scarcely keep my countenance, and help laughing at the enormous absurdity of this event!

Here we are, all on our knees. Here is the Archbishop of Canterbury prostrating himself to the head of his church, with Kielmannsegge and Schulenberg with their ruddled cheeks grinning behind the defender of the faith. Here is my Lord Duke of Marlborough kneeling too, the greatest warrior of all times; he who betrayed King William – betrayed King James II – betrayed Queen Anne – betrayed England to the French, the Elector to the Pretender, the Pretender to the Elector; and here are my Lords Oxford and Bolingbroke, the latter of whom has just tripped up the heels of the former; and if a month's more time had been allowed him, would have had King James at Westminster. The great Whig gentlemen made their bows and *congées* with proper decorum and ceremony; but yonder keen old schemer knows the value of their loyalty.

'Loyalty,' he must think, 'as applied to me – it is absurd! There are fifty nearer heirs to the throne than I am. I am but an accident, and you fine Whig gentlemen take me for your own sake, not for mine. You Tories hate me; you archbishop, smirking on your knees, and prating about heaven, you know I don't care a fig for your Thirty-nine Articles, and can't understand a word of your stupid sermons. You, my Lords Bolingbroke and Oxford – you know you were conspiring against me a month ago; and you, my Lord Duke of Marlborough – you would sell me or any man else, if you found your advantage in it. Come, my good Melusina, come, my honest Sophia, let us go into my private room, and have some oysters and some Rhine wine, and some pipes afterward; let us make the best of our situation; let us take what we can get, and leave these bawling, brawling, lying English to shout, and fight, and cheat, in their own way!

The party made its way to London a few days later with all possible pomp. A procession of more than two hundred coaches-and-six stuffed with nobility rolled along after the king and the Prince of Wales. George Augustus had been allowed to share his father's triumph. The Duke of Marlborough, remembering Oudenarde, was among the Whig potentates who insisted upon it. The duke himself, brought back from disgrace under Queen Anne, was reinstated on the spot as captain-general of the armed forces. Stuart supporters, chief among them Henry St John, Viscount Bolingbroke, and Robert Harley, Earl of Oxford, found themselves exiled to the far fringes of the crowd.

At Southwark, the Lord Mayor and assorted aldermen, sheriffs and municipal officers made a great fuss over the new king. A ceremonial sword was handed over, then handed back, and everyone clattered on to the Palace of St James's through a delightfully sunny English September afternoon.

Between the arriving king and his kingdom lay a gulf, apparent even in the day-to-day trivia of royal housekeeping. The incident of the carp was illustrative. When he looked out of his bedroom window, the king beheld the royal park, prettily watered by the royal canal, which was abundantly stocked with royal fish. He expressed a desire for fresh fish on his table. The ranger of the park, Lord Chetwynd, obliged. Some fine, fat carp were sent along the very next morning. His Majesty was most pleased, until an aide explained to him that he was expected to give Lord Chetwynd's messenger five guineas for the king's own fish, caught in his own canal, in his own park.

In the mind of George I, the king's prerogatives were unlimited. He was an absolute autocrat in Hanover. He refused to believe he was anything less in London. The idea that an English monarch's powers might be limited – especially in decisions relating to his own household and lands – simply never occurred to him.

Contretemps continued to plague him. When he wanted to enlarge Kensington Gardens by gouging out a largish chunk of Hyde Park, the king was genuinely surprised by the public outcry. His bafflement increased when he was told he could not, without disastrous consequences, turn St James's Park into a vegetable plot for the royal kitchens. He was more than a little offended by the uproar over his demand for an increase of five hundred thousand pounds in his Civil List.

For some odd reason, getting satisfactory seafood to his table posed a problem. George could not stomach the English oysters; the fresher they were presented, the more disgusted he became with their unaccustomed taste and lack of flavour. It took weeks before someone realized the king preferred his shellfish elderly, downright rank, to English sensibilities. How he avoided poisoning himself, no one could figure out.

A certain amount of pillaging was expected in every court, but the king's German retainers swarmed in like pirates – stealing, swindling, promoting bribes. Each tale of German mischief was more outrageous than the last, but the king turned a blind eye. One story concerned a Hanoverian cook who asked His Majesty to be returned to Germany. 'Because they steal here too badly,' he complained. 'We were so careful in Hanover.' His royal master refused to permit the trip. 'Bah! It is only English money – steal like the rest!' he told the scamp, 'and be sure you take enough.'

George's black servants displayed a profitable talent for tall tales. Mahomet was famous for his story of the amazing death of the queen of Prussia, George I's sister. For a few shillings, the grinning valet would regale his listeners with details of the agonies she had suffered after being poisoned with diamonds. He swore he had poked his fingers through the queen's stomach – worn tissue-thin by her diet of deadly gems.

Infinitely more brazen than George I's servants were his mistresses, who looted openly and shamelessly. When they learned of the existence of 'the great wardrobe' and 'the board of green cloth' – commissary departments for the royal household – the Elephant and the Maypole placed gargantuan orders for furniture, silver, china, draperies, food, beer, wine, candles and fuel.

A veritable river of beer was needed to slake the thirst of the countess of Darlington and her servants. From four and a half gallons in June 1715, her brewery allowance, by June 1717, had reached the staggering quantity of sixteen barrels a month. This, in addition to a torrential outpouring of sherry and claret.

Both mistresses clamoured for supplies so loudly and so constantly that the harried commissary clerks threw up their hands in 1718, recommending separate kitchens and annual household allowances of three thousand pounds apiece. Never satisfied, the Duchess of Kendal negotiated an additional candle and fuel allowance, on the ground that the king took his nightly supper in her apartment.

Sharing honours in corruption with the royal mistresses were George I's German personal staff, Baron von Bernstorff (who had helped in the divorce, and had once served George's uncle, the duke of Celle), Baron Johann Caspar von Bothmer, and Jean Robethon, his Huguenot private secretary. For their industry, George elevated Bernstorff and Bothmer to the House of Lords and made Robethon a baronet.

'Coronets and garters, bishoprics and embassies, lordships of the Treasury and tellerships of the Exchequer, nay even charges in the Royal Stud and Bedchamber' were for sale, according to the historian Lord Thomas Macaulay.

In the first wave of bribe-givers was James Brydges, Duke of Chandos. Chandos scattered tips like a sailor in 1714 and 1715, handing 250 lottery tickets to Bothmer, four hundred guineas to Robethon, three thousand pounds to the countess of Darlington, a ring 'perfect in its kind' to her daughter, and sundry gifts of wines and sweetmeats to everyone in sight. His generosity bought Chandos's friend, a man named Thomas Phillpott, the cashiership of the salt office. Other, even more profitable appointments were paid for. Chandos's gifts added up impressively over the five years ending in February 1720: nine thousand five hundred pounds each, to the countess and the Duchess of Kendal, nearly three thousand to Bernstorff, and one thousand three hundred to Bothmer.

Chandos was only one in a multitude of open-handed courtiers from whom the duchess of Kendal collected incredible fortunes. George I himself settled on her a quasi-respectable pension of seven thousand five hundred pounds a year, a sum she regarded as her right. There was, later on, the household allowance as well. When the post of master of the horse fell vacant, she persuaded her lover to hand over that salary, too. (George no doubt considered it appropriate payment for mounts of a different kind!) Comfortable incomes to anyone else, but not to the acquisitive duchess.

After the insurrection of 1715, the duchess made an impressive profit from the rebel family of Bolingbroke, who clambered back up out of their general disgrace by clinging to the Maypole. For five thousand pounds she enabled Bolingbroke's father to become a viscount. For an additional four thousand pounds she secured the Bolingbrokes a high-salaried customs post. Finally, for an eleven thousand-pound bribe contributed by Bolingbroke's new French wife, the duchess stage-managed her repentant Jacobite husband's return to England.

The duchess meddled in Parliamentary budgets and City financial deals, always to profitable effect. She received secret subsidies from abroad. There were long-distance bribes from America to pay for colonial governorships. Her name was prominent on the French ambassador's payroll, although it is doubtful that she did Louis XV much good. She lined her purse with offerings from the Habsburg court in Vienna.

'She was in effect as much Queen of England as ever any was,' according to Sir Robert Walpole, 'though she would sell the King's honour for a shilling advance to the highest bidder.'

Schulenberg at fifty-six, Kielmannsegge at forty, were a pair of gloriously decrepit public figures. London instantly took them to its heart; not since Nell Gwynn, Barbara Castlemaine and Charles II had the mob been offered such a delightful opportunity to taunt the whores of royalty.

The two mistresses drew a chorus of billingsgate whenever they appeared in public. Eventually the duchess, provoked beyond endurance, shouted in broken English from her carriage window, 'Good pipple, why you abuse us? We come for all your goods.' A wit in the crowd snapped back, 'Yes, damn ye – and for all our chattels, too!'

George I naturalized his women and ennobled them with the most profitable titles in the royal purview. Fat Kielmannsegge was content to become the Countess of Darlington. At first, George honoured Schulenberg with a brace of Irish estates, creating her Baroness of Dundalk, Countess and Marchioness of Dungannon and Duchess of Munster – with little in the way of attendant incomes. The Maypole quickly realized that collecting Irish rents was a chancy proposition at best. She sulked until George gave her property closer to London. He made her Baroness of Glastonbury, Countess of Feversham and, elevating her to the rank and title by which she is remembered, Duchess of Kendal. Fevered with ambition, the duchess aimed higher still. From her Viennese connection came the grandiloquent title of Princess of Eberstein, conferred by a grateful Emperor Charles VI!

The awful old dollies drained the last shilling from their new estates and, given the opportunity, they stole outright. Queen Anne's personal possessions were scattered about St James's when George I inherited the palace, booty untouched by Anne's onetime favourite, the grasping Duchess of Marlborough. Without a by-your-leave, the Elephant and the Maypole pawed through all the drawers and cabinet doors, seizing the queen's jewel boxes as they went. Years later, George II had to rent the diamonds his queen wore to her coronation; all that survived of poor Anne's legacy was a single short strand of pearls.

The Maypole had her admirers, including the great Walpole, and her corrupt dealings were, in general, sordid but kindly. Courtiers who crossed her, however, did so at their peril.

An anonymous letter in Mist's *Journal* observed, in 1721, 'We are ruined by trulls, nay, what is more vexatious, by old ugly trulls, such as could not find entertainment in the most hospitable hundreds of old Drury.' Blazing with anger, the duchess brought the insult to the attention of Parliament. Nathianiel Mist was fined and imprisoned.

In the most famous instance of her vengeance, the duchess brought total ruin to a man named John Ker of Kersland. A spy and minor functionary in Queen Anne's time, he claimed to have been instrumental in bringing about the succession of the House of Hanover. George I dropped him when he ascended the throne, with a trifling gift of 'one hundred thalers and two medals'.

Ker tried to obtain the post of governor of the Bahamas, but the Maypole beat him to the appointment, selling it to a rival. To her credit, she tried to negotiate a compromise with him. Ker would not be bought off. He publicly denounced

one of the foreign concubines . . . whose notorious rapacity even extended to the Colonies in America, where they appointed and continued governors at pleasure, not only exacting vast sums but receiving the revenues ordered by the public to support them.

The publicity was too much for the Duchess of Kendal. Within days, Ker was prosecuted by the chancellor. In his memoirs, he protested

the torrent of corruption that inundated the Court. . . . From the Lord Chancellor downwards, never has the law been more distorted in any case to suit political views than it was in that in which this infamous woman was plaintiff.

Contemporary accounts accused the Maypole of pursuing Ker 'to prison and even beyond the grave'.

George I seemed oblivious to his public shame. A field officer all his life, he conducted his English reign in much the same way as a military campaign in hostile territory. He bivouacked away from home as comfortably as he could, between frequent return trips to Hanover, Herrenhausen, Osnabrück and the other German landscapes he loved. (One of his first acts was the repeal of the regulation barring English sovereigns from foreign travel.)

For advice he listened to his German councillors. For comfort he turned to the duchess and the countess. There were quick amours on the side (the Duchess of Shrewsbury, a marvellously wanton Italian, was one such adventure) but George stuck mainly to his tried and true German imports. The Duchess of Kendal's apartments were conveniently located in the palace, and he hurried there daily for an odd variety of amusements. (At least part of the time, the Maypole entertained him with paper cut-outs.)

To confound their English competitors, his mistresses mounted guard on George I with a vigilance that amounted to mania. When the king went abroad in the city in his sedan chair, six footmen went ahead, six yeomen of the guard marched on either flank, and the Elephant and the Maypole covered his rear – each in her own sedan chair with attendants. The crowds loved it. If their destination was the opera, the king shunned the on-stage box reserved for royals, preferring to sit in the cozy darkness of an ordinary box with one mistress or the other, or one of his illegitimate daughters.

George was a music lover, his only claim to artistic sensibility. He was especially fond of the music of George Frederick Handel. The composer crossed from Hanover ahead of his royal patron and would survive him to score musical triumphs under George II. Created for the first George, however, Handel's elegant Water Music will be forever remembered, a twilight serenade for the monarch and his mistresses as they floated up the Thames aboard the royal barge to a dinner engagement in Chelsea. Handel followed in a vessel filled with musicians. On a fine, cool evening in summer, George I's 'bivouac' among the English had its tuneful compensations.

In September 1715, a year after his arrival, the monarch's misgivings about his fickle new subjects were put to the test. Jacobites raised the Stuart standard in the Scottish Highlands. Even to eighteenth-century observers, it must have seemed a quaint way to go about conquering a nation – James Stuart's supporters actually tied a flag to a pole, stuck it in the ground and sat back waiting for an army to show up. They hoped to rally the clans of Scotland and the disgruntled Tories of England. The rebel force they attracted was unpromising. According to an eye witness:

There were country gentlemen from Angus and Aberdeenshire, riding on stout horses, with sword and pistol, each dressed in his best laced attire, and each attended by servingmen, also armed and also on horseback. Then there were Highland gentlemen in the more picturesque garb of their country, with obeisant retinues of clansmen on foot. The mass of the army was composed of Lowland peasants, with arms slung over their plain gray clothes, and of mountaineers, nearly naked, or at least wearing little more than one shirt-like garment. Two squadrons of cavalry, which Huntly had brought with him, excited, under the name of light-horse, the derision of friends and foes; being composed of stout bulky Highlandmen, mounted on little horses, each with his petit blue bonnet on his head, a long rusty musket slung athwart his back, and not possessed of boots or pistols, those articles so requisite to the idea of a trooper. On arriving at Dunblane, this puissant body of cavalry took two hours to dismount; and it is the opinion of one who observed them, that, if attacked by an enemy, they would have been as long before they were in readiness to receive him.

The fighting, such as it was, was over before James Stuart, the Old Pretender, put in an appearance. His rebels took over Scotland easily enough, but their chieftains fell to bickering over the invasion of England. The enterprise petered out in jealousies and feuding. In November, despite forces that outnumbered the government two-to-one, the Jacobites collapsed the same day before two separate royal armies: General Wills's troops at Preston and the duke of Argyll's regiments at Sheriffmuir. The Old Pretender arrived from France in December, fifteen months late with his challenge to King George. As bullheaded as his father, he fully expected to be crowned James III, ignoring the fact that his rebellion was evaporating like highland mist. Prince James set up housekeeping in the Palace of Scone. The announced coronation date – 23 January 1716 – came and went. Scots and Englishmen foolish enough to rally to him threw down their arms and went home. By February he was back in France licking his wounds.

Reality did not wither Thackeray's inventive powers as he envisioned what might have been. He described the critical moments in which the Jacobites flubbed the capture of Edinburgh:

> Edinburgh Castle might have been in King James's hands, but that the men who were to escalade it stayed to drink his health at the tavern, and arrived two hours too late at the rendezvous under the castle wall. There was sympathy enough in the town – the projected attack seems to have been known there. Lord Mahon quotes Sinclair's account of a gentleman not concerned, who told Sinclair that he was in a house that evening where eighteen of them were drinking, as the facetious landlady said, 'powdering their hair' for the attack on the castle. Suppose they had not stopped to powder their hair? Edinburgh Castle, and town, and all Scotland were King James's. The north of England rises, and marches over Barnet Heath upon London. Wyndham is up in Somersetshire; Packington in Worcestershire; and Vivian in Cornwall. The Elector of Hanover and his hideous mistresses, pack up the plate, and perhaps the crown jewels in London, and are off via Harwich and Helvoetsluys, for dear old Deutchland. The king – God save him! lands at Dover, with tumultuous applause; shouting multitudes, roaring cannon, the Duke of Marlborough weeping tears of joy, and all the bishops kneeling in the mud.

George I's personal reaction to this bumbling adventure was predictable: he wanted to see the leaders' heads stuck up on pikes. Sir Robert Walpole and his brother-in-law Charles, Viscount Townshend, supported him, but there was hot debate in the cabinet, the first crack in the united Whig front. The Earl of Nottingham resigned. George, tough old campaigner that he was, can be forgiven his bloodthirstiness; in the end he was merciful to the rebels of 'the Fifteen'. Some went to prison and there was a certain amount of casual robbery by government troops, but no Scots hanged. Harsh penalties were reserved for the English. Lord Kenmure was executed and the king's hangers-on gobbled up the estates of other wealthy Jacobites.

The realm secure, the court returned to its peacetime preoccupations, of which the liveliest was trollop-watching at St James's.

Among the ladies of light virtue who streamed in were some celebrated relics of the past. Certainly the most intriguing confrontation was between the surviving mistresses of three previous English monarchs who chanced to appear at court on the same day. Charles II's French mistress Louise de Kéroualle, whom he created Duchess of

Portsmouth, awaited her presentation to George I alongside William III's Elizabeth Villiers, the Countess of Orkney, and James II's Catherine Sedley, the Countess of Dorchester. The last old lady spoke for them all, when she exclaimed, 'God, who would have thought that we three whores should have met here!'

German Brunhildas now began to flock across the Channel to vie for the king's favour, often competing with their English sisters on bluntly physical grounds. One arriving valkyrie, the countess of Buckeburg, ridiculed the puny charms of the English, whom she said scurried about the palace:

> pitifully and sneakingly . . . whereas those that are foreigners hold up their heads and hold out their breasts and make themselves look as great and stately as they can.

Lord Chesterfield observed the same inflationary tendencies at work, noting:

> The standard of His Majesty's taste made all those ladies who aspired to his favour and who were near the statutable size strain and swell themselves like the frogs in the fable to rival the bulk and dignity of the ox. Some succeeded and others burst.

New contenders, German or English, who hoped to replace the two permanent mistresses, were doomed to disappointment, for the Elephant and the Maypole held on to the king with a grip of iron. The Elephant, especially, proved impervious to changes of the royal heart. If less active politically than the Duchess of Kendal, the Countess of Darlington reigned with a beefy magnificence calculated to discourage tarts of lesser tonnage.

She displayed, perhaps, an excessive tenderness in regard to her reputation. At one point the countess complained to the king that the Prince of Wales was spreading stories accusing her of flirtations in Hanover. To give Prince George Augustus the lie, she whipped out an official-looking document signed by her husband, certifying that she had always been a faithful wife. Into which chamberlain's keeping the certificate was given, in which state archive it was kept, and on which hilarious occasions its contents were proclaimed to the court, are not recorded.

Chapter Five

The Feud

The Elephant's critic, the Prince of Wales, provided the court with its other major diversion: the pitting of father against son for political fun and profit.

When the new court assembled in 1714, the German and English contingents fumbled endlessly as they attempted to make themselves understood to each other. Just how garbled communications were, can be gathered from the plight of the German midwife who served Princess Caroline in her first English confinement. Convinced that the princess's English ladies-in-waiting intended to hang her, should she fail in her mission, the woman refused to proceed. A Cabinet minister interceded – Lord Townshend, in fact. He frantically shook her hand and 'made kind faces at her' until the terrified woman could be persuaded to attend her patient. Sad to say, the princess's child was born dead. There was no hanging.

In such a Babel, the prince and princess were a welcome relief. They both spoke English and generally tried to please. Given the slightest encouragement, the prince gushed that the English were:

the best, the handsomest, the best-shaped, the best-natured, and lovingest people in the world, and if anybody would make their court to him, it must be by telling him he was like an Englishman.

The princely couple made their court to the king but could not please him. For years he used every stratagem he could think of to snub, embarrass and make life intolerable for them. As they were packing for the trip to England, he ordered his son to leave behind his grandson Frederick Louis, a hostage in Hanover to the prince's behaviour in England. The boy was raised by a series of tutors, each worse than the last. Princess Caroline and her daughters were brought along to London only after the English ministers made it abundantly clear that the royal family was expected to be a family, not a bachelor garrison.

Money was a favourite weapon in the scrimmaging between father and son. Before 1714, the couple was kept virtually penniless, dependent on the generosity of the prince's grandmother, the dowager Electress Sophia. When the family set up in London, George I was forced, with great reluctance, to approve a Parliamentary income for his son. He shaved the amount from one hundred thousand pounds to fifty thousand, hardly enough to support a princely establishment. This frugality was imposed at the same time that he was personally collecting seven hundred thousand pounds a year from the Civil List. The Commons, baffled, restored the prince's allowance.

The king begrudged every penny. He hated his son's success with the English and found it acutely humiliating to depend on the prince's bilingual abilities in Cabinet Council meetings. (Of the Whig secretaries of state who ruled England, no one spoke German and only Charles Spencer Sunderland and James Stanhope, the foreign minister, spoke any French worth mentioning.)

Ill-feeling between father and son smouldered in the background through the months of the Jacobite rebellion. When, at last, the monarch departed for his first visit to Hanover in July 1716, George I flatly refused to name the Prince Regent in his absence. Instead, the prince was given the creaking title 'Guardian of the Realm and Lieutenant', last used in the fourteenth century. George Augustus was left completely powerless. Forbidden to touch foreign affairs, he could not fill the meanest vacancy in the royal household, appoint the lowliest lieutenant of the guards or transact business of any importance whatsoever. All this was trumpeted in every direction to embarrass him. As he left London, the king added the right touch of petty nastiness by relieving the prince's best friend, the Duke of Argyll, of his command.

Politicking went into high gear. The king took the French-speaking Lord Stanhope with him, leaving behind Lords Sunderland, Walpole and Townshend. He set the last two to watch his son's every move, making them personally accountable for any delinquency. Sunderland's health suddenly demanded an immediate cure in the spa at Aix. Permitted to cross the Channel, his ailment improved with miraculous speed. He left Aix for Hanover, bursting with the news that Walpole and Townshend, far from acting as the prince's wardens, were actively plotting with him against the king. From London, Baron Bothmer confirmed the report. Since his keepers constantly hovered at George Augustus's side, their presence only served to confirm the toadies' stories. Fuelling the feud on the London end were Argyll and his brother, who had the prince's ear. They correctly branded Walpole and

Townshend as the spies they were. Walpole, in his turn, was honestly alarmed at the negotiations King George undertook in Germany with the French, fearing a sell-out of English interests to benefit Hanover. He drew the king's wrath by pushing for his early return from Hanover or – dread thought – for a Parliament summoned by the prince.

Worst of all, the Prince and Princess of Wales committed the political sin of becoming popular. With the royal cat away, the royal mice played at reigning, attracting a coterie to Hampton Court. Sunderland reported drawing-rooms, musical parties and gala receptions. The king purpled to hear of thrones being set up under red damask canopies. According to the tattling minister, there was princely dining in public (George I did not do so until 1717). He whispered of princely progresses in the gilded state barge, before a cheering populace. (Sunderland failed to mention the reason for the barge trip – the princess's confinement at St James's, where her child was stillborn.)

A telltale snort of royal displeasure came with orders from Hanover booting Lord Townshend upstairs, to the position of lord-lieutenant of Ireland. When the king returned in March 1717, he immediately sacked Townshend; the Irish job was notorious as a prelude to disgrace. Walpole, who knew a disaster when it fell on his head, resigned. George Augustus and Caroline tiptoed off to their country place at Richmond.

The king brooded. He finally found the perfect occasion to revenge himself on his son in November 1717, when Princess Caroline was again brought to bed in St James's for the birth of her second son. If anything, the royal storm was more violent for breaking so late. Very properly, the Prince of Wales selected, as the baby's godfathers, his father and his uncle Ernest Augustus, Prince-Bishop of Osnabrück and Duke of York. The king was to appear in person, his uncle by proxy. When the king arrived in the princess's chambers for the christening, he dragged along his personal choice of co-sponsor. It was the duke of Newcastle, his lord chamberlain, whom the prince detested. The prince dared not lose his temper in the king's presence but, seething with anger after the ceremony, he shook his fist at Newcastle. 'Rascal, I find you out,' he shouted. Newcastle went pale. In the prince's thick accent, he heard the speech as 'I will fight you,' a challenge to a duel. Knowing the reputation for ferocity the prince had earned at Oudenarde, Newcastle was scared out of his wits.

He scurried off to Sunderland for advice, interrupting the earl's daughter's wedding to pour out his fearful story. Sunderland, who would do almost anything to injure the prince, advised him to tell the king.

George I's anger, when he was told, was frightening. He was transformed from an easy-going, elderly, somewhat retiring monarch into a murderous ogre who, as far as his ministers knew, was capable of anything. On his order, the prince was arrested without a hearing and confined under guard. He made sure his son got the message, by sending a committee of three dukes to announce his incarceration. The furious little prince gave the ducal trio a tongue-lashing, which ignited another royal explosion when they reported back to their master.

Despite their rough treatment by the prince, the king's emissaries were moved by the plight of Princess Caroline. George's first order was to lock up his son in his own chambers but the princess, still weak from her labour, clung to her husband so pitifully that his advisers persuaded him to allow the couple to remain together in her apartment. His wife's entreaties melted the prince, who sent a series of pleading notes to his father. The letters were phrased, to use Caroline's words, 'as humbly as he could have done to the Almighty Himself'. Messengers trotted back and forth, but His Majesty was unmoved. Only after four days of princely captivity did someone in the Cabinet remind the king of the Habeas Corpus Act, the English law of the land which made it highly irregular if not downright illegal to keep his son imprisoned, even when the prison was St James's.

Something would have to be done with the prince. The king muttered that he would know perfectly well what to do with him if they were in Hanover, a remark that sent an uneasy shiver through his listeners. They all remembered Sophia Dorothea and the disappearance of Königsmarck.

When the king finally reached his decision, he sent a letter to his son and daughter-in-law giving them until sundown to get out of St James's. He ordered the Prince of Wales ejected forthwith, the bed-ridden princess to follow by the end of the day. His note to his son ended with a royal edict of astounding cruelty. 'You are further charged to say to the Princess from me,' the king wrote, 'that it is my will and my grandson and grand-daughters stay at St James's.'

The day degenerated into melodrama. Princess Caroline fainted again and again as she was half-carried out of the palace in such a state of hysterics her ladies-in-waiting feared for her life. She had good reason to panic. Her newborn son was taken from the desperate woman by main force, and her five-, seven- and nine-year-old daughters shrieked in bewildered terror as they watched their mother being dragged away. Next day the king ordered the tots, including the infant, to be taken to Kensington Palace and placed in the care of the widowed Countess of Portland. By February, the baby was dead.

The crisis, for it was nothing less, grew uglier day by day. Earl Cowper, the king's lord chancellor, resigned in protest. He argued that only the gravest misconduct could justify taking the children from their parents. Cowper's replacement as chancellor was Chief Justice Thomas Parker. Parker tried to collect on a royal demand that the prince pay nineteen thousand pounds a year for the support of the children he was forbidden to see. George Augustus and Caroline, understandably bitter over their baby's death, put up a legal fight and won. The king then vented his spleen on the little princesses, stingily arguing over every shilling he paid for their care.

As in most Guelph domestic dramas, there was a streak of savagery lurking behind the public bombast. King George acted in deadly earnest; his intent can be judged from the letters of Lord Stanhope, preserved by the Duchess of Kendal and unearthed years later by the memoirist Lord John Hervey. Murder was in the air, or at the very least, kidnapping.

'*Il est vrai c'est votre fils,*' Stanhope wrote to the king, referring to the Prince of Wales, '*mais le Fils de Dieu même a été sacrifié pour la salut de genre humain.*' ('It's true he is your son, but the Son of God himself was sacrificed for the good of mankind.')

And again, in a passage that gave rise to a fantastic story of abduction to the Americas, Stanhope suggested, '*Il faut l'enlever; et my Lord Berkeley le prendra sur un vaisseau, et la conduira en aucunie partie de monde que votre Majesté l'ordonnera.*' ('He must be carried off and my Lord Berkeley will take him aboard a ship and carry him to any part of the world Your Majesty orders.')

As he plotted against his son in secret, the king continued to abuse him before the world. He notified official Europe of the affair in mortifying detail as he decreed his son's disgraced status. No one, domestic or foreign, received by the Prince and Princess of Wales would henceforth be welcomed to St James's. Any person employed in the prince's modest establishment forswore the hope of royal favour. The couple were to be denied royal courtesies and treated as private citizens.

In despair, George Augustus and Caroline set up housekeeping at Leicester House and in the country at Richmond Lodge. An Opposition formed and flocked to comfort them. Walpole and Townshend took the lead, conveniently forgetting their quondam activities as spies for the king. Walpole took getting used to, so loud, pushy and foul-mouthed even in an age of overripe vocabularies, that Caroline could not, at first, bear him in her presence. Her attitude changed when she realized his crude country manner masked a serpent's cunning. He bubbled constantly with plans to frustrate the government. In no time at all the politician and the princess became intimates. The prince distrusted Walpole but delighted in everything that pricked his father. He swallowed his dislike and welcomed his wife's new confidant.

England now had two powerful political camps, both Whig. In the trenches of the Whig 'outs', Walpole and Townshend gleefully set in motion a battle plan. They obstructed progress in Parliament, sniping and bushwhacking every move the Whig Establishment made – all the while secretly sending word to King George of the attractive cut-rate prices they would charge, in terms of political appointments, to switch their loyalties. The courier for this backstage manoeuvring was none other than the Maypole. The Duchess of Kendal adored Townshend. Although she was cold to Walpole and charged the brothers-in-law dearly for every kind word she dropped in the king's ear, she was trusted and admired by both.

Even with the duchess intervening, there was no quick solution to the personal feud. After six months, his advisors managed to wring a concession from the king permitting his granddaughters weekly visits from their mother, but the guerrilla warfare between father and son showed no signs of abating.

The king connived without ceasing against his son, to no avail. Encouraged by Stanhope and Sunderland, he attempted to seize the prince's hundred thousand-pound income. Parliament would have none of it. He tried to strip the prince of the Hanoverian electorate, if he accepted the English throne. The Act of Settlement forbade it. At Stanhope's and Sunderland's prompting, he backed the Peerage Bill, which would have frozen the number of peers and taken away the prince's right to appoint new ones on his accession, the most valuable patronage a new king can dispense. Walpole defeated it in the Commons. His Majesty raged over the setback, excluding Walpole and Townshend from the court 'forever', and even banning them from the Newmarket races on the days he attended.

George I was reduced to name-calling in the streets. When his son fell in love with his wife's lady-in-waiting, Henrietta Howard, the king dispatched her drunken, disreputable husband to make a display of his cuckolded state outside Leicester House. Howard squalled for his wife's return. A crowd gathered, realized the king had put him up to it, and laughed Howard out of countenance.

The private quarrel had striking public effects. England's system of Cabinet government was born out of it, a constitutional development directly traceable to the day the English-speaking Prince of Wales was barred from meetings of the Cabinet Council. Without his son to translate, George I lost interest completely and ceased to attend. Always before, even such invalid monarchs as William III and Queen Anne felt it imperative to hear their ministers' arguments in person. Under the new system the Cabinet meeting became a prelude to the presentation of current business to the monarch for his approval by a 'prime' minister.

King and prince were reconciled in 1720; that is, Walpole got them into the same room at the same time. Everyone concerned with the feud was weary of it and wanted a change: Princess Caroline wanted her children back; the Elephant and the Maypole wanted a holiday in Hanover; the government wanted the prince on display in the king's absence, if only as a figurehead 'Guardian and Lieutenant'; the king, true to form, wanted money.

With a total annual income of almost a million pounds, George I's bankbook was in deplorable shape; he had incurred debts of six hundred thousand pounds in three short years. Stanhope and Sunderland, who had no entrée to London's financiers, desperately needed Walpole, whom the money-men loved. With encouragement from the Maypole, they persuaded His Majesty to forget the Peerage Bill and receive the man who could fill his pockets with cash.

Walpole manipulated father and son shamelessly, giving each of them to understand the other had given in. For instance, he loudly insisted to King George that the trouble-making prince and princess be forbidden to live in St James's. With equal vehemence, he assured the prince that he would force the king to allow his son and daughter-in-law to live outside the hated palace walls. One squabble after another was defused in much the same way. By a stroke of luck, little Princess Anne came down with something that looked very much like small-pox, frightening both her parents and grandfather. Her mother was permitted to rush to her bedside and in the emotion of the moment, the king accepted an appropriately contrite letter from the prince.

With help from the princess at Leicester House and the Maypole at St James's, a private reception was arranged in April 1720. Princess Caroline actually got her husband down on his knees for the king's entrance. George I greeted his daughter-in-law amicably enough, '*Vous *êtes bien-venue, Madame. Je suis ravi de vous voir ici.'* One look at his kneeling son and he burst forth in a last fit of anger. He hissed at the prince, *'Votre conduite . . . Votre conduite.'* Somehow, they managed a handshake but the public kisses and embraces required of them next day during a thankskging service in the Royal Chapel nearly choked them both. Thereafter, they maintained an icy truce. At palace functions Princess Caroline made a great display of chatting up the king, but the two men exchanged not a word.

After suffering through the whole, horrible, hurtful mess, one would think the Prince and Princess of Wales would be incapable of treating their own children with anything but lifelong tenderness. Sadly, exactly the reverse was true. In one of those family coincidences around which psychologists love to weave theories, George II repeated his father's cruelty in 1737, when he booted *his* son Frederick, the Prince of Wales, and his princess out of St James's, also following a royal birth. Happily however, this time the baby lived, Frederick's children being allowed to remain with their parents.

Chapter Six

Bubbles and
Water-melons

A cease-fire in the royal feud was declared in the nick of time. While the king and the prince scuffled, far more dangerous events were stirring in the London Exchange, that demanded Sir Robert Walpole's full attention and energies. A rascally group called the South Sea Company concocted an historic stock swindle which sucked in untold millions of pounds despite everything Walpole could do. The scheme very nearly brought the country to financial ruin in 1720.

In January of that year, Walpole planted himself squarely in the company's path when they dazzled the Commons with a proposal to take over the national debt of nearly thirty-one million pounds. For this burden, they would charge the government only 5 per cent a year! Walpole attempted to persuade the Commons, hellbent on shedding the debt, to turn it over to the more responsible management of the Bank of England. He failed, shouted down by the chancellor of the exchequer, John Aislabie.

Towering behind Aislabie was a familiar, skeletal figure. The Duchess of Kendal, bought and paid for by the South Sea financiers, was busily whispering to the king in favour of the debt manipulation. She campaigned from the high ground of her apartments at St James's. Walpole, newly and grudgingly in the king's favour following his reconciliation with the Prince of Wales, was forced to operate out of the Parliamentary cloakrooms. He fought a losing battle. Marshalled against him was not only the Maypole, but Aislabie with his oratory, the entire House of Commons and, subsequently, the Lords. No bribe went unpaid in the company's march to financial glory. The Maypole delivered the *coup de grâce* to Walpole's opposition when she put the king himself on the South Sea payroll, as a governor of the company.

George I, as might be expected, pocketed a fat fee for the use of his name.

The gang of merchant pirates who proposed this miracle cure for the country's financial ailments was first recruited in 1711 by Walpole's old Jacobite antagonist, the earl of Oxford. Oxford's group coped, after a fashion, with a ten million pound debt left by the departing Whig ministry of the time. The company took its 6 per cent cut from duties turned over to it on wines, vinegar, Indian fabric, silk, tobacco and other imports. Their 1711 deal put just enough coin in the South Sea Company's till to make the 1720 proposition sound credible. This time, however, the directors were out to line their pockets.

Shakily propping up – and propped up by – the national debt scheme was the company's only other asset, its charter to trade in the South (American) Sea. Oxford and his cronies plugged this pipe-dream incessantly. According to the company's publicity, a kindly King Philip V of Spain would allow free access to a company ship – or was it two ships? – or a merchant fleet? – to trade in the Pacific ports of Mexico, Peru and Chile. Soon, a mighty mercantile armada would sail into Philip's South American empire, unload honest English goods and sail out again stuffed with immense amounts of Peruvian silver and Mexican gold. All who bought a bargain-priced share or two in this venture would collect dividends of 300 per cent – or was it 400? – or even (lucky simpleton!) 1,000 per cent.

King Philip of Spain, if anyone had bothered to ask him, wanted the South American silver and gold for himself. His only traffic with the South Sea Company was something called the *assiento* contract, under which the Londoners agreed to supply his American colonies with African blacks for thirty years. They were, bluntly put, slavers. Their prospects depended on a heavily-hedged promise by the Spanish king to allow one small colonial trading ship a year to take on a strictly limited cargo. Kindly Philip insisted on one-fourth of the profits, plus a tax of 5 per cent on everything else. Exactly one trading ship did slip into a South American port in 1717. There was a political ruckus between England and Spain in 1718 and the trade ended almost before it started.

In eighteenth-century Europe, however, any contact with the Americas was automatically assumed to be a key to the riches of El Dorado. Both the British and the French became temporarily unhinged by visions of American wealth at almost exactly the same time. In Paris between January 1719, and October 1720, the Scots banker John Law rose and fell, promoting his notorious 'Mississippi' scheme and flooding Regency France with printing-press money. England was swept by an investment fever between April and December 1720, a foolishness so identical it is difficult to remember the two events were unconnected. Over Robert Walpole's violent objections, the South Sea Company's non-existent ships filled with silver and gold – and dozens of other get-rich-quick schemes which sprouted up around the central fraud squeezed millions out of the public and came to be known historically as the 'South Sea Bubble'.

Parliament passed a bill accepting the company's debt proposal on 7 April 1720. The nation discarded the last shred of its good sense in an orgy of speculation that lasted eight months.

Even as the debt bill made its way through the necessary readings in Parliament, the company spread a rumour of an English–Spanish trade treaty. Their diplomatic fairytale boosted the quotes on South Sea stock to 300 per cent. A few weeks later the directors promised a midsummer dividend of 10 per cent. The stock bounced up to 400, then 550 – where it stood at the end of May. On 28 May, something triggered a spontaneous four-day buying surge. The worthless paper soared to nearly 900. At this point, there was a scary dip. It took emergency buying by the company itself to stop the skid at 750.

The rumour factory was put back to work. According to the great Bubble historian, Charles Mackay, in the next two months the stock, carried along by ceaseless ballyhoo,

. . . finally rose to one thousand per cent. It was quoted at this price in the commencement of August. The bubble was then full-blown, and began to quiver and shake preparatory to its bursting.

Mackay's account, *Extraordinary Popular Delusions and the Madness of Crowds*, written in 1841, described the bubble hysteria that seized Exchange Alley and all London:

It seemed at that time as if the whole nation had turned stock-jobbers. Exchange Alley was every day blocked up by crowds, and Cornhill was impassable for the number of carriages. Every body came to purchase stock. 'Every fool aspired to be a knave.' . . . Every person interested in the success of the project endeavoured to draw a knot of listeners around him, to whom he expatiated on the treasures of the South Seas.

Whig and Tory alike were caught up in the delirium. Excepting only

Walpole and a few wise heads around him, Whig 'outs' were as deeply involved as 'ins'. Noble speculators scrambled after the wealth of the joint-stock companies as eagerly as the meanest jobbers in Exchange Alley: the Duke of Bridgewater unveiled a 'civic improvement' dodge; so did that master of bribery, the duke of Chandos.

> Persons of distinction, of both sexes, were deeply engaged in all these bubbles; those of the male sex going to taverns and coffee-houses to meet their brokers, and the ladies resorting for the same purpose to the shops of milliners and haberdashers.

No less a personage than the Prince of Wales headed up one of the bubbles, a copper company which was indicted in June at the instigation of the South Sea directors. Since George I was a South Sea governor, the directors hoped to please him by ruining his son. The prince, tipped off, pulled out with alacrity – and a profit of forty thousand pounds. Others in the court shared his gift of timing. Sarah, the duchess of Marlborough, invested shrewdly. The Elephant raked in substantial bubble profits, although she was an amateur in comparison with her rival, the Maypole. Both the favourites, along with other court insiders, sold out their shares before they left with the king on his Hanover holiday.

Increasingly, however, there were losers – family fortunes collapsed as the summer went on. Subsidiary bubbles around the stupendous central swindle became so pernicious, in July the government outlawed more than a hundred of the worst. Mackay's book listed the most brazen.

More than a few of the bubbles arose from the pages of the alchemist's recipe book. One proposed 'extracting silver from lead'. A second envisioned 'the transmutation of quicksilver into a malleable metal'. A third sought 'to make deal (pine wood) boards out of saw-dust'. Others dreamed of 'planting mulberry trees in Chelsea Park to breed silkworms', or voyaging 'to discover the land of Ophir and to monopolize the gold and silver that country is still believed to produce'.

The swindles included one promoter's appeal for one million pounds sterling to finance 'a wheel for perpetual motion.'

A 'futures' cheat became the rage of Exchange Alley when 'Globe Permits' went on sale. These, according to Mackay,

> . . . were nothing more than square pieces of playing-cards, on which was the impression of a seal, in wax, bearing the sign of the

Globe Tavern . . . with the inscription of 'Sail-Cloth Permits'. The possessors enjoyed no other advantage from them than permission to subscribe at some future time to a new sail-cloth manufactory . . . These permits sold for as much as sixty guineas in the Alley.

Mackay reserved his keenest admiration for a bubble proprietor of breath-taking effrontery:

But the most absurd and preposterous of all, and which shewed, more completely than any other, the utter madness of the people, was one started by an unknown adventurer, entitled,

> *'A company for carrying on an undertaking of great*
> *advantage, but nobody to know what it is.'*

. . . The man of genius who essayed this bold and successful inroad upon public credulity, merely stated in his prospectus that the required capital was half a million, in five thousand shares of one hundred pounds each, deposit two pounds per share. Each subscriber, paying his deposit, would be entitled to one hundred pounds per annum per share. How this immense profit was to be obtained, he did not condescend to inform them at the time, but promised that in a month full particulars should be duly announced, and a call made for the remaining ninety-eight pounds of the subscription. Next morning at nine o'clock, this great man opened an office in Cornhill. Crowds of people beset his door, and when he shut up at three o'clock, he found that no less than one thousand shares had been subscribed for, and the deposits paid. He was thus, in five hours, the winner of two thousand pounds. He was philosopher enough to be contented with his venture, and set off the same evening for the Continent. He was never heard of again.

Blatant as these smaller bubbles were, people rushed to invest in them. The total amount sought from the public by the subsidiary bubbles before the government shut them down was upwards of three hundred million pounds sterling. The South Sea fraud itself, when an accounting was at last demanded, dwarfed them all. Before the final totting-up, thousands of deluded souls were wiped out, the economy disrupted and some provincial towns reduced to starvation by the closing of bankrupt shops and industries.

The great South Sea Company bubble began to leak in earnest in

August, deflating to a flabby 700 per cent per share by 1 September. In a public meeting on 8 September, the company's directors manufactured vast quantities of hot air to puff it up again. They read reports. They patted each other's backs. They called for confidence, as company directors always do. To their astonishment, there was bedlam in Merchant Taylors Hall. The news had broken that Sir John Blunt, the chairman, and his closest friends, among them the Duchess of Kendal and the king, had sold out. By evening, South Sea stock was quoted at 640.

Revelations in the meeting itself made things worse. Anyone who could do simple arithmetic quickly realized that the ten million pounds reported as running cash, could not possibly keep afloat two hundred millions in outstanding stocks.

By the end of September, the South Sea rogues were pleading for the Bank of England to take on their bonds. The Bank officers, persuaded in part by Walpole, finally agreed to ignore the abyss which now yawned in Exchange Alley and offered a subscription of three millions 'for the support of public credit'.

For the space of a single morning, it worked. Money poured into the bank. Then a run began on the bank itself. Mackay described the now-uncontrollable panic:

> In spite of all that could be done to prevent it, the South Sea company's stock fell rapidly. Their bonds were in such discredit, that a run commenced on the most eminent goldsmiths and bankers, some of whom, having lent out great sums on South-Sea stock, were obliged to shut up their shops and abscond. The Sword-blade company, who had hitherto been the chief cashiers of the South-Sea company, stopped payment. This being looked upon as but the beginning of evil, occasioned a great run on the Bank, who were now obliged to pay out money much faster than they had received it in the morning. The day succeeding was a holiday (the 29th of September) and the Bank had a little breathing time. They bore up against the storm; but their former rivals, the South-Sea company, were wrecked upon it. Their stock fell to one hundred and fifty, and gradually, after various fluctuations, to one hundred and thirty-five.

October was a month of chaos. King George's crown was in far greater danger from the collapse of the bubble than ever it had been from the insurrection of the Jacobites. Near-riots erupted every time a known 'South-Sea man' poked his nose out of doors. Feelings were particularly violent because the *nouveaux riches* who ran the company had made insolent asses of themselves when the boom was at its height – like the haughty idiot who publicly announced he would feed his horse on gold.

At meetings in every town in England, petitions were quickly filled demanding punishment for the directors and their government cohorts. In Parliament Lord Molesworth made a savage speech, calling for the revival of the Roman punishment for patricides: he wanted the South Sea officers sewn into sacks and thrown into the Thames.

By the time a nervous king rushed home from Hanover in November, the South Sea bribes were the talk of London. It took gall, but George's mistresses came back to face down the bribe lists being read out in Parliament. The names of the duchess and the countess were inscribed there for all to see, right behind Lord Sunderland, John Aislabie and Charles Stanhope, one of the secretaries of the treasury and a relative of the king's confidant, Lord James Stanhope.

Knight, the treasurer of the South Sea company, fled to the sanctuary of Brabant (modern Belgium), leaving behind a heap of fragmentary records too tantalizing for Parliament to ignore. In his notes on the first round of bribes, Knight put down the Duchess of Kendal for ten thousand pounds in stock, the Countess of Darlington for another ten thousand pounds, and her two nieces for ten thousand pounds apiece.

The Maypole, up to her withered old chin in the scandal, intervened to cut off Knight's capture. She hastily dispatched a series of notes imploring her friend the Austrian empress to frustrate the pursuing English bailiffs. Vienna owned the States of Brabant. Knight found himself detained – in considerable comfort – in a Brabant prison. His English pursuers howled without, powerless to ship the absconder home to testify before Parliament.

Knight's sanctuary, and the duchess's part in securing it, raised a storm in London. The penny press fulminated. Members sought to bring questions in Parliament. One caricature that circulated by the thousands, entitled 'The Brabant Screen', showed Knight with his baggage, pausing in flight to receive a safe conduct from the duchess, who crouched behind a screen.

Her quick thinking kept the key witness's voice out of the Parliamentary hearings. She sheltered the court from total ruin and the king, most likely, from abdication. The scraps of evidence Knight left behind were black enough. He receipted Charles Stanhope for ten thousand pounds, Sunderland for fifty thousand pounds. The championship grafter was John Aislabie. His account with Turner, Caswall and Co., the South Sea 'money-launderers', totalled nearly eight hundred thousand pounds!

All this was only the first round. There were later generosities to Sunderland, Aislabie, Stanhope and persons of equal quality and virtue. The shameful roll-call continued, a chronicle of corruption spewed out by a company in which the king had owned a major interest.

Charles Stanhope was the first to be tried, which sent his relative Lord James rushing about button-holing friends. The House listened sympathetically, ignored Stanhope's prodigious gains and acquitted the rascal. Bankrupt Londoners were not pleased. Angry mobs suddenly collected in the streets. With the spectre of revolution striding the corridors, the MPs were considerably harsher the next day with Aislabie.

The chancellor pleaded lamely that 'the spirit of bubbling had become so universal that the very Bank became a bubble'. The House found him guilty and clapped him into the Tower. His punishment was cheered, as were other stiff penalties that followed, mainly in the form of huge fines levied against the company directors. In a 'joyous' mood, the mob danced around bonfires.

There were casualties. Lord Stanhope had an apoplectic stroke over an argument in Parliament. He died in 1721. George I mourned him for his French and his friendship, but was considerably relieved to have one less witness to the corruption in his court. Sunderland resigned, then died in 1722. Inevitably, there was a heart attack or two and at least one suicide was laid to the scandal.

By the end of 1720, however, the Bubble horrors were receding. Walpole pushed through common-sense legislation to put South Sea finances under the Bank of England's supervision. Under his goading, the government scraped together an eight million pound dividend which was parcelled out to the hardest-hit investors. He earned the gratitude of Sunderland, whom he kept from the Tower, if not from death. The king, too, was in his debt. Walpole's blustering defence stopped the House inquiries short of George I and his mistresses.

The public meetings and muttering street crowds disappeared. Petitions no longer circulated. Grumbling, the nation somehow suffered through a monumental financial hangover. Walpole's legislative remedies were never put to use, as restored faith in credit brought about a general recovery.

In 1721, Sir Robert Walpole was accepted by George I as his first lord and head of the ministry.

Walpole switched loyalties smoothly, abandoning the cause of the

Prince of Wales. The new 'prime' minister, although he never used the term, actually won a certain amount of peace and quiet for George Augustus and Caroline. He convinced the king his son had been harmlessly put to pasture and the prince, if somewhat miffed by the defection of Sir Robert, spent the next seven years safely out of the line of royal fire. George Augustus's three little daughters stayed in the king's custody, but generous visiting privileges were extended to their mother and father. When a son, William Augustus, was born in April 1721, his grandfather allowed the baby to remain with his mother. Two daughters, Mary and Louisa, born in 1723 and 1724, also stayed in the family circle.

In a famous gaffe in a family given to them, George I brought Princess Caroline a present from one of his trips to Hanover – 'Peter the Wild Boy', a half-savage little fellow who had been found loping about the German forests on all fours. If the king had in mind to conciliate his daughter-in-law after his brutality toward her children, it was an awkward gesture, from the king of awkwardness.

In his sixties, George I still had a roving eye. He took his first English mistress, Anne Brett, who was more resourceful than most of his concubines. Her rooms adjoined the palace gardens at St James's. For easier access to the flower beds (and, one presumes, moonlight strolls with her royal lover) she had a door installed in the garden wall. The king's eldest granddaughter, Princess Anne, was outraged. On her orders, workmen bricked up the door. Anne Brett scarcely had time to have the bricks torn down, when the accession of George II made the door, and her moonlight strolls, superfluous.

Although George I strayed with Miss Brett and others, there was never a doubt as to the supremacy of the Elephant and the Maypole. Fat and lean, the Germans had come to England with him. Old and dilapidated, they stayed at his side. Their 'nieces', the royal bastards, were married advantageously. The duchess's eldest daughter Petronilla, in particular, made a brilliant match. Created countess of Walsingham, she wed Lord Chesterfield, who achieved enduring fame with his letters.

Unaccountably, the Maypole began to hanker for holiness, attending as many as seven Lutheran services in a single Sabbath. Spotting her in congregations was becoming a popular London pastime, when she was brought up short in her quest. The minister of the chapel in the Savoy refused to give the old lady the Eucharist, on the grounds that she was living in a state of adultery.

If they remained beyond the pale of respectable society, the vigilance of George's two mistresses never relaxed. They fiercely guarded their master from undue familiarity with outsiders, even his first lord. After some initial awkwardness over languages, the two chief men of the realm had grown close, spending hours together in a rustic retreat in Richmond New Park. The boisterous minister and his silent sovereign hunted, dined, consumed endless bowls of punch together – and worried the Maypole to distraction with their intimacy. Trusting no one English, Walpole least of all, she was frantic over possible royal indiscretions. She recklessly demanded that his German servants cut off the king's punch. Devoted to her he might be, but George would not be hen-pecked. After a shouting match, the supply of punch was restored.

The chief joy of the king's life remained his trips abroad. He was planning his fifth excursion to Hanover when a fatal prediction was heard from a prophetess of the time. If his imprisoned wife should die, the crone said, so would the king. Duchess Sophia Dorothea died on 13 November, 1726. Although George I was hale and hearty at sixty-seven and his mother Sophia had enjoyed marvellous health until she was eighty-four, he chose to believe the prophecy. In what must have been his only show of emotion to his son and daughter-in-law, he wept uncontrollably as he said goodbye to them in June 1727, certain he was starting on his final journey.

Only the Maypole made the trip with him, for the Elephant had waddled her way into the hereafter in 1725. In Delden, Holland, the royal vacationer made a rest stop at the home of a certain Count de Twillet. George I enjoyed the evening hugely. He consumed a mammoth supper and topped off the meal by eating 'several water-melons'. Understandably, he spent a miserable night. The next day, 10 June, he insisted that his coach press on towards Hanover despite his physical distress. The Duchess of Kendal lagged behind, for one reason or another. A contemporary account by Coxe described the king's symptoms when he reached Ibbenburen:

> He was quite lethargic; his hand fell down as if lifeless, and his tongue hung out of his mouth. He gave, however, signs of life by continually crying out as well as he could articulate, 'Osnabrück! Osnabrück!'

It was clearly an apoplectic attack. The coachman whipped the horses onward. Some witnesses argued that His Majesty never reached the city and died on the road. At least one account reported the death of

George I at Osnabrück in the palace where he was born, in the arms of his younger brother, the prince-bishop. It was a nice thought.

At first, the Maypole dismissed the report of King George's death. A second messenger convinced her. She collapsed, screaming, beating her breast and tearing her hair. In the maddest disarray, she sped ahead of the rest of the royal party to Brunswick, where she disappeared and remained in seclusion for nearly three months.

When her greed inevitably overcame her grief, George II was kind. She was allowed to return to her fortune and her estates in England, where she divided the remainder of her days between her property in Twickenham and a pretty retreat at Isleworth, Middlesex. The duchess died there in her bed at the age of seventy-six, on 10 May 1743.

Thackeray, as usual, had the last word on her late paramour, King George I, the founder of the House of Hanover:

> It is said George promised one of his left-handed widows to come to her after death, if leave were granted to him to revisit the glimpses of the moon; and soon after his death, a great raven actually flying or hopping in at the Duchess of Kendal's window at Twickenham, she chose to imagine the King's spirit inhabited these plumes, and took special care of her sable visitor. Affecting metempsychosis – funereal royal bird! How pathetic is the idea of the duchess weeping over it! When this chaste addition to our English aristocracy died, all her jewels, her plate, her plunder went over to her relations in Hanover. I wonder whether her heirs took the bird, and whether it is still flapping its wings over Herrenhausen?

Part II

THE FISHES' DAUGHTER

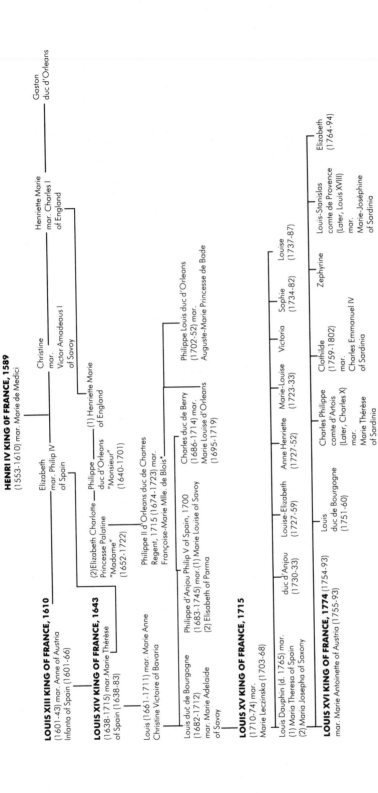

The House of Bourbon in France (From 1598 to 1793)

* Other prominent legitimated and ennobled children of Louis XIV and Mme. de Montespan: Louis-August, duc de Maine Louise-Françoise, Mlle. de Nantes Louis-Alexandre, comte de Toulouse

Chapter Seven

'Le Roi est mort!'

L ouis XIV and his great-grandson Louis XV were a pair of very bad French kings for whom die-hard royalists have been trying to make excuses for the last two hundred years. Apologists for the *ancien régime* protest that they and their relatives held the throne of France for eight centuries, as if sheer survival were synonymous with good government and not, as was the case with the Bourbons, a pretext for generations of misrule.

Louis XV became king at the age of five, a pretty child who captured the hearts of Frenchmen. The dynasty's record notwithstanding, he remained for many years their royal darling, *Louis le Bien-Aimé* (Louis the Well-Loved). He grew to be the handsomest man in Europe, and one of the laziest. Talented men governed for him. They, and he, were satisfied to preserve the outward forms of absolute monarchy, without a great king at the centre. The last caretaker, Cardinal Fleury, died in 1743. At that moment, when he might have begun his personal rule, Louis lacked the strength to gather the reins of power – and they were picked up by a brilliant mistress. To understand fully such a ruler, we must examine, as part of his reign, this period of protracted adolescence. He emerged from thirty years spent in the hunting forests and boudoirs of France a *roi fainéant*, an idler-king. It was a role his great-grandfather Louis XIV would have regarded with revulsion.

Louis XIV, who lived between 1643 and 1715, called himself the Sun King, and meant it. The sun was the symbol of Apollo, and the king, who acknowledged no earthly peers, found comparison with the Greek god appropriate. To provide France's new deity with a suitably celestial setting, he built the Palace of Versailles. The gargantuan château in the suburbs of Paris cost well over sixty million pounds sterling (one hundred and sixty million dollars), figured at present-day exchange rates. Its completion was a crushing humiliation for other rulers of the day, who rushed to build overblown baroque palaces of their own. Lacking funds for a Versailles, some of them had to make do with facsimiles of Louis's lesser palaces at Marly, Trianon and Fontainebleau.

The entire civilized world imitated the little French king. He had himself sculpted in grandiose bronze, mounted on a war horse, for all to admire. Replicas of the statue appeared, with the heads of other kings attached, in royal squares all over Europe. Because he spoke French, his fellow monarchs spoke French. They ignored the implication that their native tongues were in some way inferior. The copy-catting became absurd. He liked to eat peas; suddenly, no fashionable table was complete without *petits pois*. Society everywhere mimicked his manners, his mistresses, his furniture and his high heels.

Try as they might, Louis's imitators could not match his extraordinarily long reign (fifty-four years), his non-stop sexuality (in his sixties his unofficial wife, Françoise d'Aubigné, Marquise de Maintenon, was forced to endure the old man twice a day), or his Olympian hauteur.

Louis XIV came by his egomania honestly. He firmly believed that Saint Remi started the French monarchy in AD 498 by anointing a Frankish chieftain named Clovis with oil flown down from heaven by a miraculous dove. Louis was further convinced he had been daubed with the same substance during his coronation at Reims. God – the Christian one – gave him the divine right to rule, and, because he provided God with such a faultless viceroy, Louis had allowed God to get the best of the bargain.

He most clearly expressed his chilling view of the world in a remark to his brother, Philippe I, Duc d'Orléans, known as Monsieur. Their conversation took place during the winter of 1709. The weather was hellish. Food was scarce, firewood scarcer. Whole families were found frozen in doorways. Monsieur was moved to pity and said as much. The king replied, 'And what if four or five hundred thousand of those scoundrels die, since they are useful for nothing, would France be any the less France?'

The France he had in mind, he created by following the programme laid down by Armand Jean du Plessis, Cardinal and Duc de Richelieu, his father's legendary minister:

> To ruin the Huguenot party, humble the pride of the lords, reduce all subjects to their duties and lift his name among foreign nations to its proper level.

Louis XIV carried out the cardinal's precepts with a vengeance.

In pursuit of *gloire*, the Sun King fomented constant wars. His aggressions tore up the continent of Europe again and again, decimated his people with hundreds of thousands of casualties and left France, at his death, staggering toward bankruptcy under a three billion pound debt.

He launched a persecution of the Huguenots after Madame de Maintenon prodded him into a formal religious conversion. Louis cared little for theology, but demanded, as a point of discipline, that every Frenchman should practise the king's brand of Christianity. He decreed 'one king, one faith, one law', and backed it up with torture and massacre. The Protestant Huguenots fled, stripping France of a generation of its finest artisans, soldiers and businessmen.

In his treatment of the lords, the king displayed a unique talent for political improvisation. During the *Fronde*, the great insurrection of his childhood, his mother and regent, Anne of Austria, fought the nobility and lost. She and her sons were driven into hiding in Paris. It was a period of boyish terror Louis never forgot. As king, he distrusted his nobles, and, learning his mother's lesson well, did not repeat Anne's mistake of confronting them directly.

To keep tabs on the aristocracy, he revived the sinister *cabinet noir*, or political police, created by his father, Louis XIII. Under a powerful Lieutenant, the *cabinet* forwarded the reports of a national network of spies to the king on a weekly basis. Their round-up of gossip, rumours, whispers and slips of the tongue and pen kept him abreast of things. *Lettres de cachet*, the infamous royal arrest warrants, took the most obvious malcontents and other undesirables out of circulation. Louis demanded more. He barricaded himself and the great families of France in the most lavish detention camp the world has ever known – Versailles. Step by step, he reduced the nation's nobles to the status of toadies, penned up in the château, squabbling with each other over the privilege of attending their king when he squatted on his *chaise percée*.

To the two thousand or more aristocrats who lived there, Versailles was the only France that mattered. Its royal master was the dazzling centre of their universe. They gave short shrift to centuries of Valois and Bourbon monarchs before Louis XIV, and considered it profoundly disloyal to conceive a world that could survive without him.

The king accepted their adulation as the new Apollo. Statues, tapestries, frescos and paintings proclaimed his divinity in every corner of the château. The acolyte had only to take a stroll in the gardens, to see the miracle for himself. Larger than life, Louis's patron deity could be seen erupting from the waters of the Basin of Apollo, personified by Jean-Baptist Tuby's heroic sculpture of the celestial charioteer. The notion was seriously advanced that Louis, like Apollo, coursed across the heaven of France's daily life, before coming to rest each night in Versailles – a tenet of faith which was conveniently realized for the observer in Hubert Robert's mythic marble sanctuary, the Grotto of Thetis. Every moment of the god-king Louis's sacred day was attended by the strictest ritual, every syllable he spoke was recorded and repeated with reverence. His bedroom, which his votaries called 'the visible centre of the monarchy', was dedicated to Apollo.

France was technically Christian, so the courtiers paid lip service to Louis as His Catholic Majesty. Prompted by Madame de Maintenon, he was a determined church-goer, who inclined to place the nation's fate in God's hands when faced with setbacks. Piety aside, the daily worship at Versailles was, stripped of its veneer, out and out idolatry. Le Grand Monarque, to his suppliants, replaced Le Bon Dieu.

His father had had no such divine aspirations. Attracted by the fine hunting, Louis XIII built two modest châteaux on the site. Saint-Simon described the first as a 'little house of cards', a small lodge erected in 1624 to shelter the king after a day in the field. He welcomed his intimates to an apartment of four rooms and a tiny picture gallery, a refuge from his overbearing minister, Cardinal Richelieu, and his beautiful, boring queen, Anne. Unfortunately, his teenaged lover, Henri d'Effiat, Marquis de Cinq-Mars, did not share the king's taste for rustication and Louis XIII found himself alone in his forest idyll. Nevertheless, he added parcels of property, notably Trianon. By 1634, he had replaced the older building with a comfortable, even elegant château of red brick and white stone. He ordered some pretty gardens planted, and gave country dinner parties there in the 1650s.

The nucleus of the château, the gardens, the park and the village of Versailles was in place in 1661, when Louis XIV ascended the throne. According to a story concocted by the royal publicists, the new king and his bride, Marie-Thérèse of Spain, went riding together and stumbled on 'the enchanted palace', a near-ruin, romantic and over-grown. The account was a fiction, but his devotion to Versailles was real. He spent fortunes improving the place, building, tearing down, rebuilding, rearranging and redecorating a series of palaces there, over a span of thirty years. The various versions of Versailles satisfied a variety of needs, inimitably his own.

The château celebrated Louis XIV's wars. Like many another monarch on the high tide of victory, he underscored the permanence of his battlefield successes by building permanent monuments in marble and brick, especially at Versailles. Its rooms were crammed with glorifications of French conquest by France's foremost painters and sculptors, who depicted Louis himself front and centre in every heroic encounter.

The Salon of Mars was typical. Charles Le Brun covered every inch of the walls and ceiling with martial allegories, culminating in a giant circular plaster relief of the king by Antoine Coysevox. The king was crowned by Glory as his war-horse trampled his enemies underfoot.

Not many steps away, the decorations of the Hall of Mirrors offered a paean to his conduct of the Dutch war of the 1670s. Panel after panel trumpeted his military genius, climaxed by an overwrought Le Brun painting of the king, who, seen crossing the Rhine,

> . . . transported as Apollo on a triumphal chariot . . . holds up Jupiter's quiver of Thunderbolts; behind him Hercules swings at the old Rhine with his club while at the same time preparations are being made to gather the keys of the cities of Holland for presentation to the king.

No battlefield fantasy on his walls could calm the fears in Louis's mind; he was devoured by suspicion of his military leaders. Personal heroism in battle was viewed with disdain. Public acclaim was discouraged. Even his own brother, Monsieur, dainty, epicene, but brave as a tiger, was summoned home when he won an unbecoming victory at the Battle of Cassel. He was never again allowed to command.

Between campaigns, Louis made the personal attendance of the *maréchaux* (and the presence of all the great nobles) the single condition of his favour. Out of sight, he was convinced, was out of control. Once they were in residence, the captive courtiers were beset by demands for ever more extravagant jewels and dress, ever more reckless losses at the royal gaming tables. The money-lenders set up shop. Debt became a way of life. The king smiled. The royal purse held salaries, pensions and estates, the royal largesse meant fiscal rescue. To courtiers feverishly searching for a hand-out, to be received by the king was to be in funds. The most dreaded phrase in the land was Louis's cool, 'I do not know him'.

Accommodations for Louis's noble hostages accounted for part, only, of the perpetual construction at Versailles. It occurred to him that this pleasant country estate could be the seat of government. Why not house France's ministries within steps of the royal bedroom, insulated by distance from Paris with its insubordinate Parlement and unruly university students? The mushrooming growth of the central palace with its wings and ancillary buildings allowed Louis to keep the political talent of France on call, quite literally, in his antechamber. The Wings of the Ministries at Versailles – the central hive of *ancien régime* officialdom – were created in 1683.

In the château, with a gelded nobility tethered under the king's own roof, his ministers within sprinting distance of the royal summons, safe from the street mobs of Paris, the Sun King held the world at bay. Versailles became the ultimate bunker.

Like most tyrants, Louis XIV expected his power to extend beyond the grave. Unfortunately, he lived too long. Bloody but clockwork-perfect successes on the battlefield were followed, in the early years of the eighteenth century, by equally perfect military disasters. From the day John Churchill, the Duke of Marlborough, led the allied armies to victory at Blenheim, Louis was battered by French defeats – at Ramillies, Turin, Lille, Oudenarde and Malplaquet.

Ramillies was a defeat exceeded only by Blenheim in its scope. The French general, François de Neufville, Maréchal and Duc de Villeroi, was as terrified of the king's reaction as of Marlborough's armies. He waited five days before sending word to Versailles. When Louis was informed, he turned, more disappointed than despairing, to the Duc de Brancas, and complained, 'God has forgotten me, and after all I have done for him!' When poor Villeroi returned to the court, the old Sun King was gentle with him, saying, 'Monsieur le maréchal, one is no longer lucky at our age.'

The hope that his successors would recoup his losses began to crumble when his son Louis died suddenly of smallpox in 1711. The new dauphin, his grandson Louis, Duc de Bourgogne, proved a spineless commander at Oudenarde. Military failure threatened to sweep away the Bourbons. In the summer heat of 1712, as enemy troops bivouacked within miles of the French capital, Louis XIV pawned his jewels and melted down his gold plate to pay for a last-ditch defence of his realm. His champion at Denain, Claude Louis Hector, Maréchal and Duc de Villars, fought brilliantly. He saved Paris and the monarchy. He was unable to shield Louis from the treaty of Utrecht.

At the treaty table, Louis blundered when he ceded the rich North American fur territories of Newfoundland and Hudson's Bay to England. The French sugar islands in the Caribbean, which he kept, seemed vastly more important at the time. Closer to home, the House of Hanover insisted that he stop sponsoring James Stuart, the Old Pretender, as the rightful ruler of England. He withdrew his patronage from the Scots prince. The allies were uneasy over the double claim of his grandson, the former Duc d'Anjou, now Philip V of Spain, to the thrones of both Spain and France. Louis grumbled, but persuaded Philip to give it up. There were lesser allied demands, some tinged with vindictiveness. The king watched in fury as Austria occupied the right bank of the Rhine. In the unkindest cut of all, he was forced to dismantle the fortifications of Dunkirk.

In the same grim year of 1712, measles killed the dauphin, the dauphine and their oldest son.

It was a peculiarity of the times that the wealthier you were, the deadlier were such commonplace infections. The duc and duchesse were attended by the finest physicians available. Their fatal error was in following the doctors' advice. The family was very nearly wiped out, murdered by constant bleeding and powerful purges. The youngest, aged two, survived. A cool-headed friend of the family, Charlotte Eléonore, Duchesse de Ventadour, snatched the little fellow out of reach of the doctors. She kept him warm, put him to suck at the breasts of a healthy wetnurse (whose milk, in all probability, brimmed with the antibodies needed to fight the disease), dosed him with Alicant wine, and prayed at his sickbed like any peasant grandmother. She became his governess and was ever afterwards cherished by the future Louis XV as 'Maman', the woman he loved most in the world.

The duchesse was at the side of the five-year-old dauphin on the morning of 26 August 1715, when he waited for hours to visit his great-grandfather's deathbed.

A mob of courtiers, avid for the dying favours of the king, stampeded past the shy little heir. He was outnumbered by the *legitimés*, as Louis XIV's illegitimate children were called. The king had given his left-hand family official standing and a place in the royal succession. His favourite bastard was Louis-Auguste de Bourbon, Duc du Maine, one of his two surviving sons by the late Françoise Athénaïs, Marquise de Montespan. The duc raked in fortunes and accepted showy military commands from his father. A more important sign of favour in the hothouse competition of Versailles was his right of precedence when he attended the *lever* and *coucher*, the daily rituals of the king's arising and retiring. He lingered at the royal ear during his final interview, ignoring the stench of rotting flesh as gangrene inched its way up his father's leg.

King Louis's last will and testament placed du Maine in charge of the new boy king's education. The appointment would prop up the duc's prestige after his father's death and add to his power as commander of the household troops, but, much as he might have liked, the dying king could not give his bastard the regency. It was an honour reserved by tradition for the nearest legitimate blood relative of the minor king, his dissolute uncle, Philippe II, Duc d'Orléans.

Orléans was one of the last grown-ups to approach King Louis before the dauphin was ushered in. As he arrived, the corridors hissed with whispers among the partisans of du Maine. The favourite bastard's duchesse, Anne Louise Benedicte de Bourbon, sneered at the measles story. She was a Condé and a midget (one of a set of sisters known as 'the royal dolls') to whom King Louis had married du Maine to consolidate his position. She saw an Orléans plot in the recent royal deaths. Orléans, like many aristocrats, dabbled in science; his interest was chemistry. In her venomous little voice, the duchesse charged him with poisoning the late dauphin and dauphine. Anyone could see, she railed, that a fresh assassination would eliminate the five-year-old heir, if Orléans assumed power.

Louis XIV himself found Orléans detestable. The royal pique dated from 1708, when the young duc, posted to a military command in Spain, had been courted by Spanish grandees who were anxious to depose Philip V. Orléans loyally shrugged off their proposals, but found his military mission frustrated at every turn by Anne-Marie de la Trémoille, Princesse des Ursins, who was Madame de Maintenon's resident agent. Madame Ursins openly pulled the strings of the Spanish throne. In a drunken rage, he raised a toast to the interfering women before his officers, 'Messieurs,' Orléans said, 'here is to the health of Captain Cunt and Lieutenant Cunt.' He was recalled from his command, and not given another.

Almost as damaging, in the old king's eyes, was Orléans's determination to parade his debauched private life. The king, who enshrined appearances, called him *un fanfaron de crimes* ('a catalogue of crime'), and did his best to gut Orléans's regency of real power by posthumously decreeing a regency council dominated by the *legitimés*. Orléans would not rule at all, but would cast a single vote in the fourteen-member council. Slyly, Louis attempted to reassure Orléans, 'My nephew, I have made a will in which I have preserved all the rights owed your birth – I have made the dispositions I felt to be wisest – if there is something that is not right it will be changed.' Orléans didn't believe a word of it, but kept his peace as his uncle slipped towards death.

It was noon before the dauphin faced the king. Louis XIV had the child lifted on his bed, and kissed him. He delivered a final sermon on the subject of majesty. It was worshipfully recorded by a courtier, Philippe, Marquis de Dangeau:

Mignon (darling), you are about to be a great king, but your whole happiness will depend on your submitting to God, and on the care you have to relieve your people of their burden. In order to do this you must, whenever you can, avoid making war; it is the ruin of the people. Do not follow the bad example I have given you on this point. Often, I have started wars without sufficient cause and continued them to satisfy my pride. Do not imitate me, be a peaceful ruler, and let your main object be to look after your subjects. . . .

It was the only occasion in living memory when Louis XIV admitted he was wrong. He kissed his great-grandson again, turned him over to the Duchesse de Ventadour, and gave the assembled court a brisk talk on the loyalty they owed the throne and its new occupant. The courtiers knew it was every man for himself from the moment Louis XIV died. According to Dangeau, they '. . . burst into tears and nothing could begin to describe the sobs, sorrows and despair of all those present'.

For the five remaining days of the death watch, the Sun King's gold and silver bedroom was kept in a constant uproar. Priests droned prayers like an out-of-tune opera chorus. Every courtier who had the *entrée* burst in with his own virtuoso lamentations. The king's womenfolk (with the exception of Madame de Maintenon) added an obbligato of wails and shrieks as they fainted away and were revived. Mercifully, there was no orchestra during the last three days; someone had the good sense to cancel the musicians who struck up a fanfare each time food came near the royal lips. The king himself added to the din, joining in the prayers with surprising strength and volume. He had always addressed God in a shout; no one knew whether he thought God was hard of hearing or that he simply assumed the attitude of command, even in conversations with his Maker. Late in the proceedings, the king murmured to Madame de Maintenon that, in view of her age (she was eighty) he would see her soon. She did not take well to the idea, and exited the death chamber.

At last, early in the morning of 1 September, gangrene won. An officer of the household guard stepped out on a palace balcony in a black-plumed hat. Sweeping the hat from his head, he exclaimed, '*Le Roi est mort!*' He stepped inside, then reappeared a moment later. His hat bore a white plume. He cried, '*Vive le Roi Louis XV!*'

Luckily, protocol dictated a cheer for the living king from the crowd below, because no one mourned the dead one. His autopsied, eviscerated shell was sealed in two caskets, the inner one of lead, the outer one of heavy oak banded in iron. It lay in the Salon of Mercury for eight days, before departing in a casually assembled, perfunctory funeral procession. The cortège marched in slow step through Paris to the Bourbon burial place in St Denis. The Parisians marked the occasion by getting exuberantly drunk. They sang and danced in the streets. A few risked the bayonets of his guards to scream curses at Louis XIV's coffin.

To start the new reign, the Parlement of Paris met in solemn session with the peers of the realm for the reading of the royal will. Like everything associated with the late king, the document was top-heavy with dignity. It was sealed, not once, but seven times, kept in a special safe opened with three keys, bricked into the tower wall of the Palace of Justice.

The Duc du Maine, who knew its contents, arrived for the reading with smiles for everyone. Louis XIV's testament would place the government in his hands, he thought, for the next eight years, if not longer. The king reached his majority at the age of thirteen, but he would have to be superhuman to shed the dependency of nearly a decade; he who ruled France now, ruled for the foreseeable future.

Du Maine and his brother, Louis Alexandre, Comte de Toulouse, were two of four contenders. Toulouse, an amiable nonentity, was interested only in gardening and the hunt. Neither his brother or the Duc d'Orléans, the third candidate, troubled to seek the comte's active support. Philip V, Louis's surviving grandson, was the fourth, faraway, possibility. Philip ached for power in France, but geography and the Treaty of Utrecht prevented him from seizing it.

As the Parlement assembled, du Maine was the odds-on favourite. He was an unattractive nominee for ultimate power, misshapen, lame, effete, a physical coward for all his battlefield posturings. In childhood he had been a prodigy, a published author at the age of seven. Traces of his earlier brilliance lingered in the personal charm that so captivated Louis XIV. The diarist Saint-Simon, who hated him, wrote:

> No one had more wit than he. No one was ever endowed with more subtle and insinuating graces, while he was all the more disarming for his natural, naive, even innocent air. No one had ever been born with vaster ambition!

The duc was a formidable intriguer. In preparation for his contest with Orléans at the Palace of Justice, he spread a wide net of obligations among his fellow nobles and the lawyers of the Parlement. The *premier président* (chief magistrate) of Parlement himself was indebted to him for his office. Nothing, the mincing bastard assured his partisans, stood between him and control of the regency council.

Orléans, on the other hand, had no party. For years, he had existed beyond the pale, defying the lofty disapproval of his uncle – and the ostracism that went with it.

His sin was not sinning, but bragging about it. In a court that lived from one pompous hypocrisy to the next, his openness was regarded as unseemly, if not seditious. Louis XIV's lifetime of expensive mistresses, his illegitimates, the scarlet army of his casual conquests were institutionalized scandals familiar to every footman. But, by the rules of etiquette, the royal philandering was politely euphemized, pensioned off, or, if what Saint-Simon called the *mécanique* of the court could handle it no other way, actually legalized.

Philippe d'Orléans, heavily sexed like all the Bourbons, not only refused to hide his tom-catting but loved to shock the prigs. His lechery amused his mother, Elizabeth Charlotte of Bavaria, Princess Palatine and Duchesse d'Orléans. Known as Madame, she was a wit and social observer whose correspondence entertained most of the courts of Europe. Unsparing of her son, she wrote, 'He is quite crazy about women. Provided they are good-tempered, indelicate, great eaters and drinkers, he troubles little about their looks.'

He was rather happily married to another of Madame de Montespan's royal bastards, Françoise Marie de Bourbon. It was an arranged marriage, and although she had inherited her mother's figure and a fair share of her good looks, the bride suffered from scoliosis, which gave her a curved spine and a crippled walk. Orléans loved her anyway and had eight children by her. She was intelligent, tolerant of her husband's skirt-chasing, but consumed by ambition. Ignoring her famous mother entirely, she promoted her royal parentage without let-up. The court wags compared her to the goddess Minerva, who had no mother, but sprang fully armed from the forehead of Jupiter.

The duchesse was not jealous, but she was a little embarrassed by the ugliness of some of her husband's whores. When she told him so, Orléans delivered a classic riposte. '*Bah!*' he snorted, '*Maman, dans la nuit tous les chats sont gris.* ('Mamma, at night all cats are grey.')'

Almost his only friend during Orléans's years in the wilderness was Louis de Rouvroy, Duc de Saint-Simon. The two men could not have been more different. Saint-Simon was honest, industrious, pious to the point of prissiness. He despaired of the rapscallion Orléans, a liar who delighted in piling whopper on whopper, an open atheist, the seducer of every woman who crossed his path, so foul-mouthed his wife could not invite people of quality to dinner.

Behind the brazen façade, there was gold in Orléans's character. The sober-minded Saint-Simon cherished his friend's virtues and eloquently defended him in his memoirs:

> M. le duc d'Orléans was of medium height at best, stout without being fat, with a noble and relaxed manner, a wide, pleasant and ruddy face, black hair, and a black wig . . . there was infinite grace in his face, his gestures, and his manner . . . [which] was kind, affable, open, and unceremoniously charming. The timbre of his voice was pleasant, and he had a particular and versatile gift for speaking with ease and clarity . . . To hear him, one would have thought he was vastly cultured, but nothing was farther from the truth . . . he forgot neither facts, names, nor dates . . . he gave the impression of having deeply studied what he had touched but lightly. He excelled in vivacious and pointed impromptu remarks, such as retorts and witticisms. . . . Although he had no inclination for backbiting or malice, he could be dangerous in his judgement of others . . . he could not help deriding those he called 'saints abroad and devils at home' and one could feel his natural contempt and revulsion for them. . . . He loved liberty, for others as well as for himself. In England, he used to say, there were no *lettres de cachet*.

Orleans's love of liberty didn't prevent him, when pressed, from fighting by the rules of *realpolitik*. In the struggle for the regency, he proved to be shrewd, resourceful and surprisingly ruthless.

He knew the key to the regent's power lay, not in the royal will, as du Maine believed, but in the Parlement of Paris itself. The Parlement, and its twelve sister parlements in the provinces, were the high courts of royal France – not to be confused with representative assemblies. Their members were mostly drawn from the landed gentry; seats were inherited or purchased, as were most of the desirable posts in the *ancien régime*. 'Spices', or mandatory fees, made judgeships lucrative; under-the-table bribes often brought immense wealth.

Uniquely, the Parlement of Paris had exercised, from feudal times, a 'right of remonstrance'. Simply put, the judges were allowed to complain to the king about his laws, as they registered them. It was the sole, narrowly limited legislative privilege permitted in autocratic France – and widely popular. Although they promoted only their own interests, the judges trumpeted the claims of 'the people' in their high-sounding speeches and gulled political naifs into believing they were democratic. Louis XIV found the judges irritating and their precious right an absurdity. He went straight to the point and abolished it.

The Parlement of Paris wanted the right of remonstrance restored. Orléans horse-traded its return for confirmation of his regency. The judges listened to him, turned a deaf ear to the ghostly voice from St Denis, and set aside Louis's deathbed plan for the conduct of the regency council. They proclaimed Orléans regent with full powers. He was pleased, but left nothing to chance. To offset intervention by du Maine, troops loyal to Orléans ringed the Palace of Justice; indeed, command of the household troops provoked an argument between the two ducs. Parlement recessed and cut short the wrangling. Orléans spread bribes among its members. When the session resumed, du Maine found himself reduced to a purely honorary superintendency of the education of the heir.

It was not a bad afternoon's work for Orléans, who only the day before had been dismissed as a scatter-brained rake.

His defeat of du Maine set the rumours flying again, as the bastard and his duchesse muttered darkly of regicide. They and their friends foully slandered an essentially kindly man. Within the hour of Louis XIV's death, Orléans had gone to his knee before the new king of France, saying, 'Sire, I come to pay my respects as the first of your subjects.' He meant what he said. His love for the royal urchin in his charge and his loyalty to his sovereign never wavered during the next eight years.

The object of all this manoeuvring, Louis XV, was suddenly the sweetheart of the nation, surrounded by a court now infatuated with the child it had ignored a week before. Perhaps the only critic of the boy king was the regent's mother, Madame. 'He would be very nice,' she wrote, 'if he would talk a little; it is difficult to extract a word. He seems to love no one except perhaps his governess.'

France's new monarch made his first official appearance when Parlement convened ten days later for one of those curiously named ceremonies, a royal *lit de justice*, or bed of justice. (So-called because the king faced the judges seated on a bed-like heap of cushions.) The king rode through Paris to thundering salutes from the cannons of the Bastille. Cheering crowds clogged every foot of his route. While the scarlet-robed parlementarians came slowly to order, an official amused the little boy in the Sainte Chapelle, by showing him sacred relics thought to be splinters of the True Cross.

Finally, Louis XV entered the Parlement chamber. He was a beautiful, delicately-featured child with enormous black eyes, cherry-red lips and masses of chestnut curls. He seemed all the more touching and fragile for the great plumes that fluttered in his hat. Prompted by his governor, the elderly Duc de Villeroi, he addressed Orléans, 'Sir, I wish to assure you of my affection – my chancellor will tell you the rest.' Orléans decreed, and the Parlement registered, the king's first business: restoration of the parlementary right of remonstrance.

The king then borrowed a handkerchief from the Duchesse de Ventador, wiped the perspiration from his face, and settled down for the interminable ceremony. He was terribly bored, but he concealed his feelings with amazing skill; even as a child, Louis XV was a remarkable dissembler. His statement, his apathy – and his feigned interest – were an eerie forecast of his reign.

Chapter Eight

The Sinner-in-Chief

L ouis XIV's will might have been written on the air, so little effect did it have on the regency. In the matter of the new king's home, for instance, he left detailed instructions. His great-grandson would move, temporarily, to the fortress of Vincennes. Mourning regalia would be removed from Versailles. When the royal apartments had been aired, refurbished, and tailored to the needs of the boy-king, Louis XV would return to the great château, attended by his court.

Orléans had other ideas. On 9 September, he made a public display of carrying out the late monarch's wishes by ordering the little king moved to Vincennes. The ninety-minute excursion became a royal progress. The regent stuffed into the state coach as many members of the royal household as he could – the Duc du Maine, the Comte de Toulouse, the Duchesse de Ventadour, the Maréchal de Villeroi and himself, all dressed in black, and the tiny sovereign, Louis XV, suited in purple velvet, the mourning colour of kings. They clattered off in a wonderful show of royal unity. The trip was slowed a little by an immense turn-out of spectators. Shouts of '*Vive le Roi!*' echoed through the autumn afternoon. If small talk between Orléans and du Maine was somewhat strained, the whole stage-managed affair came off splendidly.

It was the last, perfunctory bow Philippe d'Orléans would make to the memory of Louis XIV.

No sooner had he settled the young king in the fortress, than Orléans floated rumours of the harsh winter ahead for anyone living at either Vincennes or Versailles. How could a delicate child be expected to survive? On 30 December, after a much-publicized conference of physicians on the state of the king's health, Louis XV was plucked from the draughty battlements of Vincennes and transferred, not to Versailles, but to Paris. He took up residence in the Tuileries, near the regent's own Palais Royal. The arrangement enabled the regent to make daily calls without wasting hours on the road.

Orléans established an intimate 'court' in the Tuileries, complete with majordomos and brilliantly-uniformed household guards, but staffed, in the main, by the king's governor and governess and a troop of doctors, cooks and nursemaids. The king's household was not to be compared with Versailles, but in the regent's opinion, the stupendous apartments of the château were unsuitable for a five-year-old.

Nor did Orléans wish to give house-room to a crowd of plotting aristocrats. Madame de Maintenon, who might have created difficulties, was, thankfully, realistic. She had been a lifelong partisan of the bastards, du Maine and Toulouse, having been brought to Versailles originally as their governess. She obliged the regent by retiring voluntarily to St Cyr, the academy for girls of which she was patroness. He expressed his gratitude by delivering the first instalment of her pension in person. The widow's eviction was followed by the departure of the 2,000-odd courtiers in residence at Versailles. The regent was gracious, but firm. Flushed out of their cubbyholes, the old court drove off to face the horrors of life in the provinces. Versailles was abandoned to the swallows and the field mice.

Among the decamping courtiers was Père Michel le Tellier, the old king's Jesuit confessor. Orléans exiled him in one of his first acts as regent. Tellier's *prie dieu* had barely grown cold before the tolerant duc amnestied the Huguenots; he also released Jansenist prisoners from the Bastille. The Jansenists, a Catholic reform group, had drawn papal wrath and Tellier's personal vengeance by their espousal of Gallicanism (religious home-rule). Their stand made them popular with all classes of Frenchmen, including a sizeable number of judges in the Parlement. Under the regent, they were not only tolerated but scored heavily against the Jesuits when the Jansenist Archbishop of Paris, Louis Antoine, Cardinal de Noailles, was picked to head the regent's 'council of conscience'.

Tellier's banishment was the signal for a revolution in private manners and morals. The priest, with the powerful backing of Madame de Maintenon, had censored the nation's virtue for Louis XIV. At his instigation, adulterers were hunted like criminals. (The king and his pious lady were assumed to be man and wife – at least there was no one foolhardy enough to question the sanctity of the royal bed.) Homosexuals were tormented, too. The king's own son, Louis, Comte de Vermandois, had been exiled. Operas and plays were banned from the court during Lent. Woe betide the courtier who whispered during mass in the royal chapel – His Majesty actually took names! Louis's list of transgressions was long and petty, and a royal frown could spell the end of a courtier's career. Tellier made certain the same self-righteous vigilance made life miserable for lesser folk in every parish in the land.

Once the regent took power, Tellier was given his walking papers. The French, famished for a taste of *douceur de vivre* after the sour old age of the Grand Monarque, went on an historic eight-year binge.

Gluttony, drunkenness and lechery were in vogue once more. Open promiscuity replaced the furtive intrigues of Louis XIV's court. Noblewomen, in particular, could not get their fill of sexual freedom. Duchesses lusted after lackeys, abbesses bragged about the bastards they had borne, mothers seduced their own sons.

The tainted ladies and their bourgeoise sisters reached the pinnacle of wantonness at the Opera balls. These enormous routs, launched by Orléans in 1716, were open to all, three nights a week. Six francs, a mask and a scrap of fancy dress gave anyone the right to commit public lewdness in the best society. Regency women attended in *décolletage* that left them naked to the waist. 'Adorned indecency' became the height of fashion – ball-goers veiled their bodies in the sheerest muslin and decorated their exposed breasts. So popular did the Opera balls become that an annexe had to be built at the Louvre to accommodate the crowds.

In the decadent spectacle of the regency, Philippe d'Orleans gloried in the role of sinner-in-chief. No more wicked than his neighbours, he was a good deal more visible. His private life became the talk of Europe. For once, the truth was as scandalous as the rumours, for Orléans's iniquities covered the spectrum from adultery to idolatry. (Despite his loudly-proclaimed atheism, he flirted, at least temporarily, with Satanism.)

He had always been a rebel. During the hypocritical reign of Louis XIV, the moral bombast that issued from the throne only incited young Philippe to greater impudence. A typical escapade involved his attendance, one Christmas night, at matins and all three midnight masses in the royal chapel. Through the long hours of worship, he kept his nose buried in his missal. When old Madame Imbert, his mother's first lady-in-waiting, murmured her approval, he gleefully scooped out of the missal a copy of the ribald tales of Rabelais he had smuggled into the king's private services!

Like many another lost sheep, Philippe's friends blamed his bad conduct on low companions. According to Charles Pinot Duclos:

> If he liked people they became his equals. Despite his talents and intellectual resources he could never suffice for himself: he needed

dissipation, noise, debauchery. He admitted into his circle people whom no one with self-respect would recognize as friends despite their birth and rank. Though he took pleasure in their company, he did not respect them, calling them *mes roués* to their face. One evening at supper, the Comtesse de Sabran remarked that when God created man a little mud remained from which was formed the soul of princes and lackeys, and the Regent laughed with delight at the *mot*.

Most accounts credited the duc's headlong plunge into perdition to Guillaume Dubois, the atheist abbé who was Philippe's tutor from the age of twelve. Dubois, the son of an apothecary, was Orléans's lifelong mentor in godlessness and by most accounts, his pimp. He arranged Orléans's marriage, over the furious objections of his mother, Madame, and took a hand in the education (and corruption) of the oldest Orléans daughter, the Duchesse de Berry. Madame likened him to a fox crouched to spring on a chicken. On the day Parlement proclaimed Philippe regent, she pleaded with him, 'My son, I desire only the good of the state and your glory. I ask only one thing for your honour – a promise never to employ that arch-rascal Dubois.'

The promise was not forthcoming. The worldly, ambitious abbé served Orléans as secretary and, quite effectively, as minister for foreign affairs. Later, he would be Louis XV's prime minister, seizing for himself the immense dignity of a cardinal's red hat. René-Louis, Marquis d'Argenson, described Dubois in his memoirs, noting that:

> his manners and conversation formed a perfect contrast with his ecclesiatical habit: he swore, blasphemed . . . said the most indecent things against religion . . . and persuaded his prince that there was not in the world real piety or true probity.

Under Dubois's tutelage, wrote d'Argenson, Orléans divided the world into clever rascals and honest imbeciles, and he employed only the former.

Another Orléans hero was Philippe de Vendôme, the Grand Prior of France, who was a left-hand grandson of Henry IV. Saint-Simon said the regent regarded Vendôme with 'admiration tending to actual veneration' because the Grand Prior paraded a series of mistresses, disgraced his holy office with irreligious pronouncements and went to bed drunk every night for forty years.

For a time, Orléans took up with the fortune-tellers and soothsayers who infested the court. His disbelief in God didn't deter him from seeking contact with the devil. He spent nights on end with a fast-talking *mousquetaire* named Mirepoix in the stone quarries of Vanves and Vaugirard, where they solemnly chanted invocations to the Infernal Majesty. Nothing came of it, but Orléans kept trying to make a diabolical connection. His mother described his interview with 'a madman in Paris who believes he can make an angel appear in a chimney'. Madame was indifferent to the sacrilege involved, but she was shocked when Philippe asked when the old king would die. On another occasion, he quizzed a sorcerer's nine-year-old apprentice on the death of the king. According to Saint-Simon, the little girl undertook to see Louis XIV's death scene in a glass of water. Her vision was accurate as far as it went, for she reported seeing Orléans with the regent's crown.

He wore the crown with a decided tilt in the company of the *roués*. Orleans coined the name *roués* for the raffish comrades with whom he shared his private life, deriving it from the punishment on the *roué*, or torture-wheel, which their conduct would have earned them under the previous administration. He presided as master of the revels when they gathered in the Palais Royal. The young libertines were joined by a corps of voluptuous women recruited from gutters low and high. Forty giant servants kept out the curious.

Their pleasures were predictable: choice food, oceans of drink and non-stop fornication. The *roués* ensured complete privacy by preparing their own supper, in dishes of solid silver. They roared their appreciation of sex shows of every description, the filthier the better, and constantly scouted for new ones. An evening might feature nude dancers from the Opera, who restaged orgies of the classical past. Or one of the *roués* who had invented a magic lantern, would consent to project his collection of pornographic lantern slides. The merrymaking was rounded out by off-colour stories, bawdy songs, and the inevitable sacrilegious speech declaimed by the host. (Orléans timed his gaudiest celebrations for holy days, Good Fridays included.) When the candles were snuffed, the party dissolved into a sexual romp limited only by the participants' stamina. Orléans, in his early forties, was tireless. He was good for half a dozen bottles of champagne or Tokay, and the favours of an equal number of attending whores. The orgies were remarkable less for their depravity than for their frequency – the regent and his companions caroused night after night. Promptly at eight o'clock every morning, without showing the least sign of wear and tear, he resumed the duties of government.

Eventually, the regent's relentless pursuit of vulgarity wore away Madame's loving indulgence. She wrote:

There is no longer a court. Would to God that the late King were alive. I found more satisfaction in a single day than in six years of the Regency of my son. Then there really was a Court, and not this bourgeois life to which I cannot accustom myself, I who have been bred at Court and spent all my life there.

She was mortified when it became plain that the regent's love for his daughter, Marie Louise Elizabeth de Valois, Duchesse de Berry, was incestuous. Born in 1696, Marie Louise was Orléans's favourite from childhood. When she was near death from smallpox, the duc threw out the doctors and risked his life by personally nursing the little girl back to health. By the time she married Louis XIV's youngest grandson, Charles de France, Duc de Berry, her father had spoiled her beyond redemption. Her husband, a plump, blond, prayerful ninny, alternated between public battles with his uncontrollable bride and shamefaced interviews with the king. His fourteen-year-old wife detested him, but did her level best to give the king a new generation of Bourbons. At fifteen, the king forced her to travel to Fontainebleau with the court, despite a troublesome pregnancy. She bore a dead baby girl. Two more babies, born dead or too frail to live long, followed. Her rancorous marriage ended in 1714 when a hunting accident killed de Berry. She devoted the rest of her short, embittered life to carnal excess.

The duchesse was tall, beautiful, passionate, in every way Orléans's lustful twin soul. Intimacy with her was probably impossible to resist, considering the cold reception he received from Philippe Louis, Duc de Chartres, his fanatically religious oldest son. The *chroniques scandaleuses* hinted that his third daughter, Louise Adélaïde, also was her father's mistress. She was the learned Soeur Bathilde, Abbesse de Chelles, who took time from her pursuit of theology and art, if one believed the rumours, for far lustier lessons. The whispers described her abbey as 'a palace of delight . . . the Abbey where Venus dwells'.

Orléans's indiscretions with Marie Louise were blatant. Childless and undisciplined, she became her father's companion in vice. She gambled recklessly, adored drunkenness, took innumerable lovers. Imitating the regent, she dubbed her circle of fellow wantons her *roués*. Her father came to dine with her lovers at the Luxembourg Palace. She came to the Palais Royal to sup with his mistresses. Orléans, a talented artist, painted her in the nude.

The duchesse played the strumpet in public with her father, taking liberties that horrified their family and the court. She spent hours closeted with him alone. When the rumours of incest flickered into life, they could not be put out.

Witnessing the ruin of what remained of his friend's reputation filled the duc de Saint-Simon with guilt. It was he who had arranged the de Berry marriage. His virtuous duchesse had somehow been dragooned into being Marie Louise's lady-in-waiting. She reported the riotous goings-on at the Luxembourg, and Saint-Simon, heartsick, recorded them in his memoirs:

> Her [the duchesse's] arrogance bordered on folly, and she was capable of the lewdest indecencies. One can say that except for avarice, she was the incarnation of all the vices, and was all the more dangerous because of her matchless cunning and intelligence. . . . She did all she could to make M. le duc de Berry, who was genuinely pious and completely honest, give up religion. . . . He had to deal with a proud, haughty, and pigheaded woman who despised him and let him know it. . . . She made herself unbearable by bragging about her vices, mocking religion and jeering at M. le duc de Berry. . . . She lost no time in having affairs, which were conducted so indiscreetly that he soon found out about them. Her daily and interminable sessions with M. le duc d'Orléans, where it was clear that he [de Berry] was not wanted, put him in a rage. . . . At each of the many informal meals she took she became dead drunk, and threw up whatever she had eaten. On the rare occasions when she held her liquor, she was just as drunk. . . . She often treated Monsieur her father with an arrogance that had many frightening implications. . . .

The regent and his daughter were fair game for the pamphleteers of Paris. One of the cleverest, François Marie Arouet, wrote obscene verses and spread it around that he knew the nursing home in Auteuil where Marie Louise planned to have her father's child. It was too much, even for the easy-going regent. He locked up the scribbler in the Bastille. Later, the writer achieved fame with a great play, *Oedipus*. Orléans awarded him an income. The young playwright, who signed himself Voltaire, remarked that he was grateful to the regent for paying for his board, but wished no part of his lodging.

In July 1719, the doctors did for the Duchesse de Berry what smallpox had failed to do. She died at twenty-four, a casualty of medical feuding between her regular physician and a rival.

Marie Louise departed her life as flamboyantly as she lived it. In March she bore the child of one of her *roués*, a pimply-faced lieutenant of dragoons named Rion. Her delivery was harrowing. The Sacrament was brought to her, to be administered conditionally on the expulsion of her lover from the Luxembourg Palace. She howled her defiance of her father, mother and Cardinal de Noailles. Then she reversed herself, and, according to Saint-Simon,

> made a vow that she would give herself up to religion, and dress in white – that is, devote herself to the service of the Virgin – for six months. This vow made people laugh a little.

She made a temporary recovery. By July, she was again at the point of death. A healer of the day was called in to give her a miracle elixir. Amazingly, she began to fight off the illness for a second time, to the disgust of the Orléans's own family physician. The angry quack dosed her with a poisonous emetic. Hauled to account before her mother, he huffed out of the sick room, pausing only long enough to bow to Marie Louise, now in her death agony, and wish her a pleasant journey!

She was dead within hours. In the autopsy, according to Saint-Simon, 'she was found to be again *enceinte*; it was also found that her brain was deranged'. The regent's grief was unendurable. Neither his wife or his sumptuous blonde mistress, the Duchesse de Falaris, could comfort him, nor did any amount of boisterous distraction ease his pain, until his own death four years later.

Chapter Nine

'Le Mississippi'

Despite his outrageous private life, the regent was an able ruler. Orléans made friends with George I of England, made Philip V of Spain back down from his new aggressions, and made a brave attempt to solve France's chronic insolvency when he gave his blessing to the visionary financial scheme the French called 'le Mississippi'.

Although English peace, Spanish war and 'le Mississippi' did not directly affect Louis XV's boyhood, they provide insights into the way government operated, in the kingdom he would shortly inherit. To twentieth-century minds, used to ponderous 'official policy', his uncle's conduct of affairs seems personalized, extemporized and sometimes quixotic. Whether it was also effective, is for the reader to judge.

Orléans set his diplomatic revolution in motion within a year of assuming the regency. He sent Dubois scurrying off to the Hague, where the despised abbé, now a councillor of state, met Lord James Stanhope, secretary for foreign affairs to the newly crowned George I. They played at being book collectors, and rearranged Europe's balance of power as they leafed through the dusty folios. Stanhope accepted Dubois's argument that France, however financially distressed, was more desirable as an ally than as an enemy. In January 1717, the Hanoverian king and the French regent unveiled the Triple Alliance of England, France and Holland. The alliance brought Europe's ancient foes twenty-three years of peace.

The dramatic volte-face in foreign policy precipitated a storm of protests from the *maréchaux*; their opposition gave Orléans the pretext he needed for an overhaul of the government.

In the early days of the regency, he had attempted to restore the nobility to eminence. Government by a series of councils was decreed, each council under the leadership of a great nobleman. The ducs and *maréchaux* were laughably incompetent. Seven decades of the Sun King's despotism had turned them into witless drones, interested only in the empty formalities of court etiquette. The greatest of events, in their eyes, was the meeting of the regency council and the Parlement in 1718 in which the regent stripped the Duc du Maine of his princely honours and took him out of the royal succession.

The 'reduction' of the once-powerful bastard was followed by dismissal of the councils; ministers known as 'the five kings', headed by Dubois, now governed France. The new-style regency, the discontent of the du Maines, and everyone's loathing for the English alliance, led to the Spanish-sponsored Alberoni plot.

The plotters' aims were fairly simple: they hoped to kidnap the Duc d'Orléans, imprison him in Spain, and declare Philip V Regent of France. The plot concocted by King Philip, his minister, Giulio Cardinal Alberoni, and his ambassador, the Prince of Cellamare, was farcical. Otherwise clever people like the Duc and Duchesse du Maine tripped over their own feet in a tangle of secret meetings, messengers, and codes no one could read. Fittingly, they were betrayed by a brothel keeper, who brought Orléans's *mousquetaires* marching into the Spanish embassy in Paris. The regent was lenient. He waved away evidence of high treason, beheaded no one, and imprisoned a few small fry. Cellamare was conducted to the border. The du Maines were exiled to separate provincial estates, where they retired from politics.

The affair did add a certain relish to the moment in 1719 when Orléans honoured his new treaty obligations to the court of St James. In the renewed conflict between England and Spain, he sent Louis XV's troops to fight the armies of Louis XIV's trouble-making grandson. The war crushed Philip V's imperial pretensions, for ever.

Fighting the Spanish was enjoyable, but finding the *livres* to pay for it was not. From the moment he took power, Orléans had been inundated by Louis XIV's legacy of debt, much of it incurred in the last, decrepit days of the reign. With foreign troops at the gates, tricksters, profiteers, and shylocks offering loans at 400 per cent interest had flocked to pick the pockets of the French king.

In one of the few harsh programmes of his easy-going administration, Orléans now brought the money-lenders to account. On the sound principle that it takes a thief to catch a thief, he authorized the Pâris brothers, a quartet of financiers only slightly less shady than most, to 'revise' the millions in outstanding letters of credit left behind by Louis XIV. The Pârises inspected each bill minutely. They offered legitimate creditors the regent's promissory notes at 4 per cent interest. Out-and-out crooks, when they were discovered, suffered confiscation, and were turned over to a Chamber of Justice for prosecution. Nearly all received fines and imprisonment. The worst offenders were sentenced to the pillory, or the galleys. There was one execution. The Pârises saved the government four hundred million pounds in 1716, the single year in which they operated. The court convicted over four thousand profiteers, mostly on tips from informers who collected 20 per cent of the take. A new tidal wave of corruption threatened to swamp the regency, as the contractors bribed anyone with judicial influence. A marquis offered to get an indicted financier off, for a hundred thousand crowns. 'You're too late, my friend,' the man replied, 'I have already made a bargain with your wife for fifty thousand.' One ingenious malefactor informed on himself – and was paid for his services!

The regent finally realized that he had no stomach for a regime financed by the activities of stool pigeons. He brought the Pârises's inquisitions to a halt. By the end of 1717, the brothers were in exile. They had kept the regency afloat, but the millions forced from the profiteers by their 'revisions', and the fraud trials, barely dented the national debt.

Orléans turned to a flamboyant foreigner, John Law. The son of an wealthy Edinburgh goldsmith, Law was anything but the popular image of a dour Scotsman. He was tall, amiable, a fascinating raconteur, and, if badly marked by smallpox, a devil with the ladies. In the nineties, during a brief English career as a beau, he gambled away his inheritance. A duelling scandal drove him out of England. He skipped to Flanders and Holland, where, despite his fugitive status, he cut a dashing figure.

Returning to Edinburgh in 1700, Law offered the Scottish parliament a credit scheme involving the establishment of a 'Land Bank'. The idea was hooted out of town, and Law with it. (The wits called it a 'sand-bank', on which the ship of state would run aground.) Checked but not defeated, he crossed the channel again, to Germany, Hungary, Italy and France. For income, he gambled, sharping at the card-tables of wealthy friends. He was, in fact, a brilliant player who raked in such winnings the magistrates of both Venice and Genoa thought it advisable to show him the city gates.

If he was forced to make his way on the fringes of respectable society, Law dreamed dazzling dreams. He laid vast financial proposals before Victor Amadeus, the duke of Savoy, and Charles VI, the Habsburg emperor. Eventually, the Scotsman gravitated to Paris and Louis XIV. Louis was out-of-pocket as always. He received one of Law's inventive petitions, and asked if 'Monsieur Lass' was Catholic. (To the French, who could not pronounce the 'w' in his name, Law was

Lass.) Law was Presbyterian. Louis instantly recoiled. However hard-pressed the Grand Monarque might be, no Protestant foreigner would be allowed to subsidize him!

The regent was not so choosy. On 5 May 1716, he issued a decree allowing Law and his brother William to establish a private bank in Paris. Law and Company opened with assets of six million *livres*, scraped together from gambling profits and the tag-ends of the Law family fortune. There was nothing makeshift, however, about Law's conduct of the bank's affairs. Alongside the financial sewers opened up by the Pâris brothers, his new institution fairly glistened with integrity, offering a sensible, attractive return on investment. A novel touch! His notes were redeemable at face value, without hedging.

The Parisian public hurried to buy as many Law banknotes as they could. According to Charles Mackay, who, in 1841, chronicled Law's career in his book, *Extraordinary Popular Delusions and the Madness of Crowds*:

Law was now on the high road to fortune. . . . He made all his notes payable at sight, and in the coin current at the time they were issued. This last was a master-stroke of policy, and immediately rendered his notes more valuable than the precious metals. The latter were constantly liable to depreciation by the unwise tampering of the government. A thousand livres of silver might be worth their nominal value one day, and be reduced one-sixth the next, but a note of Law's bank retained its original value. . . . in the course of a year, Law's notes rose to fifteen percent premium, while the *billets d'état*, or notes issued by the government . . . were at a discount of no less than seventy-eight and a half percent. The comparison was too great in favour of Law not to attract the attention of the whole kingdom, and his credit extended itself day by day. Branches of his bank were almost simultaneously established at Lyons, Rochelle, Tours, Amiens, and Orleans.

To such a pillar of business virtue, the regent could refuse nothing. In 1717, Orléans sanctioned the use of Law's banknotes as official currency.

Law saw greener pastures across the Atlantic. In August 1717, he petitioned the regent for, and was granted, exclusive trading rights on the Mississippi, in France's New World colony of Louisiana. Law formed the Mississippi Company and mounted a high-powered publicity campaign to sell shares in his new enterprise.

If one believed Monsieur Lass (and who did not?) the innocent natives of the Mississippi ran to thrust treasure upon European traders in return for worthless trinkets. Posters went up all over Paris, picturing the exploration of gold, silver and copper mountains. They described the quest for a fabulous boulder of solid emerald. Real-life 'Indians' (bogus, of course, but no one had the slightest idea what an 'Indian' looked like) made public appearances.

Public expectations soared higher with every preposterous claim. The wealth of the Americas was suddenly within everyone's grasp, for the purchase price of one of Law's stock certificates. Law gave the scheme a final push into the stratosphere, when he tied the stocks of the Mississippi Company to the hitherto solid currency being issued by his banks.

'Le Mississippi' was born.

Within weeks, the nation was caught up in a delirium of speculation, triggered by the first experiment in finance capitalism ever attempted in France. Instant riches beckoned to courtier, bourgeois shopkeeper, and chimney-sweep alike. One had only to dig up the gold and silver coins under one's floor boards and exchange them for the dependable notes of Law's bank, and the spectacularly profitable shares of his Mississippi Company. Law's boom was self-perpetuating. Shares in 'le Mississippi' could only be paid for with Law banknotes, in a proportion of three Law notes for every four invested.

'Le Mississippi' doubled one's money; in three months, a fifty *livres* share was worth a hundred. Second and third issues (called 'daughters' and 'granddaughters' because only holders of the original shares could buy in) offered even higher returns. The competition for shares in 'le Mississippi' was ferocious. Their value sky-rocketed. At the peak of the trading, a five-hundred-*livres* share was quoted at eighteen thousand *livres*!

By 1719, The Company of the Indies, as it finally became known, had absorbed all French trading rights in the East Indies, China and the South Seas. Law became the nation's most important 'tax farmer', when he took over collection of indirect taxes on salt, tobacco, and the like. In the same year, Law and Company became the Royal Bank of France. The Scotsman was transformed into a kind of river-god of the Mississippi, from whom all economic blessings flowed, and around whose altar clustered the enraptured French. He reigned supreme from June 1719, to February 1720, months in which the strangely coincidental 'South Sea bubble' swept England. The two nations competed with extravagant tales of 'bubble' madness.

In the rue Quincampoix, where Law's bank was situated, there was daily pandemonium. Law looked down from his office, when he was there, on a sea of shoving, shouting speculators that filled the tiny street building-to-building. He loved to toss fistfuls of money into the crowd, to see them scramble for it. Neighbouring shops that leased for a thousand *livres* a year, brought a thousand a month. Shopkeepers offered standing room, pen, and paper to speculators at astronomical daily fees. A local hunchback, the story went, rented his hump as a writing desk. Soldiers had to break up near-riots when business closed at sundown.

Law moved his headquarters to the Place Vendôme, where booths and tents were erected to accommodate the stock trading. The croupiers of Paris added to the general hubbub by setting up roulette tables in the centre of the square. Pickpockets and footpads appeared. The neighbours complained. Law was forced to move once again. This time, he bought an historic mansion, the Hotel Soissons, from the Prince de Carignan. The prince kept title to the garden acreage at the rear, where he rented out five hundred tents to the stock-jobbers – netting a monthly income of a quarter of a million *livres*. The daily carnival roared on, attracting would-be millionaires from every corner of France, and, as the word spread, every country in Europe.

Law and his family were courted by the highest levels of regency society – the ladies, especially, laid traps for the gallant banker. Madame, that keenest of observers, reported in her letters that:

> Law is pursued to such a point that he knows no rest, night or day. A duchess kissed his hand in front of everyone. If the duchesses behave this way, what will other women kiss?

One woman, hell-bent on investing, tracked him for days in her carriage. She upset the vehicle in the financier's path with a shriek. When Law rushed to rescue her, she confessed her stratagem. Law laughed and obliged her with Mississippi shares.

With easy money in every pocket, Paris was the capital of extravagance as never before. The *nouveaux riches* went on a shopping spree for wardrobes, carriages and mansions. Merchants flocked in with the costliest clothing and jewels, furniture, paintings, tapestries and statues. The regent took the lead in conspicuous consumption, by purchasing a diamond 'as large a greengage, of a form nearly round, perfectly white, and without flaw, and weighing more than five hundred grains'. His bauble set the nation back two million *livres*.

Violence had its vogue, with murders committed for Mississippi shares. One assassination in particular shocked society, a stabbing in a tavern in broad daylight, committed by a distant relative of Orléans, Antoine-Joseph, Comte de Horn. The regent showed extraordinary rectitude; despite pressure from the family, he let the death sentence stand. On Good Friday 1720, de Horn and an accomplice were broken alive on the wheel.

As the craziness mounted, Saint-Simon and old Maréchal Villars seemed to be the only two sceptics left in Paris. Villars lectured the mob from his carriage and was nearly stoned. Saint-Simon wrote:

> Everybody was mad upon Mississippi stock. Immense fortunes were made, almost in a breath. Law, besieged in his house by eager applicants, saw people force open his door, enter by windows from the garden, drop into his cabinet down the chimney! People talked only of millions!

The boom replenished some of the noblest fortunes in the nation. The Duc de Bourbon, one of Louis XIV's *legitimés*, was a glittering example. By shrewd manipulation of the 'system', he rebuilt the château of Chantilly, founded a legendary stable with 150 racehorses imported from England, and bought enormous estates for himself in Picardy.

The end, when it came, was more painful, if that was possible, than the bursting of the 'South Sea bubble' in London. Unlike the English example, in which investors were swindled by hundreds of 'bubble' companies, the French were ruined by *'le Mississippi'* alone. All France schemed and cheated in a single, high-flying enterprise. All of France's dreams shattered in a single crash.

The 'system' went out of control in March 1720, when a spat developed between Law and Louis Armand, Prince de Conti. In January, the financier had accepted the regent's appointment as Controller General of Finance, following a lightning conversion to Catholicism. He now acted with high-handed disdain, denying de Conti the additional Mississippi shares he wished to purchase at an advantageous price. The prince sent a caravan of wagons lumbering into the courtyard of Law's bank where, under protest, they were loaded with fourteen million *livres* in gold, in exchange for de Conti's Mississippi shares. Louis Henri de Bourbon, Prince de Condé, known as 'Monsieur le Duc', was next. The vulpine Condé had only recently burrowed his way into the government, but he could not resist de Conti's greedy example. He exchanged twenty-five millions in shares.

The regent, beside himself with anger, had Condé on the carpet. 'Is this the way to uphold the interests of the state?' Orleans asked him. 'Is it not a means of destroying the bank to withdraw twenty-five million as you have done, or fourteen million as Monsieur le Prince de Conti has done? What do you need so much money for?' Condé's reply was sullen but succinct: 'I have a great love of money.'

The regent could lecture as much as he pleased, but the damage was done; when the public heard of the princes' withdrawals, they raced to follow suit. Smuggling became the national pastime. Speculators sent their plate and jewellery to safety with friends abroad, or shipped bullion outright. A jobber named Vermalet heaped up a farmer's cart with gold and silver coins. He covered his treasure with a layer of cow dung, put on a peasant's smock, and drove the cart to Belgium. The country haemorrhaged its gold to banks in England and Holland.

In the regent's name, Law published edicts forbidding the hoarding of metals, their sale to foreigners, and, at the last, the possession of more than five hundred *livres* in coin. In vain. Nothing could stop the panic, once it broke.

The government flailed about, searching for a gesture to restore confidence. In desperation, the regent rounded up six thousand hooligans and derelicts, clothed them and handed them picks and shovels. He paraded the ragtag army through the streets for days on end, announcing that they would soon embark for America to dig up more gold. There were grim giggles at the stunt, but no one believed the story.

By the end of May, after dozens of proclamations and almost daily meetings of the ministers, payments in specie were outlawed.

The mood in the streets turned ugly, quickly.

The bank offered a trickle of silver in June. The building was instantly mobbed, and the silver evaporated. Bank officials were reduced to handing out copper. Bagful by back-breaking bagful, it was lugged away by those fortunate enough to bully their way up to the tellers' windows through the unbelievable crush. Men climbed trees and hurled themselves bodily into the massed crowd, in the hope of securing a better place in line. On 9 July, an attempt to storm the bank failed when soldiers fired into the crowd. They killed one man. On 17 July, according to Mackay:

The concourse of people was so tremendous that fifteen persons were squeezed to death at the door of the bank. The people were so indignant that they took three of the bodies on stretchers before them, and proceeded, to the number of seven or eight thousand, to the gardens of the Palais Royal, that they might show the regent the misfortunes that he and Law had brought upon the country. Law's coachman . . . was sitting on the box of his master's carriage in the court-yard of the palace . . . the mob immediately set upon him, and thinking Law was in the carriage, broke it to pieces. . . . The president [of the Parlement] . . . informed the councillors that Law's carriage had been broken by the mob. All the members rose simultaneously, and expressed their joy by a loud shout, while one man, more zealous in his hatred than the rest, exclaimed, 'And Law himself, is he torn to pieces?'

The regent did his best to protect the Scotsman, allowing him to hole up in the Palais Royal as 'le Mississippi' plummeted through a dizzying series of devaluations. By October, the new millionaires of the previous spring were facing fines for their manipulations. The government ordered option holders to make good their pledges. Hundreds fled to avoid paying. As his 'system' crumbled, Law, with the regent's permission, retired to one of his country estates, then set out for Italy. To his credit, Law refused financial help; his own fortune, now forfeit, was tied up in French real estate. In Venice, he returned to gambling to support himself and, eventually, died a pauper. His brother William was imprisoned in the Bastille with a handful of other insiders, but was later released.

A deadline was set for turning in three billion *livres* of worthless banknotes and stock certificates outstanding. Shares in the Company of the Indies were now worth between 5 and 15 per cent of their face value. Eight hundred clerks toiled in the Louvre until 20 March 1721, doling out the pittance in exchange for bits of paper once worth more than two billions. With a national groan, the French tore up the rest, burned them, or gave them to the children to play with.

Two postcripts bear mentioning.

At the height of the emergency, when Law sought to register special coinage powers with the Parlement, they refused. It was the latest in a long string of obstructions the lawyers had thrown in the regent's path. Orléans held a *lit de justice*, rescinded the right of remonstrance, and exiled the fractious parlementarians to Pontoise. His regency emerged from the crisis stronger than it entered.

At the final tally, an amazing fact became apparent. Because Law had insisted that shares of 'le Mississippi' be paid for with his own banknotes, by a mysterious alchemy of finance, he had succeeded in paying off half the national debt!

Chapter Ten

An Orphan at the Orgy

N ews of the Mississippi débâcle, like most events of the day, was heard in the nursery court at the Tuileries very faintly, if at all.

By common consent of his keepers, Louis XV, the future of France, grew up in isolation. What he learned of the great world, he learned from his uncle Orléans, who made dutiful visits to keep him informed. The regent merrily announced Dubois's English peace. The seven-year-old commented, 'I did not believe abbés could be so useful.' When the Spanish war began, he eagerly followed battlefield reports, like any small boy. Sometimes, he played a public, if largely ceremonial, role; when the czar came to call from Russia, his meeting with Peter the Great was an occasion of the highest importance. The giant Romanov swept the tiny Bourbon high in the air, roared imperial greetings and roundly kissed him. Louis was terrified, but uttered not a whimper. He knew an adult court surrounded his uncle at the Palais Royal, but of the dissolute social life of the regency, he was totally ignorant. An orphan guest at his uncle's eight-year orgy, the little king might have inhabited another planet.

When he was seven, the Duchesse de Ventadour, his '*maman*' who protected him from all harm, was replaced. Custom dictated that his boyhood be supervised by an all-male staff.

At the transfer of custody, suspicion ran deep, even against such a paragon as the duchesse. Louis was brought before a grim-faced committee of doctors and high court officials presided over by the regent. Stripped to his skin and inspected like a prize calf, he was pronounced sound of limb and wind, and released from the duchesse's care. It was his official introduction to life with his governor, the Maréchal de Villeroi. Louis refused to eat, and there were midnight sobs into the royal pillow, but he gave an iron display of self-control in public. The following day, he presented '*maman*' with a casket containing farewell tokens, a cross of diamonds and a superb pearl necklace.

Madame, who reported the parting in her letters, looked in on him frequently. She described the future sovereign with immense pride:

> It is impossible for any child to be more agreeable than our young king; he has large, dark eyes and long, crisp eyelashes; a good complexion, a charming little mouth, long and thick dark-brown hair, little red cheeks, a stout and well-formed body, and very pretty hands and feet . . .

It was natural to adore such a beautiful child, but Madame's judgement of his character was not swayed by superficialities. The shrewd old woman spoke her mind:

> His gait is noble and lofty, and he puts on his hat exactly like the late King. . . . He has sense enough, and all that he seems to want is a little more affability. He is terribly haughty and already knows what respect is. His look is what may be called agreeable, but his air is milder than his character, for his little head is rather an obstinate and wilful one. . . . To tell you the truth the child has been very badly brought up. He is allowed to do whatever he likes for fear of making him ill; but I am sure if he were corrected he would be less violent and that they are doing him a very bad turn by letting him behave as capriciously as he likes, but everyone is keen to gain the goodwill of the King, however young he may be.

Half a century of king-worship generated by Louis XIV had given his great-grandson the status of a demigod in the public mind. Louis's care was the making and breaking of courtiers. Under Villeroi, they were driven by fear. They feared for Louis's well-being, feared their critics, and feared royal retribution in the future. He was allowed a carefully screened playmate or two, but most of his time was spent with grown-ups whose nervous attention to his every smile, frown and fever (for he was delicate) erupted into hysterical scenes.

The king's play could create a major crisis. A pavilion was erected on the terrace at the Tuileries to shelter him and his romping companions. Louis decided to create his own band of knights, 'The Order of the Pavilion', and issue medals to the children; Villeroi ordered medals struck by the royal silversmith. The Duc de Mortemart, First

Gentleman of the Bedchamber, insisted that he, not Villeroi, was in charge of play medals and silversmiths. In a moment, the duc and the maréchal were at each other's throats, shouting and cursing. The regent himself had to be called to settle the quarrel. Louis got his medals, but the two men were blood enemies from that day forward.

Awake or asleep, someone danced attendance on the youngster. When he fell out of bed one night, the *valet de chambre* literally hurled his body to the floor, cushioning the king from injury. On another occasion, mischievously, Louis hid himself under the bed until a general alarm was raised. He emerged from his hiding place giggling, while the staff suppressed the urge to paddle the royal bottom.

Old Villeroi, possessive to the point of paranoia, began to imagine evil influences in every corner. Even Madame was not above suspicion. She wrote,

> The King had the colic the day before yesterday, and yesterday I gravely went up to him and put a little piece of paper into his hand. Maréchal de Villeroi asked me in a pompous voice, 'What note are you giving the King?' I answered equally seriously, 'A remedy for the colic.' The Maréchal: 'Only the King's physicians may prescribe for the King.' I answered, 'As to that, I am sure that Monsieur Dodart would approve. It is even in verse and to be sung.' The King grew embarrassed, read it secretly and began to laugh. The Maréchal said, 'May I see it?' I said, 'Yes, it is not secret,' and he found the following words,

You with your collywobbles	Happy, happy to be rid of them
With your rumbling winds	Oh poor unfortunates, to set
They are dangerous	them free
And to rid yourself of them	Fart
Fart	Fart, you can do no better
Fart, you can do no better	than to
than to	Fart
Fart	Happy to be rid of them.'

> Everyone laughed so hard that I was almost sorry to have played the joke. The Maréchal de Villeroi was quite put out of countenance.

Madame could make jokes about the boy's bowels, but no one else dared.

In July 1721, Louis was laid low by something a good deal more serious than colic. He displayed the symptoms of a routine eighteenth-century 'bug', complete with headache, sore throat and fever. When the Duc de Saint-Simon arrived, the regent was already there. With the Duchesse de la Ferté (sister of the Duchesse de Ventadour), the two men watched an apothecary dose the child with medicine. Without any warning, the duchesse cried, 'He is poisoned! He is poisoned!' and nothing Saint-Simon could do would shut her up.

The 'madwoman', as Saint-Simon called her, created pandemonium. The Duc du Maine, with his black suspicions of Orléans poison, had been exiled, but there was no shortage of overwrought courtiers to squawk and flutter at the bedside. The older ones remembered the poison trials of Louis XIV's time, in which Madame de Montespan herself had been implicated.

After five days of hysteria, all the attending physicians were reduced to impotent hand-wringing save one, named Helvetius. He proposed a bleeding from the king's foot. The blood-letting did nothing for the king's illness, but the malady had evidently run its course and little Louis began to recover. The bleeder was a hero.

From the center of the uproar, Saint-Simon wrote:

> I was exceedingly glad that I had refused to be the King's governor, though the Regent had over and over again pressed me to accept the office. There were too many evil reports in circulation against M. le duc d'Orléans . . . was I not his bosom friend – known to have been on the most intimate terms with him since childhood – and if anything had happened to excite new suspicions against him, what would not have been said? . . . What joy was mine when I remembered I had not this duty on my head!

Villeroi, the chief poison-monger, now took charge. (It is a mystery of the regency why Orléans permitted him to keep his post as long as he did.) He prolonged the child's convalescence, preening himself in the sickroom for six weeks while he grandly dispensed permission to visit the patient to members of the court, the Parlement, and the foreign ambassadors. At last, he ordered *te deums* in every church in Paris and trotted out the invalid for thanksgiving ceremonies at Notre Dame and Sainte Géneviève. In August on the feast of Saint Louis, the king's name day, there was a fête with musicians and fireworks, in the gardens of the Tuileries. People stood on the surrounding roof-tops to gawk. Louis, made utterly miserable by the prolonged furore, tried to hide himself in a corner.

The maréchal tugged him to the window, crowing, 'Look, my master, all that crowd, all these people are yours, all belong to you; you are the master of them: look at them a little therefore, to please them, for they are all yours, they are devoted to you.' Louis gave in. He trotted meekly out to the terrace with Villeroi, where they listened to a concert.

Saint-Simon loathed the maréchal:

> He was the least liked of anyone at Court because people found in him only a mass of fatuousness, of self-interest and smugness, of boasting about the King's favour and about his great successes. . . . He had read nothing, knew nothing, was completely ignorant in every field, given to shallow jokes, much wind and all completely empty.

Villeroi knew how to cater to the boy's vanity, but very little else. A courtier born (his father had been Louis XIV's governor), he was a disastrous general, a lady's man and gossip. His plan to prepare Louis for kingship consisted mainly in reviving the grovelling rituals of the *lever* and *coucher*. The king was encouraged to leave his affairs, like his bed-clothes, in the hands of others. Louis, who needed little excuse for indolence, was glad to oblige. He began to face his public duties wearing the silent half-smile which would become his trademark, a mask for his boredom with affairs of state.

He was prickly in defence of his dignity, demanding the exact measure of respect due to a king of France, however youthful. The regent, who might have been overbearing, inspired his gratitude by treating him with deference. Dubois, who should have known better, earned his hatred by condescension.

Out of his boredom emerged an ugly streak in the king's character. He was given to little cruelties, to his courtiers and to animals. At first sight of the Bishop of Metz, he cried, 'Oh, what an ugly man!' 'What a badly brought up little boy!' retorted the bishop, and turned his back. On another occasion, an attendant complained of a gouty foot; young Louis ground his heel into it, asking if he had stamped on the right one.

In 1720, he began to ride and shoot pheasant and partridge, the start of a lifelong dedication to the hunt. This was desirable, but his treatment of his pet cat Charlotte was not. When she littered, he gleefully tortured to death three of her four kittens. (His page, the Marquis de Calvière, recorded the episode.) There were other stories, equally unappetizing.

Moments like these might been written off as boyish prankishness, but there was more. The young king was amused by all things relating to death, corpses, graves, funerals. His obsession became an international embarrassment. Dubois was forced to write to the Doge of Venice:

> . . . all the malicious talk you have heard on the weakness of the king's temperament and on his melancholy is completely false. His health is perfect.

There were few antidotes available to counteract his morbidity. Madame, affectionate but outspoken, was one. Another was Louis's preceptor, Bishop André Hercule de Fleury. The Jesuit-educated Fleury had originally come to court in 1679 as almoner to Louis XIV's queen, Marie-Thérèse. At her death, he was rewarded with the diocese of Fréjus, a remote district in southern France where he spent the next seventeen years. The Sun King's will brought him back to Paris at the age of sixty-two, to give his great-grandson a gentleman's education.

Louis's apprenticeship in government was supervised by Dubois (now a cardinal, although his elevation had been lost in the July 1721 tumult over the king's illness). He ushered in advisors from the foreign, war and finance offices. The regent himself spent frequent mornings with the king. From the age of ten, Louis was encouraged to attend the *Conseil d'État*.

Fleury's staff of tutors filled in the blanks, familiarizing him with the arts and science. Religious instruction was reserved to the bishop himself, who assigned copybook exercises using old-fashioned moral maxims and parables.

Fleury accomplished several pedagogic goals during his years as the royal tutor. Louis, who was teachable if not brilliant, picked up the smattering of geography, history, mathematics and Latin necessary to his profession. The bishop taught him that kings answered to God for the well-being of their subjects. He drilled into his young charge the belief that sin, especially sexual sin, brought eternal damnation, especially to sexually sinful kings.

Fleury laid on the piety with a trowel, but he was sensible enough not to bury his pupil in scholarship. The tall, country cleric with his fussy manner and gentle discipline made ample provision in the king's schedule for sports and play. He was as anxious that Louis should become a fine horseman as an accomplished Latinist. Louis learned to love old Fleury despite his moralizing.

The bishop was political discretion itself. Answerable to Villeroi, he avoided intrigue completely, making a point of his loyalty to the maréchal. Once convinced that the preceptor was his man, Villeroi, who was interested in Louis solely for his exhibition value, let Fleury take charge of most of the boy's day. Only clever old Dubois, remembering his own rise to power as the tutor of Philippe d'Orléans, realized how total was the boy's dependence on Fleury. Fleury dispensed prayers, praise and fatherly affection. Uncle Orléans, the regent, who bored Louis to death with his talk of Paris and politics, took second place at best in his affections.

Chapter Eleven

The Return of the Chameleons

Although the sinks of Paris were more to Orléans's liking than the pomps of Versailles, the regent was forced to reopen the suburban court in 1722. Great events now rushed upon him. His nephew's coronation was just ahead. So was a possible royal betrothal, and the attainment of Louis's majority in 1723.

Such opportunities for spectacle were not to be missed, but they demanded splendours the city's palaces could not provide. Europe must be impressed, even intimidated, by the advent of a new king of France. Only Versailles was equal to the occasion. From Versailles, Louis XIV had exited into history. From Versailles, Louis XV, his successor, must make his entrance upon the world's stage. Heralded by a supporting cast of courtiers and servants, Louis arrived on 15 June and, with Fleury to prompt him, began memorizing his lines.

Versailles was as much a colossal theatrical backdrop as a practical dwelling. As it emerged from the dust sheets, the Sun King's fantastic château still echoed to his imperious speech and step, and the applause of the throngs who came to view his fifty-four year performance. With a new royal star in residence, it would again attract a daily attendance of six thousand or more.

Their carriages streamed out from the capital on three broad avenues which converged in an arrow-shaped plaza before the château. The commonest members of the king's audience booked special jitneys called 'chamber-pots' for the ride. The cavalcade was brought to a halt by two sets of gilded grilles and gates; at the inner barricade, all but a handful of the élite were forced to dismount and walk the final yards to the palace doors. The visitors saw ahead of them the king's stables (housing more than twelve thousand royal mounts and carriage horses), then wings and colonnades receding into the distance, rank on rank, like a stage setting designed for giants. Finally, the tremendous château itself could be seen, stretching to the left and right a full fifteen hundred feet, the longest, grandest façade on the continent of Europe. At the exact centre was the bedroom of the king. The architecture, moatless, turretless, defenceless but dominating by its sheer immensity, set the style for royal residences from Hampton Court in England to the Schönbrunn Palace in Austria.

A cluster of satellites had sprung up around the château: pleasure pavilions, among them the celebrated Orangerie and Ménagerie, the Chapelle Royale, vast office buildings, two convents, the Grand Commun (a staff residence), and the separate, extremely lovely, palace of the Grand Trianon.

The formal gardens of Versailles, André Le Nôtre's much-imitated masterpiece, provided a cool green belt of manicured *parterres* and immaculate walkways to the rear. Beyond lay Le Nôtre's *petit parc*, a dense wood cunningly planted around outdoor rooms or *bosquets*. These forest sanctuaries included an open-air ballroom and an astonishing water theatre. The Versailles labyrinth entangled explorers, particularly young ones, in a fairyland maze peopled with painted lead figures from Aesop's fables. Regiments of sculptures in marble, bronze and lead, personifying the thousand deities of the pagan pantheon, marched in Olympian rows through the gardens and into the distant woodlands. Water was the centre-piece of most outdoor displays. Piped to the arid heights of Versailles from springs up to ninety miles away, it lapped the edges of the lagoons and the grand canal, spilled carelessly from fountains and basins, and glittered skyward in towering water jets.

To the south, west and north spread the dark reaches of the hunting park, the original reason for the château's existence. Its natural paths had been widened into broad, shady *allées* to accommodate the wagons of provisions, the carriages packed with spectators and the massed phalanxes of huntsmen and retainers, who made up the royal hunt.

The royal décor set a new standard for extravagance. No European palace, and few in the fabled East, could rival Versailles for the opulence of its furnishings and decoration – nor had Louis XIV allowed the world to forget it. He gave enormous fêtes in 1664 and 1668, complete with illustrated guidebooks, for the sole purpose of showing off his treasures. Year after year, the court journals, the *Gazette de France* and *Mercure galant*, sighed in admiration over the god-king's good taste – displayed, presumably, in his avatar as an interior decorator. When he made Versailles the official seat of government in

1682, his personal suite in the château was unveiled to the public. A new word was added to the language to describe the king's quarters: *l'appartement*. It was to *l'appartement* that Louis XV returned in 1722.

He found it as enormous, draughty, and uncomfortable as it had seemed the day he attended the dying Louis XIV there, in 1715. Seating, what there was of it, was reserved for the royal family. There was precious little carpeting. Vast expanses of bare, cold parquetry faced the footsore courtier, who was expected to remain upright, except for occasional evenings when portable chairs, stools and tables were brought in for the king's receptions. Cabinets and consoles lined the walls. Mainly the work of Gobelins craftsmen, they were marvels of gilt metal and rare wood, elaborately inlaid with tortoiseshell and precious stones, their shelves laden with magnificent knick-knacks. Draped above and between the cases were Gobelins tapestries and brocades worked with pure gold thread, the wall-hangings punctuated, in turn, by heavily carved mouldings, mantles, doorways and cornices, all gilded to the last inch.

The suite was crowded with masterpieces, a *grand cabinet* of royal collections distinguished by the superb pictures Louis XIV had inherited from his unofficial stepfather, Jules, Cardinal Mazarin. The king's bedroom was hung with paintings by Domenichino, Rubens, van Dyck and Guido Reni. Titians dominated the Salon of Mercury. In the Salon of Diana was the heroic bust of the Sun King by Bernini.

The rooms of *l'appartement* culminated in one of the western world's truly overwhelming public spaces, the Hall of Mirrors of Versailles. Louis XIV's accustomed throne-room was a deliberately long, narrow gallery thirty-odd feet wide and nearly two hundred and fifty feet long. As they paced its length toward the king, diplomats were struck silent by the hall's sweep of marble and gold, bathed in sunlight by seventeen windows arching upward a full story and a half to the celebrated Le Brun ceiling. Seventeen great mirrors opposite duplicated into infinity the windows, and their views of the gardens below.

To the left and right of *l'appartement*, the public rooms and lesser state apartments of Versailles numbed the senses with acres of baroque: the suites of the queen, Monseigneur the dauphin, the royal princesses, the royal mistresses, the princes of the blood, and the greatest of the royal ministers.

Tucked in between, jumbled on top of each other in closet-sized cells the meanest peasant would have scorned, often with little but a screen, a clothes chest, and a wash basin to demarcate their floor space from their neighbour's, were two thousand and more courtiers, male and female, who gave the château as their address. In this tenement of the privileged, every square inch of living space was coveted, every amenity contested. The corridors swarmed day and night with a restless multitude who prowled the palace with a single purpose – to catch the eye, or better yet, the ear of the king.

As the new court settled in, old hands complained of the changes from the heyday of Louis XIV. The famous solid silver furniture was gone. A visitor in 1687 counted ninety-one major items of silver in the king's suite and seventy-six more in the Hall of Mirrors – a tonnage of tables, chairs, mantles, mirrors, vases, candelabra, chandeliers, incense burners, braziers and fireplace fittings that was the envy of the continent. In the king's bedroom, a solid silver balustrade separated the aristocratic elect from the aristocratic rabble. An eight-foot high solid silver throne, topped by a figure of Apollo, was the seat of majesty.

The gleaming display had lasted only two more years, until 1689. That year, despite a victorious campaign season, the king was unable to meet his soldiers' payroll. Without hesitation (or publicity), Louis XIV sent his silver furniture to the mint to keep his *blitzkrieg* rolling through the Palatinate. Two decades later, when military reversals backed him against the walls of Paris, he repeated the stratagem, melting plate and pawning jewels to finance a last defence.

If such a haphazard approach to budgetary matters has an all too familiar ring (the *dix-huitième* was a century of deficit financing by nearly every monarch in Europe) the French king's talent for wanton waste stands unique and uncontested. It can, perhaps, best be illustrated by the flower pots of Trianon.

Trianon in the 1670s had been a simple, sylvan pavilion, a garden retreat for the king. It became a full-blown palace in the 1680s. There was nothing exceptional in that, or in an enormous enlargement of the Trianon flower beds. It was unthinkable, however, for the royal nature lover to smell the same flowers twice. The gardeners invented an ingenious system of 'beds' made up of pre-planted stone pots. The pots could be buried and unearthed in seconds; entire alternate plantings were prepared and held at peak of bloom for the king's visits. If he lingered to spend the night, the flowers whose fragrance he breathed in the morning were replaced, as if by magic, before sunset. Someone counted the number of pots used in this floral sleight-of-hand. Ten thousand pots were changed, for each new royal sniff.

A statistics-lover went further and counted all the pots – including empties, those planted with seedlings, and plants in various stages of growth and bloom. According to the minutely-detailed memoirs of

Charles Philippe d'Albert, Duc de Luynes, one million, nine hundred thousand pots were employed.

Such giddy extravagance, the king's publicists insisted, was actually good for business! Among the fairy-tales concocted to justify the prodigalities of Versailles is the myth that well-heeled royal guests were so enthralled by the first, blinding sight of the château's contents, that they spent their second day at court writing orders to French manufactories whose products were on display. Much is made of Louis XIV's visit to the Gobelins, and, decades later, Madame Pompadour's sponsorship of Sèvres china-making, to prove that the ostentation of the court was somehow vital to the economic health of the nation. The truth is, no exports of tapestries or hand-painted china ever made the slightest impression on the French national debt. Louis XIV's reign was a never-ending search for ways to stave off financial disaster. In his pursuit of solvency, he became the ultimate corrupter of the French body politic, shamelessly selling titles, offices, military commands, embassies and judgeships, and creating new ones by the hundreds.

His best customers were wealthy bourgeoisie anxious to join the aristocracy. Since the noble estate was, more often than not, bankrupt, the king was at a loss to understand the hunger for titles. Nicolas Desmarets, Marquis de Maillebois, his controller general, explained to him, 'Your Majesty ignores one of the finest prerogatives of the King of France, which is that when a king creates an office, God instantly creates a fool to buy it.'

The hunt for fiscal dodges became somewhat less desperate under Louis XV, who was able to shrug off restraints on his spending because the nation remained profitably at peace. The pace of excess never slackened. The two wastrel monarchs were assisted in 123 years of squandering by their queens, their mistresses, their numerous children, legitimate and illegitimate, and an army of voracious courtiers.

The 'chameleons, wind-sniffers and tablecloth-hangers', as the courtiers had once been called, returned to the château in the spring and summer of 1722. They scampered back from their provincial estates to attend the soon-to-be-anointed king, who, himself, made the move with pleasure. A sturdy, athletic twelve-year-old, Louis found himself released from the suffocating city to the thrills of the chase in the park of Versailles. At Versailles, one hunted daily if the king wished it. The boy king did.

The hunt became Louis's passion. It would be one of the two occupations to hold his interest during his fifty-one-year reign (the other was women). He is said to have run down more than six thousand stags; at his peak, he averaged 175 a year, which he personally brought to earth. He was keen, hard-riding, indefatigable. In the saddle with companions his own age, he captured, for a few hours, the illusion of freedom.

Inside the château, he was a prisoner of protocol. Technically, the monarch was the final arbiter of the *mécanique* of the court; in reality Louis was an apprentice cowed by chamberlains he did not like or even know, as he mastered the convoluted ritual of kingship invented by Louis XIV. Operating under Maréchal Villeroi, the high priests of minutiae were forever judging the length of a lace cuff, deciding the perfect tempo for a new quadrille, or – in moments of genuine crisis – settling questions of precedence among Louis's courtiers.

To the paranoid courtiers of Versailles, precedence was the breath of life. Precedence told you where you ranked below the king. Precedence told other courtiers whether they, in turn, ranked above or below you. Who was privileged to stand inside the king's bedroom balustrade, and who was not, set Cardinal de Rohan and Cardinal de Tencin to feuding. Which lady preceded which, provoked a public brawl between Madame de Ruppelmonde and the Duchesse de Gontaut-Biron, who tried to walk ahead of her. According to the journal of Edmond-Jean Barbier, their cat-fight was enlivened by shrieks of 'strumpet' in earshot of the queen, and reached a climax when each woman told the other, literally, to 'go fuck herself'!

Such vulgar battles for precedence, tricks and bribes to gain the *entrées* to the king's presence, the pushing for place that passed as devotion, continued for another fifteen years. It was 1738 before Louis XV plucked up the courage to reserve a few hours of his day from the public treadmill of arising, dining, receiving, presiding, dismissing and retiring, and had a suite of rooms – the *petits appartements* – declared off-limits to all but his intimate circle. During his first three years at Versailles, however, the proposition that the king had a right to a private life was inconceivable. He was bowed and beckoned this way and that by courtiers who came and went almost as quickly as he learned their names, shuffling and reshuffling like the face cards in a playing deck.

A politically important, if personally distressing, new face belonged to his first cousin, the Spanish infanta Anna Maria Victoria, whose betrothal to Louis was negotiated by the regent in 1721. Known affectionately as Mariannita, the princess was intelligent, beautiful, captivating, and five years old. There would be a minimum delay of eight or nine years before the marriage could be consummated. Louis, a sexually precocious eleven, was already squirming in the grip of a fiery Bourbon puberty. He burst into angry tears and poured out his anguish to Fleury. Nothing could be done. Red-eyed and sullen, he was forced to give his consent to the *Conseil d'État*.

As they arranged the marriage with Madrid, the regent and Cardinal Dubois conveniently forgot the thirteen-year War of the Spanish Succession, which had been fought for the sole purpose of keeping a single pair of Bourbon hands from grasping the French and Spanish sceptres. The regent's own English treaty of 1717 had led to French and Spanish blood-letting, ended scarcely two years before.

The two men knew their match-making might ignite another war, but they ignored the risks, enticed by the prospect of diplomatic prizes for everyone involved. The regent, who lacked ambition for himself, could not resist the Spanish offer to wed his daughter, Louise Elizabeth, Mademoiselle de Montpensier, to the heir to the Spanish throne, the prince of the Asturias. There was even a windfall for his virtuous friend, the Duc de Saint-Simon. The duc persuaded Orléans to send him to Spain to collect the signed contracts and the infanta. While he was there, the Spanish king made Saint-Simon's second son, the Marquis de Ruffec, a grandee of Spain.

With howls of protest sure to be heard in London, Berlin and Vienna, Orléans and Dubois tried to keep the treaty quiet. The Spaniards leaked the news. Most Europeans were aghast. The French loved it. When, in March 1722, the infanta and her retinue arrived from Madrid, the welcoming courtiers found her 'fair, pink and white'. She so beguiled Madame that the old princess forgot to be nasty. She declared the king's little Spanish fiancée to be angelic:

> I am sure that you couldn't find in the whole world a more charming and beautiful child than our pretty infanta, and she makes observations that would be creditable to a person of thirty years. 'They say that when one dies at my age one is saved and goes straight to Heaven. I should be very happy, therefore, if the good God would take me.

Louis, for one, would have been delighted to see her depart heavenward immediately. The child entered her earthly kingdom perched on Madame de Ventadour's lap, clutching a doll. Louis met the carriage and conducted the infanta to her apartments in the Louvre. He displayed little enthusiasm for his bride, still less for her doll. Fleury comforted him as best he could.

Within the month, scandals in the king's personal retinue jolted the court, demonstrating to the regent how futile was his notion of a prolonged period of royal chastity. With the reopening of Versailles, scores of new courtiers had thronged to the king's side, introducing a worldliness unknown in the Tuileries. Sexual temptation slithered in. Two of the youngest, handsomest tempters were Villeroi's own grandchildren. The diarist Mathieu Marais recorded the spicy details in July 1722:

> They live in the most open debauchery at Versailles. The princes have declared mistresses . . . [and] the maréchal de Villeroi has been pained to learn that the duchesse de Retz, his granddaughter, has had lovers of every social condition since she has been at Versailles . . . she tried to seduce the King himself . . . attempted to handle him in a very hidden place. Upon which the maréchal exploded with anger against the duchesse and sent her away from Court on the spot.

There was much more, and much worse. Marais wrote,

> There are also orgies of young gentlemen together which they don't bother to conceal. The young duc de Boufflers, the marquis de Rambure and the marquis d'Alincourt having walked to a secluded wood, the duc de Boufflers decided to rape Rambure but couldn't manage it. D'Alincourt said he wanted to carry out his brother-in-law's attempt. Rambure agreed to it and went through with it.

D'Alincourt was Villeroi's grandson; he and the other youths were Louis's closest companions, avid huntsmen who roamed the forest at his side almost every day. Sodomy in the woods was not regarded as particularly wicked, but the idea that the trio might seduce the king was daunting. Should he develop a taste for boys, the deviation would interfere little with the perpetuation of the dynasty (the Bourbons, whatever their predilections, were reliable sires) but homosexual favourites were historically far more troublesome than the worst royal mistresses. Alarming memories still survived of the assassination plot against Cardinal Richelieu instigated by Louis XIII's favourite, Cinq-Mars. Even after 150 years, the picture of Henri III, surrounded by his beautiful, vicious *mignons*, caused an official shudder.

The incident threw Villeroi into a panic. He made everything as embarrassing as possible by asking for *lettres de cachet* against the offenders. His grandson was exiled to Joigny and the Duc de Boufflers ordered to Picardy. The Marquis de Rambure, whom Marais described as 'passive in every way', was thrown into the Bastille. The scandal was painfully public, a secret only from the king. When Louis noticed gaps in his circle of friends, he was told that they were being punished for vandalizing the fences in the park, whereupon a new euphemism entered the language. Sodomists were now called *arracheurs de palissade* ('picket-fence pullers').

Villeroi himself was gone within a fortnight. The daffy old man, who had somehow convinced himself that the king's ear was his alone to dispense, refused to allow the regent to see the boy in private. It was the last straw. On 10 August, on Orléans's orders, the captain of the guard scooped up the maréchal into a carriage bound for Lyons.

Fleury, who had pledged to serve only as long as the maréchal, quietly left the court. Louis was devastated. His young friends had vanished into thin air; now the two older men closest to him disappeared, too. Typically, he was too timid to to demand their return. His official coming of age and the end of the regency were only a few weeks away, but, childlike, he retreated into sulky tears. The regent was kind. His men searched out Fleury, whose flight was really a strategic withdrawal. The bishop was brought back. The king brightened.

It was Fleury who carried Louis's sword belt when, late in October, he was forced to endure his coronation. The shy new French sovereign faced the court and the nation on the high altar of the Cathedral of Reims, where he was anointed, sermonized, deafened by musical tributes, and engulfed in a twittering sea of courtiers.

The bishop was a comforting presence again in February 1723, when Louis was declared an adult in a *lit de justice* before the Parlement. The tutor's growing power was evident, when he was asked to join the newly organized King's Council. This was the old Council of Regency in a new suit of clothes, with Cardinal Dubois still prime minister under Orléans. Fleury's council seat was no empty honour. He was present during all Orléans's private talks with his nephew.

Death now made inroads on the king's official family. Cardinal Dubois, despite a dangerous infection, foolishly took a military review on horseback. During the ceremony, his abscess burst. Terrified, he finally gave in to the regent's pleas and submitted to the skills of La Peyronie, the renowned *chirurgien*. He died the day after, 10 August 1723, at the age of sixty-six. His cardinal's hat provided no immunity from syphilis and the surgery of the time.

The old pagan was true to his beliefs, or lack of them. He made a five-minute confession to a handy Franciscan, for form's sake, and died without the Eucharist. His heirs received about two million *livres*; his patron, the regent, a service of gold plate. The Parisian rhymesters ignored his successes as prelate and politician and chose to salute his career as Orléans's pimp:

> *Ci-gît que Vénus eleva*
> *Et que Vénus terrassa.*

> Here he lies whom Venus raised
> And whom Venus laid low.

Marais added a wry eulogy of his own:

> This great cardinal, Prime Minister of France, is encased in lead like the others, although he did not even have the consolation of carrying his private parts into the next world, for the surgeons had cut everything off.

The Duc d'Orléans, never one to stand on dignities, offered to take up the prime minister's duties. The young king accepted, but the arrangement lasted only four months.

In December, Orléans was sharing a fireside afternoon with his mistress, the Duchesse de Falaris. On impulse, the atheist duc asked her if she believed in God, heaven and hell. She said she did. If that was so, how could she continue living in a state of sin? Her reply was simple, 'I hope God will forgive me.'

They were the last words Philippe, Duc d'Orléans, ever heard. He slumped to the floor, dead of a stroke at the age of forty-nine. Lecher, adulterer, incestuous father, orgiast, tippler, actor, composer, painter and political liberal (before that term was known), he was the victim of his vices. Much of his early popularity had melted away after the financial disaster of 1720 and the former regent was mourned by practically no one. Ironically, his place was taken, not by Fleury, but by Louis Henri de Bourbon, Prince de Condé, the same greedy 'Monsieur le Duc' who had precipitated the Mississippi crash by withdrawing his millions from John Law's bank.

Condé was a startling compendium of physical defects: one-eyed, stork-legged and short-trunked, scrawny as a cadaver, he resembled nothing so much as a malevolent crane. When he heard of Orléans's death, he ran the entire length of the palace to reach the king first with the news. Gasping, he dropped to his knees before Louis, begging him for the prime minister's post. The self-effacing Fleury discreetly nodded. Louis appointed Condé on the spot.

He was an inept minister. Even in the case of Louis's marriage to the infanta, he solved the king's dilemma by accident. Plainly, Orléans and Dubois had blundered, and the king was unhappy. Condé launched a search for eligible European princesses. With a census-taker's faith in numbers, he drew up a list of 99, dividing them by religion – 25 Catholics, 3 Anglicans, 3 Orthodox, 13 Calvinists, and 55 Lutherans. The list narrowed to 17, then to a handful. He attempted, unsuccessfully, to palm off two unmarried sisters. The English candidates were dropped for religious reasons. The infanta of Portugal was believed to carry the blood of a degenerate stock. The Russian candidate was scratched because of her lowly origins; her mother had been, originally, Peter the Great's camp whore.

When Louis showed his impatience with Condé, his lists, and his excuses, the duc's scheming mistress, Madame de Prie, unearthed the daughter of the ex-King of Poland, Princess Marie Leczinska. The princess was originally intended for Condé himself, who was widowed and needed an heir. He would not, however, consent to Marie. She was considered a commoner because Stanislas, her father, had been an elected king only, for five brief years. But, if not fit to be a Condé bride, why not queen of France? With nudging from de Prie, Condé impudently passed along the princess's portrait to the king.

Marie was small, thin, homely, and lacked majesty, but she had an advantage over the Spanish infanta. In 1725, she was twenty-three years old and Mariannita was nine. Louis, who was fifteen and a half, said yes. His Spanish child-bride was shipped home to an enraged King Philip. There was an enormous uproar at Versailles, where the new betrothal, to a 'princess' with no royal blood, was considered a national disgrace. Rumours were floated that Marie had webbed fingers and suffered from epilepsy and scrofula, but the king, dizzy with desire for a wife, any wife, listened only to Condé. The minister dispatched the news of their good fortune to the Leczinskis, who were living on a meagre French stipend at Wissembourg in the Alsace.

'Down on our knees in thanks to God!' Stanislas ordered his threadbare family.

'Why, Father, are you called to the throne?' asked Marie.

'Heaven is still more gracious,' he replied. 'You are Queen of France.'

Madame de Prie hurried south. As the mistress of the man who was placing Marie on the throne, she preened herself shamelessly before the tiny Wissembourg court. She inspected the trousseau, and with calculated cruelty, offered Marie some of her own chemises. (Sweetly sensible, Marie accepted them.) De Prie instructed the artless princess in the fine points of court etiquette during her journey to Strasbourg, where a proxy wedding was held. The Duc d'Orléans filled in for the groom.

On 17 August, Marie started her progress to Fontainebleau, where Louis waited to take his vows in person. The trip was a rainy nightmare. Marie's party struggled through endless torrents, on roads which became an impassable quagmire. Thirty horses at a time were hitched to the royal coach to drag it out of the ruts. It was 4 September before the caravan lurched into Moret, to join Louis. Like the travellers, the king and his party were covered in mud. Despite all, the king could barely contain himself at the sight of his bedraggled bride. His ardour was obvious. At his command, the wedding at Fontainebleau was dazzling. The bride wore purple velvet and ermine, the groom was outfitted in gold brocade and diamonds. When Marie was presented with the *corbeille* (wedding gifts), she touched everyone by distributing them to her ladies with the comment, 'This is the first time that I have been able to make presents.'

In a court which regarded every royal erection as an affair of state, there was no question of delicacy on the wedding night. M. le Duc monitored the proceedings hour by hour. The triumphant matchmaker reported that His Majesty 'proved his tenderness seven times'.

Queen Marie's fits were malicious gossip. She was healthy and had the conventional number of fingers; indeed, she picked out tunes on the guitar, the viol and the harpsichord. She dabbed at the eighteenth-century equivalent of painting-by-numbers pictures (complicated bits were completed for her by a court painter). She liked to read. She disappointed, nevertheless.

Although she spoke fluent German and French, she had no small talk. At dinner, she wolfed down each meal as if it were her last, which proved embarrassing because the queen, like the king, ate alone and on public display. Superstitious to a ridiculous degree, she was so afraid of ghosts that a lady-in-waiting had to lull her to sleep at night. (This, with her strong new husband in the same bed!) The newlywed king was alone in his enthusiasm for his queen.

When the beauties of the court were discussed, he loyally commended her, '*La reine est encore plus belle.*' *Belle* or not, no one could deny the queen's ability to do a queen's duty; starting with twin daughters, Marie gave birth to ten children between 1727 and 1736. In 1729, she presented her husband and the court with that most precious of French national treasures, a dauphin. Altogether, five of her daughters and two of her sons lived (although the little Duc d'Anjou did not survive childhood). With such a track record, and with Fleury's warnings of hellfire ringing in his ears, it was seven years before Louis XV kicked over the traces of a marriage that made him a laughing-stock.

The queen sighed, '*Toujours coucher, toujours grossesse, toujours accoucher.*' ('Forever bedded, forever pregnant, forever in childbed.') She mistook Louis's constant randiness for deep love, and, for a time, endured the burdens of childbirth with joy. When his boredom became too obvious, and his conjugal visits too routine, she began to invent excuses. She denied him her favours on high feasts of the church, then on miscellaneous saints' days. When the saints deserted her, she simply outlasted the king on her knees, murmuring her nightly prayers until he gave up in disgust. For a while, the young husband contented himself with barbed messages, traced with his finger on a misted mirror. Then came a night, reported by Jean de Bourgogne, when she denied him once too often. Unusual for Louis, he was drunk. He shouted to Marie, 'Madame, you shall pay for this.' He sent his *valet de chambre*, Dominique Guillaume Lebel, racing through the corridors in search of the first available (and willing) woman he could find. She was a maid of the Princesse de Rohan, who delightedly obliged her sovereign, and gave birth, nine months later, to the first of Louis's recorded bastards. He was 'Dovigny le Dauphin', who later became a mirror merchant and a popular playwright. Having made his point, Louis strayed no further. The queen's pregnancies and pieties continued.

If Marie could be difficult, her father, ex-King Stanislas, was unfailingly debonair. One of the agreeable surprises to arrive in the queen's train, the penniless father-in-law now lived in comparative luxury in the château of Chambord.

Just for a moment, when the crown of Poland was vacated in 1733, he heeded the call to glory. More for his daughter's prestige than his own sake, he smuggled himself into Warsaw, where the nobles enthusiastically elected him king. He accepted. The Russians invaded, and the major powers had their excuse for a lively year of campaigning. French armies were dispatched against the Austrian emperor, on the Rhine and in Italy. Stanislas was left to fend for himself, sustained by a trickle of funds and a handful of *mousquetaires*. The Warsaw Diet, their pockets stuffed with Russian bribes and their city ringed by cossacks, reversed themselves and elected the Russian-sponsored candidate, Augustus III. King Stanislas, with eight hundred supporters, defied the Russian armies at Danzig, where he waited for a French naval squadron which never came. He finally bolted as the Russians closed in, driving himself to safety in a peasant's cart. The city was overrun after a 135-day siege.

Stanislas took his defeat philosophically, accepting as a consolation prize the duchy of Lorraine. Not so his daughter, who could be snappish when vexed. Fleury, on one of his economy drives, replaced the expensive water cascade at Marly with grass. Soon afterwards he was trying to comfort Marie over her father's defeat. 'Believe me, madame, the throne of Lorraine is better for your father the king,' he insisted, 'than that of Poland.' 'Yes,' the glum little queen retorted, 'just as a grass plot is better than a marble cascade.'

Stanislas's court of Lorraine, established in 1737, became one of the century's civilized perfections. Voltaire was a pampered guest. He toasted his host, 'It is impossible to be a better King or a better man.' The king complained very little, despite his shabby treatment by the French, and continued to give his daughter sound advice. Discover whom your husband trusts, he told her, and put your trust in him.

Her father's counsel was not enough to keep Marie out of trouble. With the best intentions in the world, she helped destroy Condé, her benefactor. The prime minister, who could not see the king except in the presence of Fleury, was bitterly jealous of the bishop. In the spring of 1726, he persuaded the queen to arrange a surprise meeting for him with Louis in her chambers. When he produced the inevitable bill of charges against Fleury, Louis was outraged and cut Condé short. Fleury, the shrewd country fox, had gotten the wind up and left the court. 'As my services appear to be useless,' he wrote to the king, 'I beg permission to end my days with the Sulpicians.'

Louis, at sixteen, France's crowned and anointed king, shut himself up in his closet with his *chaise percée* for a good cry. His infantile behaviour horrified the Duc de Mortemart, First Gentleman of the Bedchamber. 'Sire,' he burst out, 'are you not the master? Order M. le Duc (Condé) to go and fetch M. de Fréjus (Fleury) this moment and you will see him back.' Louis stopped snivelling and instructed Condé to restore his friend. Fleury returned next day from his country estate at Issy, to effusive greetings from the king. 'I hope you will never leave me again,' Louis pleaded. Fleury never did.

Condé left in June, taking with him Madame de Prie, who was exiled despite her position among the queen's ladies. It took weeks of patching-up by Fleury, before the king and queen were reconciled. The king did not again give Marie his trust.

After a clean sweep of Condé's faction, Fleury took charge of the government. Louis made a pretence of personal rule, announcing that he would act as his own *Premier Ministre* in the style of his great-grandfather. It was typical of Fleury to forego the title, but his power was without limit or reservation. From the age of seventy-three, already a doddering ancient by the standards of the time, Fleury ruled France, mildly and with mild success, until his death at ninety. In economics, he gave the nation two decades of prosperity mainly by giving it peace. He firmed up the shaky French currency, halted the constant haemorrhaging of the national treasure into military adventure, and gave the French bourgeoisie a chance to do what it did best – create wealth. Fleury was joined by the great English minister, Sir Robert Walpole, in smoothing over the destructive rivalry between their nations. Their peace policy broke down only in 1740, when a jingoist outburst on both sides of the Channel plunged England and France into the War of the Austrian Succession. The bishop was moderate even in religion; only after receiving his cardinal's hat did he feel obliged to do battle with the Jansenists and their supporters in the Parlement. The controversy ended in a bad-humoured truce in 1731, and smouldered on throughout the reign of Louis XV.

The court hated Fleury, blaming the hard-working minister for the king's laziness. It was true that Fleury held sway, but it was not he who snatched up the sceptre, it was Louis XV who let it drop. René-Louis, Marquis d'Argenson, who, much later, would become the secretary of state for foreign affairs, bitterly sketched the old man in his journal in 1731:

One of the most absurd spectacles is the prelate's *petit coucher*. Although he is in sole command, his only title is Minister of State. All France, from the usual idlers to those who have business, is at his door. His Eminence enters and passes into his cabinet. Then the door is opened and you see the old priest take off his small-clothes and carefully fold them; a shabby dressing gown is handed him and then his shift; he takes a long time combing his four white hairs. He discourses, chats, babbles, makes bad jokes interlarded with sugary commonplaces. The good man imagines that this is a consolation for the poor folk who press to see him; he cannot give them a more propitious moment without interfering with business.

Fleury was unassailable. He took no bribes, amassed no fortune, fattened no relatives on the payroll. He was humble, treating provincial nobodies as deferentially as he treated princes of the blood. The courtiers who dreamed of dislodging him ground their teeth. Fleury ignored them and worked. Louis played. He took an active hand on the rare occasions when the old man was indisposed. D'Argenson commented:

> . . . he works with his Ministers, does it admirably, and reaches just decisions. . . . People wonder if he will continue to work, or if his activity since the illness of the Cardinal is like the fervour of the young priest. We must remember that he is almost without passions or dominant tastes, and apathy leaves a void which has to be filled. Business is presented to kings without thorns. Their Ministers arrive with the work neatly arranged and he has merely to say Yes or No. No effort is required.

Any hopes d'Argenson may have had of the king taking control were soon dashed. He described the dilettante master of France in 1739, when the king was twenty-nine:

> He rises at eleven, and leads a useless life. He steals from his frivolous occupations one hour of work; the sessions with the Ministers cannot be called work, for he lets them do everything, merely listening or repeating what they say like a parrot. He is still very much of a child.

The marquis's opinion was shared by everyone who came in contact with Louis. In 1740, a very bad year when inflation and near-famine brought crowds into the streets of Paris, he set the monarch and his minister to paper again:

> The Cardinal is at his wits end and his resignation is expected day to day. When the King passed through the capital he was greeted with cries of *misère, du pain, du pain*. ('Misery! Bread! Bread!') When Fleury drove through Paris, women seized the bridle of the horses, opened the door of his carriage, and screamed, '*du pain, du pain, du pain, nous mourons de faim.*' ('Bread! Bread! Bread! We die of hunger!') He almost died of fright and threw coins to the crowd. The King was momentarily upset when he sensed the mood of the capital, and his duty to himself and his people struggled with his duty to the Cardinal. Though he does not feel bound to sacrifice his kingdom, he

thinks it would kill the Cardinal to substitute his arch-enemy Chauvelin. Moreover he esteems his talents, though everything is going to pieces and the Cardinal has become odious to the whole kingdom. Insensible to the public plight, more infatuated than ever with his old tutor, incapable of action, the King amuses himself and hunts, his mind a blank. Nine-tenths of the Court think him an imbecile who will never come to anything. Our nation is desperate, enervated, annihilated, and only the Farmers General [tax collectors] are alive. The moment comes when the King will govern himself or rather will choose the Ministers he needs and will work with them, though it needs the faith of Abraham to believe all that. Every day the dilemma is more urgent; the King counts for much or for nothing.

What the king counted for most, was women. Louis XV loved to fornicate almost as much as he loved to kill deer. Fleury came close to spoiling everything with his insistence that God would deny France a dauphin if Louis broke his marriage vows. Louis believed the bishop, until the dauphin arrived. The king interpreted his son's birth, in robust health, and the arrival of the Duc d'Anjou within a year, as signals from heaven that he was free at last to sow his wild oats.

Chapter Twelve

'J'aime ta soeur'

I n 1732, Louis XV embarked on his celebrated career as a womanizer. Although he was, by every account, one of the handsomest men in Europe, he began by seducing three of the ugliest women in France.

The king's faithfulness to his wife had became tiresome, especially to those closest to him, a group of young bloods known as *les marmousets* (urchins). His rectitude didn't keep them from hunting with him at the Château de La Muette, the royal lodge on the edge of the Bois de Boulogne, or deter them from spiriting him off, incognito, to balls and the opera in Paris. They eagerly attended his *petits soupers*, evenings in the new fashion, arranged by Marie Victoire Sophie de Noailles, Comtesse de Toulouse. Related to the king by her marriage to his *legitimé* uncle, the comtesse was the perfect hostess, rich, respectable, and genuinely pleased with his company. She was his neighbour at Versailles. He needed only to descend a private staircase to her ground-floor suite, for amusing evenings of food, wine and conversation.

If the general tone she set was innocently gay, her coterie was far from virtuous. Among the ladies was Condé's notorious sister, Louise de Bourbon-Condé, Mademoiselle de Charolais, who longed to add the king to her string of lovers. Some years before, Mademoiselle de Charolais had figured in a great court scandal with another of the guests, Louis François Armand de Vignerot du Plessis, Maréchal and Duc de Richelieu, the lecherous great-grand-nephew of the cardinal.

When Richelieu was in heat, absolutely nothing held him back. He attempted to seduce Louis XV's mother, the dauphine, Marie Adélaïde of Savoy, Duchesse de Bourgogne. Louis XIV, who had short patience with assaults on the royal family, had him hauled off to the Bastille.

Jail was only a trifling inconvenience. Richelieu's prison harem included Mademoiselle de Charolais and the late Duchesse de Berry. The high-born hussies fought for his favours, and when separate visiting days became awkward, declared a truce and serviced him together, in the Bastille. The story gained piquancy from the fact that he dressed his mistresses as nuns! The kinky duc was now Louis XV's boon companion, still darting from conquest to conquest, driven by a galloping case of satyriasis. Louis shared his itch, but lacked his initiative; he was twenty-three before he ventured outside the marital fold.

There was little to keep him chaste. Queen Marie was trapped in Versailles by her endless confinements; custom dictated that the queen did not leave the château when pregnant. She awaited her thirtieth birthday enveloped in middle-aged fat, her only release from the tedium of her life, a gobbling love affair with food. 'What should you do when you're bored?' she asked a courtier. 'Give yourself indigestion. At least it is something to do!' Her idea of a light meal was twenty-nine courses, plus fruit. Because she ate in public, her gluttony became, in later years, a perverse sight-seeing attraction for visitors, among them Giacomo Girolamo Casanova. Casanova was fascinated by her appetite, and by her table conversation. On the day he attended, she debated the merits of chicken fricassee with Comte Ulrick Frederick Lowendal, one of France's war heroes.

Louis shared Marie's love for the pleasures of the table, if not her obsession. (To his courtiers' consternation, he enjoyed brewing coffee and cooking 'little stews'.) It was at the table, at La Muette, that he first hinted at his adulterous intentions, with a toast '*À la maîtresse inconnue.*' For the identity of the 'unknown', the assembled company needed only to glance at their fellow guests. There sat the object of the king's desire, Louise Julie de Mailly-Nesle, Comtesse de Mailly. Although Madame de Mailly moved in the rarefied society around the king, she was far from wealthy, having married her cousin, a lieutenant in the Scottish Guards. Their poverty was Louise's dowry from her father, the Marquis de Nesle, who had wagered away the family fortune. Their consolation was a family tree with roots that extended back to the eleventh century.

Madame de Mailly was no vestal. She came to the king tested and certified by the Marquis de Puysieux. The marquis had high praise for all her qualities except her beauty, for she was homely in the extreme. Her big mouth and big nose were set in a long, equine face, above an ugly throat, breasts and arms. On the credit side, she was tall, and had fine eyes and beautiful legs. She was loud, raucous, graceless, but an attractive companion despite all her faults, cheerful and good-hearted.

When their friends arranged a tête-à-tête, Louis found her posed on a sofa, revealing a voluptuous expanse of leg, complete with undone garter. As reported by Richelieu in his memoirs, the bashful king stood frozen. Louis's first *valet de chambre*, Bachelier, who was in on the scheme, simply took his master under the arms and threw him into the young woman's embrace. Louis, used to horseplay with his valets, made no objection. Madame de Mailly hesitated the respectable moment with Louis's hand up her skirt, then forced herself to oblige the king.

D'Argenson gave the fledgling amorist somewhat higher marks. In his version of the crucial meeting, Madame de Mailly waited for the king concealed by a screen. She emerged, complaining that her feet were cold. She moved close to the fire. Louis took her foot in his hands to warm it. His fingers moved to her leg, and then to her garter, before she cried, 'Oh, dear! If I had known Your Majesty had me come for this, I should not have come.' The king brushed aside her protests and went into action.

Keeping a mistress was a game with fairly well-defined rules, but it took nearly five years for Louis to get the hang of it. From 1733 to 1738, he bounced back and forth between the queen and Madame de Mailly, rushing to Marie to sire his last three daughters, and 'giving up' his mistress annually so he could publicly receive Easter communion.

It was Louise de Mailly's unique contribution that she broke down the king's painful shyness. She untied the royal tongue, but she failed to untie the royal purse strings, for her own shyness in money matters was the despair of her relatives. D'Argenson wrote:

> She seems out of touch with her family, who are greedy for favours and fortune. Her ugliness scandalizes foreigners, who expect a King's mistress at any rate to have a pretty face.

It was 1736, three years after the initial seduction, before Louis helped her financially. He presented her with twenty thousand *livres*; at current rates of exchange, about forty-five thousand pounds sterling (ninety thousand dollars), or fifteen thousand pounds a year (thirty thousand dollars). The king spent more, in a hot summer, for ice to cool his wine. If his largesse was less than princely, it simply never dawned on Louis that the world expected him to support his mistress more lavishly.

Her station as the acknowledged *maîtresse* was established when Louis's legitimate daughter, Princess Louise-Marie, was born in July 1737. During the frequently lengthy delay between births and christenings, royal newborns were known by numbered nicknames. According to d'Argenson:

> they came to tell the king about the birth of yet another daughter [and] asked him whether she should be called Madame Septième (Madame the Seventh), and he answered Madame Dernière (Madame the Last) from which people have concluded that the Queen will be neglected indeed.

She who caused the neglect, in the opinion of the court, came very close to being an ideal mistress. Madame de Mailly was as devoted to Louis XV as la Vallière had been to Louis XIV. She was fun-loving, undemanding, so placid by nature that she sometimes got on Louis's nerves. One day, she calmly continued her needlework while he tried to interrupt with small talk. Infuriated, he cut her tapestry into bits with a knife. Her one flaw was her vanity. She had taste, dressed expensively, and, despite her formidable ugliness, sat for her portrait sixteen times. Yet, in her rivalry with the dowdy queen, she never allowed herself to preen. Queen Marie repaid Madame de Mailly's respect with spite, but, at Louis's insistence, went along with the fiction that the comtesse was *her* intimate, not his. She kept Louise as a *dame du palais* until the king dropped her, and allowed succeeding mistresses the same position in her retinue. Louis blandly included his women in his evenings with his wife. When he retired for the night, the current favourite would beg leave to do the same; the queen, with suppressed fury, was helpless to deny her permission.

In 1738, a miscarriage led to the final rupture between the king and queen. Following her failed pregnancy, Marie developed a phobia about venereal disease, insulting both the favourite and her husband when she implied that Madame de Mailly was infected, and that the pox was being carried to her second-hand by the king. One night, d'Argenson reported, Louis spent four hours in her bed, with the queen 'refusing his desires. The King left at three o'clock in the morning, saying, " 'Tis the last time I will essay this adventure." '

His conjugal visits ceased. An eight-room suite was fitted out for Madame de Mailly on the third floor of the château, connected to the king's own rooms by a private stair. (Called the Staircase of the Dogs, because the royal pack was kennelled nearby.) Louis himself abandoned the stately austerities of the Salon of Mercury in favour of a comfortable, second-floor bedroom created from the former Billiard Room. His bedroom was flanked by a study, bath and dining-room, all decorated in the gracefully curved and carved style which would become known as Louis Quinze. The suite looked out on an interior courtyard, the Cour des Cerfs. (The two-storey arrangement was the first introduction of the *petits appartements* which eventually honeycombed the north wing of the palace. In time, a fourth-floor apartment housed Madame de Mailly's sister, the Duchesse de Lauraguais. Louis's château-within-the-château had kitchens on each floor, workshops, libraries, a distillery, and on the roof, a summer dining-room, a terrace and a lilliputian park with trees, caged birds, paths, and fountains.) In the king's quarters, the planners took a headlong leap into modernity, when they installed a *chaise à l'anglaise*, flushed with running water!

Indoor plumbing was as far as he was willing to go in his break with the past. The mummified ritual of kingship bequeathed to him by the Sun King continued to consume astonishing amounts of his time and energy. Louis's new dining-room, novel and delightful as it was, did not supplant the king's public dinner, it only allowed him to take a private supper. He went daily at one o'clock to the Antichambre de l'Oeil-de-Boeuf to take food before his subjects, as prescribed by Louis XIV. Louis sat alone, under the adoring gaze of a select group, picking at an endless parade of dishes prepared solely for display. Guardsmen protected his napkin, which awaited the monarch's fingers on a perfumed pillow in a miniature gold ship. Ten servants were deployed to bring his meat from the kitchens. As the carvers bore the useless joint of beef through the corridors, courtiers in their path swept their hats from their heads, bowing deeply to the passing dish. Asked why, they solemnly replied, 'The King's meat!'

For another thirty years, Louis XV slavishly plodded through the twice-daily *lever* and *coucher*. (Utterly empty ceremonies, they were preserved by the court, and participation in them fiercely defended, for the opportunities they gave the nobles to converse with the king.) The night-owl monarch varied the hour of the *coucher*, so courtiers often arrived breathless from a foot-race down the corridors. They solemnly performed their offices, disrobing the royal person, exchanging shoes for slippers, unfolding and presenting the royal chemise and robe, lighting the few steps between the royal prayer stool, armchair, toilette and bed with the royal candlestick – carrying out the intricate, intimate ceremonial in a kind of lunatic close-order drill behind the balustrade in Louis XIV's cavernous bedroom. As the *coucher* proceeded, so did the *entrées*: the assembled court came forward to bid the monarch good-night – the *familières* (his family), the *grandes entrées*, the *premières entrées* and, at long last, the *entrées* of the chamber. Louis meekly submitted to everything, acknowledged each murmured salutation, and allowed himself to be tucked in. He then slipped away to his own bed in the *petits appartements*. The next morning he retraced his steps to the *lever*, where, waking from a feigned sleep, he performed the entire, preposterous charade in reverse.

In his passion for the proprieties, Louis sometimes outdid even his hypocritical great-grandfather. He was too intelligent, however, not to appreciate the comedy in the pretence. When Madame de Mailly's new apartment was being prepared, he held a public conversation to the effect that the quarters were intended for the Marquis de Meuse. The marquis went along with the joke, loudly proclaiming his joy at being lodged so near the king. The Duc de Luynes recorded Louis's reply, 'I'm closing the passage to my apartment.' Then, tongue in cheek, he gave the nobleman a detailed description of 'his' apartment, concluding with, 'Your bedroom will be furnished: you will have a bed, but you won't sleep in it; you will have a *chaise percée*, but you won't use it.'

Appearances were maintained at all costs, yet the search for novelties was unceasing, as the courtiers, especially the king's mistress, sought to fend off the king's ever-present ennui. Madame de Mailly, casting about for new faces, introduced her sister, Pauline-Félicité de Nesle, Marquise de Vintimille. She had no reason to fear a rivalry for the king's affections, since Madame de Vintimille, who was hot-tempered and even uglier than her sister, suffered from a body odour so putrid her husband had deserted her. The marquis said she had the soul of a devil in the body of a billygoat. Their virtuous sister, Hortense, Madame de Flavacourt, described Vintimille, *'Elle avait la figure d'un grenadier, le col d'une grue, une odeur de singe.'* ('She has the figure of a guardsman, the neck of a crane, and the stink of a monkey.') She was marking time in the convent of Port Royal when the summons came to join Madame de Mailly at the king's side.

Louis was not in the least put off by the marquise's tantrums or her malodorous affliction. For the second time he selected a big, masculine, homely woman as his mistress. He bought Choisy, a pretty hunting box, for their trysts, and, by 1739, his interest in the impoverished de Mailly was fading. D'Argenson wrote, maliciously, that her chemises were

> worn out and full of holes, and her lady's maid is badly dressed, which is the sign of true poverty. Just the other day, she didn't have five écus [about forty pounds sterling or sixty-five dollars] to pay up when she lost at quadrille.

In 1740, Louis told de Mailly to go. Madame de Vintimille took her place.

The new *maîtresse* was a prickly handful: haughty, greedy, and intriguing. She barged into politics, the first of Louis's mistresses to nag him about his listless dependence on Fleury. Vintimille demanded that he dismiss the cardinal, and take an interest in the army. She fought with everyone, so publicly that Louis scolded her before the assembled court.

'I know very well, Madame la Comtesse,' he said, 'what must be done to cure you of it. It would be to cut off your head. It would not even be too bad for you, since your neck is so long.' He could not resist a morbid parting shot, 'Your blood would be drained and replaced by the blood of a lamb.' His dressing-down had no effect. The quarrelsome Madame de Vintimille managed to lose the few friends she had, before she was brought to bed with Louis's child, in September 1741, in the apartments of the Cardinal de Rohan at Versailles.

She became wretchedly ill. Despite the ministrations of Madame de Mailly, who rushed back from her convent retirement to nurse her, she died from puerperal fever, six days after giving birth to a son, the Marquis du Luc. There were black hints that she had been poisoned. Madame de Mailly cared for the infant, who so resembled his father he was called 'Le demi-Louis'. The king was 'inconsolable'. It amused him to mourn, so he ordered her death mask moulded in wax and wept over it. In days, he returned to the hunt – and, temporarily, to de Mailly.

Of Madame de Vintimille's passing, d'Argenson noted:

The people of Versailles made merry at her death . . . the death of this ugly beast, whereas La Mailly was such a good woman. [They] came up and seized it [her corpse]; they offered all manner of indiginities to her unprepossessing body, which had been left uncovered, a barbarous act that implied scant respect for the king. The procession [to the Recollets, where she was buried in the Chapel of Saint Louis] was the occasion of much popular derision.

Madame de Mailly's restoration to favour was perfunctory, a comfortable convenience for the king, who quickly found her tedious. She was pathetically in love with him but hopelessly unimaginative in her attempts to keep him. Trying to postpone the inevitable with liquor, she staged drinking 'orgies', as the court would have them, in the *petits appartements*. When the footmen had carted away his fellow tipplers, the king was left with little but a series of hangovers and a bumper crop of gossip. Dear, desperate Louise resigned herself to sharing him, once again. She sent for ugly sister number three, Adélaïde, Mademoiselle de Montcarvel, the youngest of the Mailly-Nesle girls. In Richelieu's memoirs:

> She was young and bold, and boasted of having carefully preserved a jewel while living with Madame de Lesdiguieres, who had brought her up in her own home. The king, surprised at the 'jewel' of Mademoiselle de Montcarvel . . . robbed her of it, and then married her to the duc de Lauraguais, whom he promoted to lieutenant-general.

The duchesse was also game for sexual experiments. To quote another tale:

> . . . According to those who knew the king's secret pleasures, one of those refinements of depravity . . . led him to covet a place between the two sisters, whose bodies, like their minds, offered so complete a contrast. . . . The duchesse was tall, heavy, badly-proportioned, but of a plumpness that invited fondling. Her bust was firm and elastic and her hips were well rounded. For the rest, she was commonplace, coarse, boisterous, devoid of grace and charm; so that, if at night she gave the king pleasures that he could not procure from her skinny sister, the latter came into her own during the day, and even Louis soon tired of merely physical gratification.

This last, from the pen of Mouffle d'Angerville, an advocate in the reign of Louis XVI, whose *Vie Privée de Louis XV . . .*, published abroad in 1781, described Louis XV's domestic arrangements in detail. Although critical of his royal subject, d'Angerville's royalist sympathies probably cost him his life in the Terror.

For miscellaneous fondlings, the Duchesse de Lauraguais was awarded eighteen thousand *livres* a year, the income from a string of stores in Nantes. The delights of the *ménage à trois* soon paled, however, and she was dismissed. In his single-minded way, Louis eyed the fourth sister, Hortense. Only she, of the Nesle sisterhood, had the strength of character to resist a royal pass. Her husband put starch in her virtue, by threatening 'to leave nothing undone to wash out any insult in blood'. The bungled seduction led to an impudent Parisian verse circulated in 1742:

La première en oubli, la seconde en poussière
La troisième est en pied. La quatrième attend
Et fera place a la dernière.
Choisir une famille entière
Est-ce être infidèle ou constant?

The first is forgotten, the second is dust,
The third is ready, the fourth waiting
To give way to the fifth.
Is it infidelity or constancy
To be faithful to an entire family?

With the fifth sister, the Mailly-Nesle family tree finally brought
forth a rose. She was Marie-Anne, Marquise de la Tournelle. Married
to the marquis at fifteen, a wealthy widow at twenty-three and on the
rebound from an affair with the Duc de Richelieu at twenty-four, she
was eager for royal favour. Richelieu, who was her uncle, remained her
advisor, which may account for her skill in securing the best terms for
herself.

La Tournelle, by unanimous verdict, was a *maîtresse* of whom Louis
and the court could be proud: she was tall, blue-eyed and beautiful,
with a creamy complexion and a sumptuous figure. She was so stately,
the king nicknamed her 'Princesse'. Before giving in to the king, she
demanded and received privileges not granted a royal favourite since
the time of Louis XIV. Like de Montespan before her, the marquise
insisted upon official standing, as *maîtresse déclarée*. D'Argenson's
journal for 5 November 1742, recorded the negotiations:

One night the King, disguised in a long coat and a square wig, went
in a blue chair to see her. His Majesty remained until four in the
morning bargaining with the charmer. Having been well coached,
and with all the coolness of an experienced harlot, she stipulated that
she should be publicly recognized as the King's mistress, on the same
footing as Madame de Montespan had been. She demanded that she
should be well lodged in a manner befitting her position, and should
not be expected, like her sister, to go furtively to the private
apartments to sup and sleep. She demanded that the King should
come publicly and hold his court in her apartments, and sup there
openly. She demanded that when she wanted money, she should be
able to draw upon the royal purse; and at the end of a year she should
receive letters of nobility, duly confirmed by the Parlement, as a

duchess; that if she became *enciente* there should be no secrecy about it, and that her children should be legitimized.

Marie-Anne's cruelty towards her sister Louise shocked even the cynics. She insisted that Madame de Mailly be exiled from Versailles, to a distance of four leagues. She had no fear of rotund sister Adélaïde, whom she kept at her side. After her years of devotion, the king treated de Mailly brutally. His last private words to her were meant to hurt: '*j'aime ta soeur, tu m'ennuis.*' ('I love your sister, you bore me.') Moments later, surrounded by the court, he gaily reminded her she was to join him at Choisy. (The remark was salt in Louise's wounds. She knew that he expected to share their blue silk bed at Choisy with her sister. Marie-Anne, however, knew how to turn a profit by playing the waiting game, and let him scratch at her door in vain.)

Madame de Mailly no longer existed for the king after she left Versailles. He nearly broke with the Comtesse de Toulouse because she defiantly sheltered the comtesse in her home. Finally, in the face of his friends' outrage, Louis did the decent thing, settling her in a mansion in the Rue St Thomas du Louvre with forty thousand a year. He ordered her debts paid, getting off cheaply because his agents cheated her creditors.

La Tournelle's upkeep was another matter. There were jewels, cash, her new suite in the *petits appartements*, and, in October 1743, her elevation as Duchesse de Châteauroux. (The event was delayed while officials scrambled to find an estate to attach to the duchy, with an income of eighty thousand *livres* a year.)

With her ducal arms came a dividend which outraged the queen more than her new rank: the right to what Madame de Sevigné called 'the divine *tabouret*', a simple footstool on which she was entitled to sit in the royal presence – resting the aching feet that were the lot of the courtier. Jean Frédéric Phelypeaux, Comte de Maurepas, a minister who detested her, drew up the documents for her elevation. In his diary, he quoted one of the verses that went the rounds:

> *Incestueuse La Tournelle,*
> *Qui des trois est la plus belle,*
> *Ce tabouret tant souhaité*
> *À de quoi vous rendre très fière*
> *Votre devant, en vérité,*
> *Sert bien votre gentil derrière.*

> Incestuous La Tournelle,
> Fairest of the three,
> You may indeed be proud
> Of this coveted footstool;
> The charms you have in front
> Well serve the charms behind.

There is little doubt that Maurepas, who d'Argenson said, 'despised God, the King and royalty' sought to provoke the new duchesse's fury, either by writing the squib himself or paying to have it written. He was the most spiteful of ministers, a thorn in the side of both Châteauroux and her successor.

Châteauroux's affair with the king was one of two topics of consuming interest to the court in 1743. She reported her progress to her mentor, Richelieu, who responded from the scene of the other great event of the day, the War of the Austrian Succession. The battles in Flanders, where he was soldiering, were almost, if not quite, as riveting as her skirmishes in Louis's bed.

Chapter Thirteen

The Warrior King

The war had broken out in 1740, despite Cardinal Fleury's best efforts at peacemaking. It was an ugly scheme by the Majesties of Europe to ambush a weak cousin, Maria Theresa, the daughter of the Habsburg emperor Charles VI. Charles, who had no son, sought to protect his daughter's inheritance by persuading his neighbours to take an oath that they would allow her to ascend the imperial throne. The Kings of France and Prussia, among others, swore to uphold Charles's 'Pragmatic Sanction'. The Elector of Bavaria, who wanted to be emperor himself, declined. When Charles died in October 1740, the oaths were forgotten. Half the continent, it seemed, found reasons to strip the young empress of large pieces of her property. Sardinia, Saxony and Spain, in cahoots with France and Bavaria, signed up for a territorial lottery, encompassing Upper Austria, Bohemia, Moravia and assorted sections of Italy.

Frederick II of Prussia, at twenty-eight, was greedy if not yet great. He made an insulting offer to buy Silesia from the empress for six million francs, throwing in his support for her husband, Francis of Lorraine, as emperor. Maria Theresa replied that she defended her subjects and 'did not sell them'. Frederick sent the Prussian army into action.

As Europe chose their sides for war, Frederick backed Charles Albert, the Elector of Bavaria, to unseat Maria Theresa. So did Fleury, reluctantly, because Louis XV was related to the elector by marriage. The English, delighted by the opportunity to kill Frenchmen after dull decades of peace under Walpole and Fleury, sided with the empress.

Frederick marched in December 1740. By January 1743, when Fleury died, he was already sidling away from the war he helped start, shamelessly playing off the king in Versailles against the empress in Vienna. For sale to the highest bidder, for treaties, troops or cash subsidies, Frederick offered no excuse. 'If there is anything to gain by being honest, we will be honest,' he wrote, 'if we must deceive, let us be knaves.'

In June 1743, King George II took personal command of the English and Hanoverian troops, known as the 'Pragmatic Army', and gave the French armies a sharp rebuff at the Battle of Dettingen. The French scoffed at bellicose little King George, accusing him of bolting the field in terror. The English said he raced back into the action on foot, after his horse did the bolting. Either way, Louis's *mousquetaires* were brought to a halt and sent floundering across the River Main toward Alsace.

Châteauroux saw an opportunity in all this, to inspire her paramour to glory. On Fleury's death, hopeful cries were heard in the streets, '*Le Cardinal est mort, vive le Roi!*' The thirty-three-year-old king told his ministers '*Messieurs, me voilà Premier Minestre.*' ('Gentlemen, I am now the Prime Minister.') He had said the same thing at sixteen, only to bow to Fleury, so not much was expected. Despite his declaration of war on Maria Theresa as Queen of Hungary, in April 1744, insiders asked, who would fill the vacuum when the king tired of playing king?

Châteauroux meant to give the lie to Louis's critics, but she had no illusions about the king. Writing to Richelieu on his support for the election of Charles Albert of Bavaria as the Emperor Charles VII, she commented shrewdly:

> Some wish him to drop the Emperor, others to support his election. I begin to feel that everyone is too much on his own and that we need a stronger will than the King possesses . . . you know the tendency to let every Ministry go its own way.

A languid woman, she spent her days stretched on a couch, rising to take the air only at dusk. She was relentless with Louis, however, prodding him to command the invasion of the Austrian Netherlands. He grumbled, 'You are killing me, Madame!' She didn't blink, 'So much the better, Sire; we must call to life a King!' When he gave in, in February 1744, she wrote:

> I hope success will make him realize how sincerely I cherish his glory. . . . now it is time to show he can reign himself . . . and my only fear is that he trusts too much in his Ministers. His judgement is better than theirs, I am sure, but he often defers to them. We must hope that he will have a will of his own . . .'

Adrien Maurice, Maréchal and Duc de Noailles, who commanded in Flanders, was her ally in luring the king to the battlefield. He wanted

Louis's presence but, eager to become a military Fleury, he tried to discourage Châteauroux from accompanying the king. He cited the financial burden of too large a royal entourage. When she complained to Richelieu, her uncle was all sympathy, but seconded Noailles. Then, the king's trip became public, and there was a rush to be included in the party. Queen Marie applied, by letter. The king suddenly became as frugal as Noailles, declining her company on the grounds of expense. The dauphin wanted to go. He was nearly fifteen, and had visions of wearing a hero's laurels to his forthcoming wedding to the infanta of Spain. In his case, Louis offered a legitimate excuse: risking the heir at the battlefront was bad policy until he had, in turn, fathered an heir.

Louis arrived at Lille with a small party on 12 May, *sans* queen, *sans* dauphin and *sans maîtresse*. In the excitement of battle, he scarcely had time to miss her. He took to the hard-riding life of an officer, which was, after all, very like his hard-riding life as a huntsman. His presence worked the promised miracle. Victory after victory, if small ones, were delivered by Noailles and his second-in-command, Maurice, Maréchal and Comte de Saxe. Courtrai fell. At Menin, Louis began to look like a hero, striding about within pistol-range of the defenders to watch his sappers at work, ordering the fortifications razed, when the fortress fell, to teach the Dutch a lesson.

By the time the French took Ypres, Châteauroux could be restrained no longer. Desperate to join Louis, she gave scant attention to a fulsome letter from Berlin, in which Frederick II gave her credit for the new Franco-Prussian treaty of alliance. Frederick realized who had created the French warrior king he now observed roaming through Flanders. He purred,

> I am flattered, Madame, that it is partly to you that I am indebted for the favourable disposition in which I find the King of France, and his willingness to form the lasting bonds of an eternal alliance between us. The esteem I have always entertained for you is now reinforced by sentiments of gratitude. I feel sure the King of France will never regret his action and that all the contracting parties will derive an equal advantage. It is unfortunate that Prussia is compelled to ignore the obligations she is under to you. However, the sentiment will remain deeply engraved on my heart. *Madame, votre très affectionné ami, Frédéric.*

The duchesse arrived in Ypres to find that the French cause was again teetering on the edge of military disaster. The Austrians had overrun

Alsace and Lorraine, and King Stanislas, the royal father-in-law, was a refugee once more, fleeing his palace at Lünéville. The Flanders armies rushed south, the king in their van, to stem the invasion of French soil. Louis snatched moments alone with his *maîtresse* en route.

They reached Metz on 4 August. The king's battlefield heroics were replaced by boudoir burlesque.

From the hour Châteauroux and her sister, the Duchesse de Lauraguais, left Versailles, their carriage had been hooted on its way with catcalls and lewd jokes. In Metz, the sniggering gave way to open hilarity when workmen tore out walls and constructed a covered bridge between the king's bedroom and the Abbey of St Arnould, which stood just across the road.

The bridge, it was announced, would give His Majesty quicker access to Mass. Needless to say, the passageway ended in the boudoir of Châteauroux, who was staying at the Abbey. No one kept count of the number of times Louis 'attended Mass', but the structure creaked and groaned with constant comings and goings. The street rabble gathered under the duchesse's windows to sing:

> *Belle Châteauroux,*
> *Je deviendrai fou*
> *Si je ne vous baise!*

> Fair Châteauroux,
> I shall go mad
> If I don't kiss you!

The bridge had been in operation only a day or two before the king fell ill. He awoke constipated, with a high fever and a violent headache. D'Angerville summed up contemporary opinion when he blamed the malaise on 'the abuse of wine and spirits . . . *his excesses in other directions* . . . [and] the fatigues of the campaign and the blazing sun which had poured on him during the march'. Modern medical opinion favours a combination of sunstroke and appendicitis. Whatever the cause, by the evening of 14 August, Louis had endured enemas, purges, blisterings, bleedings and leechings – and was, plainly, *in extremis*.

Richelieu tried to declare the sick-room off-limits to all but the physicians, the valets, the *maîtresse* and himself. Louis, Duc de Chartres, the priggish son of the late regent, and a prince of the blood, exploded.

'What!' he thundered, 'A servant like you dares to refuse admittance to your master's nearest relative?' He kicked open the bedroom door and burst in with a delegation of senior officers. One look at the patient and Chartres demanded that confession, absolution and the last rites be undertaken at once. None of these was possible while Châteauroux remained at Louis's side. The king's concubine must go!

Châteauroux found herself confronted first by Louis's Jesuit confessor, Père Perussot, then by his chaplain, Fitz-James, Bishop of Soissons. The bishop sternly demanded expulsion of the duchesse and her sister not only from the bedside, but from the town of Metz. 'I think I may be doing wrong, Princesse,' groaned the king to Châteauroux. 'You must go. I am dying.' The women were unceremoniously hoisted into a carriage and rushed out of town, as a crowd pelted them with rotten vegetables.

If Châteauroux wanted proof of her success in promoting Louis as a national hero, she had it now. The French saw their king ride off to do battle for the nation. Now he lay at death's door, and because of this strumpet, he was in danger of eternal damnation. When she halted briefly at Bar le Duc and Sainte-Ménehould, citizens shrieked curses, hurled offal and threatened her safety. Her carriage ran a gauntlet along the eighty-league route back to Paris.

As news of the king's condition spread, the people succumbed to what can only be described as a national fit of hysterics. The Duc d'Orléans rushed to the shrine of Sainte Génevière in Paris, where he outstripped the wailing congregation with

> the special bitterness of his tears and the violence of his sobs. It was here, before the remains [of the saint] that suddenly and spontaneously Louis XV was proclaimed '*Louis le Bien-Aimé*'.

Everywhere there was open weeping for the newly 'beloved' king. Masses in the thousands were said for his recovery.

At Versailles, Queen Marie borrowed pocket money and gathered up the dauphin and the royal daughters. She set out for Metz convinced that she was on her way to her husband's deathbed. Her party included the dauphin's tutor, Alexis de Bois Rogues, Duc de Châtillon, who gave prayerful thanks when he got word of Châteauroux's dismissal, and delivered moral lectures on the subject to his royal pupil. The foolish man went so far as to prostrate himself before the dauphin, saluting him as king. At Sainte-Ménehould, the queen's carriage passed that of the fleeing Nesle sisters. Marie did not deign to recognize them.

In Metz, the Bishop of Soissons grew reckless. He now demanded, as his price for administering the last rites, a public confession from the king – the same degrading *amende honorable* usually forced on criminals before their execution. Louis, weak and frightened, agreed. The details of his private life were recited to the courtiers in attendance and to a gawking crowd of townspeople the bishop dragged into the royal bedchamber. As quickly as couriers could carry the news, the king's lurid confession was proclaimed from the pulpits of France.

Not only France, but France's allies were thrown into a furore by Louis's illness. Prussian Field Marshal Samuel von Schmettau, attached to French headquarters, rushed a hysterical dispatch to his master that Louis was dying of an abscess of the brain. When Frederick eventually got full details, he was especially scornful of the Bishop of Soissons, whom he termed 'a fanatic imbecile'.

The queen arrived at the bedside on 17 August. The king awoke to her weeping, embraced her, and addressed her in the only way he could: 'Madame, I have caused you much undeserved grief; I beg you to forgive me.' 'Ah, Sire,' Marie replied, 'do you not know you have never needed my forgiveness? It is God alone you have offended, and I beg you only to concern yourself with Him.'

Just when it seemed there was no end to the indignities he must endure, Louis's illness broke, on 26 August. He began to mend, but slowly; after such a mortal malady, even his robust constitution needed weeks to return to normal. It was November before he had the strength for the journey back to Paris, via Lüneville and Strasbourg.

Queen Marie, sighing and simpering, pleaded to go with him, apparently convinced that their deathbed reunion indicated a desire on his part to return to her arms. She decked herself out in pink ribbons and blushed with happiness when she encountered her husband. Louis, flabbergasted, rushed her back to Versailles, denying her request to visit her father in Lüneville. The dauphin gave him his excuse; the boy had obligingly picked up a fever that his father now decreed was dangerous in the war zone.

As the royal family departed, the extent of the military mess his illness had triggered, began to emerge. During the crisis, Noailles bungled a major drive against Prince Charles of Lorraine, the Empress of Austria's brother-in-law. The prince and his army were allowed to escape to take up the defence of Bohemia, eluding a timid, confused pursuit, crossing the Rhine, and burning strategic bridges behind them. Noailles's personal conduct on the battlefield was so craven that the Parisian mob nailed a wooden sword to the door of his house and made up insulting songs about him. King Frederick complained. When Louis felt strong enough to rejoin the army, the cowardly maréchal was left behind. Noailles's career was ended, his dream of becoming councillor to the king gone up in battle-smoke.

Louis arrived at the front as a small force under Louis de Bourbon Condé, Comte de Clermont, captured Frieburg, the capital of Austrian Breisgau. Winter cold set in almost at once, forcing a suspension of military operations, and Louis embarked on the last leg of his journey to Paris. He was grimly thankful for Frieburg. The King of France would enter his capital on a note of victory, however modest.

At the gates of Paris, triumph suddenly engulfed him. It was unanticipated and, in an age of cynically manipulated crowd scenes, completely spontaneous. Paris had gone mad, according to d'Angerville, at the first news of his recovery:

> The courier was almost suffocated by the mob. They kissed his horse and even his boots . . . there was not a workman's society but ordered a Te Deum and France was given up for more than two months to rejoicings and festivals.

Barbier described the scene in his journal,

> A Te Deum was sung at Notre Dame. . . . There was a fireworks display at the Place des Grèves carried out in the most splendid and varied manner by Italian workmen. The streets of Paris were brilliantly illuminated . . . on the Pont Neuf, in the public squares and elsewhere, there were hogsheads of wine, which were distributed with polonies and bread. In front of each of these . . . was a platform for five or six musicians who discoursed music.

His delirious subjects firmly believed that their young king had saved the nation. He had been a sinner, a philanderer. (Was there a soul in France who had not heard the scandal from the parish pulpits?) Brought back from the abyss by their prayers, he was now repentant, victorious over France's enemies and handsomer than ever. Who could resist 'Louis le Bien-Aimé '? D'Angerville picked up the narrative:

> His path was a succession of triumphal arches, and these not merely stage properties, but permanent monuments. Every tree on the road bowed beneath the weight of spectators . . . a rich noble of his suite, affected by such worship . . . scattered handfuls of money, but none stooped to pick it up. All the crowd wanted was to salute the king, who was actually addressed by 'the ladies of the fishmarket'.

Genuinely touched, Louis could only murmur, 'How sweet it is to be so loved. What have I done to deserve it?'

At a crossroads, a lovely face in the multitude caught his eye. It was the Duchesse de Châteauroux, trying in vain to maintain her incognito. She wrote to Richelieu of the joy she felt when he smiled in recognition, before a bystander's hiss sent her fleeing in tears, '*Voilà son putain!*'

The sight of her reminded him that there were scores to settle, with the sanctimonious little clique who had exposed him to public shame. Without Châteauroux to give him courage, however, the royal retribution was pigeon-hearted. Unable to retract his confession, too timid to strike directly at the duc de Chartres, he vented his anger on small fry. His largest target was Bishop Fitz-James, whom he ordered into a mild sort of 'diocesan arrest' within the boundaries of Soissons. He banished M. de Balleroy, a loudly pious relative of the bishop who was secretary to the duc. The dauphin's tutor, the Duc de Châtillon, was impossible to overlook. For his sermons to the boy on royal concubines – and the unbelievable gaffe of hailing a new king before the old king was dead – he was summarily dismissed. The king allowed himself a public snort of disgust as he cast the duc from the court: 'Really, he imagined himself the first officer of state!'

His treatment at the hands of the righteous did not destroy his faith, nor did he flag in his formal duties, but the Duc de Luynes noted:

> . . . the King has got into the habit of no longer praying on his knees, neither in the evening nor in the morning, contrary to the practice of a lifetime. One must suppose he says his prayers in bed, but the public is no longer a witness. One would have thought that the present moment would have been a good one to start thanking God on his knees again . . . one can only hope that it is feebleness which prevents him from kneeling.

Feeble the royal knees might be, but not the royal loins. He burned for Châteauroux. On 25 November, hateful Maurepas was forced to make his amends to the favourite, by carrying Louis's letter of invitation to her; the comte was received at her bedside, where she was laid low by fever and headache. Understandably, no momentary ailment was going to keep her from the king. The next day she ignored a soaring temperature to bathe and perfume herself for the trip to Versailles. Her visit was shrouded in such secrecy, there is conjecture whether the reunion actually took place. An ecstatic hour with Louis, if she managed it, cost her dearly, for it was followed by her final illness.

The symptoms, early on, were remarkably like the king's during his illness at Metz. The duchesse's case rapidly worsened, into eleven days of the tortures of peritonitis, ending in convulsions. The doctors bled her nine times. In desperation, strange healers were consulted, among them the Comte de Saint-Germain, a protégé of the diplomat Maréchal Belle-Isle, who was summoned from the laboratory where he manufactured potions and face creams. He had the good sense to refuse to treat her, although he claimed to possess the elixir of life. Fearing royal displeasure, he decamped soon afterwards for England and India, only to surface again at Versailles during the reign of Châteauroux's successor.

Châteauroux died in agony on 10 December. She was twenty-seven. The Duchesse de Lauraguais kept the death watch, but Madame de Mailly was admitted only after her sister expired, to kneel and sob beside the corpse.

Instantly, rumours of poison floated through Versailles. Richelieu, her uncle, ex-lover and closest confidant, cast a suspicious eye in the direction of Maurepas, but concluded, in his memoirs, that she was literally loved to death by her master, dying, '. . . *of immoderate and violent indulgence . . .*'

The market women returned their own verdict on the duchesse. Their loyalty was never lightly given, and, for a king they considered a moral backslider, their scorn was boundless. They gloated over the favourite's death, sending a defiant message to the throne: 'Since he has taken back his whore, he shall not find another *Paternoster* for him in all Paris.'

Even dead, Châteauroux figured in farce. Madame Jeanne Campan, who was a reader to the king's daughters and chronicler of Marie Leczinska, described the restless nights the duchesse's sudden death caused the superstitious Polish queen. One night in particular, a woman of her suite told stories into the wee hours to lull her to sleep. Nothing worked. The woman asked the queen, 'Are you feverish? Shall I call the doctor?' 'Oh, no, my good Boirot,' Marie answered, 'I am not ill. But that poor Madame Châteauroux – if she were to come again!' Boirot whooped, 'Jesus, Madame, if Madame de Châteauroux should come again, it will certainly not be Your Majesty she will be looking for!'

Louis, for a day or two, was as awestruck as his queen. He saw the wrath of the Lord in Châteauroux's death, ceased dining publicly and shut himself away behind the doors of the *petits appartements*. After his fashion, he tried to mourn her, although he was most depressed by the inconvenience her death caused him. 'Here I am,' he told the duc de Gontaut, 'unhappy till I'm ninety.' His lamentations were brief, soon soothed by a return to the hunt and by the preparations for his son's marriage.

Military campaigning was suspended, so the court turned its official attention to a single tremendous project during the winter of 1744–5: the state wedding of Louis Auguste, the timid, serious, good-looking, sixteen-year-old dauphin of France, to Maria Theresa Raphaella, the ugly, red-haired, twenty-year-old infanta of Spain. (She was a sister of the Spanish princess Louis had jilted in 1725, to marry Marie Leczinska.) Their union was a major venture in international diplomacy, another attempt to consolidate the power of the two Bourbon thrones. A proxy ceremony was staged in Madrid in December. The bride and groom participated in person at Versailles in February. The nuptial balls, the banquets – and budgets – were in the most prodigal tradition of the Bourbon court. A kingly hand was required to initial the bills.

In actuality, the royal wedding was a side-show, compared to the real business of the season: the selection of the next royal *maîtresse*. The supply of Nesle sisters being exhausted, the king's mock-fidelity came to an end and hopeful young women of the court scrambled in pursuit of the royal hunter, now transformed into the royal quarry. In the account of l'Espion Chinois:

> All the fair women of Paris took the field and . . . availed themselves of every device of art and nature to attract the opposite sex. Everyone was busy . . . dressmakers, hairdressers, trimmings-makers worked day and night. . . . never were such sales . . . they bathed and perfumed themselves in readiness for any eventuality. From finery they passed to other means of attracting. Before they heard of the Favourite's death, the women of Paris enjoyed good health. Now they found themselves afflicted with terrible headaches, and most of them went to Versailles for a change of air. The chief thing was to be seen by the king and to speak to him. The usual resource of writing was not neglected . . . [and] innumerable billets-doux were written to the Prince.

The noble ladies relied on age-old stratagems of seduction. Unfortunately, they lacked imagination, a quality possessed to an acute degree by the mistress of the château d'Étoiles, a country estate close to the hunting park of Sénart, and the royal hunting-box at Choisy. She was bourgeoise, twenty-four, and understood clearly that, being low-born, she had no hope of being formally presented to the king.

George I, founder of the English House of Hanover, arrived at Greenwich with his two 'dragon mistresses' and speaking no English in 1714.

George I's residence at St James's was more a bivouac in enemy territory than a reign. The apartments of the Duchess of Kendal, one of his mistresses, were conveniently located in the palace. (Royal Collection)

Sir Robert Walpole was 'the one golden result' of George I's reign, keeping the peace. In 1721 he became George I's first prime minister. (The National Portrait Gallery, London)

The Duchess of Kendal helped to defraud the nation at large in the financial swindle of 1720 known as the South Sea Bubble, an eight-month frenzy of speculation which nearly destroyed the English economy. During the resulting scandal the 'Maypole' sheltered the court from total ruin and the king from abdication. (Guildhall Library, London)

Louis XV became king at the age of five and remained a permanent adolescent: handsome, athletic and without any purpose in life more serious than the pursuit of game.

Jeanne Antoinette Poisson d'Étoiles, the 24-year-old wife of a minor official, who would rule France for twenty years as the Marquise de Pompadour and became France's last political mistress and certainly the most powerful. Here is a testimony to her elegance from her special protégé François Boucher. (Victoria and Albert Museum)

Frederick the Great reviewing his troops attended by his General Officers. The mutual hatred of Frederick the Great and Pompadour ignited the Seven Years War. It was, however, ironically Frederick the Great who memorialized her: she was one of the women he mocked by erecting their statues to hold up the dome of his palace at Potsdam. (The Hulton Picture Company)

The Palace of Versailles was built by Louis XIV, the Sun King, to provide himself with a suitable celestial setting. Its rooms were crammed with glorifications of French conquest by France's foremost painters and sculptors. Later Madame de Pompadour supervized the armies for the Seven Years War from here. (A.F. Kersting)

Catherine II proclaimed herself the spiritual heir of Peter the Great. She was actually a German interloper on the Russian dynastic scene who ruled by her wits and embarked on a strategy of conquest to expand Russia to the ancient borders of Byzantium. She was a magnet for men from her earliest adolescence and her name is synonymous with royal licentiousness. (Engraved by R. Woodman; National Portrait Gallery, London)

Gregory Orlov, another royal favourite to whom it was said Catherine remained faithful for nearly fourteen years, was lavished with fortune upon fortune. Their eventual parting was sweetened by breathtaking generosity from Catherine which included the Marble Palace and two hundred paintings to adorn it. The Marble Palace is one of the foremost examples of early classic architecture in Russia. (Novosti Press Agency)

Catherine's favourite of favourites, Gregory Potemkin, loved medals. Catherine bestowed on him the Order of Saint Alexander Nevsky as well as making him a Knight of the Order of Saint Andrew and giving him the Order of Saint George. He finally became Prince Gregory Alexandrovich Potemkin-Tavrichesky with Russia's four greatest provinces under his personal rule. (Novosti Press Agency)

Undiscouraged, she bought a phaeton and taught herself to drive it. Again and again, she contrived to drive into the path of the royal chase, confronting Louis in her little cart, retiring each time from his presence in adorable confusion. Manoeuvres in the field successfully completed, she pressed home the campaign by securing an invitation to the masked ball at Versailles celebrating the dauphin's marriage.

In the Hall of Mirrors on the night of 25 February, Louis appeared in an unlikely disguise: a potted yew tree. He and eleven identically costumed friends trooped into the ballroom in mid-evening, like ambulatory shrubs suddenly crashing the party from the garden outside. The prank was supposed to preserve the king's incognito, but the pretty young woman of the forest encounters had private information. She knew which yew was royal and appeared before him, costumed, naturally enough, as Diana. The goddess's crescent moon glittered on her forehead, she bore a dainty bow and quiver, and offered her sovereign a superb *décolletage*. D'Angerville quoted Louis's greeting: 'Fair huntress, happy are those who are pierced by your darts; their wounds are mortal.' The young woman blushed, and dropped her handkerchief. For a moment, she appeared to lose her nerve. What was lost was the king's heart. He gallantly retrieved the scrap of lace and tossed it to her as she fled into the crowd. A moan of despair went up from the other ladies in the ballroom: 'The handkerchief is thrown!' Louis's face was a study in desire.

She had contacts at court, albeit humble ones. The dauphin's first valet, Binet, was a cousin; a groom named de Bridge was a friend. They quickly informed His Majesty of the mystery woman's identity. His Diana was the wife of Charles Guillaume le Normant d'Étoiles, a member of a prominent Parisian banking family and the director of public works.

The seduction, if seduction is the word for a sexual encounter so reciprocal, was brief. Louis, whose hormones were ungovernable at best, existed in torment until he bedded her. She was one of those women to whom men of power are irresistible; over time, she would prove to be as deeply infatuated with the kingdom as with the king. At a tumultuous masked ball at the Hôtel de Ville a few evenings later, he never left her side. She resisted a little, for form's sake, fending him off in the hire-cab they took to her mother's house. Binet brought her to the *petits appartements* for an interview tête-a-tête. Louis heard her terms. (Forewarned, she avoided the appearance of pushiness or greed.) They consummated the affair to their mutual delight. Within days, she withdrew from her marriage bed.

D'Étoiles, understandably in love with so desirable a wife, took it badly. His servants were forced to hide the weapons in the house. He wrote a despairing letter to his wife Jeanne, who read it to the king, who was thoroughly annoyed. (It was the only time on record that she allowed her personal troubles to intrude.) The husband was appointed a *fermier générale* (tax collector) and persuaded to take a business trip. He went quietly, but he never spoke to his wife again.

In April, she was observed in public at Versailles itself, first attending a Rameau ballet, and then at a performance of the *Comédie Italienne*. Looking utterly ravishing, she occupied a box directly opposite the king and queen. In the same month, the painters, drapers and furniture movers began to renovate Madame de Mailly's old apartment. In September, Madame d'Étoiles, now created a marquise, was received at court.

She took charge of Louis's life and kingdom for the next twenty years. Born Jeanne Antoinette Poisson, she would be known to the ages as the Marquise de Pompadour.

Chapter Fourteen

The Fishes' Daughter

S he was the cleverest tart who ever lived, skilled in all the tricks that quicken the pulses of men, and kings. In another age, under another star, the Marquise de Pompadour would have had an immense success on the stage. She sang, delightfully, 'a hundred ditties' of the day. She played several instruments, and accompanied her songs on the harpsichord.

Pompadour was graceful without affectation; a joyful dancer, she managed to tempt Louis, who disliked it intensely, into joining her on the ballroom floor. Although she tired easily, her horsemanship was superb. (Nothing less was possible, if she was to keep pace with France's huntsman king.)

An amusing story-teller who could be, at times, outrageously funny, she was witty, well-read, a beguiling conversationalist. Voltaire himself applauded her acting in amateur performances at the château d'Étoiles and, later, at Versailles itself. Connoisseur and designer, she created the rooms and gowns that set off her delicate, porcelain beauty. (One of her kinder nicknames was *La statuette de Sèvres*, for the figurines created under her patronage, which she so resembled.)

The testimony of her elegance is with us still, in the paintings of Jean Marc Nattier and her special protégé, François Boucher. She confounded the well-upholstered ladies of the court with a slim, supple new silhouette. Their hairdos looked fussy, compared to her simple, gently waved coiffure. (In the sun, her light brown hair shone like a helmet of gold.) Her face was an exquisitely boned, classic oval. The eyes dominated, huge, thickly lashed, set off by milk white skin. Perfect teeth, whiter still, forever flashed in the gayest of smiles. Georges Le Roy, head huntsman of Versailles and a man with a keen appreciation for beauty, was smitten by her eyes, which he sought to describe in his diary:

... it is difficult to say exactly what colour they were; they had neither the hard sparkle of black eyes, nor the dreamy tenderness of blue, nor the special delicacy of grey; their indeterminate colour seemed to lend them to all forms of seduction and shades of expression. Indeed her expression was always changing, through there was never any discordance between her various features ... her whole person was half way between the last degree of elegance and the first of nobility.

Nobility she lacked, certainly the four hundred years of aristocratic lineage considered necessary for a place in the court of the Bourbons. Louis attempted to remedy the defect by reviving for her the Marquessate of Pompadour with its coat of arms of three castles on a field azure. His attempt failed.

To her critics, the new favourite was an orchid blooming on a dung-heap. She was the daughter of a scamp, François Poisson, who had his fingers in a number of unsavoury pies: he was a petty profiteer and butcher to the Invalides, an agent of the notorious Pâris brothers. By the time Jeanne Antoinette was four, Papa Poisson had promoted his family from drab digs on the Rue de Cléry to comparative affluence on the Rue de Richelieu. He wriggled his way up to a post as equerry to the Duc d'Orléans before his luck deserted him in 1725, when he was caught out in a black-market wheat fraud, and fled to Germany.

Poisson had barely crossed the German border before his wife took a banker, Charles-François le Normant de Tournehem, as her lover and protector. She had already achieved a certain notoriety. Barbier recollected Louise Madeleine de la Motte Poisson as 'one of the most beautiful women in the country, and very clever'. To d'Argenson, she was 'a well-known prostitute of the Palais Royal'. Although 'uncle' Tournehem adored Jeanne Antoinette, the child was too much underfoot in the new household, so Louise shipped her off to the fashionable convent school at Poissy for a year. When she returned, her mother had already picked out a suitably rich son-in-law, le Normant de Tournehem's nephew and heir. Madame Poisson also listened seriously to a fortune-teller who predicted, when Jeanne was nine, that her daughter would be the mistress of a king! She nicknamed the girl Reinette ('Queenie'), and completed her schooling at home. Contemporary journals held Madame Poisson's mothering suspect. She groomed her daughter to be, not just a young lady of social accomplishments, but something which greatly resembled a performing doll. In d'Angerville's words:

Madame le Normant d'Étoiles was just a beautiful woman if she so desired, or beautiful and vivacious, together or separately, having acquired these arts from the lessons her mother had procured for her from actors, famous courtesans, preachers and lawyers. The diabolical woman had gone to all the professions that call for subtle and varied expressions for private instruction, in order to make her daughter really 'a morsel fit for a king' . . . She could weep – like an actress. She could be at will superb, imperious, calm, roguish, a tease, judicious, curious, attentive, by altering the expression of her eyes, her lips, her fine brow. In fact, without moving her body, her mischievous face made of her a veritable proteus. . . . Unfortunately, her lips were pale and withered; she had so habitually bitten them that she had severed the tiny blood-vessels, thus causing the dirty yellow colour they bore, except when recently bitten.

With acid hindsight, Charles Augustin Sainte-Beuve summed up, 'She had been taught everything but morals, which would have stood in her way.'

Jeanne was married at nineteen to le Normant d'Étoiles. Both parents attended her wedding. Papa Poisson had returned home by 1741, the fraud charges somehow quashed; he was sensibly silent about the banker's attentions to his wife. The wedding gifts from Tournehem included a house near the Rue St Honoré, forty thousand a year and the château d'Étoiles, where the couple lived in wealthy, contented obscurity.

In Paris, Madame d'Étoiles had a small success in the society of the time. She (but not her mother) was received in the salon of Madame Geoffrin. Her singing diverted, among others, Jean François Hénault, the president of the Parlement of Paris and an intimate of the queen. She drew an interesting company to the château d'Étoiles; the stuffy local aristocrats stayed away, but a top-rung selection of the Parisian *bourgeoisie* was willing to journey out, including the intellectuals of the day. A weekend with Madame d'Étoiles might include charming amateur theatre, in which one's elegant hostess was likely to appear in a starring role. The playwright Prosper Crébillon, who had been her dramatic coach in girlhood, came. So did Fontenelle, Maupertuis and Montesquieu. Voltaire was a frequent dinner guest.

She became pregnant in 1742 or 1743, with a little boy who died. Her second child, an adored daughter, Alexandrine, was not yet a year old when Madame d'Étoiles attended the ball at Versailles.

With the ball, and the royal favour that followed, her world turned topsy-turvy. The Parlement of Paris was persuaded to issue a discreet decree of separation to Monsieur and Madame d'Étoiles. Husband Charles decamped to parts unknown, to lick his wounds. During the spring and summer, long, passionate love-letters from the king arrived daily. (They bore his imprimature, 'Discreet and Faithful' – from the most faithless of men.)

Louis's couriers arrived with the dust of the battlefield on their boots. Despite the embarrassment of Metz, he had developed a liking for the sport of war, and rode off in May to a second season of campaigning, accompanied, this time, by the dauphin. His moment of glory came at Fontenoy, a village in Flanders near the Escaut river. Here, Maréchal de Saxe with an army of fifty thousand men fought an equal allied force under George II's son, the young Duke of Cumberland. Saxe, the bastard son of the King of Poland, was typical of the mercenaries who gave the French army its backbone, a Saxon and Protestant who made his way as a professional cavalry officer. Previously in Flanders, he contented himself with patching up the mistakes of his senior commander, the cowardly Maréchal de Noailles. At Fontenoy, so ill with dropsy he had to fight from a wicker carriage, he entered the pantheon of great French warriors.

When the tide of battle turned against the French, the timorous Noailles pleaded with Louis XV to flee; Saxe brushed him aside and sick as he was, mounted a horse to lead the final attacks. In nine bloody hours, he finally brought the British forces to a halt. (The Parisians cackled with derision over the story that at Fontenoy, the Duc de Biron, a cavalry hero of the battle, changed horses three times, Saxe changed his shirt three times, and Noailles changed his pants three times.) Saxe followed up his success with a string of French victories in the Austrian Netherlands from Tournai to Ostend.

Louis's part in Fontenoy is equivocal. Under the illusion that he was impervious to battle accidents, the French king ventured so close to the action, an English cannon ball ploughed up the earth only yards away. 'I want nothing from these people,' he commented melodramatically, 'Pray return it to them.' He was buckling on armour to lead a cavalry charge when Saxe finally argued him into safety at the rear. Even then, the maréchal had to assign men to keep the royal person out of harm's way – stationing three battalions at a bridge over the Escaut, should the king's escape become necessary. Victory wiped away the king's blunders, with everyone else's. He wrote the expected drum-head letter to his wife, and toured the battlefield. For all his gruesome delight in corpses and funerals, he had no stomach for the wholesale dead heaped on every side, and he preached a pious sermon on the subject to the dauphin. On 7 September, the royal party returned to Paris to Te Deums even louder than those which celebrated Louis's recovery from illness at Metz.

The court and the public agreed it was a greater victory than any scored by his great-grandfather. Voltaire rushed to create his poem *La Bataille de Fontenoy*, an unblushing publicity hand-out set in verse. His apple-polishing continued; in his opera 'The Temple of Glory', he trumpeted the victorious arms of his sovereign, casting Louis as the Roman Emperor Trajan. Voltaire lost his head completely at the opera's premiere, leaped up and hugged the king, only to be hauled away by Louis's guards. Louis caught his breath, forgave the playwright his act of *lèse majesté* and ordered him released.

Louis was princely to Saxe, creating for him a new rank above all his other maréchaux. Saxe was appointed governor of Alsace, enriched with an income of forty thousand *livres* a year, and given the legendary château de Chambord, reportedly designed by Leonardo da Vinci. A good courtier, he said publicly that the king's presence was 'worth five thousand men' but, when the campaign season opened in 1746, he worked every stratagem he could devise to keep the monarch away from the battlefield.

While Louis postured in Flanders, Madame d'Étoiles studied his court with furious intensity. A tiny company of knowledgeable friends gathered around her, to help smooth the transition to life at Versailles. Elizabeth Charlotte de Semonville, Comtesse d'Estrades, the plump niece of le Normant de Tournehem, was there. Voltaire, dumbfounded by his luck in knowing the new favourite, appeared with verses and unsought advice. The king, conscious of the pitfalls, remarked, 'It will amuse me to undertake her education', and sent his old friend, Louis Antoine, Maréchal and Duc de Gontaut-Biron, to tutor her. A young lawyer, Collin, was hired as her secretary. She, herself, recruited a penniless courtier, the cherubic abbé François Joachim de Pierre, Comte de Bernis. (Bernis, a graceful bellettrist, phrased her replies to Louis's letters.)

Gontaut-Biron and Bernis drilled her meticulously. Both men had spent most of their adult lives threading their way through the social labyrinth of Versailles and they understood how impenetrable it could be to an outsider. Madame d'Étoiles's abilities as an actress were put to good use, mastering the special vocabulary, the gliding walk, the profound curtsey of the court. A quick student, she memorized the innumerable details of protocol that applied to each of the two thousand and more courtiers among whom she would now be required to move. By 14 September, when she was formally presented, she faced her royal lover as if she had always lived in *ce pays-ci* ('this country'), as its residents called Versailles.

It was impossible not to admire the little bourgeoise's virtuosity, but no one was deceived, not the royal family, or the court, or the infinitely more snobbish common citizenry. The dauphin stuck out his tongue when she was presented to him, and, out of earshot of his father, called her Madame Whore. The courtiers muttered against *La Bourgeoise*. For two decades, the pamphleteers and quatrain-writers never let her forget her lowly origins. She was 'the fishes' daughter', sprung from the family Poisson, and they showered her with the coarsest slanders they could concoct.

A whole class of lampoons came to be known as *poissonades*. Ostensibly dashed off by street scribes, they were more often than not authored by the courtiers of Versailles – another weapon in the never-ending warfare of intrigue which raged through the halls of the king's château. This sally, penned to embarrass the favourite on her arrival, was fairly mild:

> *Cette petite bourgeoise,*
> *Élevée à la grivoise,*
> *Mesurant tout à sa toise*
> *Fait de la cour son taudis-dis.*
>
> *Louis malgré son scruple*
> *Froidement pour elle brûle;*
> *Et son amour ridicule*
> *A fait rire tout Paris-ris.*
>
> *On dit même que d'Estrade*
> *Si vilaine, si maussade,*
> *Aura bientôt la passade*
> *Dont elle a l'air tout bouffi-fi!*

> This nobody,
> Brought up to be a merry wench,
> Measuring everything by her own standard,
> Makes of the court her slum.
>
> Louis, despite his scruples,
> Madly burns for her;

And his ridiculous passion
Makes all Paris laugh.

It is even said that d'Estrade,
So ugly and disagreeable,
Will soon be a passing fancy,
And her pride is all puffed up.

Greedy d'Estrades was a tempting target with her jowly face:

Si vous voulez faire,
Dans le temps present,
La plus mince affaire,
Il faut de l'argent.
Parlez à d'Estrades, elle recoit un écu,
Lanturlu!

Si vous voulez être
Sur de la trouver,
Et la reconnaître,
Sans le demander,
Cherchez le visage le plus semblable à un cul,
Lanturlu!

If, nowadays, you wish to arrange
The least little business, you need money.
Speak to d'Estrades, she receives an écu;
Fiddle-de-dee!

If you would be sure of finding
And recognizing her without asking,
Seek the face that is most like a behind,
Fiddle-de-dee!

A few years later, Pompadour ousted the Comte de Maurepas. Like as not, Maurepas wrote these farewell lines to himself:

On dit que Maman Catin,
Qui vous mène si beau train
Et se plaît à la culbute
Vous procure cette chute.

De quoi vous avisez-vous
D'attirer son fier courroux?
Cette franche péronelle
Vous fait sauter l'echelle.

Il fallait, en courtisan,
Lui prodiguer votre encens;
Faire comme La Vallière
Qui lui lèche le derrière!

It is said that Mother Strumpet,
Who rushes you along at such speed
And delights in upsets,
Has brought about your fall.

Whatever made you bring down
Upon yourself her fierce rage?
This brazen hussy
Has made you hop the twig!

As a good courtier
You should have loaded her with flattery
Like La Vallière,
Who licks her ass!

The reaction of Louis César de la Baume le Blanc, Duc de la Vallière, is not recorded. (He was a Pompadour protégé, the producer of her amateur theatricals.)

As the snubs and insults rained down, the marquise bore them in silence, and embarked on a campaign to endear herself to the royal family.

The Duchesse de Châteauroux had only contempt for Louis's dull, fat, unpleasant queen and showed it. Pompadour was her instant toady. At her presentation, she gushed, 'Madame, I burn with a passion to please you.' This could have been accomplished easily enough, by leaving the queen's husband's bed. Pompadour attempted the impossible, setting out to win over Marie despite their awkward domestic situation. Pompadour was the least devout of women, but for many weeks, she pleaded to take part in the queen's religious activities. She sent bouquets and little gifts. Louis, who could deny her nothing, was persuaded to invite his unwelcome spouse to his retreat at Choisy. It was Pompadour who intervened to have the queen's shabby apartments redecorated. With relentless kindness, she wore her mistress down.

At last, she was given a public place in Marie's carriage, as the court left on an excursion to Fontainebleau. The queen succumbed completely and invited the favourite to dinner beforehand. If not yet admitted to the prim circle of *dames du palais de la Reine*, she sat down to cards in Her Majesty's presence. So it went, with variations, as she worked on the dauphin and Mesdames, the king's daughters.

Two deaths that occurred in her first year as favourite illustrate the iron control she exercised over herself in her affair with Louis – and the lengths to which she would go to curry favour with the *familières*.

The king might be morbid, but he hated mourning, because custom forbade him gambling and the hunt, his favourite amusements. Therefore, when Pompadour's mother died on Christmas Eve 1745, after a long, terrible cancer, he astonished the court by permitting his new *maîtresse* a few days of retirement and daughterly tears. Pompadour quickly sensed royal fidgets, however, and the famous 'yellow colour' he exhibited when bored. He proposed postponing a trip to Marly. She shrugged off her private tragedy without a second thought, insisting that the trip go ahead. 'The death of my mother,' she told him, 'is not important enough to disturb the court and the ladies who have made expenses for Marly and would regret not going.'

Six months later, the dauphine, Marie-Thérèse of Spain, died suddenly, after childbirth. The dauphin, married only a year and deeply in love, set up a tremendous howl. In an embarrassing deathbed scene, the athletic king was forced to wrestle his corpulent son away from the dead princess. Louis then turned tongue-tied, helpless to comfort the prince. Louis Auguste waddled off to mourn in seclusion. Pompadour saw an opening to gain favour. She coaxed and wheedled until she brought father and son together in a two-man carriage on a court excursion, riding out in uneasy, but sympathetic, intimacy. The dauphin's attitude, if still disapproving, softened considerably.

Official mourning for the dauphine, conducted at Choisy, gave Pompadour her first opportunity to play hostess to the king. Made desperate by wager-less, stag-less days in hushed, black-draped rooms, Louis began to mutter about rejoining Maréchal de Saxe and the army. Saxe wrote from the front appealing to Pompadour, with whom he was friendly, to discourage the king from campaigning. Louis's foolhardy conduct at Fontenoy was still a painful memory.

Pompadour suggested a royal visit to Crécy. Located near Dreux, this was the first of the many estates she would purchase during her years as favourite. The hospitality she offered was informal, because the château was being remodelled under the supervision of her brother, Abel, and the architect Jean Caillteau, the younger Lassurance. Pompadour's gift for improvisation was equal to the occasion, turning rooms filled with workmen and scaffolding into the setting of a fascinating house party. Louis, who loved a good table, was treated to incomparable meals by the great chef Benoit. Better still, his *maîtresse* involved him directly in her planning for the estate, offering the sketches of the new wings for his approval, seeking his advice on the dairies she proposed to build, the stables, an amphitheatre, a windmill, cascades. The king even designed a green and gold uniform for the male guests. Louis enjoyed himself immensely, before the party climbed back into its coaches to return to Versailles, and the next amusement on Pompadour's programme. It was obvious from the beginning that Pompadour would dominate the king's daily life. How quickly she did so, was astonishing. Mistress of the revels to the King of France, she was everywhere at once, organizing, consulting, planning the pleasures of her lord.

Louis XV asked nothing better of life than distraction. Restless, moody, essentially frivolous, he was so ill-suited to the throne that Frederick the Great wrote to Voltaire describing him as 'a good man whose only fault was that he was king'. Coming from the eighteenth century's most distinguished villain, the adjective 'good' may or may not have been a compliment, but the Prussian king was accurate in his estimation of the French king's professional qualifications.

Despite thirty years of attempts at indoctrination by his ministers, Louis's grasp of great affairs was superficial. He had no understanding, whatsoever, of the effect his government had on the lives of ordinary Frenchmen. As a young man, he visited Paris in a bad year, and was struck by the poverty and famine he saw. Someone told him the people's suffering was caused by the extravagance of the court. Rushing back to Versailles, Louis fired eighty of his gardeners. Someone else told him that the eighty gardeners and their families would starve. He rehired them, and, irritated, returned to the hunt.

One of the most damning descriptions of Louis XV was written by Madame Campan, who actually liked him:

He was very expert in a number of pointless matters which only occupy the attention if there is nothing better; for instance, he was very adroit at knocking off the top of an egg with a single stroke of his fork; so he always ate eggs when he dined in public, and the gapers who came on Sundays to watch him dine returned home less struck with his fine figure than with the dexterity with which he broke his eggs.

He carved ivory very skilfully, and he had a talent for draughting. Born in humbler circumstances, he might have been mildly successful as a craftsman or an architect. Asked to lead the greatest nation in Europe, Louis XV was grotesquely beyond his depth.

Chapter Fifteen

An Audience of One

At thirty-five, the hunt was the king's whole life. Politics bored him. Dining, gambling, gossip, and sex were only marginally interesting. The pinnacle of his pleasure was each day's kill. In his obsession with blood sports, Louis was not alone. The chase dominated noble life, the preferred outdoor recreation of the aristocracy, and the curse of every farmer who lived next to a forest. It was a pastime with a deadly purpose. The nobleman on horseback – cavalry – was the ultimate weapons system in eighteenth-century warfare. The hunt was monarchy's physical fitness programme for its mounted killers, an enjoyable method of keeping them in fighting trim between campaigns, setting them to slaughter stags, boars, wolves, bears and small game when their human prey was out of season.

Louis had few peers in the field. Possessed of an iron constitution, he rode horses, dogs and friends into exhaustion. The hours the animals needed to recover their strength at the end of the chase, he gave grudgingly, but he absolutely refused to acknowledge that his human companions needed an occasional day of rest. He roamed without ceasing a small circuit of royal estates near Paris which possessed fine game parks: Choisy, Compiègne, La Muette, Fontainebleau and Versailles itself; or he was the sought-after guest of the owners of great hunting preserves at châteaux like Chantilly, the Condé stronghold, or Rambouillet, the home of his great friend, the Comtesse de Toulouse. Louis was oddly incurious about the rest of his kingdom, nor did he ever, to anyone's knowledge, consider peacetime travel abroad. The only breaks in his never-ending pursuit of game were his wartime visits to the army.

Pompadour did not seek to interfere with Louis's hunting, but, having no wish to become a camp-follower, she did discourage his campaigning. She offered, instead, a fabulously expanded bill of entertainment at home, a life stage-managed as if it were a continuous *divertissement* presented to an audience of one. Never a dull moment, if she could prevent it, cast its shadow on the king's day.

Her sexual performance was, of course, the subject of immediate, intense speculation. The valets and maids remembered the buxom Nesle sisters. The royal stallion and his fairy sprite, they whispered, were badly matched. Louis made his conquest, only to find his encounters with his exquisite *maîtresse* somewhat mechanical, and not nearly as frequent or as prolonged as he wished. Keeping up with Louis's sexuality drove her to despair; she dosed herself with love potions, and constantly experimented with silly aphrodisiac diets. At one point, she lived on celery, truffles and chocolate flavoured with triple vanilla and amber. She was plagued by miscarriages. (What would she not have given, to bear the king's child!) In exasperation, Louis swore she was 'cold as a *macreuse*' (a cold-blooded game bird).

Cruel but true. The poor creature was so cold-blooded, she kept her fireplaces blazing in mid-summer; even with her rooms at Saharan temperatures, she habitually buried her hands in a muff. It was her good luck that the king, too, enjoyed overheated rooms. For all her energy, Pompadour was sickly, suffering from colic, migraine, insomnia and constant colds. She coughed blood from girlhood. When she moved from the quarters she inherited from Madame de Mailly in the *attique du nord* to a ground floor suite, a chair-lift had to be rigged to spare her the climb to her lover's chambers. In later years, the palpitations with which the marquise was afflicted developed into a serious heart condition. Bouts of illness forced her to take to her bed, one or two days a week.

All of these flaws, in a less resourceful hetaera, would have ended her reign almost before it began. Pompadour was undaunted. To keep the king's infatuation fuelled, she worked with what she had.

One of her first projects was to create the *Théâtre des Petits Cabinets*. In the wine shops, there was outrage over this new extravagance. The grumblers ignored the fact that a weekly bill of plays, operas and ballets had always been presented to the court, under the aegis of *Les Menus Plaisirs*, supervised by the Duc de Richelieu. But Pompadour's theatre was exclusive, with seating for twelve or fourteen august persons only. To the greatest of Louis's courtiers, inclusion in the tiny audience, or among the players, was bliss. Not to be bidden was bitterest humiliation. At length, the queen attended. The prissy dauphin, himself, performed.

Its productions decorated and costumed by the finest artists available to the court, notably Boucher, the miniature playhouse opened in the *Galerie de Mignard* off the *Cabinet des Médailles*. For the opening production of Molière's *Tartuffe*, in mid-January, 1747, there were clandestine rehearsals at Choisy. The entire project was kept a wonderful secret known only to a tiny group of insiders. Invitations to the opening night were a source of great satisfaction to the king, who vented his natural spite on courtiers who were not, at the moment, in high favour. Maréchal de Saxe was invited to attend, as were the marquise's brother Abel, le Normant de Tournehem and a handful of others. The Comte de Noailles, Governor of Versailles, was snubbed. So was the Prince de Conti, and a couple of thousand courtiers who would have gladly committed murder to obtain seats. To make the curtain, Louis actually broke away from the afternoon's chase, galloping back to the château before the kill. The play, starring the Marquise de Pompadour, was enthusiastically received, and a full season of presentations was planned.

Pompadour's theatre succeeded on its merits: the plays and operas performed were new, the 'amateur' casts and musicians were often better than the professionals in Paris, and the actress-manager-star was quite breathtaking. (Thrilled by his *maîtresse's* impersonation of Prince Charming, Louis kissed her in public, saying, 'You are the most delicious woman in France.') In 1748, performances moved to a stage with seating for forty, designed by Gabriel and erected beside the Ambassadors' Staircase. When protests against its cost grew embarrassing, the project was 'officially' abandoned and shifted elsewhere, to Compiègne and the tiny playhouse at Pompadour's château de Bellevue.

Altogether, the merry troupe had a run of five years, offering more than sixty plays, operas and ballets. The playbill was kept soufflé-light in all the *petits théâtres:* comedies like Dufresney's *L'Esprit de Contradiction*, and Guesset's *Le Méchant*, frothy operas such as *Acis et Galatée*. The queen saw Pompadour perform in La Chausée's *Le Préjugé à la Mode*, and the opera *Bacchus et Erigone*. The fortunate few who attended were unanimous in their applause.

The critics had axes to grind, as critics nearly always do. Chief among them was the Duc de Richelieu, back from the wars and a ringleader of the anti-Pompadour movement. *Son Excellence*, as he was called, was held in high regard, for he had just conquered the duchy of Parma. This especially pleased Louis, because the duchy provided a respectable seat for his eldest daughter, Louise-Elizabeth (known as Madame Infante), and her husband, Don Philip, who was the third son of the King of Spain.

Richelieu, whose snobbishness matched his lechery, had every reason to expect that a trumpery marquise like Pompadour would not last long at Versailles. He mounted a guerrilla action against her. The nastiest titters over her family, her manners, her clothes, her conversation, could all be traced to him. He invented excuses to deny her access to the warehouses of *Les Menus Plaisirs*, filled with furniture, props and costumes she needed for the *Théâtre des Petits Cabinets*. All the while he danced attendance on the new *maîtresse*, radiating smiles and pretty compliments. Pompadour eventually complained. That same afternoon at the king's *debottée* (literally, 'un-booting') at the end of the chase, the king asked the duc, quite casually, how many times he had been in the Bastille. Richelieu instantly understood the royal message. 'Three times, sire,' he answered. Harrassment of the marquise ceased forthwith.

Louis fully appreciated Pompadour's gifts as a hostess. In the age that invented the salon, she soon made the *petits appartements* the most fashionable salon of all. From Madame de Mailly's time, the courtiers had been accustomed to gather outside Louis's study door in the early evening in hopes of an invitation to supper. Now, a new goddess reigned over the inner circle and gave to a precious evening in His Majesty's company a *cachet* beyond all other prizes. After the chase, the king emerged from his study for a moment, glanced about at the noble hopefuls, and retired to write out the evening's guest list. Few were chosen, usually less than twenty, when the door-keeper called out the names.

Madame saw to it that the actual meal was simple but elegant; it was served almost family style, by two or three servants, to maintain the air of easy intimacy. Conversation, light and piquant as the menu, was the key to the king's approbation – and a return invitation. Dinner ended when Louis led the pleasant little crowd into his private salon for coffee, which he prepared himself, and gaming. Those not at the tables were invited to be seated, a tremendous privilege in the presence of the monarch. The evening passed in this friendly, rather sedate atmosphere until about midnight, time for the formal *coucher*. Louis and Pompadour exited, she to her boudoir, he to the ritual of retiring in his great-grandfather's bedroom. The guests made their way into the public rooms of Versailles, to bask in the envy of their fellows.

So much quiet respectability, even enlivened by the high jinks of rakes like Richelieu, tended to pall on the king. Pompadour added spice to the proceedings with newcomers, among them the Comte de Saint-Germain. The imposter surfaced again from self-exile in England and India, still getting by on face creams, fake miracles, and the outrageous assertion that he had lived for centuries. He spoke familiarly of the court of François I, and claimed to know the secrets of alchemy. Louis believed him. In the account left by Madame du Hausset:

> Some days afterward, the King, Madame de Pompadour, some lords of the court and the comte de Saint-Germain, were talking about his secret for causing the spots in diamonds to disappear. The King ordered a diamond of middling size, which had a spot, to be brought. It was weighed; and the King said to the comte, 'It is valued at two hundred and forty pounds; but it would be worth four hundred if it had no spot. Will you try to put a hundred and sixty pounds in my pocket?' He examined it carefully, and said, 'It may be done; and I will bring it to you again in a month.' At the time appointed, the comte brought back the diamond without a spot, and gave it to the King. The King had it weighed, and found it but very little diminished. The King sent it to his jeweller by Monsieur de Gontaut, without telling him anything of what had passed. The jeweller gave three hundred and eighty pounds for it. The King, however, sent for it back again, and kept it as a curiosity. He could not overcome his surprise, and said that Monsieur de Saint-Germain must be worth millions, especially as he had also the secret of making large diamonds out of a number of small ones.

Saint-Germain had successfully used the king as a decoy to steer other gullible souls his way. Without doubt, His Majesty's diamond was genuine. Heaven protect the unwary who heard the story and were induced to turn over their gems to be purified and enlarged by the comte's magic. (The bogus comte kept the king's confidence, eventually operating as his personal agent!)

Pompadour recruited glamorous new companions, and she was first with the news of the court. She became Louis's gossip, peddling titbits from her rapidly spreading network of informants. Nicolas René Berryer, chief of Louis's secret police, and Robert Jarrelle, his snoopy royal postmaster, became her close friends. She appointed herself editor of the dossier Jarrelle fetched from Paris every Sunday. Louis had revived the peeping and letter-opening of his great-grandfather's reign, not out of fear of conspiracy, but because he found the sexual foibles of his courtiers titillating; his *maîtresse* sifted through the bulky submissions, retrieving the gamiest items for their mutual enjoyment. The reports were written with the panting fervour of a pornographic novel: Louis's police spies spent days ferreting out the latest seductions and venereal infections; which nobleman carried a 'dozen English riding coats' (condoms) at all times; which lady of dubious quality was a 'baptismal font in which every passerby can wash his hands'; which celebrated stud (the Prince de Conti) faked his ejaculations.

Jarrelle's dossiers also recorded the graft, bribery and outright theft which gnawed at the foundations of the court. Even with evidence in his hands, Louis lacked the courage to prosecute the offenders. He only became a shade more disillusioned. 'The thievings in my household are enormous,' he told an official, 'But there is no remedy. Too many powerful people are involved. But calm yourself, the evil is incurable.'

Chief among Louis's new pleasures were Pompadour's multitudinous building and decorating schemes. Sadly, few of her residences have survived. Once, they dotted the countryside in golden profligacy: Crécy, Montretout, La Celle at St Cloud, Bellevue, the Hôtel de Réservoirs (connected by a corridor to Versailles itself), her mansion in Paris, the Hôtel d'Evreux (now the Elysée Palace), Champs (which the king hated), St Ouen, Ménars in the valley of the river Loire.

She bought each château (only Bellevue was built for her from the ground up), remodelled and redecorated it, filled it to bursting with furniture, artworks and her collections, surrounded it with superb gardens, and promptly abandoned it. Like a discontented magpie, she fluttered on to the next promising homestead, and the next glittering bit of treasure. Louis's hours with her were filled with plans, sketches and samples, fabric swatches and paint chips.

Furnishing her many mansions, Pompadour became a major influence in the decorative style which came to be known as rococo. She infected the king with a chronic case of shopping fever. At his ease in her boudoir, he presided over twenty years of royal patronage unmatched since the time of the Caesars. The *petits appartements* became the ultimate marketplace for the artists and artisans of France. Only the cream of each craft need apply; she would have nothing that was not one-of-a-kind, designed for her alone. The specially woven curtains for the windows of the Hôtel d'Evreux were rumoured to cost five thousand *louis* apiece. *Ebenistes* such as Oeben and Cressent created the unique, curvaceous furniture that filled her houses, and became the signature of the age of Louis Quinze. The brothers Martin offered their lacquer. Aubusson and the Gobelins wove tapestries and carpets. From the hands of Verbeeckt and Rousseau came carvings, panelling from Pineau, wall decorations from Huet.

She collected. How she collected! The instinct to adorn the nest brought the expensive miscellany flooding in, and the *livres* pouring out. She made excited little speeches to Louis as the presentation boxes and packing crates yielded up priceless crystal, engraved gemstones and cameos, gold boxes, silver goblets, *objets* of every sort.

Porcelains, especially, arrived in an endless stream. These exquisite trifles were her lifelong passion: vases and plates, statuettes, chocolate cups, patch boxes, sugar bowls, cellars – and the china animals she collected by the thousands. Agents gathered them in India, China, Korea, Japan and, closer to home, from the Meissen works in Saxony and the royal manufactory at Vincennes. (Eventually, to indulge her, Louis moved the Vincennes manufactory, complete with its staff and their families, from its original site to the village of Sèvres near her château of Bellevue. The marquise became its official sponsor. The king found it amusing to hold annual sales of Sèvres ware in Versailles, playing sales clerk himself, with a smile for those who placed large orders.)

A new generation of French sculptors and painters lined their pockets with royal largesse. At Bellevue, Pigalle's nymphs played in a grotto with Coustou's serene Apollo. Falconet carved for Pompadour; after her death Catherine the Great would spirit him away to create his masterpiece, the equestrian statue of Peter the Great, in St Petersburg. The painters were a roll call of the rococo: Oudry and Pierre, who lavished their talents on Pompadour's dining-room walls; Carle Van Loo, who painted her as a Turkish sultana; Louis's special discovery, Jean Baptiste Chardin; and the cranky, brilliant Maurice Quentin La Tour, who was insufferably rude to the king when he sat for his portrait, and got away with it.

Everywhere, luscious flesh poured from the brush of François Boucher. *Décorateur* extraordinary, he filled room after room with his *pastorales*, created the costumes and scenery for the marquise's *petits théâtres*, dipped into pornography, at her request, to enliven Louis's bedroom. In idle moments, he tinted Madame's fans and decorated her missal.

Fortunes were made by humbler citizens, the gardeners and husbandmen. At Versailles, Compiègne and Fontainebleau, she created rustic 'hermitages' long before Marie Antoinette fancied life as a shepherdess. For Pompadour and Louis, they were tranquil retreats from the crowds and formality of the royal palaces – garden pavilions in an Eden she filled with an incredible variety of trees, bushes and plants her agents transplanted from the most exotic points of the compass.

For a woman who spent half her life with a head cold, she was passionate about smells. Her gardens were skilfully arranged symphonies of scent, thrown off by orange and lemon trees, oleanders, lilacs, jasmine and myrtle, rose trees in a hundred romantic varieties, and beds of every fragrant flower that patience, skill and unlimited funds could bring to bloom. Vegetable gardens supplied her kitchens (she sliced off a chunk of the Champs Elysées to plant parsnips and cabbage for the Hôtel d'Evreux in Paris); barnyards housed cows, goats and donkeys (she thought asses' milk was a therapeutic drink); henhouses sheltered the tropical birds the king liked to breed. The oases were repeated, with expensive variations, around each hermitage and mansion. Wherever she and the king might conceivably meet out of doors, she created a carefully manicured setting of colour, perfume and country charm.

It was clearly impossible for the marquise and her royal lover to supervise spending on such a vast scale and have time left for anything else. In the time-honoured tradition of her post, the new *maîtresse* sent for her relatives; it was a blessing for France that they were so few. Uncle-in-law Tournehem suddenly appeared as *Directeur-général des Bâtiments du Roi* (Superintendant of Crown Buildings). Juggling the ledgers and looting the royal purse to pay for Pompadour's far-flung acquisitions, he warmed the seat for eighteen-year-old brother Abel François Poisson. Abel was quickly created the Marquis de Marigny. (Court wits dubbed him – and he mocked himself – as the Marquis de Marinière ('Fishy'). Marigny, predatory, rude, but quick to learn and eager to climb, was dispatched to Italy to acquire culture, under the tutelage of the artist Charles Nicolas Cochin. The other blood relation to join the marquise was Papa Poisson. He was ennobled, provided with a fat estate but kept at arm's length, socially. The old swindler's manners were too crude for the court. There was the unforgettable moment when he confronted a new footman who sought to bar his way to his daughter's apartment. 'Rascal,' sputtered the head of the house of Poisson, 'learn that I am the father of the king's whore!' Thereafter, he was welcomed by the marquise only in private, although they remained close until his death ten years later.

Pompadour's defenders are fond of claiming that her legacy to the nation would have been immense, had not the leaders of the French Revolution broken up her bequests in distress sales. The Goncourt brothers hailed her as the Queen of Rococo. It took two lawyers to sort out her estate, and eight months to sell it off. Her commercial protégés, the tapestry weavers, drapers, furniture makers, goldsmiths, china-painters, shop-keepers and gardeners, shed tears of frustrated avarice when she died. The question stubbornly persists: is it reasonable to suggest that the wealth of France was wisely invested in bric-à-brac?

In the taverns, threadbare Frenchmen had good reason to snarl, 'daughter of a leech, yourself a leech!' Overtaxed, underfed, they heard rumours of the cost of a mansion like Bellevue with fury. Its Lilliputian theatre, decorated *à la Chinois*, cost fifty thousand crowns. Officially, the treasury was poorer by two and a half million *livres* for the completed château, but the crowds who gathered to watch its construction knew differently. Eight hundred workmen on the site for two and a half years may have boosted the bill as high as seven million.

From the otherwise niggardly Louis, who allowed Madame de Mailly to appear in ragged chemises, the marquise enveigled an ever more generous torrent of gold. Madame du Barry, later, outshone her predecessor with single extravagances, such as her famous diamond-covered bodice, but for sustained success in separating royal lover from royal *livres*, Pompadour must remain the uncontested champion of the *ancien régime*. She told Madame du Hausset, 'He doesn't mind signing for a million, but he hates to part with little sums out of his purse.'

Pompadour's personal allowance was a modest thirty-three thousand *livres* per annum (about seventy thousand pounds sterling, or one hundred and fifty thousand dollars). Her income bore not the slightest relation to her expenditures; she showered a hundred thousand *livres* on a single three-day royal visit to Crécy. In the twenty years she enjoyed Louis's favour, she managed to extract a total of thirty-six million *livres* from him; in modern currency, about eighty million pounds sterling (one hundred and sixty million dollars), or nearly four million pounds (eight million dollars) a year.

It was the scale of things, finally, that provoked the people's bitterness. Their fathers had groaned at the expense of Louis XIV's stupendous château at Versailles, but they were expected, under Louis XV, to foot the bills for a series of refined but distinctly un-monumental mansions and pretty cottages. They paid dearly for whims that sometimes did not last a day. The flower beds of Bellevue were a case in point. The château opened in December, a month in which nature refused to furnish Pompadour with flower beds in full bloom. Undeterred, she found a way to import the flowers she needed for the king's inaugural visit. As she welcomed Louis, the gardens of Bellevue ravished the senses with a spectacle of colour and fragrance – each blossom hand-crafted and perfumed by the china makers of Vincennes. The astonished king took the china flowers for real ones. A charming deception, rewarded by a gasp of appreciative laughter. Who among the guests had the impertinence to question the cost?

Chapter Sixteen

In the Cave of the Griffin

A pinchpenny attitude brought down Pompadour's first opponent among the ministers. He was Louis's comptroller of finances, Philibert Orry, Comte Vignory, Seigneur de la Chapelle. More or less honest, he survived in his post for fifteen years, until he foolishly questioned the bills he was asked to pay by the king's new *maîtresse*. Moreover, he was a foe of the Pâris brothers, her Papa's former employers and close friends of the family Poisson. Even if the Pârises' hatred and his own stinginess did not spell his ruin, his portfolio as superintendant of crown buildings did. It was the position Pompadour coveted for her brother Abel. Exit Orry in the winter of 1745. Enter Jean-Baptiste de Machault d'Arnouville, a comptroller who was willing to approve the squandering, if not the squanderer. With Machault came le Normant de Tournehem, to fill in at the public works desk until the Marquis de Marigny returned from his education in Italy.

In the same season in which she drew first blood, the Duc de Luynes wrote of Madame de Pompadour:

Everyone seems to think she is extremely polite. Not only is she not ill-natured and never speaks evil of anybody, but she forbids such talk in her presence. She is bright and talkative. Far removed up to now from arrogance . . .

Pompadour turned an amiable face to the royal family, the ministers and her fellow courtiers, bewildering the world with her modesty and kindness. She let it be known that her patronage could be had for the asking, by those who offered their friendship in return. The protégés hurried to her side.

At first, her coterie was dominated by writers, artists and financial types. Voltaire, despite the king's horror of his godlessness, was awarded posts (and incomes) as Gentleman of the Bedchamber and Historiographer of France. He was elected to the Académie Française in 1746.

The politicians, scenting opportunity, quickly formed ranks in her boudoir. Those who did not, learned the marquise could be a formidable enemy, when crossed.

In the spring of 1747, she nailed up her second trophy, the first of the hated d'Argenson brothers, Louis's foreign minister, René Louis de Voyer, Marquis d'Argenson. He was anti-Spanish, and Madame Infante, married to a Spanish prince, loathed him. He bridled at Pompadour's increasing interference, which she had no intention of discontinuing. The women joined forces to ask for his dismissal. D'Argenson was abruptly sacked, even as the court applauded him for arranging the second marriage of the dauphin, to Marie-Josèphe of Saxony.

Louis and his new minister, the Marquis Louis de Puysieulx, disgraced the nation in 1748 at the peace congress of Aachen, which ended the War of the Austrian Succession. Thanks to Maréchal de Saxe, the French dealt from considerable strength at the treaty table, but Louis timidly gave away territory the maréchal's armies had bled to take. He withdrew his *mousquetaires* from the Austrian Netherlands. His ally, Frederick of Prussia, stubbornly kept Silesia. When the Treaty of Aix-la-Chapelle was concluded, it recognized Maria Theresa's right to the Habsburg throne, and her husband's election as the Holy Roman Emperor Francis I. Frenchmen, cheated of their conquests, sneered that they were 'working for the Prussian king'.

The Duc de Richelieu, a veteran campaigner, openly damned Aachen as 'a masterpiece of stupidity, if not of corruption'. Saxe, the hero of Fontenoy and the Lowlands, wrote:

France, by giving up her conquests, was warring against herself. Her enemies remained as powerful, only she was weakened, with a million subjects less and almost no finances.

The maréchal carried his complaints to the grave in 1750, dying at the age of fifty-four. Rumour had it that the great cavalryman, a celebrated womanizer, drew his last breath astride. A verse commemorated his death:

Whores will weep
and Englishmen will laugh,
The time has come
for Maurice's epitaph.

Louis, stung by his commanders' reaction to the treaty, huffed that 'not being a merchant, he did not choose to bargain'. Such a diplomatic disaster might have been expected to ruin Pompadour, whose ambush of d'Argenson had put Puysieulx in charge. It did not. The king sullenly turned from his professional advisors to confide in, and listen to, his brilliant paramour.

In April 1749, she matched wits with the minister of marine, Jean Frédéric Phelippeaux, Comte de Maurepas. Maurepas was one of the truly dangerous men of Versailles, a pamphleteer and gutter poet of uninhibited vileness. He had earned the dying hatred of the Duchesse de Châteauroux with his libels; now he used the same tactics in an attempt to topple a favourite of infinitely greater intelligence and tenacity.

Maurepas openly mocked Pompadour's family, her breeding and her morals, but the king continued to find him amusing. He had known the witty, impudent minister all his life, and was too loyal and too lazy to discipline him. Pompadour retaliated by meddling in Maurepas's conferences with the king, one day criticizing his policies, the next day demanding that he retract a *lettre de cachet*. Maurepas protested, 'His Majesty must command it . . .' The king gave in to her, telling his minister to 'do what Madame suggests, please'. There came a royal interview from which the *maîtresse* actually dismissed him. 'Monsieur de Maurepas,' she sighed, 'you are turning the king yellow. Good day to you, Monsieur Maurepas.' The king was silent. Maurepas left. From that moment, his feud with Pompadour was open, and lethal.

He struck at her with a *poissonade* in which he bared the marquise's most heartbreaking secret, a medical infirmity which threatened to end her sexual relations with the king. At thirty, Pompadour suffered from leucorrhoea, a condition commonly known as 'whites', or *fleurs blanches*. In all probability, she had sustained a serious tear in the cervix of the womb during the birth of her daughter Alexandrine. Now, her inflamed vaginal tissues gave off a profuse white discharge, an embarrassment for any woman, a personal disaster for a royal concubine. With this horrid condition poisoning her intimate moments with Louis, she was reduced to tears when she discovered the following note under her table napkin at Marly:

> *La marquise à bien des appas,*
> *Ses traits son vifs, ses grâces franches;*
> *Et les fleurs naissent sous ses pas;*
> *Mais, hélas! ce sont des fleurs blanches.*

> The marquise is, indeed, attractive;
> Her face is bright, her graces are real,
> And flowers spring up beneath her feet
> – But, alas! they are white flowers.

The moment she read it, she knew the filthy thing was all over Paris and Versailles. She was equally certain its author was Maurepas. Pale with fury, she confronted the minister in his apartments.

'I will not have it said of me that I have the ministers sent for; I come to fetch them,' she began. 'When will you know the authors of these songs?' (Maurepas served also as minister for Paris, the ostensible source of the *poissonade*.)

Maurepas smiled, 'When I will know, Madame, I will tell the king.'

'You hold the king's mistresses in very small account, Monsieur.'

He bowed low, turning the knife. 'I have always respected them, Madame, *of whatever kind they might be*.'

Pompadour reported the conversation to Louis, but even the comte's insolence was not enough to dislodge him. She embarked on a campaign of carefully staged hysterics, pretending that she lived in mortal fear of Maurepas. Was he not the rumoured poisoner of the Duchesse de Châteauroux? Her retainers watched the cooks in the kitchens. She refused food if the minister was in the room. Her physician, armed with an antidote, slept in the next room at night. When Maurepas scoffed at her play-acting, she made common cause with Richelieu, submitting a memorandum to the king that accused the minister of embezzling navy funds.

Maurepas riposted by pointing out the extravagances of his accusers. He finally ventured too far in his public defiance, when he exclaimed before witnesses, 'I bring ill luck to all of them . . . Madame de Mailly came to see me two days before her sister took her place, and everyone knows I poisoned the duchesse!'

The king sent him packing at one in the morning. Maurepas's estate at Pontchartrain was too close to Versailles, so Louis ordered him into exile at Bourges.

In September, 1749, the king underscored the triumph of his *maîtresse* over his minister by taking Pompadour to Le Havre to inspect the fleet

Maurepas had formerly governed. She was received in state by the locals. Louis spent a memorable day or two hunting at the Duc de Bouillon's château de Navarre. The trip accomplished little else except to provoke anger in Paris over its expense.

Riots broke out in the capital in the spring of 1750. According to Barbier, they were triggered by the disappearance of a child. There were lurid rumours of depraved courtiers at Versailles who bathed in the blood of babes as a cure for leprosy. The Parisians nearly killed Berryer, the police chief. For good measure, they raised a great cry against the king's immorality in general, and Pompadour in particular. Soon, she could not venture to the Paris opera without being mocked from the stalls, nor attend dinner parties in the city without mud being hurled at her carriage. Louis's answer to the unrest was to retreat further into his *maîtresse's* elegant fantasies. He ordered a road built, the Chemin de la Révolte, which bypassed Paris when he journeyed to Compiègne. 'I do not see why I should go,' he sulked, 'where people call me Herod.'

After Maurepas, there was never again a question of Pompadour's power, only whom she would befriend and whom she would strike down. As Louis's confidant and his surrogate, all appointments were secured through her, all fortune spilled from her fingers. An admirer, Emmanuel, Duc de Cröy, wrote:

> It was most agreeable to deal with such a pretty prime minister, whose laughter was enchanting and who was such a good listener . . . there was perhaps not a single office or favour that had not come from her.

Business to be presented to the monarch was reviewed first by Pompadour, in a cabinet meeting conducted daily in her boudoir. There was one chair. The *maîtresse* occupied it. The ministers, some of ducal and princely rank, stood.

Her pre-eminence was attested by her enemies and her friends alike. The Marquis d'Argenson, bitterly watching her success from his exile, observed in March 1748, 'She sells everything, even regiments. The king is increasingly governed by her.' He continued:

> She arranges, she decides, she behaves as though the king's ministers were hers . . . more than ever she is the First Minister. She dominates the king as strong personalities dominate weak ones.

Edmond de Goncourt, her most influential biographer in this century, was disgusted by her avarice:

A daughter of the *bourgeoisie*, Madame de Pompadour forms her reign and dream after the image and standard of the *bourgeoisie*. All-powerful as she is, her will cannot fashion itself to greatness; and the government of her caprice betrays the meanness and littleness of the order from which she springs. It is more often than not but a meddling and haggling direction . . . she brings also to her office and her role the villainies and the appetites of her family and her race: she has in her the blood of the tax-collector . . . she does not govern, she grabs. In her hands, the monarchy is no more than a list of benefices, and you see her presuming on her favour and attracting everything to her – money, honours, territory, pensions, places, stipends, decorations, graces, remainders. She is the first favourite to be dishonoured by scandal, and by the cupidity and insatiability of her method of collection of her fortune . . .

She interfered in every phase of the government. Browbeating the Parlement was no more difficult than commanding the cabinet, and she had the lawyers on the carpet when it suited her. An account of one such encounter was set down in 1757 by the Président de Meinières, to whom she refused an official post for his son, on the grounds that Meinières was fuelling the quarrel with Louis over Papal policy. She out-reasoned and out-talked the président, who did not give in to her demands, although he carried away a vivid memory of his hostess:

Alone, standing up near the fire, she looked at me with an air of hauteur which will remain imprinted on my memory all my life; holding her head up straight without bowing, she looked me up and down in the most imposing fashion in the world.

Increasingly, it was Pompadour who spoke for France to foreign dignitaries. Charles Joseph, Prince de Ligne, the veteran Austrian diplomat, was nonplussed when he was received by Louis's paramour: 'After paying my respects to all the royal family, I was taken to a sort of second queen, who had the air of being the first.' D'Argenson, again, confided to his diaries:

She tells departing ambassadors, 'Continue, I am very pleased with you; you know I have long been your friend.' She said recently to the foreign ministers, 'For several Mondays, it will not be possible for the king to see you; as I suppose you will not come to Crécy to visit us.' That 'us' (*nous*) likened her to the Queen.

Dufort, Comte de Cheverny, who was the *Introduceur des Ambassadeurs* and who adored her, described her *lever* at Compiègne:

> . . . the ambassadors, except the nuncio, after being presented to the royal family, went to her reception. Nobody understood so well how to treat everyone in a fitting manner. To avoid etiquette, she received at her toilette. The arts, the talents, the sciences, paid her homage. The talk was gay and natural though not profound. Her conversation was adapted to each of her visitors.

All this political hubbub, added to the endless personal demands of the king, would have tired an Amazon. D'Argenson noted, without sympathy, 'She cannot stand up to the life she leads – late hours, spectacles, always thinking how to amuse the king.'

The lady herself wearied, and admitted it. In a letter to the Comtesse de Lutzelbourg, she lamented:

> The life I lead is terrible; I hardly have a minute to myself. Rehearsals and performances, and twice a week, continual journeys to the Petit-Château or La Muette, etc. Enormous load of indispensable duties, Queen, Dauphin, Dauphiness, three daughters, two Infantas; you can judge whether it is possible to breathe. Be sorry for me.

One day, she cried out to her maid, Madame du Hausset, that her life was 'like that of the early Christians, a perpetual combat!'

Let there be no mistake, she was a willing martyr. The English memoirist, Lord Augustus Hervey, described Madame de Pompadour at the peak of her career, as 'the handsomest creature I think I ever saw, and looking like a rock of diamonds'.

To her protégé, the abbé de Bernis, she quipped, 'Not only do I have all the nobility at my feet, even my little dog is beset with homages.'

She knew, better than anyone, how fleeting was public adulation. Much more frightening was her awareness that her position was forever at risk, as long as there were beautiful women in the court and Louis had eyes in his head. The knowledge was torment when, in 1751, her doctor's orders and her own inclinations forced her to leave the king's bed.

By 1752 there was a challenger. She nearly drove Pompadour out, in an intricate plot which was the very model of a court intrigue. The girl was Charlette Rosalie Romanet, Comtesse de Choiseul, a niece of Pompadour's closest friend, the Comtesse d'Estrades. Pompadour had actually sponsored the girl's wedding at Bellevue, loaning the château for her honeymoon. Fat little d'Estrades, in a twisted fever of jealousy, repaid Pompadour with betrayal. She became the mistress of her friend's sworn enemy, the minister of war, Marc-Pierre, Comte d'Argenson (brother of the exiled foreign minister). D'Argenson, on d'Estrades's advice, picked the precise moment Pompadour's love-making began to falter, to thrust Madame Choiseul-Romanet into the king's path. Eighteen and essentially brainless, the dewy young thing required hour-by-hour coaching from Auntie d'Estrades. Louis got her pregnant, but she withheld a complete surrender until he agreed to present her as *maîtresse déclarée*. During the autumn visit to Fontaine-bleau, she somehow obtained Louis's promise in writing, to banish Pompadour. Breathless, her dress still undone, she rushed from the king's embrace to d'Argenson and her aunt, crying, 'Yes, yes, I am loved! He is happy. She is to be sent away.'

Pompadour's rescue came from a most unlikely source. Etienne François, Comte de Stainville, the challenger's cousin, overcame his dislike of Pompadour to advance himself. He filched the crucial letter from Madame de Choiseul-Romanet and presented it to the marquise. Pompadour staged a teary scene in which she confronted Louis, letter in hand; the king, who hated indiscretion above all social sins, banished Madame de Choiseul-Romanet.

The girl died soon after, when her royal bastard was delivered stillborn. D'Estrades remained in Pompadour's orbit until the favourite caught her red-handed at her spying. *Finis* d'Estrades. Soon afterwards, the king made Pompadour a duchesse. Pompadour, deeply in Stain-ville's debt, had him appointed ambassador to Rome. It was the start of a long, profitable association between the ugly, witty courtier and the great *maîtresse*.

His fingers scorched by Madame de Choiseul-Romanet, Louis decided that he cared little for the intricate amusements of courtly seduction. The duchesses, comtesses, and marquises who elbowed each other aside to insert themselves into his bed presented unwanted complications. In his forties, he demanded physical release, frequently and without finesse. His ideal partners were simple, virginal and very young. (Virginity was especially desired, Barbier reported, because Louis had once contracted gonorrhoea from a butcher's daughter. His procurers sought girls of certified purity, who had not yet menstruated, much less copulated – warehousing them here and there, until their sexual bloom made them interesting.)

With Pompadour's blessing, Louis established the Parc aux Cerfs, the 'Deer Park' of dark legend. It was inspired, in all probability, by a conversation between the king and the Duc de Richelieu. 'How is it,' Louis asked his lecherous friend, 'at sixty-five you have the same desires as at twenty-five?' Richelieu answered, without hesitation, 'Sire, I frequently change the object. Novelty produces the desired result.'

Louis XV's novelties were brought to him, as early as 1752, in a tiny suite in the *attique du nord* at Versailles. This *trébuchet* (bird trap) proved to be impractical; his *grisettes* were too noisy, disturbing the insomniac Madame de Pompadour who slept immediately below. She suggested establishing a convent for them, but a less elaborate scheme was soon worked out to secure the first of a cluster of royal houses of assignation in the Parc aux Cerfs district of Versailles. Once a breeding farm for Louis XIII's stags, the area had become a spill-over suburb for courtiers unable to secure decent apartments in the main château. No. 4, Rue Saint-Médéric, a few hundred yards from the Orangerie, was fairly typical of the king's houses, a one-storey residence of four rooms, with a garden and a high wall. In it, his girls were looked after by an 'abbess', Madame Bertrand, assisted by two maids, a cook, a coachman and a porter. Charles de Mather, marquis de Valfons, who described the Parc aux Cerfs from the vantage point of a trusted staff officer, reported:

> There were two or three occupants at the same time, who had no communications with each other . . . each had her own little house . . . they received no one.

The girls were recruited from lower-class families in Paris and other cities by Lebel, his fellow valets, Berryer's police officers and female agents. While in residence, they were treated well, dressed becomingly (some came away with diamonds!), and their health carefully monitored. They were allowed teachers, to introduce them to the social graces. There were amusements. They had a private box at the *Comédie*, with a grille.

The names of Louis's nymphs have been lost, for the most part – their residence in the Parc aux Cerfs was too transient. A few were briefly memorable. Iris de Bomango was so devastated by the stillbirth of her baby, that she fled to a convent of contemplative nuns, where she became Soeur Clothilde. An English rose, who caught Louis's eye as a lady-in-waiting to the Duchess of Devonshire, used her earnings while in the Parc aux Cerfs to return to London and open an entirely respectable school for young ladies. The statuesque Mademoiselle Romans nearly broke Pompadour's heart with the beauty of the bastard son she bore the king. (The child, abandoned and later rescued from years of misadventure as a foundling, eventually became a priest.)

One of the most celebrated residents was Louise O'Murphy, the beautiful daughter of an Irish shoemaker of Paris. She was brought to the king's attention at thirteen, supposedly by that master seducer, Casanova, who claimed to have had her painted in the nude. She occupied the house in the Rue Saint-Médéric for several years, and became the favourite model of the painter Boucher. O'Murphy was eventually discharged because she broke the king's incognito. Louis posed as a Polish aristocrat, with entrée to Versailles, and no one was supposed to know the identity of the master of the house. (Hundreds of people actually did know, but Louis had to have his pretence.) When O'Murphy departed, she was given an extremely handsome retirement, of four hundred thousand *livres*. All her sisters in sin retired well, if not so generously rewarded, following pregnancies. (Their 'dowries' ranged from ten thousand to one hundred thousand *livres*.) Some of the *accouchments*, conducted in another house on the Avenue de Saint Cloud, were supervised by Pompadour and her maid, Madame du Hausset. Girls from the Parc aux Cerfs were usually told that their babies were born dead. The children were given annuities and put up for adoption by respectable couples. Their mothers were settled in marriages to wealthy men who considered the king's bordello an excellent finishing school. For the backstairs entrée such accommodations gave them, there were always bridegrooms eager to take the king's leavings. Few were disappointed, for there was no decline in the quantity or quality of girls who arrived and departed from the Parc aux Cerfs as the years went on.

The actual numbers have been hotly disputed, from a 'few dozens' cited by Louis's partisans, to eighteen hundred, charged by the Revolutionary historian J.L. Soulavie. The street wisdom of Paris was blunt, as always, and ruefully admiring: 'We are all Louis XV's bastards!' D'Angerville, in his *Vie Privée*, offered a sour financial indictment of the Parc aux Cerfs, estimating the cost of Louis's lust in the millions:

Independent of the injury which this abominable institution did to morals, it is dreadful to calculate the immense sums which it cost the State. In fact, who could sum up the expenses of that series of agents of all kinds, both principal and subordinate, exerting themselves to discover the objects of their researches – to go and fetch them from the extremities of the kingdom – to bring them to the place of their destination – to get them cleaned – to dress – to perfume them – and, in a word, to supply them with all the means of seduction that art could imagine. Add to this, the sums given those, who, not having the happiness to rouse the languid sensations of the Sultan, were not the less indemnified for their services, for their discretion, and especially for his contempt; – the reward due to those more fortunate nymphs, who gratified the temporary desires of the Monarch; . . . and we may judge that there was not any, one with another, who had not been a charge of a million, at least, to the public treasury. Let us only reckon that two in a week passed through this sink of infamy, that is to say, a thousand in ten years, and we shall have a capital of a thousand millions.

It was left to an Englishman, Thomas Carlyle, in his history of the French Revolution a century later, to denounce the royal appetite with a proper thunderclap of Old Testament rhetoric:

Thy foul harem; the curses of mothers, the tears and infamy of daughters! Miserable man! Thou 'hast done evil as thou couldst'; thy whole existence seems one hideous abortion and mistake of nature; the use and meaning of thee not yet known. Wert thou a fabulous Griffin, *devouring* the works of man; daily dragging virgins to thy cave; clad also in scales that no spear could pierce: no spear but Death's? A Griffin not fabulous, but real!

Between the revulsion of the nineteenth century and the lame excuses of the twentieth (that Louis XV was no better or worse than his times) probably lies a middle ground of judgement. In the fifteen years of Louis's visits to the Parc aux Cerfs, there was none of the cheerful, sociable vulgarity of his uncle Orléans, drinking and whoring with his *roués* in the Palais Royal; no affairs in the grand manner, of the kind which would later occupy Catherine of Russia; there was only a rich, middle-aged libertine, hurrying to his secret house to mount a faceless, nameless, barely pubescent girl, repeating his assignation with a different child night after night, selfish, debauched, and utterly alone.

The Parisian wags saluted Pompadour for her part in the unsavoury business, with a *poissonade*. It was a mock epitaph, somewhat premature, but merciless in its verdict:

> *Ci-gît qui fut vingt ans pucelle,*
> *Huit ans catin,*
> *Dix ans maquerelle.*

> Here lies one for twenty years a virgin,
> Eight years a whore,
> And ten years a pimp.

Chapter Seventeen

Petticoat II

Frederick the Great put the Marquise de Pompadour in her place, and Europe paid for his impertinence in blood.

Did the Prussian king owe courtesy to the French king's whore? The question was a travesty of protocol, but the fury it provoked in the *petits appartements* of Versailles helped to plunge the great powers into the Seven Years War. The overt causes of the conflict were less personal. Quarrels flared up over the bungled treaty of Aix-la-Chapelle. Hotheads in Vienna demanded vengeance for the Prussian conquest of Silesia. French and British territorial rivalries threatened to boil over in North America and India. But the fuse that sputtered under the treaty disputes and colonial skirmishes, and eventually ignited the last great war of the *ancien régime*, was Frederick's sardonic remark to Voltaire, '*Je ne la connais pas*'. ('I do not know her'.)

The cut was taken to heart, painfully, by a favourite who thought herself impervious to insult. Maurepas was gone, and with him the most vicious *poissonades* and pamphlets. Few of her enemies at Versailles dared to challenge her openly. The curses of the common people counted as little as the mud that occasionally spattered her carriage in Paris. Only the contempt of royalty could humiliate her.

Pompadour's self-control was remarkable. Not even personal heartbreak was allowed to distract her from her chosen rôle. When her daughter Alexandrine died in June 1754, a sorrowing Papa Poisson followed his grandchild to the grave within a fortnight. Two members of Pompadour's tiny family were abruptly swept away, yet a few weeks later, the Duc de Cröy marvelled at her gaiety, as she directed a royal *voyage* to Compiègne.

It was an altogether different matter, when Frederick II wounded her pride. The unwitting agent of the snub was her illustrious protégé, Voltaire. Frederick, an enthusiastic poet and political essayist, was a Voltaire disciple. In 1749, the playwright succumbed to years of royal flattery by mail, and accepted the king's invitation to visit him at his palace of Sans-Souci. Frederick welcomed him with cries of pleasure, springing up from the banquet table to kiss Voltaire's hand. When the writer presented Madame de Pompadour's compliments, his host was deliberately offensive. '*Je ne la connais pas.*' He went further, 'I do not think the King of Prussia need be circumspect towards a *demoiselle* Poisson, particularly if she is arrogant and lacking in the respect due to crowned heads.'

Frederick could hardly be blamed for his pique. Pompadour had been cool to his initial overtures in 1747, shrugging aside his envoy, baron Johann Chambrier. She ridiculed the Prussian king to Louis in private. Personal barbs began to fly in earnest after the peace of 1748, when the Prussian king noticed that his French subsidies were drying up. Through the grapevine of international gossip, Frederick tweaked Louis with references to *Mademoiselle Poisson* ('Miss Fish'). If he was in a particularly mischievous mood, he spoke of the reign of 'Petticoat II'. He amused himself by writing obscene verses about Pompadour, and paying French hacks to publish clandestine 'revelations' of the private life of the French king and his *maîtresse*. He christened his favourite bitch 'Pompadour'. Everyone knew the dog slept in Frederick's bed.

The mud-slinging was all the more demeaning, when compared to Frederick's gallant correspondence with the late Duchesse de Châteauroux at the time of Louis's victories in Flanders. Châteauroux was nobly born. Pompadour was not, nor could Louis's conferring of ducal dignities change her origins.

Louis joined the fray, with some long-distance sniping of his own. Frederick offered a small pension to the writer d'Alembert. Louis made a public joke of his stinginess. At Versailles, the Prussian was commonly referred to as 'the monster of Potsdam', or 'the Attila of the north'. Louis scorned him as

. . . a madman ready to risk everything to win . . . although he has no morals, no religion and no principles. He wants to create a stir and he will. After all, Julian the Apostate did.

The attack on Frederick's irreligion was an angry reaction to the sanctuary he granted to French Huguenot refugees. The charge of immorality referred to Barberina Campanini, the Italian dancer who was the object of the Prussian king's one attempt at heterosexual philandering. (To everyone's surprise, he squandered thousands of thalers on the girl. Voltaire said it was because she had the legs of a young boy.) More degrading than Campanini, in Louis's view, were the good-looking valets and guardsmen who satisfied Frederick's homosexual appetites.

Louis's denunciations sounded thin, coming as they did from a Catholic monarch who could not receive the Host, because he was the proprietor and sole patron of the Parc aux Cerfs. In his monumental nineteenth-century *Histoire de France*, Bon Louis Henri Martin wrote of Louis XV:

> He was persuaded that a king who sustained the cause of the Church could not be damned for his private sins. He dreamed of a Holy War from the recesses of the Parc aux Cerfs.

Like many ineffectual men, Louis XV sought refuge in grandiose daydreams. Somehow, he would change the world with a magnificent gesture – to the awed surprise of the officials who dominated him in real life. The idea obsessed him from the death of Cardinal Fleury until his own death, thirty years later.

To realize his dream, Louis played at espionage, creating a network of royal agents known as the *secret du roi*. The existence of his apparatus, which often worked at cross-purposes with official French policy, was suspected, but never proved, by his ministers. They were alone in their ignorance. The Prussians and Austrians both knew – the Austrians going so far as to return decoded messages from the French king to his ambassador.

(Pompadour tried, with mixed results, to worm her way into Louis's secret of secrets. She nagged the Prince de Conti, in whom Louis confided, for information. When she got nowhere, she picked Louis's pocket for his secret mail. Once, she fed the king an opiate, stole his key and rifled the drawers of his desk. She had no more success, by all accounts, than the French government.)

Apart from teaching Frederick II a lesson, two projects, both quixotic, dominated the *secret du roi*. The first pipe-dream was inspired by the king's cousin, Louis-François de Bourbon, Prince de Conti. Conti had inherited a claim to the throne of Poland from his father, who was elected king by the Poles in 1697 but never enthroned. Louis, aggravated by Polish politics since King Stanislaus fled Danzig in 1733, took up Conti's claim. (If not Conti, he favoured, as an alternate candidate, one of his daughter-in-law's brothers. The widowed dauphin had taken as his second wife Marie-Josèphe of Saxony.) In Louis's Polish fantasy, Conti would reign in Warsaw, France would gain a new ally in the East, and Louis would preen before his doubting ministers.

The Empresses of Russia and Austria and the King of Prussia would, presumably, gnash their teeth.

His second will-o'-the-wisp was nothing less than the invasion and subjugation of England. He was abetted in this silliness by the Broglie brothers, comte and duc, both senior army officers and both blindly dedicated to an all-out confrontation with the British. Together, the king and his dotty *maréchaux* envisaged a second Norman conquest. The world would turn in wonder to the king of France, revealed once and for all as a military genius, and as the true, favourite son of the Church. Europe's damnable Protestant power would be brought to heel.

The agents of the *secret du roi* whom Louis trusted to bring about these historic triumphs were an incompetent lot, stumbling through their paces in Austria, England, Holland, Naples, Poland, Turkey, Sweden and Switzerland. They were directed by Charles-François, Comte de Broglie, who assumed overall responsibility after an initial cloak-and-dagger assignment in Warsaw. Broglie doted on secret ciphers, disguises, dark-of-night meetings and the paraphernalia of spying almost as much as his master.

Their chief Russian operative was the chevalier Douglas, a Scottish Catholic who prowled the streets of St Petersburg as a fur merchant. At Louis's suggestion, Douglas spent days reducing his reports to near-microscopic dimensions, sending them home in a false-bottomed tobacco case. Fur-trade names like 'lynx' and 'ermine' were codes. In years of spying on the Russians, Douglas yielded results as minuscule as his messages.

Jean-Pierre Tercier, the first clerk of the foreign ministry, was a trusted agent. He displayed considerable promise, but had the bad grace to die prematurely. Louis suffered through a tense day or two, when it was learned that Tercier left behind a desk stuffed with correspondence of the *secret du roi*. He organized a backstairs raid on the ministry, to foil the curiosity of the foreign minister, the Duc de Choiseul.

On the English front, the Marquis de la Rozière, an army engineer, scouted the French and English Channel coasts to plan transport and logistics for an invasion force. A courier carrying his reports was picked up by the French at Calais. The king was forced to rescue the captive from his own police.

By far the most embarrassing of Louis's spies was his London agent, Charles Géneviève, chevalier d'Eon de Beaumont. Army captain of dragoons, war hero and female impersonator, d'Eon first went snooping in St Petersburg, where, as 'Lia de Beaumont', he claimed to be the confidant of the Czarina Elizabeth. Sent to London to prepare for the great invasion, he was wildly indiscreet. At one point, he published his correspondence, involving the French foreign ministry in a major scandal. D'Eon quarrelled with Tercier and Louis XV, and eventually became a somewhat unwelcome legacy to Louis XVI. In 1775, that king sent Pierre-Augustin Caron de Beaumarchais, the creator of Figaro and another agent of the *secret du roi*, to try to reason with him. D'Eon flirted, won over Beaumarchais, and blackmailed the king into paying him a pension, in return for the secret documents he had hoarded over the years. When the spy visited France in 1777, Louis XVI was forced to pay for a trousseau for his appearance at court. The transvestite swept into Versailles in a blue taffeta gown trimmed in puce, needing a shave, hair powdered and piled high. He ended his days in London, maintaining his female disguise until his death at the age of eighty-three.

The spies, and their penny-dreadful exploits, accomplished next to nothing. To Choiseul, who guessed what was afoot, the *secret du roi* was harmless entertainment for the king, obtained at bargain rates. (For the three decades of its existence, the *secret* cost the French taxpayers only eighty to one hundred thousand *livres* a year.)

Louis's vision of a Holy War against Prussia actually began to take shape in June 1755, when the British commander Edward Boscawen captured two French men-of-war, the *Alcide* and the *Lys*, off Newfoundland. Frederick, ever the friend of superior firepower, hastened to negotiate a new treaty with George II, providing Austria's gifted chancellor, Count Wenzel Anton von Kaunitz, with the diplomatic opening of a lifetime.

As Vienna's envoy to the Bourbon court in 1750, Kaunitz had become an intimate of Pompadour. They were blossoms from the same hothouse. The epicene Austrian was so terrified of fresh air that he took his riding practice indoors. He limited his diet to boiled capon, required four valets to powder his wig, foppishly wore as many as nine black silk coats – and was as devoted to decorating as Pompadour herself. He had wit. He likened his 1748 offer of an alliance to foreign minister de Puysieulx, to 'trying to make a canary digest an ox'.

In 1755, Kaunitz, who was intimately aware of the *secret du roi*, knew exactly how to approach the French king – with a thrilling secret intrigue. Louis XV would at last have his longed-for moment on the stage of history, when he turned Europe's system of national alliances on its head. Catholic France, allied with Catholic Austria, would render Protestant Prussia helpless.

Kaunitz by-passed the French foreign ministry completely and sent Austria's ambassador Count George Adam Stahremberg to seek Pompadour's help in laying the empress's proposals before Louis XV. At Stahremberg's urging, the virtuous Maria Theresa sent her most affectionate, personal greetings to Louis's official concubine. Though their existence has since been disputed, Thomas Carlyle insisted that Pompadour sighed over a series of letters written in the empress's own hand '. . . various little Notes from Imperial Majesty . . . which begin, *"Ma Cousine"*, *"Princesse et Cousine"*, *"Madame ma très Chère Soeur".'* Whether Maria Theresa herself set pen to paper is beside the point. Her sentiments were eloquently conveyed to the marquise through Stahremberg and Kaunitz. Catering to Pompadour's passion for collecting, the empress sent her a dainty lacquer writing-desk, worth seventy-seven thousand *livres*. It was decorated with a miniature of Maria Theresa set in precious stones.

The Austrians turned Pompadour's head completely. What happiness, after the insults of Frederick II! She met with Stahremberg in deep secrecy in the Babiole, or summer house, on her Bellevue estate. The third party to their conversation was her pet, Bernis, fresh from a tour of duty as the French ambassador to Venice. Bernis was a new man entirely, no longer '*Babet la bouquetière*', as Voltaire had once called him, because of his resemblance to a pretty Parisian flower-seller. Very grave and responsible, an amazingly good diplomatist despite a tendency to whine, he took up the Babiole negotiations for the king, under Pompadour's direction.

Stahremberg broke the news of Frederick II's flirtation with the English, quickly confirmed by French representatives in Berlin. The Austrian suggested a simple mutual defence agreement to offset the new Prussian-English axis. There was an enticing mention of a later trade of Parma, Madame Infante's tiny duchy, for the more spacious principality of the Austrian Netherlands.

In January 1756, Frederick actually signed the Treaty of Westminster. The English went on the offensive in North America and India. Louis retaliated with financial aid to help Maria Theresa take back Silesia from Frederick. All this was greeted with horror by Louis's heavily pro-Prussian ministers. Nevertheless, on 1 May 1756, Stahremberg, Bernis and Louis's foreign minister, Antoine Louis Rouillé, Comte de Jouy, signed the First Treaty of Versailles, which included a mutual pledge of twenty-four thousand men to defend each other's territory.

Pompadour was the guardian angel of the new alliance, to whom,

Stahremberg said, 'we owe everything'. From Vienna, Kaunitz wrote to the empress's '*très Chère Soeur*':

> . . . I must thank you for having been my guide. I must add that their Imperial Majesties do you full justice and entertain for you all the sentiments you could desire. . . . what remains to be done is too important for you to withhold your collaboration, to leave the task unfinished, and not to render you forever dear to your country. . . . I believe success to be assured, and no one will feel greater pleasure than myself in the fame and satisfaction you will derive from your services.

The Seven Years War began with Prussia's invasion of Saxony in August 1756. Frederick's excuse that he was only protecting Prussia from a plot by Russia and Austria, was angrily brushed aside at Versailles – he had marched into the homeland of the French dauphine Marie-Josèphe. Within days, Austria had her twenty-four thousand French *mousquetaires*, to help defend the dauphine's Saxon relatives.

Pompadour's patriotism knew no bounds. In her daily meetings with the ministers, it was plain that she intended to proceed from her triumphs in diplomacy to management of the war itself.

Her plans shattered to bits on the knifeblade of a ragged man named Robert-François Damiens. He was one of the thousands of spectators who came king-watching to Versailles every day. Late in the afternoon of 5 January 1757, he darted through a crowd of courtiers and guards who surrounded Louis in the marble court, as the king waited for a carriage to take him to Trianon. Damiens stabbed him in the right side with the shorter, penknife blade of a two-bladed knife. (The particular blade was important. Damiens would insist at his trial that he used the little blade, because he wished only to rouse the king to action, not to kill him.) Because it was bitterly cold, the king was muffled in a fur-lined overcoat, coat, vest, shirt and flannel undershirt. The layers of clothing kept the knife away from vital organs – it penetrated only three inches into the king's body – and cleansed the blade. Louis thought, as did many in the court, that the knife had been poisoned.

Because the court was at the Trianon palace, it took some time for messengers to fetch the queen, the dauphin, and Louis's doctors. The dauphin's own surgeon, Prudent Hevin, was in Versailles and was the first medical professional to reach the wounded monarch. Typically, he bled Louis – to treat a heavily bleeding wound. Louis, laid out on a bare mattress, dazed and hurting, called for a priest. He had been at his confession for an hour when the family rushed in.

'I am assassinated, madame, I am assassinated,' he told the queen. To the dauphin, he offered a brief sermon, 'You were born more fortunate than I. Administer this kingdom with the wisdom God gave you. Make your people happy.'

The king's first surgeon, Germaine de la Martinière, arrived with the party. He looked at the wound and pronounced it superficial. His opinion was shared by Hevin and the royal physician, François Quesnay. Quesnay said that such a wound would not have prevented another man from attending a ball.

Despite the doctors' optimism, Louis was convinced that he was dying, and on his way to the Seat of Judgement. Removed to his bedroom, he stayed prostrate, sighing and groaning, reinforced in his misery by the wailing of the queen and his daughters. For eight days, he refused to open his bed-curtains. Finally, a grizzled royal huntsman, the Marquis de Landsmath, took matters into his own hands. He strode into the sickroom. 'Get those mourners out of here,' he demanded. When the royal family left, he thrust a chamber pot into Louis's hands. 'Piss,' he ordered. Louis's urine was bloodless. 'Spit in my hand.' There was no sign of blood. Landsmath ripped open his own jerkin, baring a chest covered with the scars of war wounds. 'Look,' he ordered the king. 'These wounds were drinking troughs for flies, and I am still here. This wound,' he pointed to Louis's injury, 'is nothing. In a week we will run down a stag together.'

Although Landsmath's lecture got him up and about, Louis huddled in his bedroom for three more days, in an orgy of self-pity. He received few visitors. Pompadour was not one of them. Brooding on the attack, he lamented, ' . . . the body is doing well, but this (with a gesture to his head) is doing very badly, and this is impossible to heal.'

Damiens, who had been arrested on the spot, was interrogated and tried before the *Grand'chambre* of the Parlement. He was an unemployed manservant, a nobody of whom it was thought inconceivable that he had plotted his crime alone. The king, fresh from his latest confrontation with the Paris Parlement, was convinced that the very lawyers who now tried Damiens, had put him up to it.

Under torture, Damiens complained of the controversy over the Unigenitus Bull of Pope Clement XI. It enraged him that the squabble between pope, king and Parlement resulted in the refusal of the last rites to Frenchmen who could not prove a previous confession to a papal-approved priest. 'One ought not to refuse the sacraments to people who live holy lives,' Damiens cried, 'and who pray to God in church every day from morning till night. . . . If they had chopped the heads off five or six bishops this (the stabbing) would not have happened.'

He insisted he only wished to prick the king into action, to relieve the people of the tax burden of the new war, and break the power of unnamed ministers whom Damiens blamed for the sorry state of the nation.

Convicted of 'divine and human *lèse majesté* ', he forfeited his life on 28 March 1757, at the Place des Grèves, in the most savage execution of the reign. The event included picturesque tortures, staged for the benefit of an enormous crowd of spectators. His executioners ripped chunks of flesh from his body with pincers. Hot lead, mixed with sulphur, wax, resin and oil, was poured into the wounds. The offending right hand, still clutching his penknife, was doused in boiling sulphur, then lopped off. Damiens's tongue, which had uttered muddled subversions during his interrogation and trial, was torn from his head. All the while, the team of executioners tried unsuccessfully to quarter their victim, whipping teams of horse into exhaustion. Eventually, they were forced to hack off his limbs, one by one. They tossed his still living, breathing head and torso into a bonfire, where he cooked for four hours like a badly tended joint of beef. Damiens's brief moment of celebrity ended when his ashes were scattered to the wind.

Casanova, among others, got up a chic execution party of friends, spent three louis to rent a window overlooking the show, and reported the details. He took note of the ladies' cries of distress ('Oh, the poor horses!'), and of the sexual play in which his companions indulged while they watched. Their fondlings did not distract them from the entertaining horrors going on below.

Damiens, who was a little simple-minded, faced his fate with astounding fortitude. Not so Pompadour, who spent the days of the royal seclusion in tearful collapse. She wept and fainted, while she waited for Bernis and his bulletins on Louis's condition. In more than a fortnight, the king did not acknowledge that she existed. The memory of Metz was vivid, when Louis, prompted by the sanctimonious dauphin, the queen and the priests, banished the Duchesse de Châteauroux. In 1757, it was Pompadour's turn to tremble at the brink. The courtiers avoided her as if she were infected with a pox. Only a tiny group of loyalists kept the vigil with her: Bishop Bernis, her young admirer, Charles de Rohan, Prince de Soubise, Madame du Hausset and doctor Quesnay, Pompadour's friend the Maréchale de Mirepoix, and one or two others. In the midst of the crisis, Pompadour's protégé Machault, now the minister of marine, turned against her. With d'Argenson, the minister of war, he cooked up orders for her to leave. While she waited for a carriage to take her to the Hôtel d'Evreux in Paris, the Maréchale de Mirepoix intervened, insisting Machault had no authority. Pompadour took her advice. She ordered her servants, who were packing her belongings, to go slowly at their tasks. On the eleventh day, Louis appeared at the private staircase. Her control returned on the instant, and she greeted him joyously, without uttering the slightest reproach. Damiens, she told him, was certainly a madman. The nation was aghast at his crime and loved its king. The very next day, Louis went hunting.

She went hunting, too. Damiens achieved his wished-for purge of royal ministers when Pompadour demanded, and got, the resignations of Louis's ministers of war and marine. Small matter that French armies were taking the field against Frederick the Great. D'Argenson was summoned before her to answer for new *poissonades* which appeared each morning on Pompadour's terrace. (The pamphlets were reaching the disconsolate king in his daily mail, and in her eyes, D'Argenson was responsible, for he held the post of police lieutenant in addition to his portfolio as minister of war.)

The minister finally stiffened under her inquisition. 'Tell the king,' he said, 'in one of those moments of kindness when he refuses you nothing, not to ask me for them (the pamphlets). I would be only too glad to hold my tongue, but I cannot when he questions me.' Pompadour exploded, 'So you would rather be a good valet and see him unhappy!' Louis banished him to des Ormes in Touraine, where he went into exile with Pompadour's erstwhile confidante, the Comtesse d'Estrades. A careerist whose service to the king reached back fifteen years, the comte complained bitterly to Valfons, '. . . can he [the king] ever forget Metz where, when he was believed to be dead and was abandoned by all, I warmed him in my arms and never quitted him for a moment? It is not his will or his heart that sends me into exile but that wretched woman who has been up to mischief.'

Machault, Pompadour's own creature until he delivered her premature eviction notice, was treated more gently. The king missed him, and wrote so to Madame Infante. Machault went, all the same, convinced that the state, governed as it was by the whim of the favourite, was in peril. He confided to his diary, 'I am an old man but I will see the monarchy in its grave before I am in mine.' Pompadour even spatted briefly with Bernis. She recovered herself in time to applaud his admission to the *Conseil d'État*. He became foreign minister in June 1757 replacing Rouillé.

One other figure, separated from Versailles by the battlefields of Europe, incurred her undying enmity. Frederick of Prussia violated the special etiquette of royalty when he totally ignored the Damiens stabbing, not once inquiring into the well-being of his brother monarch. His pay-back would be devastating, if the Second Treaty of Versailles, signed in May, was any indication. Under Pompadour's prodding, Louis pledged France to field one hundred thousand men against Frederick, and to pay a twelve million *livres* annual subsidy to Vienna. In a suitably belligerent mood, Pompadour turned to the direction of the armies that poured across the Rhine.

For his loyalty, she owed a debt to young Soubise, and Pompadour always paid her debts. Now, she set about giving him regiments to command, and his chance at glory. Soubise talked a good war, but the commander in Germany, Louis Charles César le Tellier, Maréchal and Duc d'Estrées, was having none of him. Pompadour campaigned to undermine Louis's confidence in d'Estrées, seeking to replace him with the Duc de Richelieu, who would accept Soubise. In the process, she claimed an accidental victim, Mademoiselle O'Murphy, the famous resident of the Parc aux Cerfs. D'Estrées's wife, infuriated by what she correctly saw as the ruin of her husband's career, bribed her way into the house in the Rue Saint-Médéric. She flattered O'Murphy into thinking she could criticize Pompadour to the king. The Irish beauty asked him, 'How are you getting along with your precious old girl?' Louis, still clinging to his transparent incognito as her 'Polish count', raged at the frightened *grisette*. 'Wretch! Who put you up to it?' O'Murphy told him. She was cashiered for her indiscretion, but with a lavish settlement. D'Estrées was abruptly relieved of his command.

Chapter Eighteen

'A Good Joke on the English'

I t was the last thing she intended to do, but Pompadour's intrigue strengthened the hand of Frederick II, who was having a bad year on the battlefield.

His first setback came in May, 1757, after the Battle of Prague. He won the battle handily, against Prince Charles of Lorraine, only to see the Austrian survivors flee into the city, bolster its defences, and frustrate his plans for a siege. A month later, the Austrian general Count Leopold von Daun subjected Frederick to personal defeat, at nearby Kolin. Taken together, Prussian losses at Prague and Kolin were crippling, nearly twenty-eight thousand men, and he was forced to evacuate Bohemia.

Late in July, Maréchal d'Estrées crushed Frederick's English allies at Hastenbeck, on the Weser river south-west of Hanover. George II's younger son, the Duke of Cumberland, faced off with his 'Army of Observation', a patchwork of English and German units, against a French force of more than one hundred thousand men. Cumberland lost. His troops scrambled to get out of Brunswick and George II's beloved electorate of Hanover.

A month later, ninety thousand Russians marched through Poland into East Prussia. Then, to everyone's amazement, the Russians halted and actually went on the retreat. The Czarina Elizabeth was ill, and her heir, the Grand Duke Peter, was Frederick's ardent admirer. Fearing Peter's accession, the Russian generals dared not win against his hero.

The Russian vacilliation allowed Frederick only a brief breathing space, before the Swedes invaded Prussian Pomerania in September. Simultaneously, the Austrians went on the offensive, winning a major victory at Moys, in Silesia. They followed up by staging a daring raid on Berlin itself.

It was at this gloomy moment in Frederick's fortunes, that Pompadour rearranged the French command. She destroyed d'Estrées's career, replacing him with Richelieu. The duc's arrival in Hanover presented the Prussian king with a golden opportunity for knavery. He wooed his new adversary with irresistible appeals to his greed, and, on 8 September 1757, persuaded Richelieu to sign the Convention of Klosterzeven.

The Klosterzeven truce was one of those infamous arrangements peculiar to eighteenth-century warfare in which a high-born commander, intent on feathering his own nest, could treat openly with the enemy to the detriment of his nation and king. As the armies settled in for the winter, Richelieu accepted an English pledge, never honoured, to lay down their arms and return home. He then collected sixteen million *livres* in indemnities from the burghers of occupied Hanover. Only four million arrived at Versailles. Richelieu built a lovely palace in Paris with the rest, which the cynical Parisians instantly labelled the Hanover Pavilion.

The truce lasted just long enough to pay Richelieu's construction bills and complete Frederick's battle plans. Louis very timidly reprimanded Richelieu, but *Son Excellence* was too busy counting his profits to pay much attention. In November 1757, he allowed the Prince de Soubise to take command of the French forces at the Saxon village of Rossbach. There was a patter of applause from Pompadour at Versailles.

Soubise commanded twenty-four thousand Frenchmen. His imperial counterpart, Prince Joseph of Saxe-Hildburghausen, was in charge of an additional thirty-six thousand Germans. On 5 November, Frederick, with less than half their strength, delivered an unforgettable lesson in tactics. He allowed Soubise the high ground, then faked a retreat before superior allied numbers. Soubise, imploring Richelieu for reinforcements, dashed down the hill in pursuit. Richelieu dawdled. Frederick turned and tore Soubise's army to shreds. The Austrians bolted, with a number of French regiments. In less than two hours, ten thousand casualties, including the capture of eleven generals, shattered the allies. Frederick lost five hundred and fifty men. Richelieu arrived, to shed crocodile tears over the disgrace of Pompadour's boudoir general. Soubise reported a military disaster more overwhelming than Blenheim or Ramillies:

I am writing to Your Majesty in boundless despair. The rout of your army is total. I cannot tell you how many of your officers were killed or captured.

The defeat at Rossbach was a national scandal. The guilt of the officers, on the spot, in no way excused Pompadour, behind the scenes. Rossbach was the result of her conniving, and everyone knew it. Madame du Hausset wrote:

> Never was the public so inflamed against Madame de Pompadour as when news arrived of the battle of Rossbach. Every day she received anonymous letters full of the grossest abuse, atrocious verses, threats of poison and assassination. She continued long a prey to the most acute grief, and could obtain no sleep save from opiates. All this discontent was excited by her protection of the prince de Soubise . . .

Pompadour cried out to Louis, '*Après nous, le deluge*' ('After us, the deluge'). Some put the words in the king's mouth, but the old French proverb perfectly expressed the despair that overwhelmed the favourite after Rossbach. Only weeks before, she had played the elegant general-issimo, setting out positions on the battle map for Louis's commanders with beauty marks from her patch box. A *poissonade* of the time, addressed to Louis de Bourbon Condé, Comte de Clermont, mocked her control of the armies:

> *Vous allez commander l'armée,*
> *Brave Clermont.*
> *Vous avez bonne renommée,*
> *Très grand nom;*
> *Mais il faut plaire à la Pompadour,*
> *Vive l'amour!*

> *Vous gagnerez une bataille.*
> *En général;*
> *Si vous ne faîtes rien qui vaille*
> *Tout est égal*
> *Songez à plaire à Pompadour,*
> *Vive l'amour!*

> You are going to command an army,
> Brave Clermont.
> You are famous and bear a great name,
> But you must please the Pompadour.
> Long live love!

You, as a general, will win a battle
But even if you do nothing worthwhile
It will matter nought
As long as you remember to please the Pompadour.
Long live love!

The same Clermont, desperately trying to salvage the French army from the shambles of the northern war in 1758, was given a Pompadour lecture on strategy. Goaded too far, he retorted, 'Be assured, madame, that an army does not move like a finger on a map.'

The campaigns of late 1757 and 1758 confirmed the military greatness of Frederick II as did few other periods in his reign. The field was his, almost from the day he lured young Soubise's regiments to their destruction. The Prussian king never allowed the allies to present a common front, defeating the French, Austrian and Russian commanders piecemeal. He mauled their armies with indiscriminate ferocity; his trademarks were forced marches, surprise attacks, superb use of his cavalry and artillery, and brilliant battlefield improvisation. Numbers alone could not defeat him. Against the French at Rossbach, in November 1757; the Austrians at Leuthen, a month later; and the Russians at Zorndorf, in August 1758, Frederick fought with half the strength of his foes and won.

Upset victories became almost routine. Frederick's English allies, repudiating Klosterzeven, added their regiments to the army of Ferdinand of Brunswick. At Krefeld in June 1758, Ferdinand led forty thousand men to victory over a French force of seventy thousand under the comte de Clermont.

It remained for the Austrian Daun, more aggressive than his fellows, to turn the tables and surprise Frederick at Hochkirch, the following October. Daun's victory brought to a halt, temporarily, the seemingly unstoppable march of Prussian arms.

For the timorous Bishop Bernis, caught between Pompadour's shrill demands for French victories and the battlefield realities of a war against Frederick the Great, it was a season in purgatory. As defeat followed defeat, Bernis filled every memorandum and every interview with Louis and the favourite with cries of doom. The bishop pleaded for peace on any terms; he wanted mediation by the Swedes. He complained about the wretched performances of the maréchaux and his fellow ministers. He groaned that overwork, insomnia and liver attacks were killing him. His whining might have gone on forever, but, in mid-summer, Boulogne, the comptroller general, upset him with a report on the calamitous state of the national finances. Bernis, panicking, closeted himself with Pompadour. During their discussion, he implied that she was bankrupting France with her stubborn prosecution of the war. Such disloyalty was not permitted; the marquise flew into a rage. Bernis entered her apartment an old friend. He left a liability, to be replaced at the earliest possible moment.

Pompadour was immediately at Louis's ear. Slyly, she urged Louis to contact Rome and fulfil Bernis's ambition for a cardinalate. It would be a poisoned benefice, because the king had not forgotten the power usurped by Cardinals Richelieu, Mazarin, and Fleury. He wanted no prince of the church on the *Conseil d'État*.

Bernis, as it happened, averted such a predicament by suggesting that he be given a second-in-command, to relieve some of the pressures that bedevilled him. The man he had in mind was the ambassador to Vienna, the Comte de Stainville. Luckily, the king did not bear a grudge, because Stainville was the same courtier who, five years earlier, scuttled Louis's romance with his cousin, the late Madame Choiseul-Romanet, and saved Pompadour from exile. As Louis's representative to Pope Benedict XIV, Stainville helped draft a much-softened Unigenitus Bull. In 1758, he knew Bernis's 'system' of the Austrian alliance better than anyone; the bishop hoped they would work side by side, sharing power in foreign affairs. Pompadour had no such illusions.

The cardinal's hat arrived and was bestowed by a grateful king. It did not take great perception to recognize the red hat for what it was, a farewell gift. Bernis was the most perceptive of men. During the installation ceremonies on 8 December 1758, a friend exclaimed, 'This is a splendid day, indeed!' Bernis replied, 'Say, rather, that this (the hat) is a splendid umbrella.' On 13 December, the king signed the *lettre de cachet* that banished him from Versailles to exile in his abbey of Vic-sur-Aisne.

Bernis's replacement took up the reins before the cardinal left the château. Stainville had arrived from Vienna in August, to be instantly created *Duc de Choiseul et Pair de France*; he now accepted the foreign ministry to universal acclaim. (Only the devout queen and the dauphin were silent, objecting to Choiseul's reputation as a freethinker.)

Choiseul had exquisite taste and owned a collection of masterpieces. He was malicious, audacious, a wit. The perfect host, he attracted Pompadour to his table three times a week. Despite his puny appearance and 'an ugly, even revolting face,' the red-headed duc was a gallant with a string of seductions to his credit, who now proclaimed his passion for his patroness. (Pompadour was flattered but did not respond; the king, hurrying off to the Parc aux Cerfs, pretended not to notice.) Choiseul's marriage, to Louise Honorine Crozat, the daughter of France's richest war profiteer, was ideal. She allowed him to squander her immense dowry without a murmur, as well as his own income of eight hundred thousand *livres* a year. The duc set the tone for the court of Louis XV in the last years of the war with a series of dinners, balls and entertainments of previously unheard-of opulence.

With France's new foreign minister came a new comptroller, Etienne de Silhouette, who took office in February, 1759. Silhouette was a master of the art of borrowing from Peter to pay Paul. When he floated a loan for seventy-two million *livres*, he rewarded the subscribers with profits confiscated from the tax collectors, the hated *fermiers-généraux*. He gave old waste new names, performing sleight-of-hand tricks with the royal expenses while he encouraged society to follow the lead of the king and Pompadour, who sent their plate to the mint. Donations to prop up the treasury had a patriotic vogue. Even the clergy pledged the gold from the altars. Silhouette levied duties on a hodgepodge of new items: carriages, livery, coffee-shops, bachelors. It became fashionable to wear dresses stripped of their ruffles. Trousers were tailored minus pockets. A new expression for austerity entered the language, *à la Silhouette*. (The comptroller's name survives to this day as the term for an outline picture filled with a void.)

To Choiseul, Silhouette's financial crisis did not exist. With France reeling toward national receivership, the foreign minister unveiled his grand stategy for the war: he seriously undertook to invade England! Choiseul described the conquest of Great Britain in heroic colours to the king and the favourite. French regiments would take ship at Brest on the combined Mediterranean and Atlantic fleets. Crossing the Channel, somehow unopposed, they would land near London and in Scotland. There would be risings. The French would sweep all before them. The whole idea was a towering folly, but, after fifteen years of plotting just such a project with his *secret du roi*, nothing could have been dearer to Louis's heart. He diverted funds from other projects, actually scaling down France's subsidy to Austria, in the Third Treaty of Versailles.

The treaty signing was in March 1759. In August, the war clouds parted briefly, and the sun shone on the allies. A combined Russian and Austrian force overwhelmed Frederick at Kunersdorf. Berlin was occupied. The Prussian king, who contemplated suicide, wrote to his minister, 'All is lost!' Then the Russians repeated their ridiculous performance of 1757; at the very instant of victory, their advance stalled because the generals feared reprisals from the heir. Frederick raised more troops. The see-saw war resumed in the north.

The invasion of England foundered before it got off to a proper start. British warships, under Boscawen, surprised the French Mediterranean fleet on its way north from Toulon. The French lost the Battle of Lagos, off Portugal, and scattered. In the north, commander Edward Hawke first blockaded Brest, then, in November 1759, tempted the Atlantic fleet out of its sanctuary to a costly defeat at Quiberon Bay. Louis's vision of sailing up the Thames as a conqueror was blown out to sea.

Choiseul faced equally appalling news from North America, where Fort Niagara and Quebec had fallen. He waved away the colonial setbacks, insisting that 'one square league in Holland is worth more than a colony'. Nevertheless, he was driven to bargain for time, talking peace to the British as he secretly negotiated the *Pacte de Famille*, the 'family compact' which would link the fortunes of the Bourbon Kings of France, Spain and Naples. In the *Pacte,* concluded late in the summer of 1761, Charles III of Spain agreed to declare war on England if the English had not made peace with the French by May 1762. Spanish sea power, Choiseul believed, would turn the tide.

It was a military year for Choiseul; in January 1761, the king appointed him minister of war and the navy, somehow overlooking the duc's authorship of the doomed English invasion plan. His post as foreign minister was officially turned over to his cousin and successor in the Vienna embassy, the Duc de Choiseul-Praslin. Choiseul-Praslin signed the papers, but policy was still formulated by Choiseul himself, who now took on all possible power in international affairs, despite Louis XV's insistence on calling his reign a personal one.

Through it all, Choiseul danced daily attendance on the favourite. He sympathized with her in her personal feud with Frederick II, clucking over the war of the gossips, which continued unabated. However hectic the pace of his generalship, the Prussian found time to taunt the French king and his *maîtresse* with new insults. In 1759, a package of his poems and jottings was delivered from Frederick's field headquarters to Voltaire. It included an ode on the cowardice of French troops, and the following salutation to Louis:

> *Quoi! votre faible monarque,*
> *Jouet de la Pompadour.*

> What! your weakling monarch,
> Plaything of Pompadour.

Pompadour raged in vain at her royal enemy. She found a comforting ear in Choiseul, who, although he had political reservations about the reversal of alliances from Prussia to Austria, regarded Frederick II with unconcealed contempt. To Voltaire, he wrote:

> . . . he is a mad dog, and we must let him bark; that is his only consolation. I pity him: lies and insults are the only weapons he will soon have left.

Pompadour's illnesses, now frequent and serious, in no way weakened her influence. Choiseul had to bow, time after time, to her direction of the war. Indeed, his first act as minister of war was to reappoint her protégé Soubise to a joint command, with Maréchal Broglie, of the French forces ranged against the British-German armies. Soubise and Broglie argued with each other, instead of fighting Prince Ferdinand of Brunswick. The prince settled their argument by defeating them both at Vellinghausen in July. Broglie roared back to Versailles, publicly blaming Soubise and his sponsors. He was sacked for insubordination. Soubise, still grimly remembered for Rossbach, was given full command. Within the year, he achieved fame with a fresh defeat, again by Prince Ferdinand, at Wilhelmsthal.

In spite of such brainless antics, the sheer weight of the armies massed against Frederick II backed the Prussian monarch into smaller and smaller corners of his kingdom. His British subsidy had dwindled from the day George III ascended the throne in late 1760. Unlike George II, the new monarch considered himself primarily British. No longer engrossed by Hanoverian affairs, he saw little reason to support Prussia. Instead, when Spain entered the war early in 1762, George III rejoiced in Britain's colonial successes – the capture of Havana, in Cuba, and Manila, in the Philippines.

The Russian Czarina Elizabeth rescued Frederick, by dying, on Christmas Day 1761. Her successor, Czar Peter III, ordered all action against Frederick to cease immediately. Prussian treaties with Russia and Sweden were concluded in May. The allied effort, and Pompadour's hopes of crushing the Prussian king, collapsed. The war was over by December.

Two peace treaties were signed in February 1763, within five days of each other: the Treaty of Hubertusburg, between Austria, Prussia and

Saxony; and the Treaty of Paris, between France, Spain, and Great Britain and Hanover.

Under the terms of the Treaty of Paris, Louis XV stripped France of an enormous empire: Canada; all territories east of the Mississippi, including Louisiana (ceded to Spain, to pay back the Spaniards for their loss of Florida to the English); India, except for five trading concessions; and Cape Breton Island. George III remembered to tip as he left the banquet, restoring the West Indian islands of Guadeloupe, Martinique, Marie-Galante and Désirade; two tiny Atlantic islands, St Pierre and Miquelon; Belle-Île-en-Mer off the Breton coast; and the West African colony of Senegal, then called Gorée.

The Duc de Choiseul, unbelievably, called the Treaty of Paris 'a good joke we have played on the English'. Neither the minister or his royal master had the faintest understanding of the riches they threw away. One segment of modern opinion, viewing the treaty from a post-imperial perspective, actually argues that Louis, by ceding France's overseas role to the British, shed also the inconvenience of administering a global domain, and wisely avoided imbroglios such as the American War of Independence. It is impossible not to imagine the reaction of a Louis XIV or a Napoleon.

Pompadour, who had eyes to see the disaster for herself, was plunged into depression. Choiseul told Madame du Hausset he feared she might die of grief. How she agonized over the aftermath of the war can be judged from her conversation with Bernis's good friend, Madame de la Ferté-Imbault, in January 1764. (The noblewoman called to thank Pompadour for restoring the cardinal to favour with Louis.)

I found her in great good looks and well-nourished, and with the appearance of health, although she complained of insomnia, indigestion, and loss of breath whenever she climbed a stair. . . . She expatiated with all the vivacity and gestures of an accomplished actress on how much she was worried by the present deplorable state of the kingdom. . . . Then, opening her heart to me in a way which she said she could do to no one else, she described her torments with an eloquence and energy that I had never before known her to employ. In short, she struck me as quite demented and enraged, and I have never listened to a more effective sermon to illustrate the miseries inseparable from worldly ambition: she seemed so wretched, and at the same time so insolent, so violently agitated, so burdened by her supreme power, that I left her presence after an hour of this conversation with my imagination convinced that no hope remained to her except in death.

Death was just ahead. Pompadour's heart condition (a dilatation of the right auricle) worsened. Constant colds and fever took their toll. Menopause set in very early. She vomited blood and steadily lost weight; her intimates watched her fragile loveliness turn skeletal. The *chansonniers* took aim at her illness, and the court whispered unforgiving verses like these:

> *La contenance eventée,*
> *La peau jaune et truitée,*
> *Et chaque dent tachetée,*
> *Les yeux froids, et le cou long, long, long,*

> *Sans esprit, sans caractère,*
> *L'âme vile et mercenaire,*
> *Le propos d'une commère,*
> *Tout est bas chez la Poisson, son, son.*

> Stale-faced,
> With yellow, speckled skin,
> Each tooth mottled,
> Cold-eyed and scrawny-necked,

> Without wit or personality,
> Mean-hearted and mercenary,
> Ill-natured gossip,
> All is low with the Fish.

At Choisy, late in February, 1764, she was stricken by pulmonary tuberculosis. She haemorrhaged badly, then seemed to regain her strength. They brought her back to Versailles, but the improvement was only temporary. Madame de Pompadour died on Palm Sunday, 15 April 1764, at the age of forty-two.

The pathetic details of her death have become part of the Pompadour legend. She sent word to her husband, asking his forgiveness, but he pleaded his own ill health, and did not come. Louis visited her daily during her last illness, but when the curé of the Madeleine heard her confession, she was not allowed his presence again. Her last words were spoken to the priest as he prepared to leave: 'One moment,

Monsieur le Curé, we will go together.' The coins had barely been placed on her eyes, when her emaciated body was thrown across a wheelbarrow and trundled away to her own mansion nearby, obeying the rule that none but the royal dead were allowed the shelter of Versailles. Despite her vast holdings, she was in financial straits; only thirty-seven *louis d'or* were found in her desk.

Finally, there was the image of Louis XV, soaking himself to the skin on his balcony, as he watched her funeral cortège in a driving rainstorm. Some have put cynical words in his mouth, 'The marquise has chosen bad weather for her journey.' Others credit him with two tears on his cheeks, as he sighed, 'A friend of twenty years. . . . These are the only respects I have been able to pay her.'

His 'friend' took her place in a line of enterprising Frenchwomen stretching back to the fifteenth century, when Agnes Sorel inspired Charles VII to reclaim his kingdom from the English. Sorel was France's first official royal *maîtresse*. Pompadour was the last of the great political mistresses of the *ancien régime*, and the most powerful. Considering her origins, a pretty, pampered daughter of the *bourgeoisie*, how she became what she became, is a tantalizing mystery. She was trained in the arts of the boudoir but in little else. With what talents, what skills, what credentials did the forest nymph of Sénart rule king, court, ministers, maréchaux and kingdom for so long?

Edmond de Goncourt believed she learned her trade out of books. The catalogue of her library numbered more than 3,500 volumes at her death, a rich potpourri of classics, languages, music and poetry. She owned more volumes of history and biography (738), than novels (718). It is no accident that her most familiar portrait pictures her with a book in her hand. Goncourt wrote admiringly:

> The library of Madame de Pompadour was not merely a woman's reading-room: it was also the favourite's arsenal and school. The most serious volumes were not there for show and parade; they completed Madame de Pompadour's education, they furnished her with the arms of government, the terms of matters of state, the knowledge of historical precedents, the art of touching politics without gaucherie, the capacity of speaking on the gravest questions . . . with the accent and almost the competence of a minister. The books on public law, the old French law, the history of all countries, the history of France taught her all that was necessary to play her part with competence if not distinction. . . . Madame de Pompadour had merely to stretch out an arm to touch the wisdom of paganism or of Voltaire . . .

Chapter Nineteen

Du Barry's Milk Cow

E ven in death, the world cursed Pompadour for the Seven Years War. No less an expert on the subject than Frederick the Great took posthumous revenge on the arrogant 'demoiselle Poisson' by erecting her statue to hold up the dome of his Potsdam palace. She was in good company. The dome was also supported by effigies of Frederick's other Furies, Maria Theresa of Austria and Catherine II of Russia.

The Prussian king's statuary joke was the most enduring memorial Pompadour would ever have. At the French court, her memory dimmed from the day she joined her daughter in the crypt of the Capuchine convent in Paris. A particularly nasty commentator wrote of the burial arrangements, '. . . the great bones of the la Trémoille family were astonished to find near them the fishbones of the Poissons.'

The public nursed its hatred longer than the court. Churchgoers, the pious royal family among them, were outraged when Louis disbanded the French Jesuits in 1764, the year of the favourite's death. Many feared the Order as a papal conspiracy; nevertheless, they blamed Pompadour. She was accused both because she was a non-believer and a friend of the Philosophes, and because of her much-publicized religious 'conversion' in 1755. The dying Pompadour, it was whispered, revenged herself on the Jesuits because they refused to absolve her of her sins.

The Society of Jesus had thousands of enemies, but Pompadour was not one of them. She said, 'I believe the Jesuits are good people. But the King cannot sacrifice his Parlement to them just when he needs it so much.' Her protégé Choiseul was less generous, because he feared a Jesuit plot against the *Pacte de Famille*. His chance to clip the Order's wings came in 1761, when they were sued by a commercial creditor.

The Jesuits made the mistake of taking the case before the Paris Parlement. The parlementarians, with Choiseul's backing, ordered the priests to pay a million and a half *livres*, plus damages. Jesuit property was seized, their schools closed, their books banned. In 1764, Choiseul pressured the king to deport them. Louis, who was a jellyfish in conflicts with the church, would not, but directed them to submit to local religious authorities. It was the mildest of decrees, but it signalled the beginning of the end. The Jesuits' chief French protectors died off, the devout dauphin in 1765, his wife, Marie-Josèphe of Saxony, and Queen Marie Leczinska, in 1768. By August, 1773, the Order was no more, abolished world-wide by Pope Clement XIV.

Victorious against the church itself, Choiseul had little to fear from the noblewomen who now fluttered and twittered around the king, hoping to succeed Madame de Pompadour. The tiny, red-haired Comtesse d'Esparbès, a Pompadour intimate, was a leading candidate. Louis was willing, if not precisely ecstatic. Choiseul refused, absolutely, to submit to a new prime minister in skirts. He handed in his resignation. Louis implored him to remain in the government. D'Esparbès was banished to her father-in-law's estate near Montauban, and Choiseul stayed on, but he correctly predicted, 'one day, Your Majesty will exile me, too.'

Basking in the royal esteem, Choiseul was hailed for the Treaty of Paris, which people thought a triumph; for rebuilding the French army and navy after the war; for the acquisition of Lorraine when old King Stanislaus died in 1766; and for the French conquest of Corsica, when the islanders rebelled against Genoa in 1770.

The great minister's nemesis appeared in 1768, the year Queen Marie died. A blue-eyed, ash-blonde beauty, she answered to the name Jeanne de Vaubernier. She would be famous as Madame du Barry. To the horror of Choiseul, Mesdames, and most of the court, the king's new *amour* was an unblushing *fille publique*. Jeanne brought to her royal client a sunny disposition, magnificent breasts, and job references from former customers among Louis XV's courtiers. The ducs and comtes she had serviced testified to her extraordinary abilities in bed. Louis himself said she made him forget he was almost sixty.

There was little about Jeanne de Vaubernier that was not scandalous. She started life as an illegitimate, baptized on the day she was born, 19 August 1743, as Jeanne Bécu, 'natural daughter of Anne Bécu, otherwise known as Quantigny . . .' Her mother had been a beauty, too, a seamstress of Vaudouleurs, a village on the border of Champagne and Lorraine. Seamstress Anne lived in a style which made the neighbours suspect she had another, less respectable source of income. Jeanne's birth confirmed their suspicions. Her father, by most accounts, was Jean Jacques Gomard, also known as frère Ange. He was a Picpus monk, who upheld the rule (but not the morals) of the Third Order of Saint Francis. When Anne Bécu had a second bastard in 1747, the neighbours' hostility forced her to move to Paris.

In the city, Anne found work, found a husband – Nicolas Rançon – and attracted a protector, a financier who was willing to pay for her little girl's education. At seven, Jeanne disappeared into the stern precincts of the Couvent de Sainte-Aure in the Rue Neuve Sainte-Géneviève, taking with her 'two pairs of sheets and six towels'.

The nuns instructed Jeanne 'in Christian piety and in arts suitable for women'. Her convent years left their mark. She would be devout, after her fashion, all her life. At Versailles, she would get good marks for her polite speech from the same snobs who ridiculed Pompadour for her lapses into vulgarity.

Jeanne emerged from the convent at sixteen, one of those disturbing young girls on whose forehead seems to be stamped an invitation to carnal congress. In 1759, Anne complained to the police that her daughter was being slandered by the mother of a hairdresser to whom 'Jeanne Rançon' was apprenticed, who had become infatuated with his pupil. The next year, Jeanne was bundled out of a household in the suburbs, where she served as a *demoiselle de compagnie*, after her mistress's hot-blooded sons took to fighting for her favours. By 1761, she was apprenticed to a milliner in the Rue Neuve des Petits-Champs, whose establishment boomed, as word of his luscious new shop-girl got around the boulevards.

The nuns' teachings notwithstanding, Jeanne revelled in her new life. At the milliner's, she took lovers and adopted a series of aliases. Mademoiselle Beauvarnier, as she sometimes styled herself, flitted from an abbé to a colonel, to a clerk, before she met Jean-Baptiste du Barry, a military contractor, at a gambling-house. She was twenty. Du Barry was forty, a handsome ne'er-do-well from the village of Lévignac in Languedoc, who called himself 'Comte du Barry-Cérès', although he had no right to the title, or any other. He was appropriately nicknamed '*le Roué*', a sobriquet which he earned by his stylish dissipations. Du Barry boasted of his excellent connections at court. He had once been an agent of the former foreign minister, Rouillé, but, unfortunately, the Duc de Choiseul had no need of a spy, so he supplemented his army and navy contracts by contracting girls for a profit.

Years before meeting Jeanne, du Barry had tried for a royal connection. In Pompadour's time, he paraded a pretty morsel from Strasburg, Mademoiselle Dorothée, before Louis XV at the theatre and the royal hunt. Pompadour was tolerant, but the valet Lebel, who procured for the king, was vigilant against poachers. Du Barry, for his part, was too greedy, asking to be made minister to Cologne. Mademoiselle Dorothée returned from her great day in the forest of Versailles empty-handed.

In 1763, the *Roué* seduced Jeanne Beauvarnier, tricked her out with a high-falutin new name, Mademoiselle de Vaubernier, and offered her company to courtiers of his acquaintance. (Police reports referred to the girl as 'du Barry's current milk cow', although she was never formally charged with prostitution.) All in all, du Barry was a good sort of pimp, who spoiled his girls and 'covered them with gold and diamonds'. He welcomed Jeanne's mother, Anne, to his house in the Rue Neuve Saint-Eustache, and provided a handsome living for the two women, including clothes, a carriage, and Jeanne's special passion, jewels. In return, Jeanne made the rounds of libertine society, meeting, among others, a brace of ducs, de Duras, de Nivernais, de Lauzun, and the ageing de Richelieu. The Prince de Ligne, the Austrian diplomat whose gallantries spanned two continents, described her with enthusiasm:

> She is tall, well-made, ravishingly fair, with an open forehead, fine eyes, pretty lashes, an oval face with little moles on her cheeks, which only serve to enhance her beauty, an aquiline nose, a laughing mouth, a clear skin, and a bosom with which most would be wise to shun comparison.

Her noble admirers soon made it fashionable to attend Jeanne's little suppers at the Comte du Barry's, which were followed, naturally, by an hour or two of *lansquenet* or *passe-passe*. The comte's skills at the table kept the whole jolly establishment in funds.

There are at least two stories of how Jeanne first met Louis XV. In one, Jeanne went calling at Versailles, to see no less a personage than the Duc de Choiseul. Du Barry, among his other interests, had a hand in supplies for the troops in Corsica, an asset he generously made over to Jeanne and her mother. Jeanne saw Choiseul to negotiate the matter. Louis saw Jeanne in the Hall of Mirrors. Lebel saw to it that an immediate interview was provided, tête-à-tête.

In a second version, Lebel gave a supper in his rooms for Jeanne and her current lover, the treasurer of the navy, Radix de Sainte-Foy. Louis played Peeping Tom 'through a secret window made in the dining room wall'. He insisted that the beauteous supper guest be brought to him the next day – by some accounts, the same evening.

(Louis had no illusions about Jeanne's chastity. To the Duc de Noailles, he shrugged, 'I am told that I have succeeded M. de Sainte-Foy.' Noailles replied, 'Just as Your Majesty succeeded Phara-mond.' The courtier referred to the many occupants of the throne between his ancient Frankish predecessor and Louis, and the occupants, nearly as numerous, of Jeanne's bed.)

In the beginning, the valet Lebel showed no hostility to du Barry's new candidate. He accepted his usual gratuity for her services, and he was convinced, like the rest of the court, that a professional like Jeanne would be a ten days' wonder, or at most, a temporary resident of the Parc aux Cerfs. Lebel reckoned without Jeanne's phenomenal erotic skills. By July 1768, when the court set out on its annual voyage to Compiègne, Louis wanted Jeanne, publicly and permanently. Lebel, who saw his income as *procureur* about to vanish, argued with his master. Louis was so enraged by his impudence, he threatened him with the fire-tongs. He frightened the valet into an attack of colic, the story goes, and Lebel died two days later.

A dead valet was the least of the obstacles Jeanne encountered on her march to official concubinage. (Indeed, her first, temporary, lodgings at Versailles in January 1769, were the rooms vacated by Lebel.) There was a marshalling of forces by the prudes of the court, and a grumbling acceptance by the king that he still must observe the proprieties. Propriety dictated that his *maîtresse* must be a married woman.

Who would marry Jeanne? Jean-Baptiste du Barry would have done so in an instant, but a wife, abandoned and half-forgotten back in the provinces, made it impossible. He drafted a bachelor brother, Guil-laume du Barry, and whisked Guillaume and his mother before a notary in Toulouse, where the old lady gave formal permission for the wedding. They rushed to Paris to have the civil marriage contract executed, on 23 July. There was a brief pause, while Jean-Baptiste secured a church and a priest.

The wedding took place on 1 September at the church of Saint-Laurent. Du Barry tried his best to keep it secret, scheduling the ceremony for five o'clock in the morning, but not everyone agreed with the need for discretion. Jeanne's father, for one, succumbed to the impulse to carry things off in grand style. Frère Ange gave the bride away, announcing himself as Jeanne's uncle, no longer a monk but an abbé, with an august, if completely fraudulent, position as 'Almoner to the King.' He dressed sumptuously for the occasion, in 'maroon *bouracan* with gold buttons, coat vest and breeches of Lille camelot, and a cassock and cloak of Saint-Maur cloth'.

The monk's deceptions were trivial, compared to the wholesale fakes contrived by Jean-Baptiste, to endow Jeanne with the four hundred years of noble descent she needed to be presented at court. It should be noted that falsifying documents to deceive the king was punishable by death. Louis XV, with a sly flash of humour, let it be known that His Majesty would tolerate any stretch of the truth, to ennoble Jeanne. Given carte blanche, the *Roué* let his imagination run riot.

To wipe away Jeanne's illegitimacy, du Barry faked a birth certificate in which Anne Bécu was properly espoused to a semi-fictional husband, 'Jean Jacques Gomard de Vaubernier'. (The paper gave Jeanne's birth date as 1746, shaving three years off her age.) The living, breathing frère Ange who presented his 'niece' at the altar rail was ignored, as the comte forged her 'father's' death certificate.

There was also the matter of the girl's name. It was Jeanne, that much was certain. She was born Bécu, but she had, by the date of the wedding, presented herself variously as Mademoiselle Rançon, Mademoiselle Lange, Mademoiselle l'Ange, Mademoiselle Beauvariner, Mademoiselle de Vaubernier, and, on one occasion, 'Dame Jeanne de Vaubernier, "spouse" of Messire Jean Comte du Barry'. Especially for the marriage contract, du Barry invented, 'the demoiselle Jeanne Gomard de Vaubernier, a minor, daughter of the dame Rançon and of the sieur Jean Jacques Gomard de Vaubernier, interested in the affairs of the king, her first husband'.

Du Barry was no less grand when it came to honorifics for his brother. A trace of nobility, if diluted, could be found in the du Barry blood; a younger brother Elie held a commission in the *régiment de Beauce* and the *Roué's* son, Adolphe, was a page at court. None of these minor distinctions justified the sudden blossoming of plain Guillaume du Barry from Toulouse, as 'the high and puissant seigneur, messire Guillaume, Comte du Barry, son of the deceased messire Antoine, Comte du Barry, and of the dame Delacaze, his spouse'. Nor could Jean-Baptiste resist giving himself honours. He signed the register as the family's other 'high and puissant seigneur' who served the crown as the 'Governor of Lévignac'.

No detail was too far-fetched. He fabricated a genealogical record tracing the bridegroom's line to the Irish house of Barrymore. It followed logically that the new 'comtesse' arrived at Versailles with the

Barrymore coat of arms and motto: '*Boutez-en-avant*'. Madame du Barry, a sentimentalist, used the device for the rest of her life, no doubt in memory of the day her scamp of a pimp delivered her from bastardy, ennobled her and made her twenty-two again.

The newlyweds parted at the church. Guillaume accepted the separation with good grace, and for the best of reasons. He was reasonably young, in Paris, and suddenly richer by a pension of five thousand *livres* a year. It was no sacrifice to exchange life with an elderly mother in Lévignac, for an apartment in the Rue de Bourgogne with a 'piquant brunette' of nineteen named Madeleine Lemoine. Madeleine bore him a son and eventually married him, after his legal wife's death.

Flimsy as her credentials were, the new Comtesse du Barry now appeared openly at court. Once formally presented, she would automatically assume the mantle of *maîtresse déclarée*. Louis rushed the arrangements, to the delight of a few rakes like the Duc de Richelieu and the outrage of everyone else.

Choiseul mounted a campaign of smut beyond anything ever directed against Pompadour. Du Barry was pictured as a dirty-mouthed, drunken slut, the king as a drooling, senile lecher. A story circulated in which she received the Archbishop of Paris and the papal nuncio in the nude, while Louis hovered at her bedside. In another tale, she had the Marquise des Rosses whipped for her insolence, while she copulated with the king. A full-blown theatrical burlesque, entitled '*La Bourbonnaise*', played to packed houses in Paris.

Du Barry, unlike Pompadour, had a boisterous sense of humour and greeted the street *chansons* with laughter. The snobs were more troublesome than the slanderers. Mesdames ostracized the first noblewoman who agreed to act as *marraine* (sponsor) for the comtesse. A second lady set so high a price, even the open-handed king backed off. Richelieu finally persuaded Angélique Gabrielle Joumard des Achards, Comtesse de Béarn, to stand with Madame du Barry. A lawsuit had left the comtesse in desperate financial straits, but even payment of her debts did not, at first, give her courage to face the ogresses of the court. On presentation day, 25 January, she pleaded a sprained ankle. Madame du Barry remained on the fringe of things, and the king, frustrated, nursed the worst of tempers.

A fortnight later, Louis stormed off to hunt the Forest of Saint-Germain, was thrown from his horse, and dislocated his right shoulder. His pain was real, but not unendurable. As his carriage returned to Versailles, he repeated the whimpering performance he gave during the

Damiens episode. One eye-witness said he 'behaved with a weakness which would have been ridiculous in a little girl ten years old'. The royal recovery, nursed by the clucking Mesdames, was normal, if depressing. It was weeks before he resumed his visits to Madame du Barry.

In April, to everyone's surprise, Comtesse de Béarn again was asked to confront the court with the king's courtesan. Her ordeal was eased considerably by the fact that, in the interim, the presentation had become a political fight between Choiseul and the 'religious' faction.

Seldom has politics made stranger bedfellows than the papal nuncio, the royal Mesdames, Adélaïde, Victoire, Sophie and Louise, the wicked old Duc de Richelieu – and Madame du Barry. The religious clique loathed Richelieu and sniffed at du Barry, but they burned with hatred of her opponent, Choiseul, the minister who had banished the Jesuits. When the presentation finally took place on 22 April 1769, it was greeted with joy in exceedingly odd corners. One priest raised a toast to du Barry at a large public dinner, as '. . . the new Esther, who ought to replace Hamon (Choiseul) and deliver the Jews (Jesuits) from oppression'.

On the great day, her appearance in the Hall of Mirrors was delayed by her hairdresser, as he added the final curls and ringlets to her elaborate coiffure. The king had begun to grumble, when the Duc de Richelieu formally announced to the court assembled, the atten-dance of the Comtesse du Barry. She entered, wearing a blue and silver gown embellished with emerald lover's knots, and half a million *livres* in diamonds. Friends and enemies agreed, with some quibbling, that she was beautiful. After delivering the required back-ward curtsies to the king, Mesdames and the fifteen-year-old dauphin – which she accomplished with grace – France's most celebrated harlot retired triumphant.

The next day, Sunday, she took Pompadour's seat in the king's chapel for Mass, and attended the dinners of Mesdames and the dauphin. The pro-Choiseul faction boycotted the Mass, but du Barry's religious supporters showed up in force, headed by the Archbishop of Reims.

The comtesse was immediately assigned apartments at the various royal châteaux, and in July, her royal swain made the Château de Louveciennes, near Marly, hers for life. In the spring of 1770, she moved into redecorated quarters in the *petits appartements* at Versailles. Her suite had been assigned to the dauphin's saintly mother, but now the king ascended the private staircase from his apartment below to help her transform it into a lovers' bower of unprecedented luxury; its furniture, hangings and bibelots brought gasps of appreciation from the most jaded courtiers. Oddly, a steady flow of *livres* was slow to materialize, and she was forced to rely for ready cash on her former lover, the *Roué*. He wrote to a friend that he nearly bankrupted himself, financing his sister-in-law's clothes, her carriage, her servants and her gambling in her first fifteen months as favourite.

It took at least that long to break down the barriers of sullen resentment put up by the *grandes dames* of the court. Both the Duchesse de Choiseul and the minister's sister, the mannish Duchesse de Gramont, wrote to Louis XV declining further invitations to his *petits soupers*. The two women, with their close friend, the Princesse de Beauvau, led a petticoat revolt against du Barry, dedicating themselves to making her life at Versailles a social hell. The hazing continued throughout 1770. Madame de Brulart de Genlis, Marquise de Sillery, a memoirist of singular gifts, described the treatment the favourite endured, starting on presentation day:

I went to the presentation of my aunt (the marquise de Montesson) and was highly diverted, for it was the very same day on which Madame du Barry was presented. It was recognized on all sides that she was splendidly and tastefully attired. By daylight, her face was *passée*, and her complexion spoiled by freckles. Her bearing was revoltingly impudent, and her features far from handsome, but she had fair hair of a charming colour, pretty teeth and a pleasing expression. She looked extremely well at night. We reached the card-tables in the evening a few minutes before her. At her entrance, all the ladies who were near the door rushed tumultuously forward in the opposite direction, in order to avoid being seated near her, so that between her and the last lady in the room there was an interval of four or five empty places. She regarded this marked and singular movement with the utmost coolness; nothing affected her imperturbable effrontery. When the King appeared at the conclusion of play, she looked at him and smiled. The King at once cast his eyes round the room in search of her; he appeared in an ill-humour, and almost instantly retired. The indignation at Versailles was unbounded, for never had anything so scandalous been seen, not even the triumphs of Madame de Pompadour. It was certainly very strange to see at Court *Madame la Marquise de Pompadour*, while her husband, M. Lenormant d'Étoiles, was only a farmer-general, but it was still more odious to see a *fille publique* presented with pomp to the whole of the Royal Family. This and many other instances of unparalleled indecency cruelly degraded royalty, and, consequently, contributed to bring about the Revolution.

However degraded they might be in Madame de Genlis's view, the Bourbons in 1770 were still the dynasty into which all Europe hoped to marry. The Duc de Choiseul made the point once again, when he betrothed the dauphin to the Austrian Grand Duchess Marie Antoinette. The pretty Habsburg princess arrived in May, to be greeted at Compiègne by the king, his grandson Louis, and Mesdames. Choiseul supervised the welcoming party and the spectacular wedding celebrations.

The party broke the journey to Versailles with an overnight stay at La Muette. The king dazzled Marie Antoinette, a sheltered fourteen-year-old, with his wedding gifts of jewellery, including an historic strand of pearls from the legacy of Anne of Austria. He was almost as attentive to his new daughter-in-law as he was to Madame du Barry, whose presence he demanded, in defiance of all convention.

Marie Antoinette saw the favourite for the first time during dinner. She asked, 'What is the Comtesse du Barry's function at Court?' A companion replied, 'To amuse the King.' 'Then,' the new dauphine replied, 'I intend to be her rival.' Only later did someone enlighten her as to the exact nature of the 'amusements' du Barry provided. If the new dauphine was shocked, she kept it to herself. She was under strict instructions from her mother to please the king in all things, so, for the time being, she treated du Barry with courtesy, if not friendship.

Choiseul had no such compunctions. Egged on by his womenfolk, he indulged in a tantrum of bad manners towards his monarch's *maîtresse*. The king tried to play the peacemaker at a special dinner at Bellevue, in interviews in his private apartments, and, finally, in a pleading letter to the duc:

> You manage my affairs well and I am pleased with you. But beware of your entourage and of busybodies. You know Madame du Barry. She is very pretty, she pleases me, and that should suffice. She feels no hatred for you; is aware of your ability, and wishes you no harm. The outburst against her has been terrible and largely undeserved. Am I desired to take a girl of birth? If the Archduchess was to my taste (the archduchess Elisabeth of Austria, whom Mesdames hoped he would make his queen) I would marry her with great pleasure, but I should like to see and know her first. The fair sex will always trouble me, but you will never see me with a Madame de Maintenon.

Choiseul could not be moved. He was the darling of the courts of Europe: Marie Antoinette felt indebted to him for arranging her marriage; her mother, the Empress of Austria, was devoted to him as the guiding genius of the Franco-Austrian alliance; they loved him in Madrid, for the *Pacte de Famille*.

The Spanish connection ruined him. His enemies – René de Maupeou, his own protégé as chancellor, and the abbé Terray, the new comptroller general – detected a bellicose Spanish accent in Choiseul's pronouncements on the dispute between Spain and England over the Falkland Islands. They complained to the king, backing up their accusations with copies of his letters to Madrid. Louis directed Choiseul to warn Spain not to expect French support if a new war broke out. Ignoring his sovereign's expressed desires, Choiseul began to mobilize French regiments, and, on 23 December 1770, told the king that war with England was inevitable. As the minister exited, the Prince de Condé arrived. He had journeyed to Versailles from Chantilly, to protest what he saw as Choiseul's war-mongering.

Du Barry's was the decisive voice to join the chorus of complainers. Her creamy shoulders shook and the exquisite blue eyes brimmed with tears, as she pleaded with her royal lover. If he could not end Choiseul's cruelties to her, he must, at least, prevent the war she feared the minister was fomenting against England to keep himself in power.

The duc was doomed. To Louis, the horrors of the Seven Years War were still fresh in memory, and on Christmas Eve, 1770, the king sent the following letter to his minister, safe-handed in the Hall of Mirrors by the Duc de la Vrillière:

I command my cousin, the duc de Choiseul, to place his resignation as Minister of State and of the Post Office into the hands of the duc de la Vrillière and to retire to Chanteloup to await my further commands. Versailles, this 24th of December, 1770.

Louis.

The duc was informed that his cousin Choiseul-Praslin, Secretary of the Navy, had also been sacked. Choiseul bowed to Vrillière and made his way out of the crowded audience chamber, smiling all the way. He called for his coach and left Versailles. He was still smiling when he arrived in Paris, where he found royal guards posted at the *hôtel de Choiseul*, to prevent farewell calls by his friends.

Louis's vindictive gesture quickly looked ridiculous. The guards could not hold back the crowds; within hours, the Rue de Richelieu was packed with coaches. People climbed on rooftops to watch the greatest noblemen of the realm defy the king to say goodbye to their hero, crowding past each other into Choiseul's vestibule.

So popular was the exiled minister and so weak the king, that within days a rival court was thriving at Chanteloup. Choiseul built a seven-storey pagoda there, inscribed with the names of the two-hundred-odd courtiers who displayed their indifference to the royal displeasure, by coming to visit. The duc radiated cheer. The closest he ever came to expressing regrets was a note to Cardinal Bernis, 'If I ever have the honour to meet your eminence again, we will discuss exile, because we are both experts on the subject.'

There was little doubt that Louis missed him. For months, when matters of importance came before the *Conseil d'État*, he would ask, 'What do they say in Chanteloup?' The stunning news arrived, in 1771, of the Partition of Poland by Austria, Prussia and Russia. He sighed, 'Ah! If Choiseul had been here.'

Horace Walpole, a canny observer of French affairs, wrote to a friend, 'Choiseul has lost his power ridiculously, by braving a *fille de joie* to humour two women – his sister and his wife.'

Women were the brilliant little duc's undoing. Du Barry's tears drove him from Versailles, and from the lavish salaries attached to his government posts. In exile, when his enormous debts came home to roost, it was again a woman, Catherine II of Russia, who delivered the death blow. The duc and his duchesse regarded the German-born empress as an usurper. They had spread dreadful stories about her for years; now, when his creditors forced him to sell his wife's inheritance, the legendary Crozat painting collection, Catherine bought it cut rate, in a spirit of pure malice.

As Choiseul's star guttered out, du Barry's was shown in the ascendant. The favourite astonished everyone by withdrawing from the political lists almost as soon as she entered. Her first, and last, trophy of the hunt was Choiseul. Thereafter, she limited her influence to helping friends, seeking cardinal's hats, for example, to reward the papal nuncio and the Archbishop of Reims. She was generous to a fault in sharing her financial good fortune.

The *louis d'or* flowed like a golden river. Her restraint in dealing with Louis, who detested greedy women, yielded a thousandfold reward. To her annual pension of one million, two hundred thousand *livres*, the king added a yearly supplement of a hundred and fifty thousand *livres*. Then, as a New Year's gift in 1770, he bestowed a brevet for *les loges de Nantes*, a cluster of stores, homes and booths atop the fortifications of

Nantes, whose rents produced another forty thousand. She was given an open draw on the treasury for 'household expenses', but it was assumed, despite all, that she would overspend. Louis could be counted on to pay overdue bills at least once a year.

Her income barely satisfied her minimum whims. She loved pleasure, adored luxury. Soon, her *lever* was thronged by the same silversmiths and cabinet-makers, tapestry weavers and porcelain-makers, painters and purveyors who formerly clustered around Madame de Pompadour. Du Barry's nesting instinct was, by contrast, easily satisfied. She furnished Louveciennes, redecorated her apartments in the various royal palaces, and settled down to adorn – herself.

In five years, she diverted an estimated twelve million *livres* (twenty-six million pounds sterling or fifty-two million dollars by present-day exchange rates) from the French treasury into her wardrobes and cupboards. The usual price of a du Barry dress from Rose Bertin's *atelier* in Paris was two to three thousand *livres*. Her annual tab at the establishment was three quarters of a million. The cost of her laces and silks alone would have underwritten the annual budget of a duchy. From Pagelle, a couturier in the Rue Saint-Honoré, she ordered a gown for the wedding of the Comte d'Artois (the dauphin's youngest brother) that cost ten thousand *livres*. Her clothes, her coiffures, her wigs, gloves and shoes, set the pace for women of fashion. Special dolls, dressed in the latest du Barry 'look', were dispatched every month by swift couriers to other European capitals, where her outfits were copied, down to the last ruffle, scrap of lace and embroidered rose.

Described by her contemporaries as an easy-going, uncomplicated woman, utterly lacking in neurotic foibles, she was the victim of a single, uncontrollable addiction – to jewellery. With expert, expensive help from the jewellers Boehmer and Rouen, she assembled one of the greatest private collections of jewels the world has ever known, rivalling the collections of Marie Antoinette and the Empress Josephine of France, and Catherine the Great of Russia.

In the eighteenth century, pearls were as rare, and prized as highly, as diamonds. Du Barry owned more than three hundred. One hundred and forty large, flawless diamonds lay in her jewel cases, alongside hundreds of smaller ones, seven emeralds of incomparable size and perfection, and three world-famous sapphires. When Louveciennes was robbed in 1791, the published list of the loot was likened to an inventory of the jewels of Golconda – including rings, pendants, earrings, watches, bracelets, tiaras, shoe buckles, stomachers, buttons, padlocks and an unbelievable miscellany of trinkets.

The jewellery purchase which brought du Barry the greatest notoriety was her famous diamond bodice. Covered entirely in diamonds cleverly mounted to simulate ribbons, bows and flowers, it cost four hundred and fifty thousand *livres*, or more than two million dollars.

If diamonds by the bucketful could buy Jeanne du Barry's love, Louis XV was convinced he had made a wonderful bargain. She was an enchanting companion, a wanton in the boudoir, a graceful blessing of his old age. She pleased him enormously, a fact attested by the rivals who pushed forward, month after month, only to fade away again. In the year 1771 alone, the Parisian bookseller and diarist S.P. Hardy enumerated the following candidates: the Princesse de Monaco, who was the mistress of Condé; a Miss Smith from England; Madame Bèche, the wife of a royal musician; a mysterious Madame d'Amerual; and the former Madame Pater, who now presented herself as the Baronne de Nieukirke. As they paraded past, Louis looked, but touched not. He gave Madame du Barry absolute proof of his devotion when, in 1771, he sold the houses in the Parc aux Cerfs.

Only one 'rival' mattered, the vivacious dauphine, Marie Antoinette. She and her mother, the Empress Maria Theresa, hated du Barry, holding her responsible for the exile of the Austrian alliance's patron saint, the Duc de Choiseul. The empress concealed her feelings rather than offend Louis XV. Marie Antoinette, at fifteen, was not so wise. Mesdames, her aunts, dropped any pretence of tolerance, now that du Barry no longer served their purposes. They persuaded the dauphine publicly to snub the favourite, and for two years between Choiseul's departure at Christmas in 1770, and the New Year celebrations of 1772, Marie Antoinette maintained an icy silence in du Barry's presence. Nothing softened her resolve, not the pleas of the Austrian ambassador, Count Florimont Mercy-Argenteau; stern letters from her mother's minister, Count von Kaunitz; or scolding notes from Maria Theresa herself.

Her miserably dull marriage to the future Louis XVI tainted her behaviour with personal vindictiveness. The dauphin was not only a plodder, he was a frigid exception to the sexual precocity of the Bourbons. The best the king could summon himself to say of his grandson was, '*Il n'est pas un homme comme les autres.*' ('He is not like other men.') Louis XVI's marriage remained unconsummated for seven years, a situation which finally forced Marie Antoinette's brother, the Austrian Emperor Joseph II, to make an emergency trip to

Paris in 1777. Joseph described the couple's difficulties in a letter to his brother, the Duke of Tuscany:

> Marie Antoinette does not carry out her duties as queen and wife in a satisfactory manner . . . Louis has erections in excellent condition; he introduces his member and remains there for two minutes, perhaps without moving, withdraws without discharging and bids her good night, saying only that he was doing it out of a sense of duty and has no inclination for it.

Somehow, no one had noticed that Louis XVI suffered from a malformation of the penis, or told him that minor surgery could relieve the problem. Joseph did. The operation was performed, and the doltish king approached the marriage bed with zest. The queen wrote to her mother:

> I live in the most essential happiness. For more than eight days, my marriage has been most perfectly consummated. The test was repeated yesterday more completely than the first time.

In a year she was pregnant. In 1781, a dauphin was born.

Marital bliss was still in her future, when the priggish dauphine set her jaw and waged war against the king's concubine. It required intervention by both Maria Theresa and King Louis before she could be brought to speak to du Barry, on New Year's Day, 1772: '*Il y a bien du monde aujourd'hui à Versailles.*' ('There are a great many people at Versailles today.') The words spoken, she lapsed into silence. Du Barry, her bruised feelings soothed, sensibly pressed the matter no further.

Their feud engrossed the court completely, because there was, for a time, comparative calm in the nation at large. The *secret du roi* came to an end – and with it adventurism in foreign affairs – when the Comte de Broglie went into exile in Normandy. He took with him his plans for the invasion of England, greatly miffed that Louis XV now wished to keep the peace.

There was peace, too, between the crown and the Parlements. A thorn in the side of the Bourbons since the days of the Fronde, the lawyers were brought to heel in 1771, by Chancellor Maupeou. He was one of their own, a former Président of the Parlement of Paris. When faced with the parlementarians' familiar threat of mass resignation, he cut the confrontation short. On the night of 21 January, Maupeou dispatched armed officers to each judge's door. Each was asked to answer yes or no, whether he would serve. Those who answered no were immediately arrested and exiled. New, co-operative 'Maupeou Parlements' were sworn in. Within weeks, they were in successful operation. (The old Parlements, with their potential for mischief, were revived by Louis XVI. Few acts of 'citizen Capet' were more destructive to the royalist cause.)

More astonishing than peace with the Parlements was that rarest phenomenon of government, a surplus in the exchequer. The comptroller general, abbé Terray, decreed the first reforms in taxation in a generation, over the protests of the nobility, whom he now made to pay. More crucially, Terray cut expenses. He abolished hundreds of titles, and with them hundreds of salaries, of sinecures invented by the king over the years, solely for the purpose of selling them. If Terray did not balance the budget, he created the prospect of fiscal sanity, by 1774.

Suddenly, in 1774, the old king was dead. Smallpox killed Louis XV on 10 May, at the age of sixty-four. His final illness lasted thirteen days, and was misdiagnosed until the third day, when the tell-tale signs could not be ignored. (The king was thought to be immune. Measles, which he had survived in 1712, was often mistaken for the other, deadlier, 'pox'.) He was a good, if demanding, patient while there was some hope of recovery, suffering blisters, enemas, purges and bleedings by the fourteen physicians at his bedside. At the end, however, the horror of his illness broke down what small courage he had been able to muster. The Duc de Liancourt, who disliked him, reported in his diary that the king's terror and cowardice were 'beyond description'. The infection felled fifty in the palace, and killed ten. Madame du Barry survived because she had been sent away, to allow him to receive the absolution of the church. Mesdames his daughters did not, by some miracle, contract the disease, although they remained at the deathbed until the last.

The quaking dauphin and dauphine were discovered on their knees, in tears, by the Duc de Bouillon, who cried to the assembled courtiers, *'Messieurs, le Roi est mort. Vive le Roi!'* The court then abandoned Versailles in a panic flight, leaving labourers to attend to the final disposition of the remains. Louis's decomposing corpse was dumped into its double casket without an autopsy, and spirits poured on, to kill the smell. The grim cortège clattered off to the Benedictines at St Denis, past catcalls from the taverns on its route. 'Taïaut! Taïaut!' ('Tallyho! Tallyho!') – roughnecks imitated the hunter-king's familiar cry.

In his exile at Chanteloup, Choiseul had set down a scathing indictment of Louis XV's character and qualifications for kingship. It is true that the duc was a discharged employee whose opinions were prejudiced, but his denunciation was grounded in unpleasant fact:

A man without heart or brains, loving mischief as children love to hurt animals, with all the faults of the meanest soul, he lacked the capacity owing to his age to exhibit his vices as often as his nature desired. Like Nero he would have been enchanted to watch Paris burning from Bellevue, though he would not have had the courage to order it. He would have liked above all to witness the executions at the Place des Grèves, but he lacked the courage to attend. If one had wished to give him the pleasure of having someone broken on the wheel in the little marble court at Versailles, I feel sure he would leave the bed of his mistress to watch the details of the execution from a corner of the window. He made up for it as much as he could by eager attendance at burials. He was constantly talking about them and about illnesses and operations. He showed satisfaction at the death of the people he knew, and if they recovered he foretold that it would not be for long. What he enjoyed in the hunt, I feel, was the destruction of life. With such a temperament it was astonishing that he did not love war; but his cowardly fear of death was even stronger than his taste for the suffering and death of others. . . . His vanity is inconceivable but he cannot give it scope, for he is rightly aware of his incapacity. Though jealous of his authority he is weakly submissive to his Ministers. He displays the most repulsive indifference to every sort of business . . . he regards the publicity of his *amours* as a demonstration of his authority. He considers the opposition to the object of his fancy as a lack of respect for himself. He feels that everyone should bow down to his mistress because he honours her with his favour. . . . His spoiling as a child and heir made him feel that he belonged to a different species. One day when talking of our pleasures and of the offence to religion they involved, he told me I should be damned. I protested that the verdict was too severe; yet it made me tremble for him, since by his own confession he seemed to have offended the Deity even more than myself, thereby causing a greater scandal. He replied that our positions were very different. He was the Lord's Anointed and God would not allow him to be damned if, as was his mission, he sustained the Catholic religion in his kingdom. As an emanation of God he could indulge his failings without crime or remorse.

Choiseul wrote for the benefit of his fellow nobles. To ordinary Parisians, a street *chanson* summed up the dead king without a wasted syllable:

> Here lies Louis the Fifteenth,
> Second of the name of 'Well-Beloved':
> God preserve us from the Third!

The king's last *maîtresse*, one of the least political of women, survived him to die as a political agent in the inferno of the French Revolution. Louis XVI and his pompous queen banished Jeanne du Barry from Versailles. For the comtesse, still beautiful, still passionate, there were lovers to relieve the tedium of exile. There were friends to receive at Louveciennes, hospitality to extend, gifts and loans to bestow, even if her circumstances were somewhat reduced. A series of accidents and misjudgements brought her, like thousands of others, into the bloody grip of the Terror. Accused of financing *emigré* conspiracies against the people, she was condemned by a rump court. She bought a few extra hours of life by telling her captors where the du Barry jewels were buried in the grounds of her château. The inquisitors took careful notes, then threw her into a tumbril. Hands tied behind her back, half-fainting with fear, she struggled with her guards all the way to the Place de la Révolution (now the Place de la Concorde). The guillotine itself, looming ahead, convinced her that she was about to die. Her shrieks were heart-breaking.

'*Vous allez me faire du mal!*' she cried, '*Oh, ne me faites pas du mal!*' ('You are going to hurt me! Oh, please don't hurt me!') In the final politics of death, Madame du Barry discovered that ignorance was no excuse.

Part III

THE
CYCLOPS

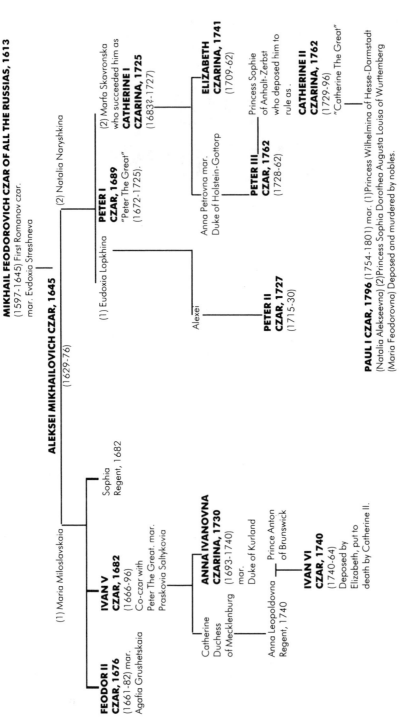

MIKHAIL FEODOROVICH CZAR OF ALL THE RUSSIAS, 1613
(1597-1645) First Romanov czar.
mar. Evdoxia Streshneva

ALEKSEI MIKHAILOVICH CZAR, 1645
(1629-76)

(1) Maria Miloslavskaia

(2) Natalia Naryshkina

FEODOR II CZAR, 1676 (1661-82) mar. Agafia Grushetskaia

IVAN V CZAR, 1682 (1666-96) Co-czar with Peter The Great. mar. Praskovia Saltykovia

Sophia Regent, 1682

(1) Eudoxia Lopkhina

PETER I CZAR, 1689 "Peter The Great" (1672-1725).

(2) Marfa Skavronska who succeeded him as **CATHERINE I CZARINA, 1725** (1683?-1727)

Catherine Duchess of Mecklenburg

ANNA IVANOVNA CZARINA, 1730 (1693-1740) mar. Duke of Kurland

Prince Anton of Brunswick

Alexei

Anna Petrovna mar. Duke of Holstein-Gottorp

ELIZABETH CZARINA, 1741 (1709-62)

Anna Leopoldovna Regent, 1740

IVAN VI CZAR, 1740 (1740-64) Deposed by Elizabeth, put to death by Catherine II.

PETER II CZAR, 1727 (1715-30)

PETER III CZAR, 1762 (1728-62)

Princess Sophie of Anhalt-Zerbst who deposed him to rule as.

CATHERINE II CZARINA, 1762 (1729-96) "Catherine The Great"

PAUL I CZAR, 1796 (1754-1801) mar. (1)Princess Wilhelmina of Hesse-Darmstadt (Natalia Alekseevna) (2)Princess Sophia Dorothea Augusta Louisa of Wurttemberg (Maria Feodorovna) Deposed and murdered by nobles.

The House of Romanov (From 1613 to 1801)

Chapter Twenty

The Cyclops

T he rulers of the Age of Reason were virtuosos at the art of public humbug. Louis XIV and his handsome, indolent successor made the social notices the only news that counted in France, luring their treacherous nobles into an impotent existence amid the glories of Versailles. Empress Maria Theresa of Austria used the reports of her piety to sugar-coat the most feudal court in Europe.

It was imperial Russia, however, which supplied the supreme practitioner of the publicist's art, the Czarina Catherine II, who trumpeted her commitment to the liberal ideals of the Enlightenment while she reigned over the cruelest autocracy in history. Not incidentally, the love of her life was her most impassioned promoter, Gregory Potemkin.

Catherine needed a good press to paper over the awkward contradictions in her sixty-seven-year career. She proclaimed herself the spiritual heir of Peter the Great but she was, in point of fact, a German interloper on the Russian dynastic scene who took power over the corpse of her husband, Peter III, put to death the last legitimate Romanov claimant, Ivan VI, and usurped the Russian throne from her own son Paul for thirty-four years. The darling of Voltaire, she was a self-styled 'republican soul' who thought nothing of condemning more than two million human beings to the slavery of serfdom for the enrichment of her courtiers. Catherine was a prude who would not countenance profanity in her presence, yet twelve lovers have made her name synonymous with royal licentiousness.

For these and other cogent reasons she might easily be set down as a pretentious hypocrite; history however commends her as Catherine the Great.

Gregory Potemkin, too, was a study in paradox. He was an ascetic and would-be monk whose multitude of mistresses included all five of his own nieces. A bona fide military hero, his most famous conquest, the Crimea, was achieved through a campaign of shameless subversion, bribery and chicanery. As much as Catherine, Potemkin created the nation we remember as imperial Russia but he was the empire builder for whom the phrase 'Potemkin villages' was coined, a by-word for colossal fakery. He was an adventurer, charlatan and by the testament of his time, a genius.

An excellent time and place to take up Potemkin's romance with Catherine is the winter of 1774, in the great, brooding Alexander Nevsky Monastery in St Petersburg. Potemkin was then one of Catherine's cavalry generals, celebrated for his dashing victories in the Turkish war to the south. He returned unexpectedly from the Russian siege of the fortress of Silistra. A hero's welcome awaited him, but he was dissatisfied with the reception he received from the empress and abruptly fled the Winter Palace to seek refuge in the monastery.

Only a short walk across the city from the palace, the ancient Orthodox cloister was as alien as if it were located on the moon. In its echoing chambers, the perfumes of the empress's ladies gave way to incense and candle-smoke, brocades and satins were replaced by monastic homespun, and the French chatter of the courtiers was drowned out by sonorous Old Slavonic chants.

Potemkin sought peace in the world of prayer, he said, but he created chaos from the moment the gates closed behind him. He staged hysterical scenes before the icon of St Catherine, where he could be found at all hours, sobbing, groaning, proclaiming at the top of his lungs his passion for the czarina Catherine herself! The monks watched in bewilderment. A scandal was always a welcome diversion, but eventually they began to doubt their lodger's sanity.

Everyone welcomed the intervention of Countess Prascovya Bruce, a confidential emissary rushed to the monastery by the empress. By the time she knocked at the visitor's portal, Potemkin's howls had reached an intolerable pitch. In their cells, the monks longed for a good night's sleep.

Their guest had reason to weep. Twelve years before, in the aftermath of the *coup d'état* that brought Catherine to the Russian throne, Potemkin had been an intimate of the 'bamboo kingdom', the gay mock-court the new empress gathered around herself. For a brief time, he was one of the young officers invited to Catherine's informal 'hermitage' evenings. These gatherings of the imperial inner circle were filled with shared pleasures, shared hopes, and, for Potemkin among others, appointments of increasing responsibility in Catherine's government.

A deadly rivalry with her lover, Gregory Gregorievich Orlov, led to

Potemkin's self-exile in the army and years of separation from Catherine. In the tumult of the Turkish war, they corresponded when they could. Potemkin dispatched battlefield scribbles. Catherine replied through her secretary. She aided his career with a certain amount of watchful favour, but Potemkin was relegated to the role of an adoring suitor thwarted by distance until December 1773, when a letter arrived at Silistra from Catherine, penned in the empress's own hand:

> My Lieutenant General and Chevalier, you are so busy, I wager, gazing at Silistra, that you have not time to read letters, and although I do not yet know if your bombardment has been successful, I am confident that everything you undertake is motivated solely by your ardent devotion to me personally, and, in general, to the beloved country which you love to serve. But since, for my part, I wish to preserve men who are zealous, courageous, intelligent and judicious, I beg you not to expose yourself to danger. On reading this letter, you will perhaps wonder for what purpose it was written. The answer is that I wish to give you confirmation of my regard for you, for I am, as ever, your very kindly disposed, Catherine.

Potemkin wondered at Catherine's purpose not at all, knowing her as he did. Her invitation was unmistakable. He requested a leave of absence from his command and sped home, fully expecting to be received as her paramour.

Never was there a less likely candidate to become one of history's immortal lovers. Even the kindest physical inventory conjures up an appalling picture. An enthusiastic drunkard and glutton, debauchery had broadened and bloated his figure into monumental fat. For the same reasons, his complexion was livid, blotched, and discoloured.

He had lost an eye, not in battle but, probably, through infection brought on by filthy personal habits. Since he scorned to wear an eye-patch, his gaping socket earned for him the derisive sobriquet of 'Cyclops'. (Many stories surrounded his maiming. In one version, Potemkin was blinded over a game of billiards in a crucial quarrel with the Orlovs. Alexis Orlov, so the story went, hurled a cue and struck Potemkin in the head. The injury was followed by the infection, loss of the eye, his flight from the court, and eventual distinction in the Turkish war.) Disfigurement and Potemkin's hatred of being stared at, brought on in its turn a grotesque facial tic.

In a court whose proudest luxury was frequent and thorough use of the famous Russian baths, he was unbelievably and inexcusably dirty.

Even his most fervent admirers among Catherine's ladies-in-waiting were repulsed by his habit of biting his fingernails to the quick.

As Catherine's favourite, his disdain for the amenities was complete. He appeared at the empress's *lever* barefoot, clad only in a grimy dressing-gown. Like some great, dishevelled, smelly barbarian, Potemkin burst upon the court with barrack-room manners so disgusting that Catherine herself was forced to post a sign in the Hermitage, pleading with her 'guests' not to blow their noses on the curtains.

Potemkin was an unlovely suitor, by any woman's standards. Catherine was not, of course, any woman. Her official portraits of the period show what official portraits are supposed to show: a matron of forty-five, beautiful in the ample fashion of the day, posed with queenly pomp and every brushful of flattery at the painter's command. Stately, noble, the empress gazes serenely into the distance, where she perceives Russia's destiny.

The portraits miss the mark by a mile. Only in the eyes lurks a trace of the engaging mischief that made her an irresistible young coquette. She was a magnet for men from her earliest adolescence.

In her diary, Catherine II looked back with remarkable detachment on the charms she possessed as Sophie of Anhalt-Zerbst, princess of a backwater German principality:

> I do not know if I was actually ugly as a child, but I know that I was often told that I was and that because of this I should try to acquire wit and other merits; that until I was fourteen or fifteen I was convinced that I was a rather ugly duckling and tried more to acquire these other virtues than rely upon my face. It is true that I have seen a portrait of myself painted when I was ten, excessively ugly, if it was a good likeness, then I was not being deceived.

She wrote with wry self-deprecation, 'I was never beautiful, but I pleased. That was my long suit.'

Becomingly modest, but inaccurate. She lacked the rose-and-ivory beauty of her mother, Princess Johanna Elizabeth, but no one who encountered the young Sophie failed to find her fascinating. She was abundantly blessed: thick chestnut hair cascaded around her pointed, elfin face; her deep blue eyes flashed with gaiety and intelligence; a quick, sweet smile of white teeth was framed in full red lips. Her radiantly healthy complexion needed no cosmetics, and was kept in bloom by a morning scrub with crushed ice. Small head held high, she already displayed the marvellous posture that would, even in old age, lead newly introduced envoys to swear she was tall.

At fourteen, Sophie was willow-slim but ripening fast, a nymph whom the handsomest of her uncles, Prince George Louis of Holstein, found bewitching. He was her first gallant, wooing her and exacting a romantic promise from his shy young niece that one day she would marry him.

She could please men with more than physical allure, a talent she demonstrated by her adolescent conquest of Frederick the Great. Her father, Field Marshal Prince Christian Augustus of Anhalt-Zerbst, was an officer in Frederick's army, albeit not a very good one. It was her ambitious mother who wheedled Frederick's recommendation of Sophie as a candidate for marriage to the Russian grand duke.

The grand duke, a nephew of the childless empress Elizabeth I of Russia, was, like Sophie, a German, the former Prince Charles Peter Ulrich of Holstein. He had recently been transplanted to the empress's court in St Petersburg, where his prospects of ascending the Russian throne rested solely on the fact that he was a legitimate grandson of Peter the Great and his aunt's choice to breed the next generation of Romanovs. There was no blood-tie on Sophie's side. When the imperial commissioners swept into the tiny family castle at Stettin, they cynically questioned her, inspected her, and packed her off to St Petersburg. She was a princess, they reported to their mistress, a German who spoke Charles Peter Ulrich's language, and she was, presumably, fertile.

For such a cold-blooded honour, Sophie's debt to the King of Prussia was immense; Frederick had plucked her from total obscurity to become, eventually, czarina. When Sophie began the long trip east to her future husband, a visit to her sponsor in Berlin was both protocol and pleasure.

To everyone's amazement, Sophie melted the misogynistic Prussian king with the 'wit and other merits' she had acquired. Frederick received the princess from Stettin with delight, so taken by her that nothing would do but she be his guest of honour at a state dinner. Her mother was loath to share the limelight with her daughter. First, she pleaded an indisposition on Sophie's part, then, the lack of a proper gown. Frederick promptly lent Sophie a dress belonging to one of his sisters. He gave the dinner and spent the entire evening engrossed in conversation with his protégée, while the rest of the party maintained a respectful distance.

The vivacious child who captivated the king was sheltered and inexperienced, but lightning-quick to profit from life's harsher lessons. If she resented being shipped off to Russia like a prize broodmare, she didn't protest to Frederick – nor did she complain about the long, gruelling expedition in her later writings. Like a sensible, marriageable princess, she was content with her lot.

When she arrived in Russia, she was unprepared for the steamy goings-on in the imperial court. Elizabeth herself casually took lovers; the 'night emperor' of the moment was a highly important personage. Oversexed, overconfident courtiers swarmed around the charming new grand duchess. Catherine, to use her newly acquired Russian name, defended her chastity and reputation from all comers, knowing her position depended on her ability to produce an heir of unblemished legitimacy.

She encountered an embarrassing obstacle; her husband was physically impotent. He suffered from a strangulated penis, a commonplace condition a physician could have remedied with a snip of the scissors, had anyone been willing to relieve the grand duke's ignorance. No one did. Peter babbled to his cronies about imaginary sexual conquests like a silly, adolescent boy. He ignored the stifled laughter when it became common knowledge that, at bedtime, the sire of future Romanovs entertained his fetching young wife with attacks by his regiments of toy soldiers.

Catherine, faced with divorce, deportation or worse, was left with only one option. Empress Elizabeth demanded a pregnancy, *now*. Catherine did her best to oblige. She abandoned her scruples and her virtue, and had her first affair.

Thirty years later, Catherine's virtue was the least of Potemkin's concerns. She was now Catherine II, imperial and dazzling, who had survived tyranny under Empress Elizabeth, terror under Emperor Peter III, a *coup d'état*, widowhood and assorted *amours*. Her lover of many years was Prince Gregory Orlov, the former guards captain who, with his four brothers, led the coup of 1762 that elevated Catherine to the throne.

The Orlovs solved Catherine's marital problems at the same time they made her czarina, by the simple expedient of wringing her husband's neck. Catherine publicly blamed Peter III's death on haemorrhoids. Privately, the bruises on Peter's throat could not be wished away; she absolved Gregory and his brothers on the flimsy ground that the regicide was a drunken indiscretion.

Now, Potemkin was bidden from Silistra, so he thought, to replace Gregory Orlov. From the mud and shelling of the Turkish front, he came at a run. In St Petersburg he stubbed his toe on reality. Orlov himself had been deposed.

Tiring of Catherine after more than a decade as her consort, Gregory Orlov philandered once too often and, for once, too shamefully. He seduced his thirteen-year-old cousin Catherine Zinovieva, the empress's namesake; worse still, he had the bad grace to be found out. The affair humiliated and infuriated Catherine, who insisted on discretion in her court, if not propriety. She honoured the debt she owed the Orlovs (or bought their allegiance, if their political power is taken into account) by retiring Prince Gregory in a shower of rubles, diamonds, palaces, estates and serfs.

Catherine quickly found consolation in the arms of an amiable cipher named Alexander Semyonovich Vasilchikov, the handsome son of an old boyar family, splendidly muscled and untiring in bed. When Gregory Potemkin arrived from the Turkish battlefront, it was Vasilchikov he found occupying Orlov's post of adjutant-general and his apartments in the Winter Palace.

Why send for Potemkin when she had an ardent new lover to warm the winter nights? Because Vasilchikov, fully clothed, bored her to distraction. Realizing this, Potemkin pressed his suit in a new flush of confidence. Catherine responded joyously, seemingly blind to the physical toll his years of dissipation had taken on her hero. She pleaded only for patience until 'a certain boring individual had been honourably dismissed'. Then she equivocated. Weeks passed, with Catherine flirtatious one day, coy the next. Vasilchikov remained at court.

Finally, Potemkin staged his retreat to the Alexander Nevsky Monastery. From his monk's cell, he bewailed his plight to all who would listen, waging a war of nerves with his on-again-off-again mistress. He made certain that daily, sometimes hourly reports of his wretched state were carried to the Winter Palace. Catherine eventually succumbed and sent Countess Bruce with her capitulation. The letter said in part:

Tell Panin that he should send Vasilchikov away to take a cure somewhere. His presence upsets me a great deal, and at the same time he complains about pains in the chest. After his cure we will send him as an ambassador where there is not much work to do. He is a nuisance and a bore.

Without question, Potemkin loved Catherine deeply – the rest of his life is eloquent testimony to the fact – but in this shrewd Ukrainian even the most exalted emotion was mixed with the bargaining instincts of a horse-trader. Within the hour that Countess Bruce broke the news of his triumph, he fell to haggling, prizing loose every possible advantage from the empress before returning to court.

Catherine's surrender had to be unconditional. Not for Potemkin was the circumspect if swift advancement of Vasilchikov, who had been raised from simple cornet to commander of the imperial bodyguard, thence to gentleman-in-waiting, chamberlain, personal aide-de-camp, and favourite.

Nor did Catherine dare suggest that Potemkin, an infamous seducer, undergo a physical examination by her physician. (Later favourites were inspected like so many animals at stud, to allay the empress's mortal fear of venereal disease.) Much less would he submit to a 'test' of his skills as a lover by the voluptuous Countess Bruce. (This initiation, which would become one of the scandals of Catherine's reign, was the practical if outrageous brainstorm of the countess, the first of Catherine's ladies-in-waiting to hold the position of *éprouveuse*.)

Countess Bruce assured him that the empress would accord Potemkin 'the highest honours' if he returned to the Winter Palace, court language which admitted Catherine was in love. With insolent cheek, Potemkin wrote to acquaint his monarch with his terms:

> If my services justify her Imperial Majesty's attention, and my sovereign's generosity and favours toward me are not exhausted, then I implore her to dispel all doubts of my unworthiness by appointing me as her personal adjutant-general. This cannot offend anybody, and I will consider it the height of my happiness, all the more so as being under Her Majesty's special protection. I would then have the honour of receiving her wise orders and, by studying them, become more capable of serving her Imperial Majesty and the beloved fatherland.

They both knew his appointment offended absolutely everyone, but she agreed. He came to her in an unprecedented leap to the pinnacle of place at court.

Potemkin emerged from the Alexander Nevsky Monastery triumphant over Vasilchikov, and over the most influential parties in Catherine's court. These included the Orlovs who had originally introduced him into Catherine's inner circle; the various supporters of her son and heir Grand Duke Paul; and her most powerful minister, Paul's former tutor, Count Nikita Panin. Panin in particular was reluctant to welcome a favourite of Potemkin's ambition and abilities, having just gone to the trouble of disgracing Gregory Orlov in order to fill Catherine's bed with the empty-headed Vasilchikov.

Experienced courtiers knew a rising sun when they saw one. Field Marshal Rumiantsev's wife wrote to her husband the day after Potemkin was received, 'A piece of advice, my treasure; if you have a request to make, address yourself to Potemkin.' The palace was still in an uproar a week later when Catherine appointed him lieutenant-general in her own Preobrazhensky regiment (Catherine herself was colonel-in-chief). In a matter of days he was transmitting imperial orders to Count Panin. Soon, Catherine gave him official status at the highest level by appointing him a member of the Grand Council.

The court dithered and realized that this was a favourite whose reach for power was more than matched by his grasp. Not even Gregory Orlov had picked up the reins of command with such exuberant self-assurance.

Orlov himself figured in a famous Potemkin anecdote of this period. The two men are supposed to have met on the palace stairs, Potemkin climbing to an appointment with the empress, Orlov descending from one. As they passed Potemkin asked, 'What's the news at court?' Orlov shrugged. 'Nothing,' he answered, 'except that you are going up and I am coming down.'

Chapter Twenty-One

Feasting with Little Grisha

No one promoted Catherine more enthusiastically, and with less regard for the truth, than Catherine herself. For three decades, she worked tirelessly to create the legend of the ruler who held a mighty empire with nothing more than liberal ideals, a lovely smile, and a widow's pathetic claim. She was utterly shameless about it: beguiling her ministers, her generals and the great Russian boyars, bending them to her will, bribing them, when it suited her, with little victories over their sweetly vulnerable sovereign.

She fooled hardly anyone. To her admirers she was 'The Imperturbable', serene and unswerving in her purposes. To her detractors, she was a tyrant, loving empire for its own sake. To everyone who approached the throne of the czars, she was the magnificent empress Catherine II, who shared power with neither her ministers, her generals, her boyars – or her lovers.

She had twelve lovers in all, and, with few exceptions, they were tall, athletic, uncomplicated, male animals. Some were blessed with the minor gifts and accomplishments that made court life bearable, some were not. Catherine gave them wealth. She gave them herself. She withheld power. Even the gorgeous Orlov, whose daring brought her to the throne in the first place, was, in the end, a supporting actor only.

Potemkin was an exception.

Catherine permitted him everything she denied the others. Soon after his début as her favourite, she let him shoulder aside Panin and the Orlovs to negotiate personally the Turkish peace treaty at Kutchuk Kainardji. It was his first appearance as a diplomatist, at which he scored a major success, and Catherine made him a count of the Russian empire. If there were any Orlov supporters left at court, she underlined the brothers' downfall by presenting Potemkin with her portrait miniature set in diamonds to adorn his coat. It was an honour only Prince Gregory Orlov had previously received. Soon after, she named Potemkin minister of war and, partially replacing Panin, appointed him acting foreign minister.

He loved medals like a child. Catherine bestowed the Order of Saint Alexander Nevsky, made him a Knight of the Order of Saint Andrew and, in 1775, gave him the Order of Saint George. His chest was soon festooned with foreign medals, too: Sweden's Saint Seraph, the Danish White Elephant, the Polish White Eagle, and the Prussian Black Eagle. Joseph II of Austria scandalized his mother and co-regent Maria Theresa when he made him a prince of the empire. (France declined to award Potemkin, a non-Catholic, the Order of the St Esprit. England huffily denied him the Garter.)

Finally, when Potemkin annexed the Crimea for Catherine in 1783, she created him Prince of Tauris (the ancient name of the territory). He was now Prince Gregory Alexandrovich Potemkin-Tavrichesky, with Russia's four greatest provinces under his personal rule. Catherine's most intimate collaborator for seventeen years, Potemkin was czar in all but name.

Luckily, Catherine was not a snob, for Gregory Potemkin came from the sweepings of Russian society. Born in 1739 near Smolensk in the tiny village of Chizhovo, he was the son of a dour, defeated army captain remembered mainly for his poverty and his young, beautiful wife. The twin verities in the Potemkin family were the Russian army and the Russian Orthodox faith. Gregory perfectly reflected this background in later life, representing, for all his flamboyance, the 'Moscow' axis of Catherine's reign, intensely Slavic, conservative, tied to tradition.

His clever mother Darya saw a way out of the family's pinched circumstances through the church. She sent her Gregory off, at the age of six, to his well-placed godfather in Moscow to be entered in a monastery. In 1756, he was one of the first students accepted by the University of Moscow. He performed brilliantly in the *gymnasium*.

When he won a gold medal for his theological papers, he received the honour from Empress Elizabeth herself. One glimpse of the wonders of the Winter Palace put theology in the shade. Two years later Potemkin was expelled from the university for 'laziness and missing classes', whereupon he joined the horse guards. In a letter to his mother, he explained: 'I will start with a military career – if I am not successful, I shall take to commanding priests.'

Among his fellow guardsmen were the Orlov brothers, who

recruited him into the conspiracy of 1762 that deposed Peter III in favour of his wife Catherine. Twelve years later, Potemkin took command of Catherine's heart and her empire.

Potemkin's ascent to favour was described with considerable eloquence in the memoirs of Charles François Philibert Masson, a busybody Frenchman who tutored Grand Duke Paul:

> Potemkin came one day, and boldly seized on the apartments of his predecessor; thus proclaiming his victory, by making himself master of the field of battle, so long disputed against him. His love, his valour, and his colossal nature, had charmed Catherine. He was the only one of her favourites who dared become enamoured of her, and to make the first advances. It appeared that he was truly and romantically captivated by her. He first adored his sovereign as a mistress, and then cherished her as his glory. These two great characters seemed formed for each other: their affection was mutual; and when they ceased to love, they still continued to esteem each other: politics and ambition united them, when Love had dissolved his bands.

Potemkin quickly asserted the Russian male prerogative in their affair, from time to time treating Catherine quite badly. The empress of Russia could be found waiting meekly in the Winter Palace for her favourite to return from drinking and gambling bouts with his friends. When petulance seized him, she pleaded in vain for admittance to his chambers.

He was quick-tempered, ferocious in his rages. When his jealousy was heated to fever pitch by stories of Catherine's previous intimacies, he accused her of taking fifteen lovers. She was forced to submit to him a 'frank confession' in writing, which recorded her romances in detail. Catherine humbly and very accurately described the circumstances of her doomed marriage to Peter III and her subsequent liaisons with Serge Saltikov, Stanislas Poniatowski, Gregory Orlov, and Alexander Vasilchikov.

> This one [Gregory Orlov] would have remained forever, [she wrote to Potemkin] had he not been the first to tire; I learnt this on the day of his departure [to the Turkish peace negotiations] . . . from Czarskoe Selo and simply decided that I could no longer trust him, a thought that hurt me cruelly and forced me, from desperation, to take a step [her affair with Vasilchikov] which I deplore to this day

more than I can say, especially at the moments when other people usually feel happy. All caresses provoke nothing in me but tears, so that I believe I have never cried since my birth as I have in these eighteen months. I thought at first that I would get accustomed to the situation but things grew worse and worse; on the other side they [Vasilchikov] sulked sometimes for three months and to tell the truth I was never happier than when they got angry and left me in peace, as the caresses only made me cry.

Now, Sir Hero, after this confession, may I hope that I will receive absolution for my sins; as you will be pleased to see, there is no question of fifteen but only of one-third of that figure of which the first occurred unwillingly and the fourth in despair, which cannot be counted as indulgence; as to the other three, God is my witness that it was not through wantonness, for which I have no leanings, and had I been destined as a young woman to get a husband whom I could have loved, I would have never changed toward him. The trouble is that my heart is loath to remain even one hour without love; it is said that human vices are often concealed under a cloak of kindness and it is possible that such a disposition of the heart is more of a vice than a virtue, but I ought not to write this to you, for you might stop loving me or refuse to go to the Army fearing I should forget you, but I do not think I could do anything so foolish, and if you wish to keep me for ever, show me as much friendship as affection, and continue to love me and to tell me the truth.

Primitive, insolent, fabulous, Potemkin was the great love of Catherine's life. If modern theory is to be believed, he and the empress were almost certainly married before the end of 1774 in St Petersburg's church of St Samson. Sworn to secrecy, only Potemkin's nephew, Count Samoilov and Catherine's servants attended the ceremony. Documentation for this tale has disappeared, but there is no blinking the fact that, in letter after letter in the years that followed, she addressed him as 'husband' and 'spouse'.

The one-eyed maverick the court maliciously dubbed 'the Cyclops' bore little resemblance to the hero Catherine saw through the rosy mists of awakening love. Memory transformed Potemkin for her, starting with the never-to-be-forgotten Russian 'white night' in June 1762, when she made her bid for the throne. Potemkin was an anonymous sergeant-major among the guardsmen who thronged out of their barracks into the silvery spring twilight to support her.

Their new czarina Catherine touched their praetorian hearts, a gallant woman clad in unaccustomed male regimental uniform, frail and infinitely appealing astride her horse. When she struggled to secure her sword knot, Potemkin broke ranks to offer his own.

Even in the turmoil of the moment, Catherine's eyes lighted with appreciation of her benefactor. Potemkin, at twenty-two, was tall, slim, dark, 'a veritable Alcibiades' with curly hair and flashing eyes. In the years that followed, time might ravage Potemkin the man, but Catherine would remain enthralled by Potemkin the memory.

He was much in her mind at her coronation in Moscow, six months after the coup was complete. When his name appeared on the honours list for promotion from sergeant-major to ensign, she edited the list in her own hand to award him a double advancement to lieutenant, with a bonus of ten thousand rubles and an estate with four hundred serfs. There was more to the gesture than sentiment. Potemkin, although he had been one of Peter III's jailers at Ropsha, was, unlike the Orlovs, clearly innocent of the regicide.

These memories lingered when he returned triumphant in 1774. There were other images from the past as well, which cast a glow over her feelings towards her new lover.

Catherine's father, like Potemkin, a military man of religious conviction, had been left behind in Germany when his wife and daughter Sophie were invited to Russia. The sternly Orthodox empress Elizabeth pointedly excluded him from her invitation because of his Protestant faith. Prince Christian Augustus wept publicly as he bid farewell to his little Sophie in Berlin, certain he would never see her again.

He intuited correctly. Elizabeth refused to allow him to witness Sophie's formal conversion to Orthodoxy and her betrothal and marriage to Grand Duke Peter. By the time Catherine was finally crowned empress in her own right, Christian Augustus was fifteen years in his grave. She felt his absence as keenly as ever.

When Potemkin's day came, his relationship with Catherine had gently paternal overtones, surprising because he was ten years her junior. They could be found sitting together by the hour, her face softly cradled in his enormous hand as he stroked her features and murmured expressions of quiet devotion.

A second phantom in Catherine's mind was that of Peter the Great. Potemkin evoked the legends of Peter, a towering figure of a man with extraordinary gifts and hunger for experience. Both men were unkempt, impatient with appearances, heroic in their tippling and wenching. Catherine was born four years after Peter's death and possessed not a drop of Romanov blood but she held the secret conviction that she had inherited the Petrine mantle. With the advent of Potemkin, she felt Peter's living presence.

Ironically, Potemkin embodied many of the best and worst qualities of her previous lovers, but blended in a mixture Catherine found altogether better suited to her taste.

Serge Vasilievich Saltikov, her first lover, had been a wily, unprincipled court intriguer, whose betrayals brought her dreadful heartache. Saltikov kissed and told, peddling details of their affair to the courts of Europe during his later career as a diplomat in Paris and Dresden. Potemkin was an intriguer without peer, deceiving, bribing and betraying everyone in his path – but never Catherine. He loved scandal. He adored tattling. But he was the empress's own gossip, bringing the juiciest news of the court first to Catherine's ear.

Count Stanislas Augustus Poniatowski, her second lover, was a weakling poet who all his life attempted to play the prince. Catherine bundled him off to Poland, in 1764, to be crowned King Stanislas II Augustus. He pined for her from Warsaw through thirty years of tear-stained correspondence, undeterred by the lovers who succeeded him. By way of contrast, when Potemkin rose to favour, he was immediately master, commanding both empress and empire. Catherine's only problem was restraining him, yet he could be as tender as Poniatowski. Potemkin penned these moonstruck lines to glorify forever his first sight of her:

As soon as I beheld thee, I thought of thee alone.
Thy lovely eyes captivated me,
   yet I trembled to say I loved.
To thee, Love subjects every heart, and
   enchains them with the same flowers.
But, O Heavens! what torment to love
   one to whom I dare not declare it –
   One who can never be mine.
Cruel Gods! Why have you given her such charms,
   Or why did you exalt her so high?
Why did you destine me to love her and her alone?
   Her whose sacred name can never pass my lips,
   Whose charming image will never quit my heart.

Gregory Orlov, Catherine's third lover, was, for all his vanity and arrogance, well suited to her physical requirements, a great, snorting stallion in bed who paced her own lusty nature. Potemkin was no less randy, giving and getting enjoyment with a zest that made her feel young again. From the first night he erupted from the favourite's secret staircase into her bedchamber, naked under his dressing gown, Catherine was swept up in a hugely satisfying physical affair. In her own words:

'There is not a cell in my whole body that does not yearn for you, oh infidel!'

'I thank you for yesterday's feast. My little Grisha fed me and quenched my thirst, but not with wine . . .'

The love notes that fluttered from Catherine to her one-eyed Lothario, jotted in state conferences, dispatched at every hour of the day and night, attested to his performance. She put it bluntly:

'My head is like that of a cat in heat . . .' 'I will be a "woman of fire" for you, as you so often say. But I shall try to hide my flames . . .'

She immortalized Potemkin with a truly dotty lexicon of pet names: 'my button', 'my professional bonbon', 'my dearest doll', 'my dear little heart', 'my darling pet', 'golden cock', 'my golden pheasant', 'dear plaything', 'my kitten', 'lion of the jungle', 'my little father', 'little parrot', 'my little pigeon', 'my marble beauty', 'tiger', 'wolfbird', and 'my twin soul'.

She sounded only slightly less foolish when she wrote about him to the world at large. In Paris, Baron Frederick Melchior von Grimm, her lifelong correspondent, received a hurried bulletin on the progress of events, 'I have parted from a certain excellent but very boring citizen [Vasilchikov] who has been immediately replaced by one of the greatest, most amusing and original personalities of this iron age.'

After the custom of the time, gifts sped between them. Potemkin had only to praise a bauble – or a palace – to possess it. And as often as not, the couriers went scurrying in the opposite direction, bearing precious burdens from the favourite to his mistress.

Catherine's largesse was, of course, the stuff of daydreams. Her lovers were rich men from the moment they set foot in her bedroom. If they sometimes exited hastily, they always exited comfortably.

Alexander Vasilchikov, for instance, left the Winter Palace after a brief twenty-two months as the favourite. The empress said goodbye with one hundred thousand rubles in pocket money and a lifetime income of twenty thousand rubles a year. Going-away gifts also included diamonds by the fistful, seven thousand peasants, and (to replace the apartment at the bottom of the empress's secret staircase) a palace in Moscow. All this was dispensed with only one stipulation from his former mistress, that he was to proceed to Moscow, four hundred-odd miles from the Winter Palace, and remain there permanently.

Gregory Orlov, to whom it was said she remained faithful for nearly fourteen years, was lavished with fortune upon fortune during his long sway as consort. As he embarked on his last, embarrassing mission as her plenipotentiary to the Turkish peace talks, Catherine dressed him for the occasion in a suit embroidered in gold and buttoned with massive diamonds, valued at more than one million rubles.

The day after he left, the Catherine Zinovieva scandal broke and he toppled from favour, but even in disgrace, the empress's generosity to him was breathtaking. Their farewells were sweetened with one hundred thousand rubles in cash; an annuity of one hundred and fifty thousand rubles; the Marble Palace, one of the architectural jewels of St Petersburg; and two hundred paintings to adorn it. Catherine ordered for him the unique Cameo Service of Sèvres porcelain, a priceless creation, each piece of which incorporates a priceless antique cameo. Finally, she created him prince, adding to his already immense holdings vast new estates and six thousand serfs.

Orlov, it must be said, was hardly parsimonious in his turn. As a parting gesture, he presented his imperial mistress with the fabulous Orlov diamond, one of the world's largest gemstones, weighing over two hundred carats. It had been part of the booty of the Persian conqueror of India, Nadir Shah. Another legend was added to its history when Catherine had it set into the imperial sceptre; like so much else in the Catherine legacy, it is today part of the national treasure of the Soviet Union.

Potemkin's gifts to Catherine put her other favourites to shame, but not by extravagance alone. He possessed a genius for the perfect gesture. No gem could light up the gloom of a bitter Russian winter as gloriously as a hamperful of fresh roses fetched from Italy to Catherine's boudoir by an army of the swiftest couriers. Or a dancer plucked from her performances in Paris and spirited across the continent to charm an audience of one in St Petersburg. Or an incredible New Year feast of red ripe cherries picked in orchards at the ends of the earth for Catherine's table. What woman, even of imperial station, could resist such gestures of love?

Adding zest to the pretty theatrics, Potemkin was, very simply, fun to be with. In a court heavy with French formality and Russian excess, Catherine's corpulent lover was a daily source of pleasure.

Their first introduction in 1763 presaged all that followed. Recruited for one of the informal evenings she called her 'hermitages', Potemkin's talents as a mimic were touted in advance by the brothers Orlov, who were then his boon companions. When they brought the young officer before the empress, he presented a hilariously accurate imitation of Catherine's own Russian delivery, studded with mispronunciations and German gutturals. There was a moment of stunned silence before his hostess broke into helpless peals of laughter, leading the company in applause. In later years as her favourite, Potemkin skewered everyone in her entourage to droll perfection, from boyars to ambassadors.

No one could entertain Catherine like Potemkin. Sometimes it was a homely little jest amid the stilted protocols of the Winter Palace – the great general snatching up a tiny coat Catherine was knitting for one of her pet greyhounds, to try it for size across his vast belly. He clowned for her, he sang, he was a master story-teller.

> Darling [she wrote to him] what comical stories you told me yesterday! I can't stop laughing when I think of them . . . we spend hours together without a shadow of boredom. It is always with reluctance that I leave you. My dearest pigeon, I love you very much. You are handsome, intelligent, amusing.

Handsome, hardly. But to the monarch who prized gaiety in her court above all things, he was a witty, light-hearted godsend. (Catherine's own performing talents were minimal. She could wiggle her ears and, on occasion, sing off-key.)

Balancing the intimate Potemkin was the public Potemkin, the first and last full partner Catherine was to have in the tricky business of governing Russia. A decade before he became her lover, Potemkin had served with distinction in the Legislative Commission, the body created by Catherine to discuss her famous 'Nakaz', the ultra-liberal (and irrelevant) policy pronouncement that began her reign. Potemkin acquitted himself well in other civil posts before departing for the Turkish war in 1768.

With his customary virtuosity, the young commander proved himself to be a soldier's soldier. General Potemkin was the hero of Foksham, where he commanded the cavalry in a rout of ten thousand Turks. He was in the thick of the battles for Braila, Larga, Kargul and Izmail. His Balkan commander, Count Peter Rumiantsev, wrote:

> Not knowing what it is to be urged into action, he of his own free will, sought every opportunity to join the fray.

Field Marshal Prince Alexander Golitsyn joined in the chorus of praise:

Russia's cavalry has never fought with such order and bravery as it does under Major General Potemkin.

Catherine, whose heart beat faster for heroes, could hardly remain cool to such a god of war. Potemkin eventually capped his army career with the rank of field marshal and the presidency of the War College, effectively commanding the entire Russian military establishment.

Paradoxically, the scandalously unkempt favourite was an impeccable officer, the very model of parade-ground spit and polish. He was an intelligent, even visionary, reformer of the antiquated Russian military system. Under his guidance, morale was boosted by the formation of national and racial battalions, including a force made up of Turkish refugees, an Albanian unit, even a Jewish battalion, the Israelovsky. Closer to the soldiers' hearts, Potemkin swept away nonsensical regulations. Short, neat hair was substituted for the Prussian-style powdering and curling then required of soldiers. New, comfortable uniforms replaced tight, impractical battlefield dress. Indiscriminate beatings were outlawed.

Although he became the favourite with the glamour of the battlefield still clinging to him, Potemkin had no intention of becoming the empress's pet war hero. Nor, for that matter, did Catherine regard him as such. She needed a champion of rarer and subtler qualities to help her cling to her perch at the top of the Russian autocracy.

Chapter Twenty-Two

Caterina Secunda

T he courtiers fawned. Her Preobrazhensky regiment raised the echoes with their cheers. Diplomats offered compliments from her fellow sovereigns. On the surface, Catherine's acceptance as empress was unchallenged. Yet in the quiet hours of the night, she needed only to turn on her pillow to see the handsome head of Gregory Orlov and be tortured by the thought that, given the right circumstances, Orlov and his swaggering brothers could snatch the imperial crown from her.

Any illusions she may have harboured on that score were dispelled by Gregory Orlov himself on her coronation day in 1762, when he boasted to the coronation party that he had placed her on the throne and could, if he wished, topple her from it in 'one or two months'. His cruelty reduced Catherine to tears until Count Cyril Razumovsky, a devoted suitor from her days as grand duchess, replied,

'Possibly. Very possibly, young man. But a fortnight before then we would have hanged you.'

The incident, ironically, lead to Razumovsky's ruin, not Orlov's. It was an omen of things to come in Catherine's reign. Gallant Count Cyril headed a faction supporting the new empress, more powerful than the guards conspiracy organized by the Orlovs; he was immensely rich, influential among the great boyars and was the grand *hetman* (military leader) of the Ukraine. In the uneasy mind of Catherine, so powerful a defender could be dangerous. At the time Razumovsky presented the claim of his heirs to the hetmanship, Catherine betrayed her old friend utterly. Not only did she deny the claim but coldly abolished the post, incorporating the Ukraine into her empire as a province.

More threatening to Catherine than the power of Razumovsky was the loathing the Orlov brothers inspired in the same guards officers who had helped them overthrow Peter III. Gregory Orlov made no secret of his disgust with playing the role of a 'Pompadour'. He talked publicly of marriage to Catherine.

The imperial guards would not for an instant countenance the commoner Orlov as official consort. The prospect of Gregory as an eventual czar and his brother Alexis as chief minister outraged even such loyalists as Count Panin. A conspiracy was inevitable. In the first year of Catherine's reign, two captains of the Izmailovsky guards, Fyodor Khitrovo and Michael Lasunsky, were tried secretly and convicted of plotting to kill Gregory and Alexis Orlov to prevent the marriage. How bitter and widespread the resentment of the Orlovs had become may be judged by Catherine's timidity in punishing the plotters. She spared them torture, prison, even fines, and simply banished them to the comfort of their country estates.

Try as she might to make light of the incident, Catherine was plainly frightened. Even Orlov took the hint, because his demands for legal wedlock ceased forthwith.

The fidelity Catherine so desperately missed in the men closest to her, Potemkin offered in unlimited measure. Their correspondence during his absence in the army confirmed her best estimate of the man as a selfless suitor who would serve his ruler as devotedly as he loved his mistress. To the hour of his death, without qualm or quibble, Potemkin was loyal.

Her ejection of Cyril Razumovsky from his private kingdom showed Catherine greedy for land. More importantly, it demonstrated her gifts as a player in the never-ending power game of the Russian court; she finessed the Ukraine with muscle supplied by the Orlovs and Count Panin.

A decade later, she gambled for much higher stakes during the First Partition of Poland with Prussia and Austria. She was on her own. Gregory Orlov, for whom her ardour was waning, was in Moscow combatting an outbreak of plague. Had he been on the scene, he would have regarded a deal with Frederick II with the same enthusiasm as a pact with the devil. Orlov was a veteran with bitter memories of the Seven Years War. The day was still to come when he and Frederick would meet and like each other. Potemkin, whose own anti-Prussian bias was more reasoned but no less forthright, was far away facing Turkish guns. It was to Catherine's credit or shame alone, that the partition took took place in August of 1772, during a rare, momentary thaw in Russian relations with Prussia. The partition, a monumental land-grab which poisoned the politics of Europe for centuries, branded Catherine as a faithless double-dealer. She was seen as a betrayer not only of a defenceless nation, but also of her own former lover, Stanislas Poniatowski.

Nine years before, the seeds of the partition were planted when the empress Elizabeth died on the very day she was to receive the keys to Kolberg, the final prize in the Seven Years War. His campaigns had brought Frederick of Prussia near to ruin. At exactly the wrong moment, Peter III succeeded Elizabeth. Peter reversed his aunt's policies and armies and snatched a lickspittle peace from the jaws of Russian victory. From that moment, his days on the throne were numbered. Hated as 'the Holsteiner' when he was grand duke, he was now cursed in the taverns for his slavish adulation of Frederick.

Catherine wrested power from her husband leading the very men whom Peter had robbed of their triumph over Frederick. She cooled the romance with Berlin but took no stronger measures. Frederick for his part remembered the determined little princess from Stettin and vowed not to repeat the military mistake of his confrontation with Elizabeth. He became Eastern Europe's 'honest broker', dangling the rich Polish plain as a distraction before both Russia and her erstwhile ally, Austria.

When the opportunity came, in 1764, for Catherine to place her former lover, Count Stanislas Poniatowski, on the Polish throne, the Prussian king's connivance made it possible. Poniatowski was a flop as a national leader. He accepted Russian subsidies from Catherine's bully in residence, Prince Nicholas Repnin, while he infuriated the Poles with empty patriotic bombast. His spinelessness actually fuelled the Polish Rebellion, forcing Catherine to prop him up with troops needed in her war with the Ottoman Empire.

Maria Theresa, the most Catholic Empress of Austria, subsidized what she saw as a Polish Catholic revolt against Russian Orthodox repression. France and, reluctantly, Prussia also stirred the pot with officer 'advisers' operating among the rebels. Finally, Maria Theresa, who loathed Catherine, followed the dictum that 'the enemy of my enemy is my friend', and struck a most peculiar blow for the Polish Catholics by sending help to Catherine's southern foe, the Muslim Turks. In 1771, Frederick the Great came to the realization that any one of these nose-to-nose confrontations between Russia and the three western powers could erupt into a general war, if nothing was done to defuse the situation.

He was preparing suitably appetizing proposals for the two enemy empresses when Maria Theresa acted first. The pious Austrian monarch, whom Catherine nicknamed 'Lady Prayerful', protested her peaceful intentions while marching her troops to the Polish border in the Carpathian mountains. She then occupied an area of Poland known as 'Zips' in January 1771.

Catherine, and even the wily Frederick, were caught off-guard by the occupation. Frederick's younger brother Prince Henry, on a state visit to St Petersburg, made a joke of the Austrian aggression to his hostess,

'In Poland one only has to stoop down to pick up a bit of the country.'

Catherine replied with a laugh,

'Why shouldn't we both take our share?'

The partition was on. After an additional eighteen months of horse-trading, the three monarchs relieved Poland of 30 per cent of its acreage and nearly five million citizens, a stunning act of international lawlessness. Frederick, whose scheming brought the partition about, grumbled about the size of his share but nevertheless managed to annex the Polish provinces on the Baltic which stood between Brandenburg and East Prussia. Maria Theresa seized huge tracts to which Austria had not the faintest claim. The sanctimonious old fraud signed the treaty of partition with tears streaming down her cheeks. When told of it, Frederick reacted with cheerful venom.

'She weeps,' he said, 'but she takes.'

Catherine claimed White Russia as her due, proclaiming that it was part of the ancient lands of Kievan Russia. To her credit, she did pay reparations of a sort to victimized Poland, even as she stationed troops throughout King Stanislas's domain and dictated a new Polish constitution.

The partition should have destroyed Catherine's liberal reputation among the French *philosophes*, but Voltaire actually applauded her for 'restoring order to a country inhabited by Catholic fanatics, the friends of Pope and Padishah'. Hailed by the Sage of Fermy as 'the Semiramis of the North', clever, literate Catherine had become the pet of the Immortals. She wrote to them, flattered them with the thought that she ruled by their humanist theories, from time to time tossed them morsels from the imperial banquet. She bought Denis Diderot's library, pensioned him and rescued the great French encyclopaedist from penury. Her agents – including Diderot – operated from the most fashionable salons in Paris to acquire masterpieces for her palaces. Polish partition or no, she remained a member in good standing of the eighteenth-century Enlightenment.

Not so easy for Catherine's friends to choke down was the great insurrection of 1773, with its revelations of the misery of the Russian masses after more than a decade of 'enlightened' rule. Unfortunately for Catherine, the Pugachevschina, as it became known, coincided with the downfall of Gregory Orlov. Potemkin was still in the wings. Either Orlov or Potemkin would have made short work of the rebellion, given their dashing records on the battlefield, but with Alexander Vasilchikov at her side Catherine was worse than alone. Her mistake in picking such a nonentity as her protégé was all too plain. Gifted as he was in the boudoir, Vasilchikov was a vastly inadequate everywhere else.

As open revolt forced the empress into brutal repression, her situation was rendered particularly embarrassing by the presence of a pair of distinguished eye-witnesses from western Europe. Baron Frederick Melchior von Grimm was the first to arrive. Her correspondent, agent, and confidant of many years standing, he could not have been personally more welcome. What Catherine dreaded were the reports he would write about the Pugachevschina in his *Correspondance Litteraire*, a fashionable newsletter read by every level of international society. More irritating still, Denis Diderot picked 1773 as the year to call on his 'good Ste. Catherine', champion of the common man.

In the provinces, Pugachev and his followers decapitated her nobles by the thousands. In St Petersburg, Baron von Grimm descended on her with his questions and note-taking while Diderot floated in with Olympian advice on the theory and practice of democracy. It is a matter of conjecture which was the greater test of Catherine's mettle.

The cossack Emelyan Pugachev led a revolt terrifying for its size and timing, coming as it did in the midst of the Turkish war. Pugachev claimed to be Catherine's dead husband Peter III, who had escaped his assassins in 1762. Peter now emerged, miraculously alive and well after a decade of hiding among the Yaik Cossacks, ready to cast out the usurper Catherine.

As a matter of fact, Pugachev was only the latest in a series of impostors, for fraudulent Peters had a way of popping up in the outlying provinces. This 'czar', however, issued a shrewd call to arms which, ironically, appropriated some of Catherine's own liberal ideas and turned them upside down. In a grandiloquent manifesto, the resurrected 'Peter' enfranchised his people, their children, and their grandchildren, granting them 'eternal freedom' from taxes and from the cruel exploitation of the great landowners. At the same time he urged their return to the old ways of Russian custom and religion, 'the ancient prayers and the long hair and the beard'. He cursed what the masses perceived as a Frenchified, ungodly court.

Before the court awakened to the threat, there was a ragged army laying waste the great estates of eastern Russia, under a leader who was reputed to have personally beheaded thirty thousand enemies.

Catherine at first shrugged off the revolt. Voltaire read her letters and noted that she was 'not in the least embarrassed by this new husband who has turned up in the province of Orenburg'. As the Pugachevschina grew, so did her anxiety. She tried to put down the rebellion with armies of ever-increasing size, troops she could ill afford to spare from the Turkish front. Her generals waged a see-saw campaign against Pugachev, sometimes retreating, more often winning partial victories – but Pugachev escaped again and again, to recruit more rebels. Finally, his looting, burning followers were only 120 miles from Moscow!

The devastation caused by Pugachev continued until 1774, a year of great Russian victories against the Turks, which freed the regiments needed to pacify the nation. When their turn came, Catherine's injured nobles were ferocious. Suspected rebels by the thousands were rounded up, beaten, branded, mutilated. There was 'a gallows in every village' and on many a river, too. Hanged peasants were floated down the Volga on rafts to set an example for those downstream. Pugachev himself was trussed up by his lieutenants and handed over to Catherine's troops. They brought him to the capital in an iron cage.

He hoped for clemency from the empress on the grounds of his personal courage. Catherine did prevent the use of torture at his trial, but ordered his public execution by the most savage traditional Russian method. The executioner was instructed to lop off Pugachev's arms and legs one by one, as a preliminary to beheading him. Bungling, or bribed, he beheaded him first. The limbs had to be severed from a lifeless body.

Catherine made her excuses to Voltaire. 'He was an extremely bold and determined man. If he had offended only myself, I should pardon him, but this cause is the Empire's and that has its own laws. No one since Tamerlane had done more harm. . . .'

To put a more honest face on it, Pugachev the false Peter challenged not a new empress nervous for her throne, but an absolute, implacable autocrat. All hope of liberal reform for the Russian peasantry was abandoned as Catherine cast her lot with the Russian nobility, declaring herself the 'first landowner of Russia'.

During Diderot's visit in 1773 and 1774 the harried empress actually found time for sixty interviews with him in five months! During their conversations, the French philosopher put forth the very latest republican suggestions for the betterment of her realm. With the Pugachevschina on her doorstep, Catherine could not part with a shred of power. As she reported it later, she was quite gentle when she set forth their political differences to her friend.

If I followed his advice I would have had to turn everything in my empire upside down: laws, administration, politics, finances. I would have had to do away with what existed and substitute castles in the air. For all that, since I listened to him more than I talked, anybody observing us could take him for a strict teacher and myself for his obedient pupil. In all probability he thought the same, for after a certain time had gone by and he noticed that none of the great changes he had been advocating had taken place in my reign, he expressed amazement and mortification. Then I told him frankly:

'Monsieur Diderot! I have listened with great pleasure to everything you have told me, with admiration for your brilliant mind. Yet with all your great principles – which I understand only too well – it is a good thing to write books but it can be a bad thing to put them into practice. In your plans for reform, you forget the difference in our situations. You philosophers are fortunate: you write only on paper, which is smooth, obedient to your commands and does not raise any obstacles to your imagination – while I, poor Empress, have to write on the ticklish and easily irritated skins of human beings.'

Diderot, the perfect guest, changed the subject. Until he departed laden with the usual imperial gifts, they spoke only of art, literature and ethics in the abstract. When Voltaire planned a pilgrimage to St Petersburg five years later, she wrote in panic to their mutual friend Baron von Grimm, 'For the love of heaven, advise the octogenarian to stay in Paris! Tell him that Catherine is only worth seeing from a distance.' She had had her fill of the Enlightenment, close-up.

Despite Poland, Pugachev, and Orlov's fall from grace, in these years Catherine began to realize her ambition to make St Petersburg a centre of civilization in the East. She envisaged a magnificent imperial capital, the envy and model of the courts of western Europe, a jewel of the eighteenth century to rival ancient Byzantium. At its heart would glitter a single blue-eyed diamond – Catherine II.

Canny publicist that she was, Catherine was aware of the importance of a majestic setting to her reputation as a grand monarch. She was now Russia's unquestioned civil autocrat, military commander-in-chief and, to the Russians who counted, meaning the aristocracy, she was *Matouchka*, beloved Little Mother of the Russian People. From Elizabeth I she inherited a series of colossal, uncomfortable palaces, for the most part sketchily decorated and sparsely furnished. The new Winter Palace was especially daunting, a magnificent shell with all the echoing charm of a baroque warehouse.

There had been little necessity to furnish it for the fanatically pious Elizabeth, whose life was one long religious progress. Elizabeth's court eternally packed and unpacked its belongings like an over-dressed gypsy tribe, as the courtiers trailed after the empress on her endless pilgrimages. Eventually, Elizabeth's reign succumbed to her diseases. Diabetic, swollen with dropsy, she spent her days in muttered conversations with her icons as she sank into premature dementia. Fear of assassination drove her to sleep each night in a different location. Her bed and dressing table, some chests of jewels, and tables to hold an ever-present, glutton's buffet of delicacies, all were dragged from apartment to apartment with her. The idea of permanently furnishing the imperial residences was simply not considered.

Some idea of the decorating problems which faced Catherine can be gained from the dimensions of the new Winter Palace. When creating Peterhof and Czarskoe Selo for Elizabeth, the architect Bartolomeo Rastrelli had made up for the shortage of fine European furniture in eighteenth-century Russia by manufacturing it in his own workshops. His ingenuity worked miracles in these smaller palaces. Such makeshifts were out of the question in 1754 when he began to rebuild the Winter Palace. Rastrelli quadrupled its size for Elizabeth, bringing into being Europe's largest royal dwelling place, the majestic house of the czars in St Petersburg.

Regrettably, its newest tenant, Catherine II, was confronted by an unfurnished masterpiece with only the thinnest sprinkling of amenities. She took possession of a thousand-plus empty rooms waiting to be made habitable with furniture, rugs and chandeliers, more than four thousand walls empty of sconces and pictures, nearly two thousand windows requiring draperies, endless miles of uncarpeted, foot-killing corridors and 117 staircases.

In a matter of weeks, Catherine's desire for creature comforts brought the latest in Louis XV *bergères, canapés, commodes, lits* and *secrétaires* trundling up to the palace gates in wholesale lots. Agents scoured the ends of the empire for tapestries and Afghan and Persian carpets. Drapers and seamstresses became a semi-permanent palace colony. Catherine's imperial settling-in made lavish western decor the latest vogue among her courtiers and put fortunes into the pockets of German furniture-makers in particular. (For one desk alone, the empress parted with twenty-five thousand rubles. It was an elaborate creation with trick panelling and a built-in music box, made for her by the master craftsman Abraham Roentgen.)

The bare walls of the Winter Palace led directly to her first acquisitions of paintings. As a grand duchess heavily in debt, she had shown little interest in old masters. Catherine's first love was her library – she was, and always would be, a reader and bibliophile. Now, however, the imperial treasury tempted and there were those four thousand palace walls to be filled.

From Berlin came word of a Polish art dealer named Johann Gotzkowsky who was anxious to unload a consignment of paintings originally destined for Frederick the Great's palace of Sans Souci. Frederick was now threadbare, in the wake of the Seven Years War. Showing off before her one-time sponsor must have been irresistible. In 1763, she bought the entire lot, a mixed bag of 225 paintings which travelled to St Petersburg by ship, crossing the Baltic directly to the palace quay on the banks of the Neva. In the crates were excellent Dutch and Flemish canvases, including a tiny group of acknowledged masterpieces by Franz Hals, Rembrandt van Rijn, Peter Paul Rubens and Jan Steen.

Catherine inspected each picture personally, felt the first thrill of pride in ownership – and was lost forever to the mania of collecting. The Berlin purchase was destined to become the nucleus of the Hermitage collection, one of the world's incomparable treasuries of painting and sculpture.

Catherine was frank to admit her ignorance as she entered the glamorous, treacherous world of collecting; there is no doubt that Frederick's reputation as an expert convinced her to make her first purchase. But, like the greatest art collectors and patrons, she had the good sense to hire good taste. She also had extraordinary luck in the men who represented her in the capitals and art centres of Western Europe. Her ambassador to the French court, Prince Dmitri Golitsyn, was a connoisseur of the first rank, whose easy entrée to the great salons of the time, especially that of Madame Geoffrin, guaranteed Catherine a listening-post as sensitive to happenings in the world of art as to the world of politics.

One of Golitsyn's first coups involved the second and most famous of her agents, the encyclopaedist and art critic Denis Diderot. Together in 1766, they persuaded Diderot's friend, the sculptor Etienne Maurice Falconet, to accept Catherine's commission to create the statue in St Petersburg which was her homage to the spirit of Peter the Great. Falconet's gigantic bronze horseman is a masterpiece of political sculpture. It looms above Peter's city bearing a dedication that tells us almost as much about the woman who placed it there, as the man it represents: *Petrus Primus, Caterina Secunda*.

Art purchases made by Golitsyn, Diderot and Count A.I. Musin-Pushkin, her ambassador to the court of St James, numbered in the thousands. It is well to remember that Golitsyn's Paris activities on the empress's behalf, and, later, Diderot's, took place under the prominent nose of Louis XV. King Louis's enmity toward the Russian czarina, for all the *politesse* with which his ministers expressed it, was a malignant fact of European political life. A few of the purchases brought off by Catherine's agents are worthy of special mention, for their political notoriety as well as their artistic merit.

In 1769, her Saxon ambassador, Prince Alexander Bieloselsky, alerted Catherine to a collecting coup to be made in Germany, where the paintings of Count Heinrich von Bruhl were offered for sale by his heirs. Von Bruhl's collection sparkled with pictures by Caravaggio, Rembrandt, Rubens, Cranach and Watteau. Catherine acquired it with particular delight because the same von Bruhl was the powerful Saxon minister with whom, as an unhappy grand duchess, she had been forced to plead for the return to St Petersburg of his young aide, her first lover, Stanislas Poniatowski.

Catherine's ability to spirit sought-after paintings out of France itself was made emphatically clear in 1772, when Diderot and Golitsyn purchased for her the celebrated collection of the French multi-millionaire Pierre Crozat. Crozat's daughter, Louise Honorine, was married to a general, Etienne Stainville, Duc de Choiseul, who was King Louis's foreign minister and a constant source of friction in the prickly relations between the French and Russian thrones. It was the duc who denied Catherine the salutation 'Your Imperial Majesty' with which Louis had addressed the Empress Elizabeth. The insult brought all official correspondence between the two courts to a standstill.

Over the years, Choiseul continued to foment hostility toward Catherine as a matter of national policy; his duchesse knew no bounds in private, manufactured scabrous stories about the death of Peter III, and branded Catherine an immoral 'monster'.

Catherine found it especially sweet, therefore, to snatch away from the duchesse of her father, M. Crozat, the four hundred famous pictures including superb canvases by Raphael, Veronese, Rubens, van Dyck and Rembrandt. It was sweeter still, in the same year, to purchase choice items from the collection of the Duc de Choiseul himself. Banished from Versailles in 1770 when the Comtesse du Barry charged him with Spanish treason, the spendthrift duc finally faced a mortifying day of reckoning when his creditors forced the sale of his cherished paintings at public auction.

For the rest of her life, Catherine bought artworks on an imperial scale – paintings by the shipload, drawings by the thousands, tons of sculptures, an exact replica of the Raphael Loggia in Rome – and yet, guided by her friends and her own instincts, bought with superb discernment. Unjustly, she accused herself of *'gloutonnerie d'art'*. But it was axiomatic in the auction rooms of eighteenth-century Europe that nothing, not rival bidders nor the hatred she inspired in the French and Austrian courts, stood between the masterpieces she wanted and the empress with the bottomless purse.

Even the Winter Palace could not absorb pictures and sculptures in the gargantuan quantities in which Catherine bought them, so, in 1764, she commissioned the building that was eventually to lend its name to the greatest of Russian art collections – the Hermitage. Before there was a building, her guests were summoned to evenings '*à l'ermite*', the French word for recluse. Shutting out the world, the empress's intimate circle gathered around her for gossip and gaiety. Catherine loved good company almost as much as the pretty treasures that arrived daily from Berlin, Paris and Amsterdam. It seemed entirely logical to bring together under one roof her favourite people and her favourite works of art.

Catherine's Hermitage gave expression to her nesting instinct. It was her whim of the moment to provide a home for her family, the three robust sons she had borne Gregory Orlov, and the heir, spindly, temperamental Paul. Commissioning the Hermitage was a last, perfunctory bow to convention before Orlov shattered what remained of her Protestant rectitude with his philandering. When she broke with him she awoke to the fact that her power was as absolute in private as in public, a realization which led to the exotic ménage she developed with Potemkin.

The design for the Hermitage was worked out by the brilliant young French architect Jean Baptiste Vallin de la Mothe, who enlivened the prevailing baroque style with graceful elements of classicism, in a new synthesis Catherine found appealing. De la Mothe built for her an intimate but spacious home on the flanks of the Winter Palace, connecting to two sunny picture galleries constructed on the roof of the imperial stables.

Here, free from the stiff constraints of court life in the Winter Palace next door, she continued to play hostess among her pictures to one of the century's truly unique shadow courts – a higgledy-piggledy assortment of diverting friends and gossips, handsome young officers of the guard, the occasional bemedalled hero on leave from the Turkish front, amusing members of the diplomatic community, actors and actresses for her private theatricals, her lovers, the heir to the throne – and the imperial bastards. This ill-assorted but amusing unofficial family gave her private life its meaning.

It was from the recently completed Hermitage that Potemkin fled to bury his maimed face in the distant Turkish war. It was to the Hermitage he returned from the siege of Silistra.

Chapter Twenty-Three

A Traveller's Wife

Potemkin took his cue from the Orlovs, and the festering hatred they inspired. He launched his career as the official favourite with a campaign to win the respect, if not the affection, of Catherine's court. His success at the treaty table of Kutchuk Kainardji did much to restore Russian national pride. Actually, the peace was shaky, but Russian fleets sailed the Black Sea for the first time, with freedom of passage through the Bosporos and the Dardanelles. He negotiated independence for the Crimean Tartars and the Georgians in the Caucasus. Somehow, he prized loose an indemnity from the Ottoman treasury. Because he knew only too well how to ignite the fiery patriotism of the Russian nobility, Potemkin won the sultan's recognition of their 'little Mother' Catherine as 'emperor'.

His performance enraptured the military in particular. They remembered the shame Peter III had brought upon them after the Seven Years War with Prussia. Gregory Orlov's arrogant, tactless failure with the Turks at Focsani they regarded with contempt. Now Potemkin, one of their own, brought home vindication of their long, bloody struggle. Catherine wrote quite accurately to Baron von Grimm:

What a good head the man has! He has had a greater share in the peace than any other man, and this intelligent creature is as amusing as the devil!

Potemkin set himself to amuse not only his imperial mistress, but the entire nation, as impresario in charge of the peace celebrations of 1775. The usual Te Deums and fireworks, banquets and balls were only the prelude to an enormous extravaganza he staged in Moscow. With Catherine still apprehensive about Gregory Orlov, following their separation, Potemkin arranged to soothe feelings in that quarter by covering Gregory's brother Alexis in glory. Alexis, just returned from the historic Russian naval victory at Cesme in the Mediterranean, was given precedence among Catherine's corps of generals as they paraded before the Kremlin. The crowd cheered themselves hoarse for the Russian warrior who had destroyed the Turkish fleet. They ignored the two hired British admirals who actually commanded the expedition and won the laurels Alexis wore, John Elphinstone and Sir Samuel Grieg.

From the golden triumphal arches in Kremlin Square, the celebrants streamed to the outskirts of the city to see Potemkin's main attraction, a fascinating war-in-miniature mocked-up in a rural pasture. He created a charming 'combat zone' for his visitors, complete in every detail. There was a tiny Black Sea filled with boats, its shores dotted with theatres, ballrooms and amusement pavilions named for famous battlefields and towns captured by Russian armies. Led by Catherine, the rejoicing Russian nobility ate, drank and danced their way through a fantasy tour of the Turkish war.

Jockeying for position in the midst of all this good fellowship and festivity was concealed, but very thinly. Potemkin choked down his loathing for the Orlovs to allow Alexis his triumph – the very man, it was rumoured, who had blinded him. To Potemkin, parades were cheap. In the power games that counted, he was not to be outmanoeuvred by any man.

A clear signal was sent to the diplomatic corps when Potemkin abruptly brushed aside Catherine's foreign minister, Count Nikita Panin, to act as official host to Prince Henry of Prussia. Prince Henry, on a return visit to St Petersburg, occupied the first rank among the foreign notables assembled for the national festivities. He decorated Potemkin with the Prussian Black Eagle. Other embassies quickly took the hint, abandoning Panin's anterooms for Potemkin's. They were met with haughty indifference; a story circulated that the new favourite refused to rise for the Comte de Segur of France, receiving him barefoot, decked out in his tattiest dressing-gown.

In an imperial capital where extravagance and eccentricity flourished, Potemkin was a phenomenon. The gossips clucked and chuckled over his exploits. Charles Masson attempted to capture Potemkin's flamboyant style:

> I leave to travellers the office of describing the pomp of his entertainments, the laborious luxury of his house, and the value of his diamonds; and to German scribblers, to relate how many bank-notes he had bound up as books in his library . . . or the cost of his sturgeon soup, which was his favourite dish; or how many miles he would send a courier for a melon, or a nosegay, to present to one of his mistresses.

Potemkin had in his suite an officer of high rank, whom he sent sometimes for a dancer, then to Astrakhan for a water-melon; now to Poland, to carry orders to his tenants; to Petersburg, to carry news to Catherine; or to the Crimea, to gather grapes. This officer, who thus spent his life travelling post, requested an epitaph to be ready for him in case he should break his neck, and one of his friends gave him the following:

> Here Bauer lies, beneath this stone,
> Coachman, drive on!

He [Potemkin] created, destroyed, or confused, yet animated everything. When absent, he alone was the subject of conversation; when present, he engaged every eye. The nobles, who detested him, and who made some figure when he was with the army, seemed at his sight to sink into nothingness, and to be annihilated before him. The Prince de Ligne, who was his tale-bearer and flatterer, said, 'There is something barbarously romantic in his character,' and he spoke the truth.

The public spectacles of 1775 served as Potemkin's formal début as Catherine's consort and co-ruler during her later reign. He would eventually orchestrate Catherine's meeting with Joseph II and the subsequent Russian alliance with Austria, the protectorate in Poland, the war with Sweden, the ultimate victory over the Turks at Focsani, and the treaty of peace with Sweden. He was Catherine's trusted broker in matters of state both great and small. He inspected her dispatches, planned alliances with her and dreamed imperial dreams with her. Always, he scooped up the bribes that accrued to his lofty position with happy greed. Not since Peter the Great had such an unlikely star shone with such blinding intensity in the Russian firmament. The Austrian ambassador, Charles Joseph, Prince de Ligne, described him vividly.

He is the most extraordinary man I have ever met. He gives the appearance of laziness yet works incessantly . . . always reclining on his couch yet never sleeping, day or night, because his devotion to the sovereign he adores keeps him constantly active . . . melancholy in his pleasures, unhappy by virtue of being happy, blasé about everything, quickly wearied of anything, morose, inconstant, a profound philosopher, an able minister, a sublime politician and a child of ten . . . prodigiously wealthy without having a sou,

discoursing on theology to his generals and on war to his arch-
bishops; never reading, but probing those to whom he speaks . . .
wanting everything like a child, capable of dispensing with everything like a great man . . . what then is his magic? Genius, and then
genius, and then more genius!

Prince de Ligne and his fellow diplomats watched the 'genius'
assemble a 'New Russia' for his mistress to rival the empires staked out
in the New World by the major European powers. In the preceding
century, Russia had fumed in landlocked frustration while Spain
crossed the Atlantic to loot the golden treasure of Mexico ('New
Spain'); France attained dominion in Canada ('New France'); and the
British crown acquired its rich American colonies ('New England').
Now Catherine and Potemkin would dispel bitter Russian envy as they
added vast new territories to the Motherland. Catherine's app-
ropriation of the Ukraine from Cyril Razumovsky in 1764 was her
first, almost accidental, step toward this goal.

Potemkin's audacious Russian plan of expansion was first publicly
enunciated, surprisingly enough, by Gregory Orlov. In a famous
speech to the Grand Council in 1769 (which was undoubtedly ghost-
written for him) Orlov revived a Russian dream inherited from Peter I.
He called for the conquest of Constantinople and the establishment of a
new Byzantine empire under Russian rule. In Potemkin's time the
scheme became known as 'the Greek project' and changed the course of
Russian history in the eighteenth century.

Catherine and Potemkin counted the spoils of Kutchuk Kainardji and
immediately eyed the Crimea. This southern peninsula, blessed with
incredible abundance, was strategically crucial if Catherine's dream of a
Byzantine empire was to become reality. The favourite wrote to his
imperial mistress with his usual candor:

> The Crimea is so located that it cuts across our borders. Whether we
> face the Turks on the Bug or in the Kuban region, the Crimea is
> always in our path. Now, imagine that the Crimea were yours, that
> this wart on the nose were removed, then all at once the position on
> the borders becomes admirable.

Potemkin's 'wart' was now undefended against the proposed Russian
surgery. After three centuries of Ottoman rule, the Crimea was
nominally independent, governed by a shaky Tartar khan. Military
occupation would have been the obvious solution to put down purely

local opposition, but no one wished to provoke a new war with the sultan. Russia was battle-weary from the Seven Years War with Prussia, six additional years of fighting against the Turks, and the ghastly upheaval of the Pugachevschina.

Empress Catherine and her Cyclops hatched a plan of conquest on the cheap. Their strategy was to undermine the Crimean khanate through spying, bribery, sabotage and general mischief-making, against the day when the khan would beg his good neighbour to the north for Russian troops to restore order in his mysteriously troubled land. To pull the strings of this inglorious plot, a master villain was needed. Catherine appointed Potemkin. As viceroy of her kingdom on the Black Sea, he was given supreme authority to develop the lower Ukraine and all her immense new southern lands. His real mission was to topple the khan.

The price of Crimean real estate proved to be unacceptably high, however, in personal terms. Because Potemkin was needed in the south as ruler, founder of cities, industrial promoter, naval architect, ambassador, and *agent provocateur*, the 'Greek Project' threatened the lovers with long, aching absences from each other. Such a situation was not to be borne with half-empty beds by either the passionate empress or her ugly, rapscallion favourite. They ended the first two years of their affair by entering into an arrangement that has added spice to histories ever since.

What Catherine and Potemkin did was worldly but not at all bizarre. Like the pretty wives of travelling men before and since, Catherine wept copious tears, kissed her spouse goodbye as he set off on his journeys, then found a handsome lad with whom to amuse herself in his absence. Potemkin, a sensible husband for all his jealous shouting, winked at the good-looking strangers he found lounging about the palace on his return and sought his own pleasures with charming companions on the road. What amazed eighteenth-century and modern observers alike was the couple's ability to maintain this cosy arrangement in perfect harmony for so many years – and that it was the husband, by and large, who picked out the young gallants who comforted his lonely spouse.

It was a simple, civilized solution to a common domestic problem. Potemkin contrived to complicate matters.

He knew some degree of freedom from each other was a political necessity. To serve his empress in distant lands, he must extricate himself from nightly duties in his mistress's bedchamber. This was no easy task because it entailed persuading Catherine, in the second year of their affair, that she must make do with a substitute while permitting her lover to wander at will. Furthermore, to Potemkin's crafty Ukrainian mind it was absolutely necessary that she, Catherine, must play him false first, putting her squarely in the wrong and making it her duty as empress to atone for her transgression by handing over the power Potemkin sought. There was also biology to be considered. Potemkin knew her plea that she could not survive a single hour without love was no idle fancy; Catherine was highly sexed.

Finally, there was the crucial problem of picking the right 'friend' to solace her loneliness. Potemkin had no intention of aborting his statesman's career at the whim of some ambitious stud whom an infatuated Catherine took seriously during business hours. Catherine's 'night emperor' in his absence must be of Potemkin's choosing, a trustworthy, warm body and nothing more. To use an accurate if ugly word, a *minion*.

In the autumn of 1775, political affairs in the south came to a head. Potemkin knew the time had come to act. A swarm of randy young officers were underfoot in the Winter Palace in the wake of the Turkish war. Despite her pledges of eternal devotion to him, Catherine had begun to eye the likelier ones. Potemkin, for his part, found the lusts of a lifetime impossible to put aside. He felt an all too familiar itch when surrounded by Catherine, Sashenka and Vavara, the three delectable nieces who arrived with the pack of relatives he brought to live at court.

Perversely, Catherine picked just this moment to remember her wifely virtue. She fidgeted, flirted a little but refused to make the first move. What to do?

Potemkin, whose best thinking was done horizontally, took to his sickbed. For most of the winter he nursed what were probably digestive attacks, 'spleen', to use Catherine's term. Potemkin's enemies whispered his illness was venereal. (There is some evidence that he put them up to it.) He protested his innocence and settled down to wait for Catherine to choose a new lover. With her horror of sexual disease, she was genuinely distressed by the rumours, forced to disbelieve them officially while acting with prudence in private.

Potemkin's ruse worked perfectly. When his digestion improved, he left on a month-long inspection trip to Novgorod. Catherine strayed at last, becoming infatuated with her secretary. Now the injured but forgiving husband could return, approve or disapprove of his wife's new friend, and assume for the first time his newest portfolio, as imperial pander.

Told of Catherine's infidelity, he was heartbroken. He despaired. She consoled. When the initial 'shock' passed, Potemkin gleefully turned the situation to profit, asking for and getting 'key money' from Peter Vasilievich Zavadovsky, the new favourite, who paid the sum of one hundred thousand rubles for the rights to Potemkin's apartments.

Zavadovsky had entered Catherine's personal service when the empress was suddenly swamped by plans for the victory ceremonies of 1775 and the grand duke's second wedding in 1776. An appeal to Marshal Count Peter Rumiantsev, Countess Bruce's brother, brought two secretaries to her side forthwith. She was delighted with both candidates.

The unassuming one, Alexander Andreyevich Bezborodko, had served with Potemkin during the siege of Silistra. An officer educated in a clerical academy at Kiev, he shared Potemkin's theological interests; this and some outstanding foreign policy papers augured well for his future in St Petersburg.

Catherinian lore, however, credits Bezborodko's success at court to a charming domestic happenstance. Late one evening, we are told, the Winter Palace was empty of all but Catherine, the indefatigable monarch finishing her day's work. She was served an impromptu meal of *blinis* and caviar in her chambers. The portion served was too large. When the deserted palace was ransacked for a suitable dinner companion, only Bezborodko could be found, the most junior of officials in the imperial service. Catherine, never one to stand on formality, engaged the young clerk in political chat as the two polished off her supper. His replies to her questioning were astute in the extreme. A brilliant career was launched between mouthfuls of buckwheat pancake. Bezborodko was to become her minister of foreign affairs, Potemkin's ever-faithful anchor in the capital, and a prince under the future Emperor Paul I.

Her other new secretary was Peter Zavadovsky, a passionate southerner, better bred and educated than Potemkin, but a fellow Ukrainian. His courage under fire had earned him a lieutenant-colonelcy at twenty on the staff of Marshal Rumiantsev. He possessed impeccable manners, charm, an athletic build and seductive good looks.

Catherine needed no pancake supper to appreciate his potential.

Zavadovsky was her flawless factotum, as decorative as he was efficient in coping with the thousand and one details of the Moscow fête and the imperial wedding. He won Catherine's gratitude and affection. Affection soon deepened into love.

When he assumed the favourite's mantle, the court was thrown into a ferment of speculation over Potemkin's downfall. Diplomats rushed the news to their home ministries, gloating over the Cyclops's 'disgrace' if he had handled them roughly, regretting it if, like the Prince de Ligne of Austria, they admired him. But weeks passed with the most effusive public displays of affection between the empress and Potemkin. The one-eyed wonder remained her chief adviser with no visible political rivals, least of all Zavadovsky. Gradually the bewildered embassies and courtiers awakened to a new set of realities. Whether in his mansion attached to the Winter Palace or on the frontiers of the empire, Gregory Potemkin wielded influence over Catherine II as never before. She addressed him in her letters with undiminished devotion, as 'beloved husband'. Yet she retired each evening on the strong young arm of Peter Zavadovsky. Potemkin was left free to romp with the niece of his choice.

This cast of characters might have remained unchanged for years except that Catherine and Potemkin failed to take into account young Zavadovsky's feelings. To everyone's surprise he fell deeply, sincerely in love with his forty-seven-year-old mistress. With love came bitter jealousy of Potemkin.

Zavadovsky resented the older man's vivid presence in Catherine's life despite his absence in the south. At the first hint of rebellion on Zavadovsky's part, Potemkin roared back into St Petersburg demanding his dismissal. They quarrelled openly. Zavadovsky was dropped amid floods of imperial tears. Potemkin made sure he was the last favourite Catherine chose for herself for the next twelve years.

Zavadovsky spent only twelve months in the empress's service, but like all her favourites he left a richer man. A French diplomat, the chevalier de Corberon, summed it up rather spitefully:

> . . . fifty thousand rubles, a pension of five thousand, and four thousand peasants in the Ukraine, where they are worth a great deal. You must agree that it's not a bad line of work to be in here.

Of the Imperial protégés, Zavadovsky was the only one to return to public life with some degree of success after leaving Catherine's service in 1777. He eventually became a senator and outlived his former mistress to serve as a minister under her grandson, the emperor Alexander. Unfortunately Alexander had little respect for him, resenting the survival of such a 'fossil' in his new regime.

Potemkin wasted not a moment in filling Catherine's bed. This time the choice fell on Semyon Gavrilovich Zorich, a major in the imperial hussars so handsome the ladies of the court called him 'the Adonis'. He was a Serbian gifted with gallantry, a spectacular physique and little else. Battlefield prowess earned him the highest Russian medal for valour, the George Cross. The empress rewarded his first night in action on more intimate terrain with a bonus of eighteen hundred peasants.

Very quickly in the sycophantic court with which Catherine surrounded herself, the favourite's position had acquired its own intricate protocol.

The first step was the selection of the presumptive favourite, conducted jointly by Potemkin and the empress. Potemkin, whose uninhibited conduct was a scandal at other times, displayed an almost dainty regard for appearances when he brought forth his candidates for Catherine's inspection. To illustrate, one suitable individual was actually dispatched from Potemkin's apartments to Catherine's with a watercolour on which Potemkin desired Her Majesty's opinion. She gave both the artwork and the messenger a minute examination. The young man returned to Potemkin bearing Catherine's verdict on himself, pencilled on the back of the picture: 'the lines are excellent; the colours less felicitous.'

Accepted, the lucky young man advanced to step two, a physical examination by Catherine's English physician, Doctor Rogerson.

In step three, the notorious 'initiation' test was conducted by Countess Prascovya Bruce, who reported her findings to the empress in detail.

Inspected, vetted and auditioned, the young man's great moment arrived, typically, at the close of a social evening in full view of the court. He was invited to escort the empress to her bedchamber, aware that his fortune would be made in the next few hours. If the first night's performance was a success, the new favourite was shown to his new apartments on the following day. A first gift of one hundred thousand rubles appeared as if by magic in a drawer.

Custom dictated that the final formality to be observed was the surrender of the hundred thousand rubles to Potemkin. Semyon Zorich shared his good fortune gladly. So did each of the young adjutants-general as they occupied the premises.

Zorich brought contentment, but all too briefly, resulting in a 'changing of the Guard' in less than ten months. This time it was Potemkin who failed to understand fully the qualifications needed for a successful candidate. With small talk that consisted almost entirely of soldiers' jokes, 'the Adonis' was excruciatingly boring. Catherine eventually told Potemkin, 'Last night I was in love with him. Today I cannot stand him any more.'

Zorich saw the inevitable coming and reacted with fury. Sir James Howard Harris, the English ambassador, wrote that the Serbian warrior planned to go out fighting. 'Of course I know I'm going to be sacked,' Harris quoted him, 'but by God I'll cut the ears off the man who takes my place.' Zorich blamed his misfortunes on his sponsor, quarrelled with Potemkin and actually challenged him to a duel! It was the excuse Catherine needed to send him his dismissal. Zorich stormed through the palace corridors to pound on the doors of her apartment. They were locked tight. Cooler heads (principally Potemkin's) prevailed and a pension, estates, and the customary gift of peasant 'souls' – seven thousand of them – smoothed Zorich's departure into exile.

Catherine recovered her composure with a brief holiday in one of Potemkin's villages in Finland. The prince ushered forward a twenty-four-year-old sergeant of the household guards. The young man, Ivan Korsak, was immediately addressed by the more stylish name of 'Ivan Nicolayevich Rimsky-Korsakov'. He was from Potemkin's native Smolensk, more sophisticated than Zorich and possessed of some scraps of education.

In Charles Masson's memoirs there is an anecdote which neatly describes his intellectual stature:

> Korsakov, the Empress's favourite, had a handsome face and was of a very elegant figure; but, possessing neither understanding nor knowledge, he was as incapable as Zorich of diminishing the influence of Potemkin. A single fact will display his character. As soon as he obtained the post of favourite, he conceived a man like him ought of course to have a library. Accordingly he sent for the most celebrated book-seller in Petersburg without delay, and informed him, that he wanted books for his house at Vasiltchikov, of which the Empress had just made him a present. The book-seller asked what books he wanted. 'You understand better than I,' answered the favourite, 'it is your business: but there must be great books at bottom, and little ones at top: as they are at the Empress's.'

Rimsky-Korsakov played the violin, wrote love songs and serenaded her, so she said, ignoring the fact that the empress was tone deaf. She described him in a letter to Baron von Grimm:

Pyrrhus, the King of Epirus! Wonder and exaltation are called forth by this masterpiece of creation. He is the despair of painters, the unrealized dreams of sculptors. When Pyrrhus takes his violin, the very dogs listen to him. When he sings, the birds come to hear him, like Orpheus. He makes no gesture, no movement that is not graceful and noble. He sends out warmth like the sun; he is radiant; he delights in all sounds of harmony; he is the personification of every precious gift with which nature in an orgy of prodigality had endowed a single human being. . . .

Creation's masterpiece lasted fifteen months, until the day, late in 1779, when Catherine found him in the arms of Countess Bruce.

There were tears, but the empress dismissed Rimsky-Korsakov no less graciously than she had the others, requiring only that he take his severance pay (diamonds worth one hundred and fifty thousand rubles, estates and peasants) and move to Moscow.

Countess Bruce left for Moscow simultaneously, but to join her husband, who was governor general there. Her duties as *l'éprouveuse* were assumed by Anna Protasova, who was related to the Orlovs, and by Catherine's chambermaid, Maria Perekusikhina.

Rimsky-Korsakov's companion in exile provided an extra fillip of scandal to his banishment. A lady flew to his side: Countess Stroganov, the gorgeous, cultured wife of one of the richest men in Russia. When Rimsky-Korsakov was first introduced to the court, the Stroganovs had just returned from a long visit to Paris. The favourite and the countess met and immediately fell in love. He could not jilt the empress. She would not desert her husband. Rimsky-Korsakov not too cleverly consoled himself in the bed of the luscious Prascovya Bruce. After they were found out and peremptorily dismissed, Countess Stroganov shed her husband and her reputation to follow him into disgrace.

It was a story with a happy ending, nevertheless, for all the world loved these lovers, particularly Catherine and the countess's husband. With astonishing forbearance, Stroganov put at his ex-wife's disposal a palace in Moscow and a handsome country estate. Rimsky-Korsakov and his beautiful paramour became the darlings of Moscow society, much admired for their musical evenings.

Potemkin had a replacement waiting in the wings. Alexander Dmitrievich Lanskoy, Catherine's beloved 'Sasha' from 1780 to 1784, was an impoverished officer in the *chevalier* guards, the unit charged with the safety of the empress herself. Unable to keep up with the extravagance of life at court, the sensitive twenty-two year old asked the War College for a transfer to the provinces. Potemkin, who was vice-president of the college, took one look and snatched up Lanskoy as his aide-de-camp – and favourite-in-waiting.

With Lanskoy, Catherine blossomed as never before. She gloried in her multiple roles of imperial sponsor, teacher, motherly adviser, cultural guide (he shared her love of painting and sculpture), and fifty-but-feisty mistress. Lanskoy was amiable, devoted, and utterly devoid of political pretensions, for that reason well-liked by the most cynical courtiers. Even Charles Masson's memoirs describe Lanskoy as:

> . . . the most beloved of Catherine's lovers, and appeared most worthy to be so. He was handsome, graceful and accomplished, an admirer of the arts, a friend to talents, humane and beneficent. Everyone seemed to share the sovereign's predilection for him.

The empress fell genuinely in love, experiencing four sublimely happy years in Czarskoye Selo, the charming summer palace where Lanskoy helped her rear her grandsons Alexander and Constantine. It was Sasha who introduced her to the Swiss teacher Frederic César de Laharpe, a fiery republican who took the boys' education in hand to mould (he thought) the world's first humanitarian despots.

Her idyll ended tragically because Catherine loved Lanskoy not wisely but too often. If the memoirs of Doctor Wickard, the attending physician at Lanskoy's death, are given credence, the luckless favourite sought to keep pace with her appetites by dosing himself with cantharides (Spanish Fly). When he fell ill in June 1784, the 'strong constitution' Catherine so admired in bed could offer little resistance in fighting off what should have been a routine sore throat; her 'man of gold' was dead in five days after a losing struggle with diphtheria.

Catherine was so torn by grief that even the grand duke and grand duchess who hurried to offer their sympathy were barred from her presence, forced to listen to her wretched sobbing through locked bedroom doors.

Prissy old Baron von Grimm, to whom she had extolled the god-like virtues of Rimsky-Korsakov, was now the recipient of a pitiful letter:

> A deep affliction has overwhelmed me, and my whole happiness has fled. I thought I should die after the irreparable loss of my best friend. I educated this young man. He was gentle, tractable, grateful and I hoped he would be the support of my old age. I have become a

desperate, monosyllabic creature. . . . I drag myself about like a shadow. . . . I cannot set eyes on a human face without the tears choking my words. . . . I do not know what will become of me, but I do know that in all my life I have never been so unhappy as now, that my best and kindest friend has abandoned me like this.

Her worried ministers sent south for Potemkin. He had little reason to mourn Lanskoy, who was the first of the favourites to replace him in Catherine's heart. There was, indeed, a nasty rumour that the young man had been poisoned on Potemkin's orders. Nevertheless, when the news reached him of Catherine's condition, he raced back to St Petersburg to comfort her. Catherine gratefully let her 'beloved husband' steer her through the emotional maelstrom, 'howling with me in my grief', as she recalled it, 'and thereby making me feel more at ease.' She placed a memorial vase in the garden at Czarskoye Selo where Lanskoy was buried, dedicated 'From Catherine to My Dearest Friend', but she felt his loss profoundly for many years.

Chapter Twenty-Four

The Prince of Tauris

W hat kept her from total breakdown was the Greek Project, then coming to fruition under Potemkin's cultivation. In 1783, scarcely a year before Lanskoy's death, the Crimea had been annexed by Russia. Potemkin now swept aside the empress's grief, engulfing her in plans for the 'New Russia'.

The annexation had been an opportunistic *tour de force* for Potemkin, who bided his time until a young, inexperienced prince, Shagin-Girei, ascended the Tartar throne. An outbreak of plague brought chaos to the new khan's domain. Invasion by a Georgian warlord quickly followed. Potemkin's southern armies, massed for months on the Crimean borders, overran the peninsula bringing 'peace and order' and Russian rule. Formal annexation, followed in a few months by annexation of the Georgian Caucasus, provoked not a murmur from the great European powers and only feeble protests from Turkey. St Petersburg erupted in an orgy of celebration. Catherine re-christened the Crimea with its ancient Greek name, Tauris. Potemkin was created its prince.

Although he possessed half a dozen mansions and palaces in St Petersburg, Moscow and elsewhere, nothing would do but that she build for him the Tauride Palace, an immense monument to his accomplishment. Potemkin's new home was designed by Russia's greatest native architect, Starov, and rose on the banks of the Neva among the most important buildings of official St Petersburg. Constructed of the most precious materials, filled with a potentate's treasury of paintings, tapestry, sculpture and furniture, it was to be more splendid than the Marble Palace of Gregory Orlov.

Catherine, typically, mourned Lanskoy in a frenzy of activity. She planned a church to commemorate him and serve as his tomb. She supervised every detail of construction of the Tauride Palace. To further distract herself, she launched into a study of comparative languages: Finnish, Turkish, Abyssinian and others. More than any other interest, however, the new land of Tauris provided a worthy outlet for her energies, as the empress joined Prince Potemkin in a prodigious effort to Russianize the territory. Together, they mounted vast schemes to create new roads, new industries, new arsenals, new harbours and the naval forces to fill them. Whole new Crimean cities sprang into being where none had existed before, with cathedrals, theatres, palaces and academies.

Despite Potemkin's temptings and proddings, it was seven months before Catherine could bear to see the favourite's apartments again occupied. This time, fortune and Potemkin smiled on Alexander Petrovich Ermolov, a tall, blonde aide-de-camp of thirty-one, whose snub nose earned him the nickname 'white nigger'. He was devoted to Catherine but obviously misinformed as to what was expected of him; after a few weeks at Catherine's side, Ermolov set himself up as an all-purpose spy and tattle, informing on her ministers and Prince Potemkin himself. Potemkin was skimming the funds for the colonization of White Russia. Everybody knew it, including Catherine, who shrugged and accepted Potemkin's lame excuse that he 'borrowed' the missing rubles. Then Ermolov confronted his mistress with evidence that the prince was pocketing a one hundred thousand ruble pension destined for the deposed Crimean khan. The empress was forced into an unwelcome confrontation.

Potemkin took his scolding with bad grace, fumed, grumbled and left St Petersburg to sulk in the country. He returned to the Peterhof for the anniversary of the empress's coronation, an evening no one was likely to forget.

Catherine had left the ballroom early, retiring without Ermolov, who was playing macao with friends. Suddenly, the assembled notables were confronted by a raging, one-eyed mountain in cloth of gold and diamonds, who bellowed his detestation of the young favourite to his face, 'Cur! White nigger! Monkey! You dare to spatter me with the mud of the gutters from which I raised you!' Ermolov's hand automatically dropped to his sword, but before he could draw, Potemkin's fist sent him sprawling. The Cyclops roared through the ballroom without a backward look, scattering guests and guards as he flung open the doors of Catherine's boudoir. The empress's ladies cowered, and Catherine herself, she later confessed, was paralyzed with fear as His Serene Highness delivered his ultimatum at the top of his lungs,

'If this nonentity remains at Court, then I quit the state's services from today! You must choose between Ermolov and me . . . or I shall not set foot in your palace.'

The storm raged for hours, with cries of anguish from Catherine as Potemkin thundered his denunciations – without a word of explanation of the disappearing pension. Finally there was the reconciliation, to which Catherine looked forward after each of Potemkin's tantrums. Seldom had the old lovers been so tender and physically passionate. Potemkin emerged among the courtiers leading a smiling empress by the hand.

Within hours, the noble Ermolov was gone. Catherine's generosity was unfailing; the 'white nigger' took with him four thousand peasants and one hundred and thirty thousand rubles.

It was June, 1785. Potemkin, whose choices for the favourite's sinecure had enjoyed mixed success, was like an inept village match-maker determined to get his couples right. In short order the heavy, aging empress, fifty-six, was paired with Count Alexander Matreievich Dmitriyev-Mamonov, twenty-six, the very guardsman summed up with the watercolour. Mamonov was aristocratic, athletic and, like Lanskoy before him, apolitical. His uncle was the same forgiving Count Stroganov whose wife had decamped with Ivan Rimsky-Korsakov in 1779. Mamonov was just the tonic Catherine needed, a fellow art-lover whom she quickly nicknamed 'Monsieur Redcoat', in honour of his officer's jacket.

Dear Baron von Grimm was the recipient of a dewy-eyed pen portrait which described,

> . . . a being who possesses the kindest of hearts together with the most honourable nature, he is clever as the devil and has an inexhaustible fund of gaiety. We hide our fondness for poetry as if it were a crime, we adore music; we have a rare ease of understanding in everything, God knows what we do not know by heart . . . we write in Russian and French with a style and character that are rare. We have two superb black eyes with uncommonly fine eyebrows; height above the average, a noble air, an easy bearing, in a word, we are as solid on the inside as we are agile, strong and brilliant on the outside.

Catherine's next letter out-gushed the last:

> We sparkle with wit, we are a marvellous raconteur, and we have a

rare gaiety. This Redcoat is . . . so handsome, obliging and well-bred you would do well to love him without knowing him.

Wit, gaiety, uncommon eyebrows and all, Mamonov was at her side in 1787 when Catherine left on a trip as momentous as the transcontinental bridal journey that brought her to St Petersburg from Stettin in 1744. Now she fulfilled her yearning to see for herself the New Russia into which Potemkin had poured every ounce of his genius and, it seemed, most of the rubles in the empire.

Catherine's Crimean journey outshone any royal progress before or since. She left St Petersburg in mid-winter, heading south with several hundred guests and an enormous entourage of servants and retainers. The party spent six months on tour, covering four thousand miles by sleigh, river galley, and carriage. Not the least of the attractions that lured the empress and her guests from the frigid Russian capital were the paradisal weeks they spent in the Crimea, which remains to this day a sub-tropical mecca for Russian vacationers.

In his arrangements for the trip, Potemkin invented a whole new vocabulary of extravagance. The imperial party's itinerary was brightened by daily fêtes and entertainments personally conceived and designed by the prince. A final accounting was never given, but Catherine's triumphal progress through her southern empire cost ten million rubles, if it cost a kopeck. The bill for the empress's holiday translates roughly into one hundred and thirty million pounds sterling.

St Petersburg cheered the empress and her guests out of sight on a sparkling January day in which the temperature plunged to seventeen degrees below zero. Accompanying Catherine was the entire court, and key members of the diplomatic corps whose presence was vital to her political purposes.

She would have spirited away her grandsons to see their imperial inheritance, but young Duke Alexander fell sick with chicken pox at the last minute. Excepting, of course, the despised heir, Grand Duke Paul, it seemed as if everyone else in the city went along. The throng of ministers, courtiers, diplomats, wives, mistresses, companions and servants filled a cavalcade of nearly two hundred sleighs. Bundled in sables and bearskins against the killing cold, they raced across the frozen countryside toward the ancient city of Kiev. From Kiev, Catherine planned to embark on the next leg of her journey by water, when the spring thaw made the Dnieper river navigable.

Regiments of imperial cavalry guarded the eight-hundred-mile sleigh route; five hundred horses were stabled at each day's destination to provide fresh relays for the sleighs; and dozens of provincial noblemen waited in jittery anticipation, their mansions and palaces conscripted by Potemkin as overnight way-stations for Catherine and her party. Day or night, an advance squadron of cooks and servitors waited at each full stop with a piping hot meal in readiness for the arrival of the main caravan. Catherine's guests dined each time on a different, precious porcelain service and the most luxurious table linens. If they were entertained in a private residence, the complete service was left behind for the owner as a token of the empress's appreciation; if they dined in an imperial mansion, the elegant 'door prize' went to one of the honoured guests. Teatime each afternoon found them merrily picnicking in the countryside as the servants dispensed glasses of tea from samovars steaming in the snow. The guests stretched their legs, changed sleighs and travelling companions and drove on. Even the early nightfall of the Russian winter was held at bay with giant bonfires which lighted the route.

No detail was too insignificant for Potemkin, no luxury was too difficult to provide. Catherine's own sleigh, built especially for the trip, was a complete, miniature *dacha* on runners, including a spacious drawing room, library, and imperial bedroom, all decorated in the most sumptuous manner. Six windows afforded panoramic views of the snowfields speeding past to the empress, Madame Protasova, and Mamonov, now in his eighteenth month as aide-de-camp. The cosy little party was often joined by the most entertaining of Catherine's other guests, who chatted, told stories and sang as they warmed themselves around porcelain stoves. The immense sleigh whipped along, drawn by thirty horses, attended by its own corps of hostlers and outriders. Fourteen other house-sized sleighs transported ministers, diplomats and assorted grandees. The balance of the party sorted itself out in less opulent but still comfortable vehicles.

Twenty-one days later, Prince Potemkin waited to welcome the holiday-makers to Kiev, where the delay until the spring thaw passed in a three-month-long court festival. Potemkin provided a glittering schedule of daily banquets, balls, receptions, theatricals and fireworks.

Catherine presided in the city's most magnificent palace. Lesser mansions, totally refurbished, completely staffed, their kitchens and wine cellars overflowing with comestibles, were assigned to the ministers and ambassadors. Seasoned courtiers were particularly keen to be invited to the empress's 'hermitage' gatherings and to the fabulous entertainments provided by the Austrian ambassador, Count Ludwig Cobenzl.

All this gala activity was centred on the venerable Kievan citadel located on the west bank of the Dnieper. Potemkin, in one of his melancholy, monastic moods, decamped from the 'High Town' to make his headquarters in Pechersky Lavra, the Monastery of the Caves, farther south on the river. He chanted and prayed with the monks, all the while stage-managing the enormous imperial party taking place in the city itself. France's charming new ambassador, Louis Philippe, Comte de Ségur, sketched the milieu that Potemkin created in his cloister:

> Whether from natural indolence or from an affected disdain which he thought useful and politic, this powerful, capricious favourite of Catherine's – who had perhaps just appeared in full field marshal's uniform covered with diamonds and edged in embroidery and lace, his hair dressed, curled and powdered like a French courtier – would now receive us wearing only a pelisse, open at the neck, with his legs half bare and his feet in slippers, his hair flat and unkempt. He would lie languidly stretched out on a broad divan, surrounded by . . . the greatest personages in the Empire, rarely inviting one of them to be seated.

In the midst of Potemkin's carnival of self-indulgence, Catherine was still trying to pass herself off as the liberal champion of the people. The Comte de Ségur was an aristocrat but an authentic friend of liberty. He had fought with Lafayette and Washington, and when he glimpsed the tattered, freezing wretches held at bayonet-point along their route, he questioned conditions in the countryside. Catherine's reply was a pearl of self-serving sophistry:

> I travel not to see places but people, and above all to be seen by them so they can feel my living presence among them and approach me with their petitions, knowing I will punish the injustices of those who have abused their authority.

No Russian peasant would have been allowed within a ballroom's length of the empress, but there were serious purposes for the sojourn in Kiev. Potemkin knew Kiev, the revered old 'Mother of Russian Cities', was a source of legitimacy for Catherine and her 'foreign' court in the eyes of the arch-conservative boyars of the provinces. The city also served as a pointer directed at the south, where the empress and her viceroy hoped to intimidate the Ottoman Empire.

Carefully planted rumours swept Europe that Catherine planned war against the sultan. The Austrian Emperor Joseph II was suspected as a co-conspirator (with some justification, in light of the 1781 treaty between Austria and Russia). England and Prussia made common cause in the event of a Russian attack. George III tried to lure Sweden into the alliance and, on the sly, subsidized the Turks.

In May, the Dnieper ice melted. So did Potemkin, who rejoined Catherine's 'travelling circus' as ringmaster and star performer when the company embarked for the river journey south. A flotilla of eighty ships had been launched for the trip, headed by seven fabulous galleys the like of which had not been seen since Byzantine times, especially constructed to transport the empress and her honoured guests.

The entire fleet was decorated in the Byzantine manner. The cabins sparkled with gilt, silks and brocade; liveried servants catered to every whim; meals were taken on solid gold plates; an orchestra on board each galley whiled away the moments between entertainments staged on the shore. Potemkin's touch penetrated to the most intimate arrangements; a mirrored panel beside Catherine's bed slipped back to provide instant access to young Mamonov's bed in the next room.

Officially rechristened, the Dnieper became once again the 'Borysthenes', its name under the Roman *Imperium*. Potemkin transformed both banks of the river for the entire two hundred and fifty mile trip to the south, providing a stupendous parade route through which the imperial ships made their way. At every turn in their stately promenade toward the sea, the voyagers were greeted with picture-postcard scenes, villages shining with fresh paint and filled with merry crowds, flowering gardens, forest glades and verdant meadows. Shepherds piped to flocks of fat sheep; youths and maidens scampered to the water's edge to present songs and dances; smartly uniformed troops of cavalry executed drills to the accompaniment of military bands; Cossacks galloped alongside the river bank to salute their sovereign. The mighty river itself yielded a musical tribute, when a barge-borne symphony orchestra floated by, playing an ode to Catherine. Day after day, the idyllic diorama swam past, numbing the viewers with an endless succession of saccharine pastorals. Catherine's attitude was coy surprise as the spectacle unfolded.

She asked Ségur, 'Is not my little household prettily furnished. Do you not find it well and agreeably run?'

No project to which Potemkin lent his name was complete without scandal. The Dnieper voyage had more than its share, including the charges that have stigmatized him through the centuries as a colossal fake. G.A.W. von Helbig, the ambassador of Saxony, was the source of the stories and of the term *Potemkinsche Dorfer* – Potemkin villages – which entered the language with lightning speed as a synonym for fraud. Friends of the prince, Ségur in particular, tried to defend him but even so kindly disposed an observer as the Prince de Ligne could not resist a malicious letter home:

> These loyal subjects certainly resembled each other strangely, and had the Empress alighted and visited one of these pleasing hamlets, she would have been disillusioned, for the whole thing was but a wonderfully devised stage-effect arranged by Potemkin. The villages were sham villages consisting only of flimsy façades, deceptive in the distance.
>
> It is a pity that the supposed inhabitants were real creatures of flesh and blood for these wretched peasants of Little Russia were forced by Potemkin to rush by cross-roads from one of the Empress's stopping places to the other, there to welcome her with songs and acclamations in her voyage along the Dnieper. Having played their parts, they were left to get home as best they could and many died of fatigue and hunger. Over a thousand villages in Little Russia lost the greater number of their inhabitants, as well as their flocks and herds, but they served Potemkin's purpose. The Empress was delighted.

Contemporary accounts gave the lie to this story; modern research has proved it totally false.

Without question, Catherine's New Russia had been hastily stitched together. Potemkin's 'new city' of Kherson had been built in six years, Sevastopol in three. Potemkin spruced up the scenery along the empress's path and gave grimy walls a fresh coat of whitewash, but the man who founded Ekaterinoslav, Kherson, Nikolaev and Sevastopol, creating them from the foundation stones up in the southern Russian wastelands, had no need for cardboard villages and treadmill actors. Regrettably, the accusation of fakery has never completely faded, casting a shadow over Potemkin's claim to statesmanship.

Waiting for Catherine at Kanev, the party's first port of call, was Stanislaus II Augustus of Poland – *né* Poniatowski, poet, failed king and Catherine's former lover. He was still besotted with the empress despite a quarter-century of separation, her repeated rebuffs and, impossible to ignore, the partition in which she, Frederick of Prussia and Maria Theresa of Austria sliced up his kingdom like a fat Polish ham.

Doggedly, he once again pleaded his cause with his former mistress. Potemkin hoped to include Stanislas's seven million subjects and excellent military machine in the Russian-Austrian treaty. Catherine longed to see his royal heels. Business was brief, curt and concluded in a single day. The empress embarked the following morning with insulting haste, leaving a perfunctory note of regret.

Old lovers, it was plain, were unwelcome in Catherine's entourage if they had the presumption to age well. Slim, erect, elegant Stanislas II was a devastating mirror held up to the empress in her corsets.

At her next stop waited a much more compatible travelling companion, the young emperor Joseph II, now seated alone on the throne of Austria since the death of his domineering mother. Joseph and Catherine knew and liked each other personally from the time of his visit incognito to St Petersburg as 'Count Falkenstein'. Although he was the brother of the arch-reactionary queen of France, Marie Antoinette, Joseph paid lip-service to republicanism and shared Catherine's friends of the Enlightenment, Voltaire and Diderot. Catherine invited Joseph along on her travels, hoping to whip up a full-blown military alliance against the Turks.

They met in Kaidak, a town immediately above the Dnieper rapids. Leaving the rest of the imperial party to negotiate the white waters of the river, they travelled ahead by carriage to the first of Potemkin's 'new' cities, Ekaterinoslav ('Catherine's Glory'). No Potemkin village this, but a vibrant metropolis. It may have been a bit rough around the the edges but the city was obviously complete, with houses, mansions, a silk industry and an archbishop who presided as the two sovereigns laid the cornerstones of a cathedral. (Potemkin boasted it would be grander than St Peter's in Rome. Sad to say, there never was a cathedral, but Catherine's namesake city survived and prospered to become the Soviet Union's mighty southern industrial centre, Dniepropetrovsk.)

Seams showed embarrassingly at their next stop, Kherson, where the empress and emperor were forced to steal into town without a welcoming cannonade. Kherson's six thousand homes had been slapped together on such shaky foundations it was feared the vibration would bring them tumbling down.

The fortress city was laid out in marshland so unhealthy that fever had killed thousands as it was being built. In the dockyards were ships of unseasoned wood, waiting to be moored beside quays that did not exist. Catherine ignored everything but Potemkin's flattery; Joseph II kept his peace and wrote confidentially of the prince's realm,

. . . he commands . . . hordes of slaves obey. Fifty thousand persons were destroyed in these new provinces by the toil and the emanations from the morasses.

A diplomatic storm suddenly blew up. Potemkin's Black Sea fleet, assembling near the mouth of the Dnieper to greet the party at Sevastopol, was suddenly faced by a squadron of the Turkish navy which came on station to guard the nearby Ottoman port of Ochakov. Catherine was told of undercover assistance given to the Turks by English and French 'advisers' in the area and erupted in anger. Both countries' ambassadors, Alleyn Fitzherbert and the Comte de Ségur, were ordered into her presence and heard themselves accused of conspiring against her with the sultan.

The squall passed quickly as the cortège rolled on into the Crimean peninsula, the land at journey's end. Here, Potemkin surpassed himself as a fabulist. According to one account, the empress's carriage was saluted at the frontier,

. . . by Caucasian princes . . . beautiful as the dreams of sculptors, who rode to meet her armed with bows and arrows. Circassian troops in silver robes riding bareback on milk-white steeds bore down on her like a dazzling cloud. When the minarets of Bashtasarai rose on the horizon . . . [the party was] surrounded by men in long, gold-embroidered robes and closely veiled women. They were led to the palace, where cool fountains played in marble recesses, and there Catherine mounted the throne of the Great Khan.

His mistress's brief rest-stop in Bashtasarai gave Potemkin an irresistible excuse for wanton spending. To billet her party for just ten days of sightseeing, the khan's palace underwent a year of redecorating. Potemkin conscripted Catherine's own gifted Scottish architect, Charles Cameron, to direct the army of workers which refurbished every square foot. They spread the marble halls with acres of precious carpets, painstakingly restored the mosaics, laid on miles of gilding, repaired the plumbing that fed the fountains and brought the gardens to perfect bloom against the precise evening of the empress's arrival.

That night, the travellers found themselves in a city transformed by torchlight within and fireworks without. Bidden to a feast worthy of Kublai Khan, they dined between bursts of applause for a fantastic vaudeville of singers and dancers, imported from every corner of New Russia. Outings and day-trips to the region's historic sights alternated with evenings of Oriental enchantment until the party set out for its ultimate destination, the seaport of Sevastopol.

There, the last and greatest wonders in Potemkin's bag of tricks were revealed. In a specially constructed pavilion overlooking the Black Sea, the welcoming banquet came to an unforgettable conclusion when curtains parted to reveal the bay of Sevastopol. Russia's newly launched Black Sea fleet, sixteen men-of-war and twenty-four frigates, lay at anchor. Regiments of Potemkin's Tartar warriors massed on the slopes from the heights to the water's edge. While the ships' guns thundered repeated salutes, the entire force of seamen and soldiers roared a great hurrah for the empress. With Joseph II in tow, Catherine was driven to the port for a formal inspection, passing through the magnificent Sevastopol naval complex of fortifications, wharves and barracks.

The naval review in the harbour was an appropriate prelude to Potemkin's finale. He fielded two entire armies, a few days later, to re-enact the Battle of Poltava for his royal guests. Full-scale, in correct uniform, and in exact detail, the troops of Peter the Great once again launched themselves against the army of Charles XII of Sweden, in the battle which established Russia as the dominant power of northern Europe in 1709.

Catherine beamed at the titanic display of Russian might. The Austrian emperor, awestruck by Potemkin's achievement, was chilled by the thought that the prince's Tartars could march in minutes, and his fleet could bombard Constantinople in a matter of hours.

Chapter Twenty-Five

Drawing the Tooth

From the emotional heights of Sevastopol, the royal tourists were brought to earth with disconcerting speed. Joseph II abruptly faced rebellions at home, forcing his hostess to make an early departure to speed him towards Vienna.

When Catherine and Potemkin said goodbye, she clung to him in a tearful outpouring of embraces and endearments. Overwhelmed by his love, his loyalty and the incredible tributes he had laid at her feet, she would willingly have discarded Mamonov to rekindle the grand passion she had shared with the Cyclops a decade before. Potemkin hastily backtracked, rejecting her advances delicately but firmly. After years spent among the beauties of the south, he had no taste at all for fat little old ladies, however imperial. The Cyclops's 'wife' drove north to Moscow in deep depression.

Disasters awaited her, political, military and private, a woeful march of events that was to continue for the next year and a half. She arrived in Moscow expecting to celebrate the silver anniversary of her reign. Instead she found herself facing a famine and a hornet's nest of resentment. Her nobles were holding off insurrection in the central provinces only by paying for grain out of their own pockets. Potemkin's prodigal spending infuriated everyone. There was audible grumbling about Catherine's lavish trip. She decreed economy measures for the court, reimbursed the loudest complainers and patched things over as best she could.

In August 1787, the sultan impudently disregarded the timetable she and Potemkin had worked out for the Russian conquest of the Ottoman empire. Her ambassador to the Sublime Porte was tossed into a dungeon. The sultan demanded instant Russian withdrawal from the Crimea. Catherine refused.

The Turks attacked in force, with a suddenness and energy that startled her and threw Potemkin into a complete funk. His foolishness was apparent to the world. Operatic sabre-rattling in the Crimea and international publicity given to the 'Greek Project' were puffs after all, and nothing more. Turkish regiments strolled north through New Russia, brushing aside such Russian defenders as they found; Potemkin had scattered his best units all over the southern landscape to parade and stage mock battles for the empress.

Catherine stubbornly named him commander-in-chief of the new war effort, ignoring the availability of two of her finest military men, Peter Rumiantsev and Alexander Suvorov. An endless stream of messages from the empress in St Petersburg to her commanding general in Kherson called for victories. She got nothing in reply but Potemkin's repeated offers of resignation.

When he finally stirred himself, months later, to besiege the port of Ochakov, his enemies in the capital licked their lips over tales of a palatial underground bunker at Kherson from which he directed the Turkish campaign. In halls decorated with lapis lazuli, the stories went, hundreds of servants, a complete orchestra and a corps of concubines recruited from among his officers' wives catered to Potemkin's debauchery. The prince of Tauris, they said, too corrupt to fight, was willing to surrender New Russia without firing a shot.

Calamities kept coming, by land and by sea. Revolt flared up in the Crimea itself, slowing Potemkin's already glacial conduct of hostilities. When Joseph II honoured his treaty obligations and launched a Balkan campaign with himself in personal command, the Turks trounced him. The Habsburg emperor limped home to face rebellions throughout his empire. His crippled army and broken health pulled the last prop from under Catherine's hoped-for assault by the Christian powers on the Muslim Ottomans.

When a great storm in the south nearly destroyed her new Black Sea navy, the sea of troubles surrounding the empress became an actual one. In the north, Catherine averted a mutiny among the officers of the Baltic fleet, only to face an attack by Gustavus III of Sweden. The Swedish monarch struck with the blessing of Britain, where it was hoped a Baltic Sea threat would foreclose any Russian adventures in the Mediterranean. Gustavus's squadrons mauled the Russians at Svenskund, sinking fifty-three ships and killing ten thousand men. Ironically, the most famous fatality of Svenskund was Sir Samuel Grieg, the same borrowed British admiral who had engineered the victory of Cesme Bay for Alexis Orlov. Swedish ships followed up, actually sailing into the Neva estuary to shell St Petersburg. Catherine, true to her nickname of the Imperturbable, ignored the noise. She refused to seek safety for herself, but moved her choicest paintings out of the Hermitage.

Her fortunes reached low ebb when Gustavus III galloped into Russian Finland at the head of thirty thousand fierce Swedish troops. The hundred thousand defenders of St Petersburg promised by Potemkin failed to materialize. A pitifully thin line stood between the Swedes and the capital; it was pure luck that Gustavus was sabotaged by his own nobles, who pulled Catherine's chestnuts out of the fire by declaring their king's war unconstitutional. Gustavus's withdrawal was temporary, but it gave the Russians time to strengthen their defences.

Long, grim months crept past before the first significant Russian victory in the south. In December 1788, it took bloody assaults and frightful casualty lists to conquer Ochakov, the tiny Turkish port near Sevastopol which Potemkin had boasted to Catherine could be overwhelmed in a single day. The empress, beside herself with joy over the faintest light in the wartime sky, wrote to Potemkin, 'I take you by both ears and kiss you in my thoughts, Grishenka, dear friend of my bosom!'

With the world crashing around her ears, the defection of Alexander Mamonov provided a note of almost comic relief. For months, Monsieur Redcoat had complained of being 'stifled' by the court, a condition peculiarly aggravated by all forms of transportation. He was stifled by the imperial sledge, so he said, as it sped toward Kiev. He was stifled on the imperial galley, despite the Dnieper breezes. When they returned to St Petersburg, his attacks became so acute that travel in Catherine's own coach made him ill. His mistress shrugged and allowed him his own stables, with personal coaches built to his own design.

Predictably, his malady began to undermine Mamonov's nightly performance, leading to tearful scenes with Catherine. He wrote to Potemkin begging to be relieved of his duties as aide-de-camp. Potemkin, ringed about by the rampaging Turkish army, shot back, 'It is your duty to remain at your post for the duration of the war. Don't be a fool and ruin your career!'

Potemkin knew, the whole court knew, what Catherine did not. Mamonov's shortness of breath was due to his panting after one of her ladies-in-waiting, Princess Darya Scherbatov. In June 1789, when the princess was too big with child for further concealment, the lovers were summoned before the empress. She was scandalized. She stormed. She wept (in private). She forgave, with a parting gift of an estate and a hundred thousand rubles. She went so far as to preside at the young people's wedding before sending off Mamonov to breathe more easily, presumably, in the country.

Just off-stage, waiting to be introduced by Potemkin's enemies, was

Plato Alexandrovich Zubov, a lieutenant in the horse guards. Within a week of Mamonov's wedding, the twenty-two-year-old Zubov was Catherine's aide-de-camp and the sixty-year-old empress was rehearsing his virtues in letters to Potemkin. She prattled on about the new paragon at her side:

> the most innocent soul with the kindest heart and the sweetest disposition in the world . . . without malice or treachery . . . modest, devoted, supremely grateful. He weeps like a child when he cannot enter my room.

With the blindness of infatuation, she insisted that Zubov shared her feelings toward Prince Potemkin:

> The child thinks you are cleverer, more amusing and more agreeable than anyone around you, but keep this to yourself, for he does not know that I know it.

Zubov, for his part, dripped acid with every mention of Potemkin's name, dinning in her ears the mistresses Serenissimus kept, his southern palaces, his multi-million-ruble extravagances. Catherine defended Potemkin, holding him up to her protégé as a master statesman, but by year's end she was completely under Zubov's spell. For the first time in more than a decade, Potemkin was forced to contend with a favourite not of his choosing. Zubov's soft-spoken manner, furthermore, masked the razor-sharp skills of a courtier. A palace brat who came to the court in his boyhood to serve as a page, Zubov grew up among the palace factions. The young guardsman prospered in the serpent's nest of court intrigue as if it were his natural environment.

If Potemkin did not instantly run scared, his friend Bezborodko did. He wrote to the prince, warning him of the pretty viper nestling at Catherine's breast.

A series of battlefield triumphs brought the nation's run of bad luck to an end. Shaking off their earlier failures, the Austrians occupied Belgrade. Potemkin took the fortress of Bender, then marched to the Dniester River and captured Akkerman. The Turks were defeated at Focsani and Rymnik. Potemkin, who usually spared his men unnecessary casualties, was willing to pay a grisly price for victory over the sultan. He sent Suvorov against a Danube fortress forty miles from the Black Sea with this curt order of battle:

'You will capture Ismail, whatever the cost.'

Storming Ismail cost more than twenty thousand Russian and thirty-four thousand Turkish lives. The armies grappled in hellish weather, so cold that it was impossible to bury the dead; holes had to be hacked in the frozen river to dispose of the corpses. When the city was taken, Suvorov was equally curt in his victory message:

'The Russian flag floats on the ramparts of Ismail.'

In St Petersburg, Catherine used the occasion to vent her spite on the British for fomenting the Swedish attack from the north. 'I hope that those who wish to drive me out of St Petersburg,' she told the British ambassador, 'will allow me to retire to Constantinople.'

Russia was obviously winning the southern war. Gustavus III of Sweden bent to the shifting wind before it could blow north and signed the Treaty of Verela in August, 1790.

Catherine's only major frustration was Poland. There, the old Prussian fox, Frederick, had outflanked her by concluding a mutual defence pact with King Stanislas while Catherine was distracted by war with the Turks and Swedes. The Polish Diet then ratified a new constitution, which actually strengthened the monarchy. It infuriated the empress. Zubov and his pack of relatives, greedy for Polish estates, egged Catherine on when she melodramatically identified the Polish reforms with the Jacobins who were turning the world upside-down in France.

The French Revolution, a hateful reversal of what she believed to be the appointed order of things, stripped away the last of Catherine's republican pretensions. Voltaire's marble bust disappeared from her apartments. She welcomed the fleeing French aristocracy, clamped down on the liberals she had once encouraged in Russia and urged Austria, England and Prussia to declare war on France – without, however, pledging a single Russian soldier.

Once the European powers were firmly tied down by their expeditions, she planned a grim vengeance on the 'nest of Jacobins' she fancied she had uncovered in Warsaw.

At Catherine's elbow as she dealt with the new forces in Europe was the most adored of apprentices, Plato Zubov. She described 'the child's' first adventures in foreign policy in doting letters to Potemkin. They were ashes on the prince's head. His influence with the empress was being challenged at the very moment something infinitely more precious was under attack – his health. Years of gluttony, drunkenness and sexual excess took their toll. His bouts of 'spleen' became frequent and agonizing. Suddenly, the indestructible, one-eyed giant was a mortally sick middle-aged man fighting off his second attack of malaria in a year.

Serving with him was Valerian Zubov, the detested favourite's brother. A flicker of Potemkin's old impertinence showed itself when he sent Valerian hastening north from his headquarters at Jassy, carrying a private message to Catherine. He was coming home, Potemkin wrote, 'to extract a painful tooth'. (In Russian, 'zub' means 'tooth').

At the first real scent of victory in the south, he dropped everything and hurried to St Petersburg and the empress. Catherine smiled her imperturbable smile and prepared a hero's welcome, but the lines were clearly drawn for combat between the favourites.

How Potemkin hoped to draw the 'tooth' was anyone's guess. The court remembered the stormy confrontation in which he had ousted the spying Ermolov. There were rumours of candidates more tractable than Zubov (Potemkin *always* had someone in mind). Bezborodko favoured Potemkin wooing Catherine personally, despite the fevers and cramps that wracked him. Potemkin was confident he could again captivate the empress as in the past. (Had not Catherine made it plain at Sevastopol that she would welcome his return as a full-time lover?)

Whatever the outcome, sick or not, Potemkin beamed his way home like a plump ray of southern sunshine, the quintessential courtier spinning glorious plans for his return to the imperial presence.

In every town *en route*, triumphal arches, parades and Te Deums welcomed the conqueror of the Turks. Catherine dispatched a delegation of official greeters from St Petersburg to Moscow; Bezborodko, bursting with the latest news of Zubov's back-biting, eagerly headed it. On Potemkin's arrival in the capital, Catherine looked at the ailing, aging Cyclops and saw what she wanted to see. If she understood how precarious his health really was, she refused to acknowledge it in public – the Prince of Tauris was a pillar of the empire. She described him a few weeks later in a letter to the Prince de Ligne:

One looks at Marshal Potemkin and must admit that his victories and his successes beautify him. He has returned to us from the army as handsome as the day, as merry as a finch, as brilliant as a constellation of stars, wittier than ever and giving every day a feast more beautiful than the last.

Estimates of Potemkin's squandering in St Petersburg that spring range from a quarter of a million to more than a million rubles. In the great rooms and grounds of the Tauride Palace he hosted banquets, balls, masquerades, receptions and firework displays that were without precedent. The masked ball which saluted the empress's sixty-second birthday in April 1791 was the last and, by all accounts, the most lavish.

Potemkin, impresario that he was, even invited the neighbours to a gala street fair outside the palace, where the common folk of the district were entertained by games, rides, fountains flowing with wine, endless barrels of Russian *kvass*, and trestles groaning with food. They returned the favour by lustily cheering his guests to the door. Catherine's carriage was engulfed in a perfect frenzy of adulation, orchestrated to the last drunken hurrah.

Charles Masson was among the bedazzled guests who stood watching the sovereign's arrival.

The Empress entered the vestibule to the sound of lively music, executed by upwards of three hundred performers. Thence she repaired to the principal saloon, whither she was followed by the crowd; and ascended a platform, raised for her in the centre of the saloon, and surrounded by transparent decorations, with appropriate inscriptions. The company arranged themselves under the colonnade, and in the boxes, and then commenced the second act of this extraordinary spectacle.

The Grand Dukes Alexander and Constantine, at the head of the flower of all the young persons about the Court, performed a ballet. The dancers, male and female, were forty-eight in number, all dressed in white, with magnificent scarves, and covered in jewels, estimated to be worth above ten millions of rubles. The Ballet was performed to select airs suitable to the occasion, and interspersed with songs. The celebrated Lepic concluded with a *pas* of his own composing.

The company then removed to another saloon, adorned with the richest tapestries the Gobelins could produce. In the centre was an artificial elephant, covered with rubies and emeralds; and his cornac was a Persian richly clad. On his giving the signal, by striking on a bell, a curtain rose, and a magnificent stage appeared at the end of the apartment. On it were performed two ballets of a new kind, and a lively comedy, by which the company were much amused, concluded the spectacle. This was followed by chorus singing, various dances, and an Asiatic procession, remarkable for its diversity of dresses, all the people subject to the sceptre of the Empress being represented . . .

Presently after, all the apartments, illuminated with the greatest care, were thrown open to the eager curiosity of the crowd. The whole palace seemed on fire: the garden was covered with sparkling stones; mirrors innumerable, pyramids and globes of glass, reflected the magic spectacle in all directions. A table was spread with six hundred covers; and the rest of the guests were served standing. The table service was of gold and silver; the most exquisite dainties were served in vessels of the greatest richness; antique cups overflowed with the most costly liquors; and the most expensive chandeliers gave light to the table. Officers and domestics in great number, richly clothed, were eager to anticipate the wishes of the guests.

Toasts were raised to the empress's glory, to Potemkin's leadership, and to fresh Russian victory in the field. Only days before, Prince Basil Repnin had forded the Danube with forty thousand troops to engage the Turks at Machin. Russian regiments had exterminated a force of more than one hundred thousand Ottoman warriors under the grand vizier. Potemkin drained his glass with sour formality, saluting another man's triumph. Catherine ignored his pleas to follow up Repnin's victory and take Constantinople itself. She placed herself completely in Zubov's camp, which favoured a quick (and weak) treaty of peace.

When they parted that night, Potemkin fell to his knees before Catherine. She was fulsome in her gratitude but sharply reminded him of the treaty to be negotiated at Jassy, the Jacobins to be exterminated in Poland. When they realized how coldly imperial the moment had become, they were both suddenly reduced to tears, the one-eyed, middle-aged courtier defeated by a stripling intriguer, the empress trapped in an elephantine, dropsical body only an unprincipled adventurer could love.

It was the Cyclops's last, theatrical bid for Catherine's heart. A few weeks later, he left for Jassy and the Turkish treaty. What strength he had crumbled during the journey as his carriage jolted over dusty, broiling summer roads. Doubled over by horrible internal pain, he ignored the advice of his own doctors and brushed aside the balms and nostrums which arrived daily from Catherine. When the pain subsided for an hour or two, the physicians looked on in helpless horror as their patient wolfed down gargantuan quantities of food. One such meal, consumed while Potemkin burned with fever, included 'a ham, a salted goose, three or four chickens [washed down with] *kvass*, mead and wines'. Between bouts of gluttony, Serenissimus existed on a hideous diet of cabbage soup and raw turnips.

Understandably, he was forced to absent himself from the Jassy treaty negotiations in a daze of illness. He eventually fled the Moldavian capital for an imagined sanctuary in Nikolaev, travelling with his favourite niece, Sashenka, and a tiny party of secretaries and physicians. His final message to Catherine was a cry of despair,

> Matouchka! Beloved Sovereign! I have no more strength to endure my torments. My only chance is to leave this town . . . I do not know what will become of me. Your very faithful and very grateful subject – Potemkin.

Somewhere between Jassy and Nikolaev, he knew his time had come. Stopping the coach, he insisted on being laid on the ground. With Sashenka wailing beside him in the dust, Potemkin died at the age of fifty-two. The members of the party searched their pockets for the gold coins dictated by Russian custom. There were none. Finally, a coachman donated a five-kopeck copper to close the Cyclops's single eye.

When the courier reached St Petersburg a week later, the news devastated Catherine. She was bled repeatedly and huddled sobbing in her bed for days before she could bring herself to make the formal announcement that the prince had died. Endlessly, she whimpered, 'Whom shall I rely on now?' She relayed this bitterest of news items to Baron von Grimm:

> A terrible blow has fallen on my head [when] a courier brought me the very sad news that my pupil, my friend, my idol I must say, Prince Potemkin of Tauride has died. I am in such a state of affliction as you cannot imagine. To an excellent heart, he added a rare understanding and an extraordinary broadness of mind. His views were always broad and magnanimous, he was very humane, full of knowledge, singularly amiable. His ideas were always unique. . . . never was there a man with such a gift for the clever word and the apt remark. . . . No one in the world could be led by others less than he. He was passionately, zealously devoted to me, scolding and growing angry when he thought it was possible to do better. With age and experience he corrected his faults. His rarest quality was a physical, intellectual and moral courage that set him absolutely apart from the rest of mankind. Because of that we were always able to understand each other and ignore those who could not do so. In a word, he was a statesman.

Chapter Twenty-Six

The Rites of Cybele

P ublic mourning for Potemkin was embarrassingly brief. Obsequies, such as they were, took place in Kherson, where his niece Alexandra erected a tomb for him in the church of St Catherine. In St Petersburg, the empress refrained from publishing a memorial, nor did she plan a monument to his memory, lest she offend Plato Zubov. She honoured Potemkin mainly by paying his debts. They were enormous, but he owned innumerable palaces and country estates, a mammoth collection of artworks, thousands of peasants and, it was rumoured, half a million rubles in diamonds. The prince of Tauris did not go bankrupt to his grave.

Following Zubov's lead, the courtiers expressed their condolences, pulled long faces for a fortnight and returned to their normal pursuits. One of them, Count Feodor Rostopchin, wrote:

> It is most extraordinary that [the prince] has already been completely forgotten. Generations to come will not bless his memory . . . for he possessed to the highest degree the art of inspiring hatred even as he scattered benefactions with a negligent hand. One would have thought his chief goal in life was always to abase others so he might rise above them. His greatest weakness was to become infatuated with every woman he met. He wished to be thought a rake and ridiculous as this was, his desire was completely satisfied.

First among Potemkin's women, the grieving empress was obliged to blink back her tears in the presence of her young lover. There were no sighs for the Cyclops, however desperately she missed the empire-builder, the battlefield genius, the courtier with his glorious gestures. The ugly, rollicking clown would mimic her court no more. The husband and lover were dust in Kherson.

Potemkin's ghost was kept alive, curiously enough, in the jealous heart of Plato Zubov, who was driven to outshine the prince in all things. Fancying himself a conqueror, the young favourite concocted a greedy new assault on Poland. He dreamed of a place in history, revived Potemkin's 'Greek Project' as an 'Oriental Project' and packed off his brother Valerian to invade Persia. Zubov sought diplomatic laurels when he negotiated the hoped-for dynastic marriage between the empress's granddaughter Alexandra and the new King of Sweden.

Charles Masson sketched the old and new favourites:

> Potemkin owed his greatness most of all to himself. Zubov owed his only to Catherine's decline. We watched him wax in power, wealth and prestige . . . as Catherine waned in activity, vigour and understanding. He was obsessed with the desire to do everything, or to seem to do it. His haughtiness was matched by the servility of those who rushed to prostrate themselves to him. Everyone crawled at Zubov's feet. He stood erect and thought himself a great man.

Catherine was old now, toothless, gasping for breath, the famous dignity of her walk hobbled by the ugly weight of Bright's disease. She walked, that is, on good days. At other times she was pushed in a wheelchair by the broad-shouldered Zubov. Special ramps were constructed to ease her movements in the Raphael Loggia and her beautiful English gardens at Czarskoe Selo. She who had once derided the empress Elizabeth's paintpots and potions now had recourse to the same vain remedies herself, but she accepted the breakdown of her body without complaint. Her formal schedule was as heavy as ever. Into the endless *levées* and receptions she waddled, 'wearing Zubov', in Bezborodko's contemptuous phrase, 'like a decoration'.

At all costs, Plato must be pleased.

His was the strong arm on which she leaned in public. His was the supple body that fired in her the last embers of passion, behind the boudoir doors. According to Charles Masson's diaries:

> Yet even in this advanced period of her life she was seen to revive the orgies and lupercalia which she had formerly celebrated with the brothers of Orlov. Valerian, a younger brother of Zubov, and Peter Solikov, their friend, were associated in office with the favourite. With these three young libertines did Catherine spend her days. . . . It was at this juncture she formed a more intimate society . . . under the name of the 'Little Hermitage'. The parties were frequently masqued and the greatest privacy prevailed . . . [as they] engaged in all sorts of frolics and gambols. In short, there was no kind of gaiety which was not permitted.

Catherine afterwards formed another assembly, more confined and more mysterious, which was called the 'Little Society'. The three favourites of whom we have just been speaking, Branicka, Protasova and some confidential women and *valets-de-chambre* were its only members. In this the Cybele of the north celebrated her most secret mysteries. The particulars of these amusements are not fit to be repeated . . .

According to another account, Zubov returned to his apartments from these encounters 'prostrate with fatigue and pitiably sad, throwing himself on his couch with a scented handkerchief'.

Masson was neither the first nor the most lurid chronicler of Catherine's sexual history. From the beginning, stories had circulated about the little Grand Duchess of Russia with the welcoming bed. Her first slanderer was her first lover, Serge Saltikov, who regaled Paris and Dresden with stories heartbreaking in their intimate details. He was followed by the Duchesse de Choiseul, who fulminated to the courtiers of Versailles against 'the usurping whore' who murdered Peter III.

Catherine's domestic arrangements were bound to come to the attention of Frederick II of Prussia. His respect for her political acumen soured as early as 1773 when she sent her lover Gregory Orlov barging into the Turkish peace negotiations. No one could be blunter than Frederick. 'It is terrible,' he complained to his brother, Prince Henry, 'when the prick and the cunt decide the interests of Europe.'

Late in 1777, fashionable London snickered over Ambassador James Howard Harris's reports of the candidates who queued up to audition for the favourite's post with the *éprouveuse*, Countess Bruce, and with the empress herself. The crisis of the moment was the departure of Semyon Zorich, 'the Adonis'. Stalwarts who rose to the occasion included young Prince Kantemir, the war minister's nephew, said to be even more beautiful than Zorich; a handsome Russian diplomat who performed during a ball at the Peterhof; and a visiting Persian prince whose 'extraordinary physical attributes' abundantly filled Catherine's specifications. When the choice ultimately fell on Ivan Rimsky-Korsakov, sighs of regret were heard across two continents as Harris's salacious anecdotes came to an end.

The measure of the men in Catherine's life became increasingly genital. When Potemkin absented himself to fight the second Turkish war, she engaged in casual liaisons with the likes of the American sailor-mercenary John Paul Jones. He bragged that the empress and he had treated each other for syphilis. Voltaire's 'Semiramis of the North' was now 'Messalina', her unflagging sexuality in old age perceived as grotesque. There were tales of experiments in bestiality conducted in the imperial stables (never proven – nor probable, given the limits of human physiology).

In her sixties, the ruin of her private reputation was of little moment to Catherine, whose public stature as the most distinguished monarch of her time was reinforced by the death of Frederick the Great and the execution of Louis XVI. Her blue eyes sparkled with all their usual zest. The famous smile might be a trifle fixed, from moment to moment, but the smile was there. She harboured no illusions when she wrote to Baron von Grimm on the fiftieth anniversary of her arrival in Russia, with a roll call of the doddering survivors of her youth.

> I doubt there are ten people in St Petersburg who remember. There is still Betzkoy, blind, decrepit, gaga, asking young couples whether they remember Peter the First. Old Countess Matouchkine who, at seventy-eight, danced yesterday at a wedding . . . the grand chamberlain Naryshkin and his wife . . . the master of horse who denies this because he does not wish to be thought so old . . . and one of my old maids, who forgets everything. These are all proofs of old age, and I am one of them.

For a moment only, this clear-eyed old woman's private world had teetered on the precipice with Potemkin's death, but her iron will permitted no regrets for what might have been. She had written to Potemkin himself that in Zubov's arms she 'came back to life like a fly that was numbed by the cold'. To her enraptured eyes her ignorant, scheming lover represented youth and the future. She let youth have its day. Plato strutted about the court with a great plume in his hat, toying with a pet monkey as he listened to his sycophants. His uniform was so tricked out with decorations, Masson thought he looked like a ribbon-seller at a fair.

Potemkin's notoriety as a philanderer was especially galling to the favourite. The moment he felt sure of the empress, Plato embarked on wholesale seductions. The ladies scurried into his bed with little urging. Potemkin, curse his memory, must not go down in legend as the greater rake; Plato Zubov would surpass him by corrupting the bride of Grand Duke Alexander, Elizabeth Alexeyevna. The grand duchess was far too intelligent to succumb, but neither she nor any of the other ladies dared to report Zubov to Catherine. The grand duke himself was forced to dance attendance on Catherine's *minion* to protect his young wife.

Zubov's erotic adventures among the ladies-in-waiting, while the huffing and puffing continued nightly in Catherine's chambers, would have sapped the energies of Casanova himself. The favorite sniffed his handkerchief, preened and swaggered forth, determined to cut a grander figure than the dead Potemkin.

Chapter Twenty-Seven

Ghosts

Z ubov eclipsed the Cyclops only in his greed.
The second partition of Poland provided the favourite with a
spectacular opportunity for booty. In 1792, he rushed Bezborodko to Jassy for peace negotiations with the sultan. The foreign
minister returned from Jassy with a ridiculous treaty and precious little
profit to show for three years of Russian battle casualties. His empress
and her favourite willingly ignored his failure because their heads were
filled with dreams of expropriated Polish wealth. As the ceasefire
disengaged troops from the Turkish front, they were immediately
moved to the Polish border.

Catherine was as eager for the partition as Zubov but, seasoned
propagandist that she was, she used the Terror in France as her excuse
for tyranny in Poland. If the Terror did not actually terrify her, she
gave a convincing performance; she smuggled passports to Louis XVI
and Marie Antoinette and suffered public agonies over the flight to
Varennes, the trials and the beheadings. She invoked memories of the
Pugachevschina and saw Jacobins behind every Polish bush. Her cries
of anguish were carefully orchestrated for a select international audience, followed by an inevitable call to arms by Czarina Catherine II,
preserver of the *ancien régime*, protector of the East from 'the hydra-
headed monster of revolution'. (It was considered impolite to remember her forty-year flirtation with the liberals of the French
Enlightenment.)

A puppet Polish group was persuaded to denounce the new constitution and appeal to the Russian empress for 'protection'. Catherine
immediately unleashed an overwhelming military force against her
former lover, King Stanislas, ordering nearly one hundred thousand
troops into Poland and Lithuania. Stanislas looked to Prussia for
protection under the treaty of 1790, but Frederick the Great was dead.
His nephew Frederick William II sold out the Polish king without a
second thought.

Betrayed by the Prussians, Stanislas wilted. His Diet sat for four days at Grodno in silent defiance of their king, Catherine's ambassador, Count Yacov Sievers, and a ring of Russian guns. The delegates were so outraged by the treachery of Prussia they refused to vote on the fate of their homeland. Finally, Sievers ratified the partition by fiat. He declared that the delegates' silence implied consent, and Poland was whittled to one third of its original size, with barely four million citizens and an army of fifteen thousand. Zubov's appetite for spoils beggared belief. He and his cronies took title to thousands of square miles of eastern Poland and most of the three million Poles enslaved in the new Russian territories.

Savaged by Catherine and pillaged by Zubov, the ancient Polish kingdom vanished from the map of Europe scarcely a year later.

To lay the ghost of Potemkin, even the plunder of Poland was not enough for the favourite. He immediately set out to wheedle Potemkin's great southern fiefdom for himself. Catherine handed over the Cyclops's beloved New Russia without a murmur, appointing Zubov at twenty-six to Potemkin's old post of governor-general. Because Potemkin had been a Knight of St Andrew, she was obliged to knight Plato, too. He now ruled more than a quarter of the empire, with great arrogance but little ability. It is not recorded whether or not he actually visited his new domain, but it is certain that two years later when the empress created him prince and gave him command of the Black Sea fleet, he had never set foot aboard ship.

The tormented Poles, meanwhile, rose in a desperate insurrection. In 1794 nobles, peasants and soldiers fought shoulder to shoulder against the Russians. First at Krakow, then in cities and towns across the Polish plain, they rallied to a superb leader, Thaddeus Kosciusko, a resourceful army officer who had served with George Washington twenty years earlier. Kosciusko was a reluctant hero. He considered the uprising premature but he won victories against the Russians despite enormous odds. The Russian garrison at Warsaw was overwhelmed. Catherine and Frederick William II of Prussia, caught napping, blamed each other for the débâcle. Leopold II, who had succeeded his brother Joseph in Austria, was determined not to be shut out and hurried forward with demands of his own. In the confusion there was a momentary spark of hope for the rebels, snuffed out only days later when Kosciusko fell wounded in the Battle of Maciejowice.

Suvorov's troops stormed back into Warsaw, massacring an entire suburb of the city on their way. Europe shuddered as the corpses of twelve thousand men, women and children were heaped up in the streets of Praga. Catherine expressed her personal sentiments by promoting Suvorov to field marshal. She shipped Kosciusko off to the fortress of Schlusselburg in Russia and offered her 'hospitality' to Stanislas; with tears of relief, the king abdicated his thirty-one year reign to become a permanent 'guest' in a palace in Grodno guarded by Russian soldiers.

The Russian empress, the Prussian king and the Austrian emperor haggled over the last scraps of Poland. Suvorov's army was in occupation so the empress had the advantage, with the power to promise much and cede little. Catherine graciously allowed Prussia to seize Warsaw and permitted Austria to take Krakow and Lubin, while great stretches of territory to the east, including Kurland and most of Lithuania, became the western frontiers of Russia. Zubov and his hangers-on, needless to say, again fattened their fortunes with sequestered Polish estates.

Her hydra-hunting at an end, Catherine now expressed joy and thanksgiving for her success in 'putting down the revolution in Eastern Europe'. The world ignored the ballyhoo and saw the partition of 1795 for what it was – conquest and massacre, brutal and inexcusable. The entire affair was a sickening betrayal of the liberal ideals she had once espoused and the policy supported by Potemkin, who felt little sympathy for the Poles but shrewdly understood the strategic value of a kingdom to the west, however weak, as a buffer state.

Eventually, Catherine wrote 'Finis Polonia' across an unrecognizable map of Europe. She had barely laid aside the quill before Prince Plato was at her side, aquiver with a plan to revive Potemkin's 'Greek Project' and transform it into an 'Oriental Project'. A grand strategy of renewed expansion in the south and east, the scheme would recoup Bezborodko's failure at Jassy, give Zubov a glorious niche in Russian history and, he hoped, obliterate the memory of Potemkin forever. Zubov had now assumed Potemkin's old dual role as foreign minister and head of the War College. He proposed to capture Constantinople with a diabolically clever flanking manoeuvre. His Oriental Project would begin with a military feint into Persia, confound the sultan's generals as Suvorov simultaneously swept down through the Balkans on the Ottoman capital, and a Russian fleet laid siege to Constantinople from the sea.

The prince persuaded his imperial mistress to commit a force of twenty thousand men to the first stage of this grandiose dream; a salient aimed at Persia and India under the command of his younger brother Valerian. Valerian, whose personal heroics had cost him a leg in Poland, was unfortunately only a lieutenant in that conflict, with talents for generalship as yet untried. He received his marching orders in February 1796. To his credit, he took Derbent and Baku (against the mildest resistance) before the expedition sputtered to a halt at the end of the summer, still hundreds of miles from the Persian border. Potemkin's Crimean occupation of 1784 remained the high tide of Catherine's Byzantine dreams.

Prince Plato chased the phantom of Potemkin at a time when a wiser man would have spent his time ingratiating himself with the future czar.

Russia without Catherine was unthinkable, but given the empress's age and infirmities, a change of sovereigns was only a matter of time. Who the monarch would be was as yet unclear. For the first time, his courtier's instincts deserted Zubov when he steeled himself to look into the future. He believed, with the empress herself, that she would be succeeded by her eldest grandson, Grand Duke Alexander.

In such a happy event, the Zubovs were assured of high place in a new court. The brothers had been the childhood companions of Alexander and his brother Constantine at Czarskoe Selo; young Valerian in particular was fondly remembered by Catherine as 'the little black boy', the grand dukes' special friend who led them in mischief-making.

Alexander's father, Grand Duke Paul, was still the legal heir to the throne. Catherine, under the system of succession decreed by Peter the Great, had a lawful basis for bypassing her son, yet she still feared the reaction of the conservative boyars. Until she could screw up the courage to reject him publicly, Paul was isolated on the fringes of court life like some sort of political pestilence.

Catherine worked to prevent his succession, but Paul had his supporters in Russia and abroad. He had grown into manhood the very image of Peter III, small, scrawny, saucer-eyed, effectively scotching the rumour that he was the illegitimate son of handsome Serge Saltikov. The resemblance to Peter, however, was only physical.

The frail, sickly boy coddled by the Empress Elizabeth's nannies had matured into a sensitive, troubled man of obvious intelligence. There were, it is true, reminders of Peter in his psychological makeup; he shared Peter's devotion to Frederick the Great and admired all things Prussian. But Paul was far from being the spectre of mad Peter as Catherine claimed, returned from the grave to bedevil her.

Paul was married at nineteen to a German princess of Catherine's choosing, Wilhelmina of Hesse-Darmstadt, who took the Russian name of Natalia Alekseevna at their wedding in 1773. On the surface at least it was a good marriage. Natalia sustained him through the last years of the Orlov brothers and the spectacular rise of Gregory Potemkin. Like Zubov, Paul hated Potemkin, but for much bitterer reasons. Potemkin had been at Ropsha with the Orlovs; Paul considered him equally guilty of his father's murder.

The grand duke was forced to swallow his hatred as Catherine showered her brilliant Cyclops with offices and honours which rightfully belonged to her son. Catherine neglected few opportunities to embarrass him. During the celebration of her forty-fifth birthday, for example, she gave the grand duke a cheap watch, while she handed Potemkin a gift of fifty thousand rubles. Paul had pleaded for that exact sum to settle his spendthrift wife's debts. Catherine's capacity for vindictiveness was surprising in a woman usually so generous-spirited; when the grand duchess died in childbirth in 1776, Catherine turned Paul's genuine grief into a nightmare by reading to him Natalia's letters to her lover, Paul's best friend.

Providentially, his second wife, Princess Sophia Dorothea Augusta Louisa of Württemberg, was a 'treasure'. Catherine trilled her praises to one of her correspondents:

> I am infatuated with this charming Princess . . . she is precisely what one would have wished: the figure of a nymph, a lily-and-rose complexion, the loveliest skin in the world, tall and well built . . . she is graceful. Sweetness, kindness and innocence are reflected in her face.

Paul fervently agreed. When Sophia, inexplicably, fell head-over-heels in love with the grand duke, his happiness was complete. She became Grand Duchess Maria Feodorovna late in 1776 and for at least a decade, they were a serenely devoted couple who held a modest court of their own at Gatchina and made the best of increasingly harsh treatment by the Empress. When their two sons were born, Catherine exercised her rights as matriarch and autocrat with the same cruelty inflicted on her by the empress Elizabeth when Paul was born in 1754. Almost at birth, Catherine snatched each boy from his mother's breast to be raised under her personal supervision and groomed for an imperial destiny. She named the infants Alexander and Constantine. She planned to replace Paul with Alexander on the Russian throne; Constantine would rule the new Byzantine Empire she and Potemkin were assembling in the south.

During the 1780s Maria Feodorovna consoled Paul for the loss of his sons by giving birth to six lively daughters, surrounding the solitary grand duke with a large, loving family of his own creation. In 1796, far too late for the empress to intervene, she presented her husband with a third son, Nicholas.

In the rosy aftermath of her 'adoption' of Alexander and Constantine, Catherine permitted the grand ducal couple a grand tour of Europe. The 'Comte and Comtesse du Nord' were received enthusiastically in 1781 during incognito visits to Austria, Belgium, France, Holland, Poland and Switzerland. (Paul defied his mother when he called on his hero, Frederick II, in Prussia.) Various courts pronounced Maria Feodorovna lovely and Paul intelligent. His praises were sung even at Versailles. According to one French account:

> The Grand Duke seemed to know the Court as if it were his own. His conversations . . . revealed not only an extremely penetrating and very educated mind, but also a subtle understanding of all the nuances of our customs and all the subtleties of our language.

There were indiscretions. Paul raged openly against his mother's advisors (meaning Potemkin) to the Viennese: 'As soon as I have some power, I'll have them flogged, I'll break them, I'll drive them out.' His frankness delighted the Emperor Joseph II, who had suffered much under a tyrannical mother of his own. A few ministers, to quote the prince de Ligne, thought Paul 'suspicious, touchy . . . playing the rebel and the victim of persecution'.

The trip was, taken *in toto*, a spirited but basically harmless performance on Paul's part, but there was the inevitable wrangle with Catherine on his return. She was outraged at his conduct, demanded an accounting of their expenses and shipped all the grand duchess's new gowns back to Paris. Paul and Maria Feodorovna retreated to their estate at Gatchina and a household far from imperial politics, which began to fill with daughters, music and books. Maria Feodorovna supplied the little girls and the music, for she loved organizing *musicales* for their small court; the bookish Paul built a superb library over the years, numbering nearly forty thousand volumes.

The girls and their mother shared his enthusiasm for Gatchina, where he created the very model of an enlightened Russian estate. He adopted advanced agricultural techniques, provided free hospitals and schools for the Finnish serfs of the estate, and founded Lutheran churches for them. Ultimately, Paul persuaded his mother to give him a battalion of troops to defend Gatchina against local brigands.

With the arrival of the troops and his Prussian military advisor, Baron Steinwehr, conditions at Gatchina underwent ominous changes. The master displayed an increasing fascination with the super-Prussian 'parade ground militarism' that had been a mania with his father. Black moods were more frequent, paranoid fears became pronounced. Terrified of assassins, Paul ordered whole forests levelled to provide an unobstructed view of all the approaches to the castle. Police sentries checked credentials before allowing even old friends into the grand ducal presence. A single visit to the Finnish front during the Swedish war of 1788'–90 was enough to produce Paul's infamous 'Gatchina system' which brutalized the tiny detachment of troops on the estate with martinet command, nit-picking, antiquated rules and liberal use of the knout. When the Bastille fell, he shared his mother's 'panic' over the events in France, except that the grand duke genuinely believed a wave of Jacobinism was sweeping across the face of Europe. In May 1794, he arrested four officers of the Gatchina batallion, firmly convinced that their short-cut pigtails were the telltale marks of revolutionary traitors.

Catherine, more than ever confirmed in her distrust of her son, only grudgingly invited Paul and Maria Feodorovna to witness the betrothal, in September 1796, of their eldest daughter, Alexandra Pavlovna, to the new King of Sweden, Gustavus IV.

It was a dynastic marriage needed to heal the hostility between the two northern powers, but it was a love match none the less. Paul's darling Alexandra was instantly smitten by her eighteen-year-old Swedish suitor, a tall, blonde, athletic prince of Vikings. As luck would have it, Gustavus was so beguiled by the sweet thirteen-year-old grand duchess he waved aside protocol and declared his love and intention to wed the girl. He wooed her at every opportunity, with the delicacy due to her extreme youth. The parents breathed a happy sigh of relief. (They had not been consulted when Prince Plato and the empress planned their daughter's future.) Catherine was enraptured with the pretty fairy tale Zubov had wrought for her benefit. Zubov preened shamelessly over his diplomatic triumph, took endless bows, and left troublesome details to his foreign ministry advisor, Alexander Markov.

The celebration ball in the Winter Palace commenced with a solemn betrothal ceremony in the throne room attended by the imperial family, ranking officials of the government, military, diplomatic and religious dignitaries. Of these last, the Metropolitan Gabriel officiated as the Orthodox grand duchess and the Lutheran king formally pledged their love.

The empress ascended the throne of Peter the Great promptly at seven, painfully corseted and gowned, walking with extreme difficulty but erect, regal, smiling. She was accompanied by the official heir, Grand Duke Paul. (For the last time, she thought. She had finally decided to proclaim a new heir on her name day, 24 November.) The successor-to-be, Grand Duke Alexander, was also at her side. At Catherine's feet sat Grand Duchess Alexandra Pavlovna, her young heart pounding as she awaited her suitor. Gustavus IV was in an anteroom for the actual signing of the marriage contract, the terms of which were being presented by Zubov's lackey, Markov.

Ignored by Zubov and Markov was a minor stipulation which suddenly caught the king's eye. Alexandra, according to the contract before him, would not be required to convert to the Protestant faith to reign as queen of Sweden, but would be allowed to remain Orthodox, with her own chapel in Stockholm and her own corps of Russian priests.

The minor stipulation was anything but minor to Gustavus. He demanded an explanation. The court and Catherine waited. There was an explosion of royal Swedish temper. Zubov was sent for. Gustavus refused point-blank to sign.

After an embarrassing, paralyzing wait of more than three hours, the favourite reappeared in the throne room to whisper his failure to the empress. Red-faced, she announced a delay in the engagement due to the king's 'indisposition'.

Catherine had to be helped from the room; the shock of public humiliation by 'the young puppy' made her ill with colic through a long, sleepless night. In the next few days, an attempt was made to patch things up, but the moment had passed. The young grand duchess was heartbroken. The empress was icy. The king was defiant as he took his leave.

With medical hindsight, it is plain that Catherine's 'colic' was a minor stroke. It continued to trouble her, especially at night. Her ulcerated legs gave her no peace. She was restless, tired, depressed. One evening she saw a shooting star and took it as a portent of her death. This, from a rationalist who all her life had laughed at superstition. Catherine correctly sensed her health was in serious danger and cut back on her official duties for the first time, keeping appointments to a minimum, appearing in public only for dinner and for Mass. She was determined to survive sound in mind and limb until 24 November, the day on which she would proclaim her new heir.

She very nearly made it.

On the morning of 5 November she went about her normal routine: ice to massage her face, extra-strong black coffee, a chat with Zubov and work with her secretaries. Death, when it came, left her without a shred of dignity. An apoplectic seizure felled her in her water closet, swift, shattering and final. After the servants extricated her mammoth body from the little room, she lingered for two more days, her face alternately purpled with rushing blood or blanched white, the poor, dry tongue sticking half out of her open mouth as she choked for air. There was no faintest stirring of consciousness, no deathbed whisper, no physical sign to convey her testament. Doctor Rogerson was summoned, bled her, consulted with his colleagues. The physicians quickly handed their patient over to the priests.

The court was plunged into chaos. Zubov sobbed wildly at his mistress's bedside. Alexander, who knew perfectly well his grandmother intended to name him her heir, stepped meekly aside in favour of his father. Paul hastened to St Petersburg through the November snows in a state approaching hysteria, torn between shock, tearful thanksgiving and the sick fear that her illness was some sort of trap set by his mother to destroy him. The young grand dukes gave their father his first moment of reassurance when he arrived that evening; they greeted him dressed in the green Prussian uniforms worn at Gatchina, which had been forbidden in Catherine's presence.

The following day, Bezborodko, who had confiscated all Catherine's (and Zubov's) papers, handed Paul a sealed envelope tied in black ribbon. It was inscribed in Catherine's own hand, 'To be opened after my death, in the Council.' Her son tossed the paper unopened into the fire and stepped into history as Paul I. He was forty-two, czar of all the Russias after a delay of thirty-four years. His mother, Catherine the Great, died the same morning, 6 November 1796, at the age of sixty-seven.

At noon Paul was enthroned in the Winter Palace chapel, where he accepted the allegiance of the Czarina Maria Feodorovna, the grand dukes and their wives, the grand duchesses, the metropolitan, the clergy and the court. With steadily rising spirits, he reviewed a regiment of guardsmen. He found their performance inadequate by Gatchina standards. The czar then retired to complete his detailed, personal instructions for the funeral.

In the days that followed, Paul settled accounts with the dead before beginning his reign over the living. Thirty-four years of private devotion to a martyred father spilled over into a grotesque public display.

The bones of Peter III were reverently exhumed from his tomb in the Alexander Nevsky Monastery and brought to the Winter Palace, where the entire skeleton was assembled, dressed in full military uniform, the imperial crown placed on the skull, and the ghastly corpus seated on the throne of Peter the Great. By Paul's order, the pitiful creature from the grave was given the submission of Imperial Russia – as representatives of every great family, every command, every monastery bent the knee, murmured the oath, kissed the skeletal fingers.

Peter's spouse, in Paul's eyes his executioner, lay in state in nearby Kazan Cathedral. No dignity was denied her, but Catherine's long reign suddenly counted as nothing, as Paul rearranged history to please his sense of decency and decorum. There had never been an assassination, a usurping empress, lovers. Paul I succeeded Peter III and honoured his widow Catherine above her female station by including her in the double funeral cortège which now paced to muffled drums across St Petersburg to the Cathedral of Sts Peter and Paul. Leading the processional in the bitter cold marched a frail old man, head high, bearing the crown of Peter III. It was Alexis Orlov, a living ghost from the drunken scene long ago at Ropsha, publicly doing honour to the sovereign he had murdered. Another feeble conspirator of 1762, Prince Feodor Bariantsky, marched slowly behind.

At the cathedral, Peter and Catherine were laid to rest in identical white sepulchres, coupled under a banner bearing Paul's final, ironic blessing: 'Divided in life, joined in death.'

The macabre spectacle was not yet finished. The Cyclops rankled in the new czar's memory; Gregory Potemkin's career, his insults, his rumoured marriage to the empress were unforgivable. Paul ordered the treasures of the Tauride Palace crated and hauled away so the building could serve as barracks and stable for the Horse Guards. The tomb at Kherson was ripped open, its contents rushed to the capital by special courier. Paul watched with grim satisfaction as the mortal remains of the prince of Tauris were unceremoniously dumped into the Moika Canal, so much graveyard refuse floating out to sea with the city's sewage.

Surprisingly, the living survivors of Catherine's reign fared quite well. There were few punishments. Plato Zubov was simply 'given permission to travel'. Paul entertained himself between the funeral and coronation by recalling Catherine's outcasts from exile and releasing her prisoners from jail. One of the Polish prisoners, a member of the illustrious Potocki family, was told, 'I know you have suffered much, that you have been mistreated for a long time, but under the preceding reign all honest men were persecuted, myself first of all.'

The only credential worth having was disgrace under Catherine; Paul could be counted on for redress. The coronation itself was the occasion for astonishing gifts to 'victims' and to Paul's supporters that dwarfed the bounty of Catherine herself. There was a certain amount of feverish relief in the air, as the nation settled down to the reign of 'the Prussian'.

Catherine was, understandably, memorialized very little in Pauline Russia, but her place in history was fixed from the moment of her death. Many attempted her epitaph but she had the last say, in the obituary she composed for herself soon after the death of Potemkin. It was vintage Catherine, a press release for posterity:

Here lies Catherine the Second.
Born in Stettin on April 21, 1729. She went to Russia in 1744 to marry Peter III. At the age of fourteen she made the threefold resolution to please her husband, Elizabeth and the nation. She neglected nothing in trying to achieve this. Eighteen years of tedium and loneliness gave her the opportunity to read many books. On the throne of Russia she wanted to do what was good for her country and tried to bring happiness, liberty and prosperity to her subjects. She forgave easily and hated no one. She was tolerant, understanding and of happy disposition. She had a republican spirit and a kind heart.
She was sociable by nature.
She made many friends.
She took pleasure in her work.
She loved the arts.

Under Paul I, Russia became a gigantic parade ground. In his four and a half years on the throne, the French elegance of Catherine's reign evaporated in the thunder of cannon, the barking of Prussian-style drill masters and the devotion to imbecilic minutiae typical of a military state. The precise length of a marching step, the number of buttons on a uniform jacket, the shape of a haircut occupied the attention of the highest councils of government. No one in eighteenth-century Russia much minded the change, except that as the new regime took hold, the fabulous patronage granted by Catherine to the aristocracy vanished. From the 'golden age' of unlimited privilege and power, they suddenly found themselves without defence against seizure of their estates, deportation and worse.

Paul's reign was finally brought down by its confusions. A famous lampoon of the period pictured the emperor holding in one hand a scroll labelled 'Orders', in the other, 'Counter Orders'. On his forehead was inscribed, 'Disorder'.

In the epilogue that was bound to happen, Plato Zubov surpassed Gregory Potemkin in his last historical role. At Ropsha in 1762, however serious Potemkin's complicity, the young sergeant could not bring himself to put to death his anointed sovereign. When the Orlov brothers strangled Peter III, Potemkin did not defend the czar, but took no part in the regicide. He was a bystander.

Thirty-eight years later, Zubov returned from exile to lead the party of nobles who penetrated the Michael Fortress to confront Paul I. On 11 March 1801, they burst into the czar's bedroom, planning to demand his abdication in favour of Grand Duke Alexander, but the sight of little Paul shivering with fright behind some hangings enraged them.

There is uncertainty as to what happened next.

According to one account, Zubov's giant brother Alexis beat Paul to death with his fists; another story, echoing the last minutes of Peter III, favours strangulation; in a third tale, the nobles struck again and again with their swords, slashing and stabbing through the draperies into the emperor's body.

Whatever the method of murder, it is certain that Plato Zubov did not, like Potemkin, stand idly by.

Sources

The Elephant and The Maypole

Ashdown, Dulcie M. *Royal Paramours*. New York: Dorset Press, 1986.

Beattie, John M. *The English Court in the Reign of George I*. London: Cambridge University Press, 1967.

Barker, Felix and Jackson, Peter. *London: 2,000 Years of A City and Its People*. New York: MacMillan, 1974.

Chenevix Trench, Charles. *The Royal Malady*. New York: Harcourt, Brace & World, 1965.

Creasy, Sir Edward Shepherd. *Fifteen Decisive Battles of the World, From Marathon to Waterloo*. New York: Dorset Press, 1987.

Joelson, Annette. *Heirs to the Throne: The Story of the Princes of Wales*. London: Wm Heinemann Ltd, 1966.

Jordan, Ruth. *Sophie Dorothea*. New York: George Braziller, 1971.

Mackay, Charles. *Extraordinary Popular Delusions and the Madness of Crowds*. New York: Farrar Straus and Giroux, 1932.

McCarthy, Austin. *A History of the Four Georges*. New York: Harper & Brothers, 1885.

Murray, Jane. *The Kings and Queens of England*. New York: Charles Scribner's Sons, 1974.

Murray, John J. *George I, The Baltic and the Whig Split of 1717*. Chicago: The University of Chicago Press, 1969.

Ogg, David. *William III*. New York: The Macmillan Company, 1967.

Plumb, J.H. *The First Four Georges*. New York: The MacMillan Company, 1957.

Redman, Alvin. *The House of Hanover*. New York: Coward-McCann, Inc., 1961.

Sinclair-Stevenson, Christopher. *Blood Royal, The Illustrious House of Hanover*. Garden City, New York: Doubleday & Company, 1980.

Sedgwick, Romney. *Lord Hervey's Memoirs*. New York: The Macmillan Company, 1963.

Sickel, Walter. *Bolingbroke and His Times*. New York: Haskell House Publishers Ltd, 1968.

Thackeray, William Makepeace. *The Four Georges*. London: The Cornhill Magazine, Vol. 2; and Smith, Elder and Co., 1860.

Trevelyan, George Macaulay, O.M. *England under Queen Anne: Blenheim*. London: Longmans, Green and Co. Ltd, 1930.

Trowbridge, Wm R.H. *Seven Splendid Sinners*. New York: Brentano's, 1910.

Turner, E.S. *The Court of St. James's*. New York: St Martin's Press, 1959.

Walpole, Horace, Fourth Earl of Orford. *Reminiscences*. London: John Sharpe, Piccadilly, 1819.

Wilkins, W.H. *The Love of an Uncrowned Queen, Sophia Dorothea, Consort of George I*. New York: Herbert S. Stone and Co., 1901.

The Fishes' Daughter

D'Angerville, Mouffle. *The Private Life of Louis XV*. (Translated by H.S. Mingard.) London: John Lane the Bodley Head Limited, 1924.

D'Argenson, René-Louis, Marquis. *Essays, Characters, Portraits, Anecdotes, etc*. London: Logographic Press, 1889.

Asprey, Robert B. *Frederick the Great; The Magnificent Enigma*. New York: Tichnor & Fields, 1986.

Barry, Joseph. *Passions and Politics; a Biography of Versailles*. Garden City, New York: Doubleday & Company, 1972.

Bernier, Olivier. *Louis The Beloved; The Life of Louis XV*. Garden City, New York: Doubleday & Company, 1984.

Carlyle, Thomas. *Critical and Miscellaneous Essays*. Philadelphia: Carey & Hart, 1845.
History of Frederick II of Prussia. London: Chapman & Hall, 1859.
The French Revolution: A History. New York: Wiley and Putnam, 1846.

Casanova de Seingalt, Giacomo Girolamo. *Memoirs* (Translated by Arthur Machen). New York: Alfred A. Knopf, 1929.

Cheke, Marcus. *The Cardinal de Bernis*. New York: W.W. Norton & Company Inc., 1958.

Clergue, Helen. *Phases of France on the Eve of the Revolution*. London: Jonathan Cape, 1922.

Dill, Marshall Jr. *Paris in Time*. New York: G.P. Putnam's Sons, 1975.

De Goncourt, Edmond Louis Antoine Huot. *The Confidantes of a King;*

The Mistresses of Louis XV (Translated by Ernest Dowson). London and Edinburgh: T.N. Foulis, 1907.

Gooch, G.P. *Louis XV; The Monarchy in Decline*. London: Longmans, Green and Co., 1956.

De Gramont, Sanche. *Epitaph for Kings*. New York: G.P. Putnam's Sons, 1967.

The Age of Magnificence; Memoirs of the Duc de Saint-Simon. New York: G.P. Putnam's Sons, 1963.

Guerard, Albert. *France in the Classical Age*. New York: Harper & Row, 1965.

Kemble, James, ChM, FRCS. *Idols and Invalids*. London: Methuen & Co. Ltd, 1933.

Kybett, Susan Maclean. *Bonnie Prince Charlie; A Biography of Charles Edward Stuart*. New York: Dodd, Mead & Company, 1988.

Law, Joy. *Fleur de Lys: The Kings and Queens of France*. London: Hamish Hamilton Ltd, 1976.

Loomis, Stanley. *Du Barry, A Biography*. Philadelphia and New York: J. B. Lippincott Company, 1959.

Lough, John. *An Introduction to Eighteenth Century France*. London: Longmans, Green & Co., 1960.

Mackay, Charles. *Extraordinary Popular Delusions and the Madness of Crowds*. New York: Farrar Straus and Giroux, 1932.

Maurois, André. *A History of France* (Translated by Henry L. Binsse). London: Jonathan Cape, 1949.

Mitford, Nancy. *Madame de Pompadour*. New York: Harper & Row Inc., 1968.

The Sun King: Louis XIV at Versailles. New York: Harper & Row, Inc., 1966.

D'Orléans, Elizabeth Charlotte, Duchesse. *The Letters of Madame, Vol. 2* (Translated by Gertrude Scott Stevenson, MA). London, J.W. Arrowsmith Ltd, 1925.

Memoirs of the Court of Louis XIV and The Regency. Paris: Grolier Society, 1930.

St. John, Bayle. *The Memoirs of the Duke of Saint-Simon in the Reign of Louis XIV and the Regency*. London: Chatto and Windus, 1876.

De Saint-Simon, Louis de Rouvroy, Duc. *Memoirs of Louis XIV and His Court and of the Regency, Volume III*. New York: P.F. Collier & Son, 1910.

Stryienski, Casimir. *The National History of France; The Eighteenth Century* (Translated by H.N. Dickinson). New York: Funck-Brentano, AMS Press Inc., 1967.

Trouncer, Margaret. *The Pompadour*. London: Hutchinson & Co. Ltd, 1937.

A Duchess of Versailles: The Love Story of Louise, Duchesse de Choiseul. London: Hutchinson, 1961.

Van Kley, Dale K. *The Damiens Affair and the Unraveling of the Ancien Régime*. Princeton, N.J.: The University Press, 1984.

Walton, Guy. *Louis XIV's Versailles*. Chicago: The University of Chicago Press, 1986.

Williams, H. Noel. *Memoirs of Madame Du Barry of the Court of Louis XV*. New York: P.F. Collier & Son, 1910.

The Cyclops

Coughlan, Robert. *Elizabeth and Catherine*. New York: G.P. Putnam's Sons, 1974.

Haslip, Joan. *Catherine the Great*. New York: G.P. Putnam's Sons, 1977.

Lincoln, W. Bruce. *The Romanovs*. New York: The Dial Press, 1981.

De Madariaga, Isabel. *Russia in the Age of Catherine the Great*. New Haven and London: Yale University Press, 1981.

Masson, Charles F.P. *Secret Memoirs of the Court of Petersburg*. New York: Arno Press & The New York Times, 1970.

Nikolaev, Vsevolod A., and Parry, Albert. *The Loves of Catherine the Great*. New York: Coward, McCann & Geoghegan, 1982.

Oldenbourg, Zoe. *Catherine the Great*. New York: Pantheon Books (Random House), 1965.

Polotsoff, Alexander. *The Favourites of Catherine the Great*. London: Herbert Jenkins Ltd, 1940.

Redman, Alvin. *The House of Hanover*. New York: Coward-McCann Inc., 1961.

Sedillot, René with Franz Pick, *All the Monies of the World*. New York: Pick Publishing Company, 1954.

Troyat, Henri. *Catherine the Great*. (Translated by Joan Pinkham). New York: E.P. Dutton, 1980.

Index

The Fishes' Daughter

The Cyclops

Alexandra Pavlovna, Grand Duchess (Catherine II's granddaughter), 286, 296, 297

Bashtasarai, 274
Betzkoy, Count, 288
Bezborodko, Alexander Andreyevich, 258, 279, 281, 286, 290, 292, 298
Bruce, Countess Prascovya, 222, 227, 228, 258, 260, 262, 287
Bruhl, Count Heinrich von, 249

Cameron, Sir Charles, 274
Cesme, naval Battle of, 252, 277
Charles XII, King of Sweden, 275
Choiseul, Étienne François, Duc de, 249
Christian Augustus of Anhalt-Zerbst, Field Marshal Prince (Catherine II's father), 225, 234
Cobenzl, Count Ludwig, 269
Constantine Pavlovich, Grand Duke (Catherine II's grandson), 263, 282, 293, 294, 295
Constantinople, 255, 275, 280, 283, 292
Crimea, the, xv, xvi, 221, 231, 252, 254–6, 265, 266, 268, 274, 276, 277, 293
Crozat, Pierre, 249
Czarskoye Selo, 232, 247, 263, 264, 286, 293, 281, 295

De Ligne, Charles Joseph, Prince, 254, 255, 259, 272
Diderot, Denis, 243, 244, 245, 246, 248, 249, 273
Dmitriyev-Mamonov, Count Alexander Matreievich, 267, 268, 269, 271, 276, 278, 279

Elizabeth I, Empress of Russia, xv, 225, 226, 231, 234, 242, 246, 247, 249, 286, 293, 294, 300
Elphinstone, Admiral John, 253
Éprouveuse, 228, 262, 287
Ermolov, Alexander Petrovich, 266, 267, 281

Focsani, 252, 254, 279
France, 221, 231, 242, 249, 253, 255, 270, 273, 280, 290, 295, 296
Falconet, Étienne Maurice, 248
Fitzherbert, Alleyn, 274
Frederick II, King of Prussia ('The Great'), 225, 226, 241–3, 248, 272, 280, 287, 288, 290, 293, 295
Frederick William II, 290, 291
French Revolution, 280

Gatchina, 294–6, 298
Golitsyn, Field Marshal Prince Alexander, 239
Golitsyn, Prince Dmitri, 248, 249
Geoffrin, Madame, 248
George III, King of England, 271
Greek project, 255, 256, 265, 276, 286, 292
Grieg, Sir Samuel, 253, 277
Grimm, Baron Frederick Melchior von, 236, 244, 246, 252, 261, 263, 267, 284, 288
Gustavus III, King of Sweden, 277, 278, 280
Gustavus IV, 296, 297

Harris, Sir James Howard, 261, 287
Henry, Prince of Prussia, 243, 253, 287
Hermitage, the, 224, 248, 250, 251, 277
Holland, 295

Izmailovsky guards, 241
Israelovsky battalion, 239

Jacobins, 280, 283, 290, 296
Jassy, Treaty of, 287, 288, 294, 296
Johanna Elizabeth, Princess (Catherine II's mother), 224
Jones, John Paul, 287
Joseph II, Emperor of Austria, 231, 254, 271, 273, 275–7, 291, 295

Kantemir, Prince, 287
Khitrovo, Fyodor, 241
Kiev, 243, 258, 268–70, 278
Kosciusko, Thaddeus, 291, 292
Kutchuk Kainardji, Treaty of, 230, 252, 255

Laharpe, Frédéric César de, 263
Lanskoy, Alexander Dmitrievich, 262–5, 267
Lasunsky, Michael, 241
Leopold II, Emperor of Austria, 291
Louis XV, King of France, 247, 249
Louis XVI, 288, 290

Maciejowice, Battle of, 291
Mamonov, Count Alexander, *see* Dmitriyev-Mamonov
Marble Palace, the, 237, 265
Maria Feodorovna, Grand Duchess (Paul I's second wife), 294–6, 208
Maria Theresa, Empress of Austria, 221, 231, 242, 243, 272
Marie Antoinette of Austria (later Queen of France), 273, 290
Markov, Alexander, 296, 297
Moscow, 231, 234, 236, 241, 245, 252, 258, 262, 265, 276, 281
Matouchkine, Countess, 288
Mothe, Jean Baptiste Vallin de la, 250
Musin-Pushkin, Count A.I., 249

Nadir Shah, 237
Nakaz code, 238
Naryshkin, Grand Chamberlain, 288
Natalia Alekseevna, Grand Duchess (Paul I's first wife), 293, 294,
'New Russia', 255, 265, 268, 272, 274, 277, 291

Ochakov, port of, 274, 277, 278
Orlov, Alexis, 223, 241, 253, 277, 299
Orlov brothers, 223, 226–8, 230, 231, 234, 238, 241, 252, 253, 262, 286, 294, 301
Orlov, Prince Gregory, xv, 222, 226, 227, 229–32, 235, 237, 240, 241, 244, 246, 250, 252, 255, 265, 287